CRIMINALLY IGNORANT

Criminally Ignorant

WHY THE LAW PRETENDS WE KNOW WHAT WE DON'T

Alexander Sarch

OXFORD
UNIVERSITY PRESS

OXFORD
UNIVERSITY PRESS

Oxford University Press is a department of the University of Oxford. It furthers the University's objective of excellence in research, scholarship, and education by publishing worldwide. Oxford is a registered trademark of Oxford University Press in the UK and certain other countries.

Published in the United States of America by Oxford University Press
198 Madison Avenue, New York, NY 10016, United States of America.

Library of Congress Cataloging-in-Publication Data

Names: Sarch, Alexander, author.
Title: Criminally ignorant : why the law pretends we know what we don't / Dr. Alexander Sarch.
Description: New York : Oxford University Press, 2019. | Includes bibliographical references and index.
Identifiers: LCCN 2018052698 | ISBN 9780190056575 ((hardback) : alk. paper)
Subjects: LCSH: Criminal liability. | Criminal law—Philosophy. | Guilt—Philosophy.
Classification: LCC K5065 .S26 2019 | DDC 345/.04—dc23
LC record available at https://lccn.loc.gov/2018052698

9 8 7 6 5 4 3 2

Printed by Books International, United States of America

To my parents—
My mother, who taught me to love thinking and talking about the big questions;
my stepfather, who taught me to love science and the value of being patient;
and my dad, who taught me to love arguing and to pursue truth at all costs.

Contents

Acknowledgments

SINCE I STARTED WRITING about willful ignorance, the topic has taken on increased political importance. Willful ignorance and related forms of motivated reasoning undoubtedly are mechanisms by which our political culture has become so divided and infused with propaganda, misinformation, and fake news that calling this the "post-truth era" no longer seems much of an exaggeration. Turning a blind eye, refusing to investigate, and otherwise manipulating one's reasoning to preserve desired conclusions—these are cognitive behaviors that help falsehoods spread online and fuel political polarization. Whether driven by groupthink, the desire to preserve a preferred self-conception, or more mundane traits like laziness or bias, we all bear a moral responsibility to remain reasonably well informed about important issues and to amplify factually accurate claims and intellectually defensible conclusions. It's a natural, all-too-human tendency to blind ourselves to uncomfortable truths and adjust our reasoning to preserve preferred conclusions. Nonetheless, we must strive to combat such tendencies and achieve better, more truth-oriented intellectual habits. We must have the courage to seek and accept facts even when they diverge from what we would wish.

That's a moral matter. What about the law? When should the criminal law demand truth-seeking and impose harsher penalties on those who succumb to the temptation to blind ourselves to realities we don't like, rationalize away recalcitrant evidence, or otherwise engage in motivated reasoning? Can bad epistemic habits make one more *culpable* in ways the criminal law should recognize? These are the sorts of questions this book tackles. I argue that the criminal law legitimately recognizes that certain extreme epistemic failings can stem from insufficient regard for others, which can merit more serious censure by the criminal law.

Good epistemic practices are a lot easier when you have lots of smart people around who support you and hold you accountable. I was extremely lucky to benefit from this in working on the present project. I was supported and encouraged, critiqued and assisted, pushed and prodded, by many exceptionally astute and kind colleagues, friends, and family. This book reflects that kindness in innumerable ways. The project would have failed without them, and I owe them a tremendous debt of gratitude. The book surely still has many failings, but those are completely my own fault.

I want to explicitly acknowledge numerous people to whom I am particularly grateful. Thanks first to Gideon Yaffe, whose help and encouragement got me started on this book in the first place. It will be obvious to anyone who reads it that I've benefited immensely from his work, and I thank him for all the critical comments and support he's offered through the years.

Thanks to Andrei Marmor, whose support, insight, and criticisms were essential not only to this book but to my broader opportunity to write it. Similarly, I owe Doug Husak a debt of gratitude for his guidance, encouragement, and terrific comments on many parts of this project.

I must also thank my fantastic colleagues at the University of Surrey School of Law. Every day I go into the office, I feel tremendously fortunate to be able to work—and be friends—with such a smart, kind, energetic, and generous group of scholars. Many of them provided lengthy written comments on numerous draft chapters, and even took part in a workshop on the manuscript. I'm extremely grateful to Josh Andresen, Hrafn Asgeirsson, Steve Bero, Ambrose Lee, Ira Lindsay, and Chris Taggart, as well as Mikolaj Barcentiwicz, Bebhinn Donnelly-Lazarov, Marie Newhouse, and Veronica Rodriguez-Blanco for their incredibly generous comments, criticisms, conversations, and support. You guys are the best.

Thanks to Jan Willem Wieland, whose own work on this topic I've benefited greatly from, for generously providing such sharp and constructive written comments.

I'm grateful to former colleagues at USC, who helped me get this project off the ground, including Jon Quong, Steve Findlay, Erik Encarnacion, Joe Horton, Greg Keating, Jake Ross, Mark Schroeder, and Gary Watson. A big thank you also to my Michigan Law School mentors, Scott Hershovitz and Gabe Mendlow, not just for their help on this project, but for all their support through the years.

Many thanks to audiences at UCL, KCL, Oxford, University of Iowa Law School, and Queen's University Law School for extremely helpful feedback on various parts of the project. I'm especially grateful to Mihailis Diamantis, Andrew Simester, Will Thomas, and Aness Webster for their valuable comments, criticisms, and guidance. Thanks also to Craig Agule, James Edwards, Stephen Galoob, Steve Garvey, Steve Schaus, Kevin Toh, Dennis Baker, Carliss Chatman, Steve Nyak-Young, Hillary Nye, Massimo Renzo, Kenneth Silver, and Bob Sullivan. Thanks as well to the editors of *Legal Theory, Law*

& Philosophy, Criminal Law & Philosophy, University of Colorado Law Review, and *St. John's Law Review* for giving permission to reprint portions of my earlier papers related to the topic of this book.

Lastly, I'm more grateful than I can properly express to my family. Thank you to my wonderful, smart, and talented parents—my mother, Bettina Skard, stepfather, John Arthur Skard, and father, Kenneth Sarch. Thank you to my awesome siblings, Natalya, Oren, Yaron, Serena, Gabriel, and Daniel. And last but not least, thank you to my lovely wife, Vanessa Reid, whose intelligence, compassion, and conversations I couldn't manage without. So much love to you all.

Introduction

THE CEO OF CarCo suspects that while the cars the company manufactures emit more CO_2 than legally permitted, middle management is doctoring the emissions tests to hide the violations. The CEO's advisers offer to carry out a large internal investigation to determine whether this is true. But the CEO tells them not to bother—the money should go to finishing up the fancy new corporate headquarters instead. He orders them to not mention this to him ever again, and they should avoid discussing the matter with any engineers or scientists who might have knowledge of the issue. Actually, the CEO's suspicions were correct: the emissions tests were fraudulent.

The CEO has been willfully ignorant. He deliberately preserved his ignorance of the fact that company employees were engaged in fraud. Were the CEO charged with aiding the fraud, his willful ignorance would be no defense. Insisting that he didn't actually know the fraud was occurring (he merely suspected it) would do him no good.

This might seem puzzling. After all, ignorance of essential facts generally *does* have exculpatory force in the criminal law. If I start punching what I genuinely believe to be a pillow and don't realize until it was too late that this was no pillow but a person, then I might avoid conviction for assault.[1] If I genuinely didn't know that the fancy new laptop

[1] Model Penal Code (MPC) § 211.1 (defining assault); MPC § 2.04(1) (defining "mistake of fact" defense).

Criminally Ignorant. Alexander Sarch.

my friend gave me was stolen, I might avoid a conviction for receipt of stolen property.[2] So if ignorance is usually exculpatory, why are things different for willful ignorance?

One way to start to see the answer is that there would be grave dangers if ignorance always did exculpate. If ignorance always precluded conviction, there would be clear incentives to commit crimes in a state of obliviousness. It would allow us to get the benefits of criminal activity without facing liability in the event of prosecution. Judicial tools are therefore needed to counteract the incentives to preserve one's ignorance about the wrong-making features of what we do.

The willful ignorance doctrine is just such a tool. It says courts may treat the deliberate attempt to remain ignorant of the criminal nature of your conduct as a basis for punishing you *as if* you knew what you were doing. Thus, the CEO of CarCo could be punished *as if* he knew of the emissions fraud. Similarly, Judge Jed Rakoff observed that in the run-up to the 2008 financial meltdown, a "top-level banker . . . confronted with growing evidence . . . that mortgage fraud was increasing, might have inquired . . . [but] if . . . the executive failed to make such inquiries, might it be because he did not want to know what such inquiries would reveal?"[3] The willful ignorance doctrine allows convicting such bankers of crimes requiring knowledge—like aiding and abetting or conspiracy to commit fraud. Indeed, Judge Rakoff argues that, given the willful ignorance doctrine, prosecutors shouldn't have been so reluctant to prosecute the executives at the heart of the meltdown.

In this book, I investigate the deeper principles behind the intuitive idea that willful ignorance is equivalent to knowledge, such that courts may pretend that actually ignorant defendants possessed the knowledge required by statute. What is the principled explanation for why a court may treat those who kept themselves in the dark *as if* they knew what they were doing?

The traditional answer offered by courts is a hypothesis about culpability: deliberately turning a blind eye to the facts that make one's conduct criminal is equally culpable as acting with knowledge thereof. This so-called *equal culpability thesis* is often invoked by courts, but rarely examined. Still, it raises fundamental questions about the criminal law. What sense of culpability is at issue here? Why is deliberately preserving one's ignorance culpable in this sense? Does self-induced ignorance always make one's conduct as culpable as knowing misconduct, or only sometimes? If the latter, when? Can *any* sufficiently culpable conduct—like cheating on spouses or taxes—suffice for treating one as if one possessed the knowledge required for just any crime, like fraud or possessing drugs? Certainly not—but why, exactly? What limits are there on the law's pretense that we know what we don't? Why does equally culpable willful ignorance support *pretending*

[2] MPC § 223.6.

[3] Jed Rakoff, *The Financial Crisis: Why Have No High Level Executives Been Prosecuted?*, N.Y. Rev. Books (Jan. 9, 2014).

that defendants had knowledge when in reality they didn't? Can we make sense of this legal fiction?

These are the questions this book aims to answer. The overarching ambition is to defend a theory of when and why the criminal law may legitimately impute mental states on the basis of equal culpability. This helps place the existing willful ignorance doctrine on a more secure normative foundation. At the same time, the theory reveals the pressing need for doctrinal reforms: the willful ignorance doctrine must be restricted to avoid punishing defendants more than they deserve.

My project is not limited to willful ignorance, however. The normative idea behind the willful ignorance doctrine—that we may impute missing mental states to defendants on equal culpability grounds—is surprisingly fertile, and, if taken seriously, grounds an array of further imputation principles. Thus, I defend several new rules, which allow certain forms of culpable but not-quite-willful ignorance (like recklessly or negligently preserved ignorance) to substitute for higher mental states like knowledge or recklessness. I also defend corporate analogs of certain imputation principles. Still, because equal culpability imputation is such a potent idea, it must be reined in by setting appropriate limits on its use. What's needed is a theory that places the idea of equal culpability imputation on a solid theoretical foundation, while also demarcating its proper boundaries.

The willful ignorance doctrine thus serves as my window into a broader set of questions about the criminal law. By generalizing from willful ignorance, I seek to justify the imputation of mental states on equal culpability grounds *in general*. This, in turn, requires elucidating the notion of criminal culpability that underwrites such imputation. Imputing mental states on the basis of equal culpability amounts to a legal fiction, and thus carries inherent risks. But not all legal fictions are unjustified—particularly if used within proper limits. Courts must be more cognizant of the theoretical foundations of such imputation principles to avoid applying them in unjust ways. My theory of when and why equal culpability imputation is a justifiable way to promote the aims of the criminal law shows how to do just this. It provides the basis for a restrained and defensible use of equal culpability imputation. While my primary focus throughout the book is US federal law, my normative project has clear implications for analogous rules in state law and other common law jurisdictions like the United Kingdom and Canada.

The book is divided into three parts: the first is about the conceptual foundations of criminal liability, the second is about the existing willful ignorance doctrine, and the third is about rules that go beyond willful ignorance. More specifically, Part I starts by introducing key concepts in Chapter 1, and then defends a theory of criminal culpability in Chapter 2, which anchors the theoretical arguments in later chapters.

Part II examines the normative basis for the existing willful ignorance doctrine for individuals. Chapter 3 argues against the most prominent attempts to justify some version of the doctrine. Instead, Chapter 4 defends a more principled account of when and why willful ignorance actually is as culpable as knowing misconduct. This reveals the proper limits within which courts should give willful ignorance jury instructions, and I show how such normatively improved jury instructions can be formulated in workable ways.

In Chapter 5, I extract from the willful ignorance doctrine a general theory of equal-culpability-based mental state imputation. This theory lies at the core of the book. The theory not only completes my defense of the legitimacy of allowing willful ignorance to substitute for knowledge but also helps evaluate and reform numerous other criminal law doctrines—including the felony murder, transferred intent, intoxication, and Pinkerton rules. I then proceed to use this theory to examine other forms of ignorance that are not strictly speaking willful.

Part III moves beyond willful ignorance. Chapter 6 argues that repeatedly recklessly preserving one's ignorance can also substitute for knowledge, provided the conditions of equal culpability are met. However, there are inherent limits to equal-culpability-based imputation. Thus, Chapter 7 argues that no form of culpable ignorance is itself sufficient for treating defendants as *purposeful* wrongdoers. By contrast, Chapter 8 argues that another form of subwillful motivated ignorance, where one is not fully aware of the risks of one's conduct, justifies treating some negligent actors as if they were reckless.

Finally, Chapter 9 considers corporations. It is not only culpable to preserve one's own ignorance, but the same can be true for preserving the ignorance of others. Accordingly, I argue that when corporate employees culpably preserve the ignorance of others within the corporation, the missing knowledge of the relevant inculpatory facts can be imputed *to the corporation*. I extend my theory of criminal culpability to corporate actors, and argue that culpably interfering with the information flow within the corporation can justify imputing knowledge to the corporation itself.

In this way, I not only seek to place the existing willful ignorance doctrine on a more secure normative foundation but also to delineate the proper boundaries of equal culpability imputation in general. The result is a comprehensive account of when the criminal law may legitimately impute missing mental states on the basis of equal culpability.

I Foundations

THIS PART INTRODUCES the questions to be examined in the book and develops the theoretical framework that provides the foundation for the ensuing discussion. Chapter 1 presents a roadmap of the main criminal law concepts we will be concerned with and takes a closer look at the willful ignorance doctrine, which is the starting point for the general theory of equal culpability mental state imputation developed in later chapters. Situating this doctrine in the broader criminal law context reveals the questions to be tackled in the book. Since the project is to analyze, evaluate and ultimately defend certain criminal law doctrines that impute mental states on the basis of equal culpability, the notion of criminal culpability requires elucidation. Chapter 2 provides my account of culpability and aims to show why it offers a particularly attractive way to think about this concept. The theory follows the tradition of understanding culpability in terms of insufficient regard, but the details are fleshed out in new ways to strengthen the view, highlight its explanatory power and reveal its normative attractions. This insufficient regard theory of culpability will serve as the basis for many of the arguments to follow.

1 Criminal Law Basics and the Willful Ignorance Doctrine

THIS CHAPTER SETS the stage. My starting point is the willful ignorance doctrine, since it is the source from which I will eventually extract my general theory of equal culpability mental state imputation. After explaining some core criminal law concepts, I introduce the willful ignorance doctrine and the normative claim it is premised on—the *equal culpability thesis*. Situating the doctrine in the broader criminal law context reveals the questions to be tackled in the book, and the chapter ends by indicating the sorts of answers I will develop.

I. Criminal Law Basics

Most crimes are defined to require an *actus reus* (Latin for "guilty act") and a culpable mental state—or *mens rea* ("guilty mind"). I will generally use the mens rea definitions in the influential Model Penal Code (MPC). While the MPC has been criticized,[1] it captures the traditional understanding of the main mens rea categories well enough for present purposes.

[1] *See, e.g.*, Paul H. Robinson & Jane A. Grall, *Element Analysis in Defining Criminal Liability: The Model Penal Code and Beyond*, 35 STAN. L. REV. 681 (1983).

The MPC recognizes four mental states one can act with: purpose, knowledge, recklessness, and negligence. On the MPC definition, a "person acts purposely with respect to a material element of an offense when" it is that person's "conscious object" to make that element obtain.[2] Thus, if my act causes death, and this result was my "conscious object"—my aim or goal—I have acted *purposely* as to the death.

By contrast, I kill *knowingly* when I don't aim at death, but do an act I believe is virtually certain to cause death. More precisely, one "acts knowingly with respect to a material element of an offense" when one is "aware" or "practically certain" that the element obtains (depending on what sort of element it is).[3] The MPC qualifies this basic definition,[4] but since the qualification is an attempt to capture the phenomenon of willful ignorance,[5] it is discussed in Section III. Generally, I adopt the MPC's basic definition of knowledge as practical certainty.

The criminal law's concept of knowledge thus is not the one found in the philosophical literature. The latter is typically taken to require justified true belief plus some fourth condition designed to avoid so-called Gettier counterexamples.[6] By contrast, one has criminal law knowledge of a proposition when one merely has high confidence in its truth and is correct—even if such confidence is not justified by one's evidence.[7] It's not surprising that the criminal law would employ this more anemic concept of knowledge because in this context subjective certainty of inculpatory facts is the main determinant of an actor's culpability (and together with truth, the main factor fixing the seriousness of one's offense). Someone who sets fire to a building while subjectively certain that someone else is inside, but whose evidence does not objectively justify that belief, is just as culpable (all else equal) as someone who lights the fire with the same subjective certainty but whose evidence *does* objectively justify the belief. Thus, the differences between the criminal and philosophical concepts of knowledge seem not to matter much for culpability. The legal concept of knowledge might be critiqued, but that is a project for another time. This book will use "knowledge" in its legal sense.[8]

---

[2] Model Penal Code (MPC) § 2.02(2)(a).

[3] MPC § 2.02(2)(b).

[4] MPC § 2.02(7).

[5] *See infra* note 53 and accompanying text.

[6] *See* Ed Gettier, *Is Justified True Belief Knowledge?*, 23 ANALYSIS 121–23 (1963); Jonathan J. Ichikawa & Matthias Steup, *The Analysis of Knowledge*, STANFORD ENCYCLOPEDIA OF PHILOSOPHY (2012) ("Most epistemologists have accepted Gettier's argument . . . that . . . truth, belief, and justification . . . are not in general sufficient for knowledge."), http://plato.stanford.edu/entries/knowledge-analysis/#GetPro.

[7] Robin Charlow, *Wilful Ignorance and Criminal Culpability*, 70 TEX. L. REV. 1351, 1374–75 (1992) ("criminal knowledge is correct belief").

[8] Can one have knowledge of future events—say, that one's conduct will be harmful? Especially UK courts and theorists often assume one can only have *belief* in future events, not knowledge. DAVID ORMEROD & KARL LAIRD, SMITH AND HOGAN'S CRIMINAL LAW 142 (14th ed. 2015) ("The judicial view is clear: knowledge is true belief and one cannot know something . . . that has yet to occur."). Not a lot except terminology hangs on this point. Still, I think this view is mistaken. All available scientific evidence suggests it's true now that the sun will rise tomorrow. Since the future-tensed proposition *the sun will rise tomorrow* is true now, there's no reason we

Next, consider recklessness. The MPC provides that a "person acts recklessly with respect to a material element of an offense when he consciously disregards a substantial and unjustifiable risk that the material element exists or will result from his conduct."[9] Thus, if I speed down a crowded street and recognize that this imposes a serious risk of death (and there's no justification for it), then if this actually kills someone, I've killed recklessly.

These definitions suggest a picture on which one's confidence in an inculpatory proposition, p, comes in degrees. The idea is that one's confidence in the truth of p may be assigned a number between 0 and 1, where 0 represents absolute confidence that p is false and 1 represents absolute confidence it is true. If one's confidence (or credence[10]) in p is 0.5, say, this corresponds to a belief that p is equally likely to be true as it is to be false. As one gains more confidence in p (which, let's suppose, is true), there is some point at which one would count as reckless were one to do the actus reus with that degree of credence in p (provided this is not justified). Call the level of confidence in p required to be reckless the "recklessness threshold." In the MPC's terminology, this is the point where the risk one is aware of becomes "substantial."[11] As one's confidence in p is increased further, one eventually reaches a point where one counts as *knowing* p for criminal law purposes.[12] Call this point the "knowledge threshold." We needn't specify exactly what likelihood

---

can't know it now. Granted, we cannot completely rule out that nuclear war will break out tonight, destroying the earth and preventing the sun from rising tomorrow. Nonetheless, this only means we cannot justifiably be 100 percent certain the sun will rise tomorrow—although we can come quite close. Surely, we can justifiably be *practically certain* that this proposition is true, as required for criminal law knowledge. Since future-tensed propositions can be true now, it's unclear why we cannot have knowledge of future events.

Still, even if I'm wrong—perhaps only *timeless* propositions (like "the sun rises") exist, which aren't true before the events they describe occur—then this makes only a terminological difference. We'd still go around making plans on the practical certainty that the sun will rise tomorrow, even if this shouldn't be called "knowledge." Likewise, we could still define crimes to impose liability in the same circumstances by distinguishing between "belief" and "knowledge." Thus, I want to sidestep this metaphysical fight. I'm happy to use whichever terminology proves best, since it makes no substantive difference. In this book, I'll assume we can have knowledge of future events because I think time-indexed propositions are perfectly sensible. (Moreover, I worry that insisting it's impossible to know the future because only timeless propositions exist, which lack truth values before the events they describe, means we can't know the past either.) But if I'm wrong, my arguments can easily be translated into terminology that separates belief in future events from knowledge of past events. The substance of my views would remain unchanged.

9 MPC § 2.02(2)(c); Ira P. Robbins, *The Ostrich Instruction: Deliberate Ignorance as a Criminal Mens Rea*, 81 J. CRIM. L. & CRIMINOLOGY 191, 220–22 (1990) ("Recklessness is conscious disregard of a substantial and unjustifiable risk, or 'conscious risk creation.' [It is] a willingness to act in the face of a perceived probability of the existence or creation of a particular fact, circumstance, or result.").

10 *See, e.g.*, Jacob Ross & Mark Schroeder, *Belief, Credence, and Pragmatic Encroachment*, PHIL. & PHENOMENOLOGICAL RES. (forthcoming) (discussing the view that "what it is . . . to believe a proposition is for [one's] credence in this proposition to be above a certain threshold").

11 MPC § 2.02(2)(c).

12 Kenneth Simons, *Rethinking Mental States*, 72 B.U. L. REV. 463, 474 (1992) ("Criminal law distinguishes recklessness from knowledge according to a single factor: whether the actor believed that the risk was merely 'substantial' (recklessness) or instead 'highly probable' (knowledge).").

one must believe p has of being true to count as knowing it—perhaps it's 90 percent certainty, 95 percent certainty, etc. The required level might also vary with context.[13]

Finally, the mens rea of negligence corresponds to the criminal failure to recognize a serious risk one *should* have recognized. On the MPC definition, a "person acts negligently with respect to a material element of an offense when he should be aware of a substantial and unjustifiable risk that the material element exists or will result from his conduct."[14] Some might say negligence is the *omission* of a mental state (i.e., awareness of risk). However, I think it is more accurate to say that negligence is identical to whatever mental state the defendant possesses at the time that *constitutes* his failure to perceive a risk he should have seen under the circumstances. For example, if I'm caught up in the baseball game on TV but ought to be aware that I'm risking injury to my child who I've left unattended on the balcony, we can say that my unawareness of the risk of injury to my child—that is, my negligence with respect to it—is *constituted* by my attending solely to the baseball game.[15]

These four mens rea are often said to form a culpability hierarchy,[16] with purpose sitting at the top, followed by knowledge, recklessness, and then negligence. The claim, more precisely, is:

> **Culpability Hierarchy**: All else equal, it is more culpable to do a prohibited act with a mens rea that is higher up in the hierarchy than an act that is identical in every relevant respect except that it was done with a lower mens rea.

The big question here is what "relevant respects" must be held fixed for all else to be equal. Surely, the magnitude of the harm caused and the obtainable benefits must be the same. But what else? One's motives in acting? One's cruelty? I offer some answers to these questions in Chapter 2, where I show how my theory of culpability helps defend the hierarchy claim. Perhaps the claim is false, but given its wide adoption in law, I think this is a conclusion we should reach only as a last resort. Better to start by seeing how far we can get in defending the law's core features, given their development through centuries of practical experience.

[13] *Cf.* Ross & Schroeder, *supra* note 10.

[14] MPC § 2.02(2)(d).

[15] The MPC clarifies that "[t]he risk must be of such a nature and degree that the actor's failure to perceive it, considering the nature and purpose of his conduct and the circumstances known to him, involves a gross deviation from the standard of care that a reasonable person would observe in the actor's situation." MPC § 2.02 (d).

[16] *See, e.g.*, Kenneth Simons, *Should the Model Penal Code's Mens Rea Provisions Be Amended?*, 1 Ohio St. J. Crim. L. 179, 195–96 (2003) ("The MPC views its four basic mental states or culpability terms as hierarchically ordered").

II. The Willful Ignorance Doctrine and Its Normative Basis

With this map of the mens rea landscape in criminal law, let me explain where the willful ignorance doctrine fits within it.

A. KNOWLEDGE CRIMES AND INCULPATORY PROPOSITIONS

To be guilty of a *knowledge crime*, one must know an *inculpatory proposition*. For example, the MPC makes it an offense to "purposely receive[] . . . property of another knowing that it has been stolen, or believing that it has probably been stolen, unless the property is received . . . with purpose to restore it to the owner."[17] The inculpatory proposition for this crime is that the property received has been stolen (or very probably has been). Alternatively, consider a hypothetical statute defining second-degree arson as the act of intentionally damaging a building by setting fire to it while knowing another person is inside.[18] Thus, the actus reus is setting fire to a building, while the inculpatory proposition (or one of them) that must be known is that someone is in the building at the time. Here's a third example: US federal law makes it a crime to "knowingly . . . possess with intent to . . . distribute . . . a controlled substance."[19] Conviction under this statute requires knowledge that what one possessed was a controlled substance. Mere recklessness toward this fact doesn't suffice. In general, the inculpatory proposition often will be a factual circumstance the knowledge of which makes the actus reus wrongful—or more so.

One complication requires clarification. In the previous examples, I talked as if for each knowledge crime, there is one single proposition the defendant must know for being guilty. This is a simplification. In reality, to be guilty of a knowledge crime, it is enough to know any of a *range* of true propositions that are sufficiently close to the crime's core inculpatory proposition. Take receipt of stolen property. Its *core* inculpatory proposition is, roughly, *this property I've received is very likely stolen*. However, real people don't think in this kind of legalese. Rather than deploying abstractions like *property* or *stolen*, people are more likely to use a description of the item they possess (e.g., this laptop, car, cellphone, etc.) and just have a vague sense that the item had a dubious source. This, too, could satisfy the knowledge element for this crime. The point is that to satisfy a crime's knowledge element, it is enough to know either (i) its core inculpatory proposition ("this property I've received is very likely stolen"), or (ii) some closely related proposition from which

---

[17] MPC § 223.6.

[18] In fact, arson statutes tend to say it's sufficient for the defendant to know a person was in the building or that he *reasonably should have known*. *See* N.Y. Penal Law § 150.15. But let's set aside that complication to get a good example of a knowledge crime. Other statutes could be used too. First-degree burglary in New York requires (among other things) that the defendant "knowingly enters or remains unlawfully in a dwelling with the intent to commit a crime therein." N.Y. Penal Law § 140.30.

[19] 21 U.S.C. § 841(a)(1).

the core inculpatory proposition is straightforwardly inferable by normal people in the circumstances ("this Gucci bag from Tony Soprano probably wasn't his"). For clarity, throughout this book I'll make the simplifying assumption that what must be known to be guilty of a knowledge crime is its *core* inculpatory proposition. Just bear in mind that, in principle, knowledge of any closely related proposition from which this proposition can be straightforwardly inferred would also suffice. From now on, I'll ignore this complication unless it makes a difference.

B. THE WILLFUL IGNORANCE DOCTRINE

Where a knowledge crime is charged, it is common practice among courts to allow willful ignorance of the relevant inculpatory proposition to satisfy the knowledge element of the crime.[20] Willful ignorance jury instructions state that the jury may find the requisite knowledge to be present if the defendant was merely willfully ignorant of the relevant proposition.[21] In a drug possession case, for example, such instructions might say that the jury can find that the defendant had the required knowledge if he was willfully ignorant of the fact that the substance he possessed was a narcotic. As the old chestnut has it, you could be convicted of knowingly possessing drugs if you transport a stranger's suitcase in exchange for $500 and you deliberately refrain from looking inside in order to remain ignorant about whether it contains drugs. Similarly, if your friend with gang ties suddenly gives you a fancy laptop and starts telling you a dubious story about where he got it, but you cut him off saying "no, don't tell me, I don't want to know," you could be treated as if you knew it was stolen.

The "willful ignorance doctrine" refers to the rule that juries may convict a defendant of a knowledge crime even if he was only willfully ignorant of the inculpatory proposition. This doctrine is a boon to prosecutors, since it gives them another route to securing convictions besides proving *actual* knowledge. The doctrine can apply in any factual setting: from not looking to see if the suitcase one has been asked to carry contains drugs to turning a blind eye to the possibility that one's employees are engaged in money laundering. This doctrine allows courts to treat such defendants as if they had the knowledge required for conviction.

Finally, the doctrine I'm concerned with should not be confused with the distinct *evidentiary rule* recognizing that proof of willful ignorance can also be grounds for the jury to infer the defendant had actual knowledge.[22] The evidentiary rule applies when the defendant's willful ignorance of p provides circumstantial evidence that he actually knew

---

[20] All the federal courts of appeals have endorsed the willful ignorance doctrine. Global-Tech Appliances, Inc. v. SEB S.A., 131 S. Ct. 2060, 2070 & n.9 (2011) (collecting cases).

[21] United States v. Heredia, 483 F.3d 913, 917 (9th Cir. 2007) (en banc) (discussing such jury instructions).

[22] *See Global-Tech*, 131 S. Ct. at 2073 (Kennedy, J., dissenting) (observing that "[f]acts that support willful blindness are often probative of actual knowledge").

p (i.e., was practically certain thereof). This is not the willful ignorance doctrine proper. Unlike the evidentiary rule, the willful ignorance doctrine applies even where both sides accept that the defendant did *not actually know* the inculpatory proposition. This doctrine still allows mere willful ignorance to be a basis for punishing the defendant as if he possessed knowledge (although it's agreed that he didn't literally). The willful ignorance doctrine thus covers conduct that otherwise falls *outside* the scope of the applicable statute. That's precisely why it's puzzling.

C. A BRIEF HISTORY OF THE WILLFUL IGNORANCE DOCTRINE

Before precisely defining willful ignorance and discussing the normative foundations of this doctrine, let me sketch the rule's history in Anglo-American jurisdictions. The English courts apparently were the first to adopt it in the criminal law. Writing in 1954, Edwards observed that "[f]or well-nigh a hundred years, it has been clear from the authorities that a person who deliberately shuts his eyes to an obvious means of knowledge has sufficient *mens rea* for an offence based on such words as . . . 'knowingly.' "[23] He noted that "[s]o far as can be discovered, the case of *R. v. Sleep* was the first occasion in which judicial approval was given to" the willful ignorance doctrine[24] (also dubbed the "connaivance" rule by English courts[25]). The court in *R v. Sleep*,[26] an 1861 case, quashed a conviction on the ground that one cannot be convicted of knowingly possessing "naval stores" without the jury finding "the prisoner either knew that the goods were government stores or wilfully shut his eyes to the fact."[27] Subsequent nineteenth-century cases solidified the rule that willful blindness can substitute for knowledge in the context of offenses like knowingly allowing "gaming" in one's licensed premises (like hotels or taverns).[28]

US law started employing the concept of willful ignorance in the nineteenth century as well, albeit slightly later than the United Kingdom. Some nineteenth-century US cases appeal to willful ignorance in noncriminal contexts—like land law[29] and commercial

---

[23] J. Ll. J. Edwards, *The Criminal Degrees of Knowledge*, 17 MOD. L. REV. 294, 298 (1954). *See also* Jonathan Marcus, *Model Penal Code Section 2.02(7) and Willful Blindness*, 102 YALE L.J. 2231, 2233–34 (1993) (offering a similar history of the doctrine); *Global-Tech*, 131 S. Ct. at 2069 & n.6 (noting "[t]he doctrine emerged in English law almost four decades earlier [than in the United States] and became firmly established by the end of the 19th century").

[24] Edwards, *supra* note 23, at 298.

[25] *Id.*

[26] [1861] 30 L.J.M.C. 170, 169 E.R. 1296.

[27] R v. Sleep [1861], 169 E.R. 1296, 1302 (Willes, J.). *See also id.* at 1301–02 (Crompto, J.) (liability cannot be avoided "where the prisoner's eyes are wilfully and deliberately shut to the truth").

[28] Edwards, *supra* note 23, at 298–99. *See* Bosley v. Davies, [1875] L.R. 1 Q.B. 84, 88 (remanding because "constructive knowledge will supply the place of actual knowledge"); Redgate v. Haynes [1876] L.R. 1 Q.B. 89, 94 (Blackburn, J.) (maintaining that "if [a licensee] purposely abstained from ascertaining whether gaming was going on or not . . . this would be enough to make her liable" for "suffering gaming").

[29] U.S. v. Mullan, 10 F. 785, 791 (C.C.Cal. 1882) ("No one could be possibly ignorant of the character of the land . . . without actually shutting his eyes against open, public, notorious, obvious facts. [Defendants] must

paper.[30] Then in 1899, the Supreme Court employed it in a criminal context. The defendant in *Spurr v. United States* was charged with a "willful" violation of a statute that prohibited bank employees from certifying checks drawn against an account with insufficient funds.[31] In setting aside the conviction, the Court held the offense would be present "if the officer purposely keeps himself in ignorance of whether the drawer has money in the bank or not."[32] This case did not strictly speaking apply the willful ignorance doctrine in the sense I am concerned with. After all, the statute in question required a "willful" not a "knowing" violation, and so this case was not clearly an instance of allowing willful ignorance to satisfy the *knowledge* element of a crime. Nonetheless, in the wake of *Spurr*, other criminal cases did rely on the willful ignorance doctrine proper in the early twentieth century.[33]

The notion of willful ignorance had acquired a strong foothold in US law by the mid-twentieth century, since the drafters of the MPC in 1962 attempted to define "knowledge" to capture the phenomenon of willful ignorance.[34] (However, as I argue later, the MPC strategy fails.[35] Willful ignorance is not knowledge.) The willful ignorance doctrine was solidified as a core feature of US federal criminal law with the 1976 case of *United States v. Jewell*.[36] There, the Ninth Circuit upheld a defendant's conviction for knowingly possessing drugs in violation of 21 U.S.C. § 841(a)(1) where the defendant was convicted under willful ignorance jury instructions.[37] *Jewell* became one of the leading willful ignorance cases, and willful ignorance instructions became known as the "*Jewell* instruction."[38]

---

have known . . . the truth, or else they were wilfully ignorant and blind to what the law required them to see and know.").

[30] Town of Lansing v. Lytle, 38 F. 204, 212 (C.C.N.Y. 1889) ("The rule which shields a purchaser of commercial paper who has not bought mala fides . . . does not protect a purchaser who willfully avoids making inquiry when circumstances of grave suspicion point to a fraud.").

[31] Spurr v. United States, 174 U.S. 728, 733–34 (1899).

[32] *Id.* at 735.

[33] *See Global-Tech*, 131 S. Ct. at 2069 & n.7 (collecting cases); Rachmil v. U.S., 43 F.2d 878, 881 (9th Cir. 1930) (per curiam) ("the offense of 'knowingly' concealing cannot be committed without some knowledge on the part of the bankrupt of the existence of the bankruptcy proceeding, unless he willfully closes his eyes to that which is obvious"); United States v. Yasser, 114 F.2d 558, 560 (3d Cir. 1940) (agreeing that offense of "knowingly and fraudulently concealing" property from creditors can be committed if one "closes his eyes" to the inculpatory facts, and ordering willful ignorance jury instructions on remand); United States v. Erie R. Co., 222 F. 444, 448–49 (D.C.N.J. 1915) (holding that if "the carrier willfully and intentionally remained in ignorance of the facts necessary to determine whether the import rate was lawful, [it must] be charged in law with the knowledge of the facts which reasonable inquiry and investigation would have revealed").

[34] *See infra* note 53.

[35] *See infra* note 53–55 and accompanying text.

[36] 532 F.2d 697 (9th Cir. 1976).

[37] *Id.* at 700 ("Government can complete their burden . . . by proving . . . conscious purpose to avoid learning the truth").

[38] U.S. v. Heredia, 483 F.3d 913, 918 (9th Cir. 2007) (approving what "many colloquially refer to the deliberate ignorance instruction as the '*Jewell* instruction'").

Willful ignorance instructions have now been approved by all US federal circuits,[39] as well as by the Supreme Court (interestingly, in a patent infringement case—though with a thorough discussion of the criminal cases).[40] The willful ignorance doctrine has become a favored tool of prosecutors, especially in the context of drug crimes requiring knowledge. At this point in US federal criminal law, there seems no turning back. A recent Westlaw search produced over 5,000 reported decisions from US federal courts containing some version of the phrases "willful blindness" or "willful ignorance."[41] Indeed, over 500 of these were reported after 2016. US law is now firmly wedded to the willful ignorance doctrine.

D. INTRODUCING THE EQUAL CULPABILITY THESIS

With this brief history of the willful ignorance doctrine in hand, let's turn to one of the main normative questions to be confronted in this book. *Why* may a defendant's willful ignorance be taken to satisfy the knowledge element of a crime? What *justifies* this practice?

There is a simple, but powerful thought underlying the willful ignorance doctrine: deliberately turning a blind eye to criminality shows one to be culpable in the same way, and to the same degree, as acting with knowledge of it does. As the Supreme Court put it, "[t]he traditional rationale for this doctrine is that defendants who behave in [a willfully ignorant] manner are just as culpable as those who have actual knowledge."[42] Following Husak and Callender, I call this claim—on which the willful ignorance doctrine is founded—the *equal culpability thesis*.[43] Courts routinely cite it as grounds for the doctrine.[44] As the Ninth Circuit said in *Jewell*, a leading willful ignorance case, "the

---

39 *See Global-Tech*, 131 S. Ct. at 2070 & n.9 (collecting cases); *see also* Marcus, *supra* note 23, at 2232 ("All the federal circuits have employed willful blindness doctrines.").

40 *Global-Tech*, 131 S. Ct. at 2069–70.

41 The search was carried out on March 31, 2017. I queried the "All Federal" database for the term "willful" in the same sentence as "blind!" or "ignorant!" (where "!" indicates a root expander).

42 *Global-Tech*, 131 S. Ct. at 2069.

43 Douglas N. Husak & Craig A. Callender, *Wilful Ignorance, Knowledge, and the "Equal Culpability" Thesis: A Study of the Deeper Significance of the Principle of Legality*, 1994 Wis. L. Rev. 29, 53 (1994).

44 *See* United States v. Jewell, 532 F.2d 697, 700 (9th Cir. 1976) ("deliberate ignorance and positive knowledge are equally culpable"); United States v. Heredia, 483 F.3d 913, 926 (9th Cir. 2007) (en banc) (Kleinfeld, J., concurring) (opining that "wilful blindness is 'equally culpable' to, and may be substituted for, positive knowledge"); United States v. Stadtmauer, 620 F.3d 238, 255 (3d Cir. 2010) (quoting *Jewell*'s observation that the "substantive justification" for the willful ignorance doctrine is the equal culpability of willful ignorance and knowledge); United States v. One 1973 Rolls Royce, V.I.N. SRH-16266 By & Through Goodman, 43 F.3d 794, 808 (3d Cir. 1994) (describing "the mainstream conception of willful blindness as a state of mind of much greater culpability than simple negligence or recklessness, and more akin to knowledge"); United States v. Rivera, 944 F.2d 1563, 1570 (11th Cir. 1991) (willful ignorance doctrine "is premised on the belief that acts conducted under . . . deliberate ignorance and acts committed with positive knowledge are equally culpable").

substantive justification for the rule is that deliberate ignorance and positive knowledge are equally culpable."[45]

In principle, one might offer other rationales for the willful ignorance doctrine. One might argue, on deterrence grounds, that the doctrine is justified as a prophylactic mechanism for preventing knowing wrongdoing. That is, perhaps punishing misconduct that very nearly but doesn't quite qualify as a knowledge crime will help deter knowledge crimes proper.[46] Alternatively, some might argue that when one has deliberately preserved one's ignorance of some inculpatory fact, one should be estopped from denying that one knew it.[47]

However, these alternative justifications are not the focus of this book. The reason is that they are not the courts' official justification for the willful ignorance doctrine. Instead, courts generally rely on the equal culpability thesis as the basis for approving willful ignorance jury instructions. We saw the Supreme Court dub this the "traditional rationale" for the doctrine.[48] In my view, the courts' preferred rationale should be taken seriously and adhered to at least as our starting point. My project, therefore, is to examine the normative principles at work in the traditional rationale. If this fails, courts may have to reach for other justifications to retain the willful ignorance doctrine. But such alternative justifications go beyond the scope of this book. My aim is to see how far we can get by remaining faithful to the courts' traditional rationale.

The traditional rationale places constraints on when the willful ignorance doctrine legitimately applies. To remain faithful to this rationale, willful ignorance toward the inculpatory proposition should satisfy the knowledge element of the crime *in all but only* those cases where the willfully ignorant defendant really is as culpable as a similarly situated knowing actor. Thus, the proper scope of the willful ignorance doctrine just is the set of cases in which the equal culpability thesis holds. So to determine when willful ignorance instructions are warranted, we need to know when the equal culpability thesis is true. Are all cases of willfully ignorant misconduct as culpable as the analogous knowing misconduct? Or only sometimes? More generally, if willful ignorance is not knowledge, but, as we'll see, a form of recklessness where one's suspicions remain uninvestigated, how could willful ignorance *ever* rise to the same level of culpability as the analogous knowing misconduct? I tackle these questions in Chapters 3 and 4 and ultimately give an account of when, and why, the willful ignorance doctrine is properly applied.

---

[45] 532 F.2d at 700.

[46] Paul Robinson, *Imputed Criminal Liability*, 93 YALE L.J. 609, 620–21 (discussing the utilitarian justification for imputation principles).

[47] Thanks to David Enoch for this suggestion.

[48] *Global-Tech*, 131 S. Ct. at 2069.

III. The Basic Notion of Willful Ignorance

Evaluating the equal culpability thesis requires elucidating the notions of both criminal culpability and willful ignorance. Culpability is the primary focus of Chapter 2, where I defend a particular version of the popular *insufficient regard theory* of criminal culpability. Its basic thought is that one is culpable for an action to the extent it manifests insufficient regard for the interests of others that are properly protected by the law.[49]

Here, let's focus on willful ignorance. To start, it is widely agreed that willful ignorance is not just a subspecies of criminal law knowledge. As seen, knowledge in the criminal law consists in high subjective certainty (or belief) plus truth.[50] The consensus among courts[51] and commentators[52] is that willful ignorance is not knowledge thus understood. This familiar point bears emphasizing because one might have thought the equal culpability thesis could be maintained just by defining knowledge so that willful ignorance counts as a type of knowledge. In that case, anyone who does the actus reus in willful ignorance would trivially be as culpable as one who does it knowingly, since the willfully ignorant defendant would herself be a knowing actor. Indeed, this is arguably the strategy employed by the MPC.[53]

However, this strategy fails.[54] As some scholars convincingly argue, one can be willfully ignorant of a proposition without having a particularly high degree of confidence

---

49 *See, e.g.*, Larry Alexander & Kimberly Ferzan, Crime and Culpability 67–68 (2009) ("insufficient concern [is] the essence of culpability"); Peter Westen, *An Attitudinal Theory of Excuse*, 25 L. & Phil. 289, 373–74.

50 *See supra* note 10.

51 United States v. Svoboda, 347 F.3d 471, 477–78 (2d Cir. 2003) (willful ignorance instruction "permits a finding of knowledge even where there is no evidence that the defendant possessed actual knowledge" (internal quotation marks omitted)); United States v. Freeman, 434 F.3d 369, 378 (5th Cir. 2005) ("deliberate indifference charge permits 'the jury to convict without finding that the defendant was aware of the existence of illegal conduct'"); *Global-Tech*, 131 S. Ct. at 2072 (Kennedy, J., dissenting) ("[w]illful blindness is not knowledge").

52 Robbins, *supra* note 9, at 226 ("deliberate ignorance is not knowledge"); Deborah Hellman, *Willfully Blind for Good Reason*, 3 Crim. L. & Phil. 301, 302 (2009) ("contrived ignorance itself is not a form of knowledge"); Husak & Callender, *supra* note 43, at 51 (arguing that "wilfully ignorant defendants do not possess knowledge").

53 The MPC commentary explains that its definition of knowledge in "[p]aragraph [2.02](7) deals with the situation British commentators have denominated 'wilful blindness' or 'connivance.'" MPC 129–30 (Tent. Draft No. 4, 1955). *See also* Marcus, *supra* note 23, at 2231–32.

54 Here's why. MPC § 2.02(7) states that "[w]hen knowledge of the existence of a particular fact is an element of an offense, such knowledge is established if a person is aware of a high probability of its existence, unless he actually believes that it does not exist." While this covers some instances of willful ignorance, it clearly doesn't cover all. As argued in the main text, one might have serious suspicions about a fact (e.g., there are drugs in the suitcase) and deliberately preserve one's ignorance thereof, but still not believe this fact has a "high probability" of obtaining. Perhaps one only believes it has a 30–40 percent chance of obtaining. This clearly is enough for willful ignorance, but falls outside the expanded MPC definition of knowledge in MPC § 2.02(7). Thus, MPC § 2.02(7) is too narrow to fully capture the phenomenon of willful ignorance.

in its truth.[55] Perhaps one merely sees the proposition's truth as *somewhat* probable—though not probable enough to be *practically certain* of it—and then goes on to deliberately avoid acquiring more information about it. This would be a case of willful ignorance that falls outside the criminal law definition of knowledge as practical certainty. (Indeed, as Husak and Callender argue, some cases of willful ignorance would not fit within *any* plausible definition of knowledge.[56])

If willful ignorance is not just a form of knowledge, what *is* it? On the most basic understanding, willful ignorance involves two components. Glanville Williams noted that a person is willfully ignorant if he "has his suspicions aroused but then deliberately omits to make further enquiries."[57] Likewise, the Supreme Court recently observed that most courts agree on "two basic requirements: (1) the defendant must subjectively believe that there is a high probability that a fact exists and (2) the defendant must take deliberate actions to avoid learning of that fact."[58] Given the broad agreement that at least these two prongs are required, I adopt the following as my *basic account* of willful ignorance:

> **Basic Willful Ignorance**: To be willfully ignorant of an inculpatory proposition p (which let's suppose is true[59]), one must
> (1) have sufficiently serious suspicions that p is true (i.e., believe that there is a sufficiently high likelihood that p is true, short of practical certainty[60]), and
> (2) deliberately (as opposed to negligently or recklessly) fail to take reasonably available steps to learn with greater certainty whether p actually is true.

Unless otherwise indicated, this is the sense of willful ignorance I will employ here. As Chapter 3 notes, one might add further requirements to this basic account to restrict it to

Here's a second problem. MPC § 2.02(7) also ropes in cases that *neither* fit the core definition of knowledge as practical certainty *nor* involve any kind of willful ignorance. Suppose the defendant thinks there is a high probability (perhaps 60 percent) that there are drugs in the suitcase. However, investigating might not be feasible and he makes no effort to preserve his ignorance. MPC § 2.02(7) would implausibly count this as knowledge too. The case actually is neither knowledge in the sense of practical certainty nor willful ignorance, as defined later. Instead, it is mere recklessness as to the fact of drugs in the suitcase. As my account in Chapter 4 makes clear, there is no normative basis for equating *mere recklessness*, without the effort to preserve one's ignorance, with knowledge. This is a second way MPC § 2.02(7) goes wrong.

[55] Husak & Callender, *supra* note 43, at 37–38.

[56] *Id.* at 51 (offering a persuasive argument to this effect).

[57] Glanville Williams, Criminal Law: The General Part 157 (2d ed. 1961).

[58] *Global-Tech*, 131 S. Ct. at 2070.

[59] It's unclear whether a person can be willfully ignorant of a proposition that is false. However, this needn't concern us, since (barring abuses) one is not likely to be charged with a knowledge crime unless the inculpatory proposition is plausibly true. (Granted one might still be charged with the *attempt* to do the knowledge crime. But since the mens rea for attempt is intent, not knowledge, willful ignorance won't figure into many attempt prosecutions.)

[60] Plausibly, what counts as a "sufficiently high probability" may vary depending on features of the context—like the amount of harm at stake.

cases of willful ignorance that seem particularly bad. For example, some federal circuits insist one's motive for remaining ignorant must be to preserve a defense against liability in the event of prosecution.[61] (Chapter 3 discusses but rejects this restriction.) Still, the basic account of willful ignorance yields the broadest version of the equal culpability thesis that is at least plausible. So this is my starting point.

Before proceeding, several clarifications are necessary. First, on the basic account, performing the actus reus of a crime in willful ignorance always makes one qualify as *at least* reckless. As Alexander and Ferzan emphasize, "[t]he prototypical willfully ignorant actor is, of course, reckless. The risk he is taking—of, say, smuggling drugs—is an unjustifiable one."[62] This follows from prong (1) of the basic account. It states that willful ignorance requires harboring suspicions that the inculpatory proposition for the crime is true (e.g., that the substance one is transporting is drugs). Thus, if one proceeds to do the actus reus in the face of these suspicions, one at least counts as reckless as to that proposition. The question we will ultimately have to confront, then, is what could raise the willfully ignorant defendant's culpability up from the level of mere recklessness to that of knowing misconduct.[63]

Not all theorists agree that suspicions of p are needed to be willfully ignorant of p. Some think one can be willfully ignorant of p without any awareness of a risk of p.[64] On this view, if one merely should have been aware of such a risk, but then went on—perhaps unconsciously—to block oneself from obtaining more information about whether p obtains, one might count as "willfully ignorant" in a broad sense. Admittedly, this might be appropriate terminology for moral evaluation. Perhaps I display a morally objectionable form of "willful" ignorance if I *should* realize my salad dressing might contain traces of seafood, but my dislike of one guest with a seafood allergy subconsciously affects me so that this possibility ceases to be salient and I don't check whether the salad

---

[61] United States v. Willis, 277 F.3d 1026, 1032 (8th Cir. 2002) (requiring that one "purposely contrived to avoid learning all of the facts in order to have a defense against subsequent prosecution"); United States v. Delreal-Ordones, 213 F.3d 1263, 1268 (10th Cir. 2000) (same); United States v. Puche, 350 F.3d 1137, 1149 (11th Cir. 2003) (same). *Cf. Heredia*, 483 F.3d at 920 (explicitly rejecting this "motive prong" in defining willful ignorance).

[62] Alexander & Ferzan, *supra* note 49, at 34. (Hellman criticizes their pure recklessness view of willful ignorance, but acknowledges that Alexander and Ferzan can respond. *See* Hellman *supra* note 52, at 311.)

[63] Note that this question also arises for Alexander and Ferzan's account. They are correct that the willfully ignorant are at least reckless. But some cases of willful ignorance are especially culpable—indeed, as culpable as the analogous knowing misconduct. We want to know what it is, precisely, about opting to remain in ignorance about the risks of one's conduct that could increase one's culpability from the level of mere recklessness to that of knowing wrongdoing. This is the question my account in Chapter 4 seeks to answer. So it can be seen as fleshing out Alexander and Ferzan's claim that willful ignorance is a form of recklessness.

[64] *See, e.g.*, Jan Willem Wieland, *Willful Ignorance*, 20 Ethical Theory & Moral Prac. 105, 115 (2017) (arguing "we need not add a suspicion or awareness requirement on willful ignorance. The latter is compatible with suspicions, but there's also willful ignorance without them").

dressing contains seafood before serving it. This broad notion of "willful" ignorance is a species of negligence (as discussed in Chapter 8).

Nonetheless, this broad notion is not the concept of willful ignorance that the criminal law employs, and the criminal law is my primary concern here. Willful ignorance matters to the law because courts allow it to substitute for knowledge of the inculpatory proposition. But to serve this function, willful ignorance must at least rise to the level of recklessness. While it is plausible that an especially egregious form of recklessness ("recklessness plus") can make the defendant culpable enough to merit treatment as a knowing wrongdoer, it is doubtful that any form of mere negligence could. Accordingly, in this book, I understand willful ignorance as the criminal law does.

Next, prong (2) is necessary to distinguish willful ignorance from other forms of culpable ignorance. Self-caused ignorance, after all, is not always willful or deliberate—it might be merely reckless or negligent. Suppose one is uncertain about some question, and while one meant to investigate, one simply forgot or was distracted from doing so. This clearly makes one count as ignorant, but one's ignorance does not seem *willful*—just inadvertent or negligent. For ignorance of some fact to be truly willful, one must deliberately decline—or, equivalently, consciously choose not—to acquire additional information about the matter. This is the law's position, and I follow this assumption too.[65] Prong (2) in the basic account captures this.

Lastly, what does "deliberately" as used in (2) mean? I take this term from the Supreme Court in *Global-Tech*.[66] Paradigmatically, to deliberately fail to investigate involves acting with *purpose*—the aim or intent—to preserve one's ignorance. Most courts adopt this meaning of "deliberately preserving one's ignorance."[67] However, some courts suggest that even when the defendant did not have purpose to remain in ignorance, a *merely knowing* failure to investigate (i.e., doing what one knows will prevent one from learning the truth, but not intending this) can also suffice for willful ignorance. This is suggested

---

[65] For example, *Jewell* says willful ignorance requires "conscious *purpose* to disregard the nature of that which was in the vehicle, with a conscious *purpose* to avoid learning the truth." 532 F.2d at 700 (emphasis added). *See infra* note 67 and accompanying text.

In principle, one might argue the law's definition should be expanded, thus making willful ignorance instructions more widely available. I discuss similar moves in Chapters 6 and 8. However, for reasons of clarity and transparency, I don't advocate altering the definition of willful ignorance. Instead, I take the legal definition as fixed, and argue that we should go beyond the existing willful ignorance doctrine in certain ways. I contend we should recognize new doctrines that allow egregious kinds of nonwillful ignorance to substitute for higher mental states. I take this tack because it's clearer and less likely to invite needless definitional fights. But nothing of substance hangs on it. We could reach the same results I argue for by changing the definition of willful ignorance, if one prefers that route.

[66] 131 S. Ct. at 2070.

[67] *See, e.g., Jewell*, 532 F.2d at 700 (requiring "a conscious purpose to avoid learning the truth"); *Heredia*, 483 F.3d at 918 ("when Congress made it a crime to 'knowingly . . . possess with intent to . . . distribute . . . a controlled substance,' . . . it meant to punish . . . also those who *don't know because they don't want to know*") (emphasis added). *See also* WILLIAMS, *supra* note 57, at 157 (willful ignorance requires that one "*deliberately* omits to make further enquiries *because he wishes to remain in ignorance*") (emphasis added).

especially by statements that willful ignorance requires "conscious avoidance" of inculpatory knowledge.[68] On this view, one could also count as willfully ignorant if one acted in ways one merely is *practically certain* will preserve one's ignorance, even if this was not one's purpose or aim. (Some courts aren't consistent on this point and slide between these two views.[69]) For clarity, I favor the second, wider approach. Still, to avoid needless controversy, I generally focus on the first, more familiar type of willful ignorance. I'll explicitly note where this wrinkle makes a difference.

IV. Clarifying the Equal Culpability Thesis

As noted, the normative foundation for the willful ignorance doctrine—its "substantive justification"[70]—is the equal culpability thesis. It claims, roughly, that misconduct done in willful ignorance in the basic sense is just as culpable as knowing misconduct. However, there are two ways to unpack this claim. One, it turns out, is far superior.

First, the equal culpability thesis might be understood as the claim that whenever a defendant D does the actus reus of knowledge crime C in willful ignorance, *there is some possible person directly guilty of C who D is just as culpable as*. This amounts to saying that a willfully ignorant D can be convicted of C as long as D is as culpable as the *least culpable knowing actor* who could legitimately be found guilty of C.

Nonetheless, this version of the equal culpability thesis—the "Indeterminate Counterpart" interpretation—raises concerns. Even if true, it would not be a defensible basis for allowing willful ignorance to substitute for knowledge. The logic of this version of the thesis suggests that anyone who does the actus reus of C can be convicted of C solely because she attains the *minimum level of culpability* required for C. However, it is unclear how to even begin determining what this minimum culpability level is for any particular crime. I doubt there is any such level for particular crimes.

Moreover, since most crimes can be committed under circumstances that do not render one very culpable, the logic of grounding the willful ignorance doctrine on the Indeterminate Counterpart thesis implies that even *very slightly negligent* actors could in principle be convicted of serious knowledge crimes. Consider a secretary bullied into doing things she knows will help her domineering boss commit fraud. While the abuse and pressure she faced greatly reduces her culpability for assisting the fraud, assume it stops just short of constituting the defense of duress to the crime of aiding and abetting

68 United States v. Ferrarini, 219 F.3d 145, 155 (2d Cir. 2000) (concluding "the jury was properly instructed that conscious avoidance could . . . be used to infer knowledge of the conspiracy's unlawful objectives").

69 *Compare* United States v. Svoboda, 347 F.3d 471, 480 (2d Cir. 2003) (willful ignorance instruction warranted when evidence "establish[es] the defendant's purposeful contrivance to avoid guilty knowledge") (internal quotation marks and citations omitted), *with id.* at 479 ("factfinder may . . . rely on conscious avoidance to satisfy at least the knowledge component of intent to participate in a conspiracy").

70 *See supra* note 44.

fraud (a crime that requires knowledge of the underlying offense). But accountants, lawyers, or bankers in everyday life who are only slightly negligent, lazy, or incompetent can very easily attain the same level of culpability in dealing with clients who actually are perpetrating frauds. By the logic of the Indeterminate Counterpart interpretation of the equal culpability thesis, this would allow the slight negligence of these accountants, lawyers, or bankers to substitute for full knowledge of their clients' fraud. But this is an implausible basis for imposing aiding and abetting liability.

Thus, a different interpretation of the equal culpability thesis is needed. Instead, it should be understood as the claim that willfully ignorant misconduct is as culpable as *the analogous knowing misconduct*. The idea is to focus on the willfully ignorant defendant's *similarly situated* knowing counterpart, as follows:

> **Unrestricted Equal Culpability Thesis (UECT)**: Suppose A1 and A2 each perform the actus reus of a given crime that requires knowledge of an inculpatory proposition, p. A1 and A2, and their respective actions, are identical in every respect except one: while A1's action is performed with knowledge of p, A2's action is performed in willful ignorance of p in the basic sense. On these suppositions, A2 is (at least) as culpable for her action as A1 is for his.

This version provides a more plausible basis for the willful ignorance doctrine. It does not face the problems of the Indeterminate Counterpart interpretation. First, it does not require determining each crime's minimum culpability level. Moreover, it is unlikely that only slightly negligent actors will be as culpable as their *exactly analogous* knowing counterparts. Accordingly, I take UECT to be the simplest formulation of the equal culpability thesis that at least is *plausible* as a basis for the willful ignorance doctrine.

Most federal courts accept UECT, insofar as they allow willful ignorance in the basic sense (not some restricted form of willful ignorance that requires bad motives for not investigating) to suffice for giving willful ignorance jury instructions. Most notably, the Ninth Circuit adopted the unrestricted approach in *United States v. Heredia*.[71] The court held that a "two-pronged instruction"—requiring only that the defendant suspected "drugs were in the vehicle . . . and deliberately avoided learning the truth"[72]—was adequate.[73] Other circuits resemble the Ninth Circuit in allowing willful ignorance in the basic sense to suffice—including the Second,[74] Third,[75]

[71] 483 F.3d 913, 920 (9th Cir. 2007) (en banc).

[72] *Id.* at 917.

[73] *Id.* at 920–21.

[74] United States v. Ferrarini, 219 F.3d 145, 154 (2d Cir. 2000) (willful ignorance requires "aware[ness] of a high probability [of the inculpatory fact] and consciously avoided confirming that fact").

[75] United States v. Flores, 454 F.3d 149, 155 (3d Cir. 2006) (willful ignorance requires "defendant 'was [subjectively] aware of the high probability of the fact in question,' and 'could have recognized the likelihood of illicit acts yet deliberately avoided learning the true facts' ") (internal citation and alteration omitted).

Fifth,[76] Sixth,[77] and Seventh Circuits.[78] (At least two circuits—the First and Fourth—have issued conflicting decisions on whether willful ignorance in the basic sense suffices.[79]) Moreover, it is plausible that the Supreme Court favors the unrestricted approach. After all, in its recent *Global-Tech* decision, when sketching the willful ignorance doctrine, the Court only mentioned the two prongs of the basic account. Indeed, some courts have cited *Global-Tech* in support of the claim that the Supreme Court does not favor the restricted motive approach some circuits favor (as discussed in Chapter 3).[80] Nonetheless, it is not clear how much to make of this, since *Global-Tech* did not expressly confront whether further restrictions to the concept of willful ignorance should be imposed.

V. The Questions to Be Answered

We've seen what willful ignorance is and how to understand the courts' traditional rationale for this doctrine—the equal culpability thesis. My aim in this book is not only to examine the justification and scope of the willful ignorance doctrine, but to use the theoretical framework we get out of this examination to investigate a range of foundational questions about the criminal law that the doctrine implicates. What are they?

Starting narrowly and working outward, one question we've already seen is that of when the willful ignorance doctrine may legitimately be applied. Trivially, this will be when the equal culpability thesis is true. But when is that? Answering this question reveals when willful ignorance grounds the imputation of knowledge as needed for conviction. Chapters 3 and 4 build an account of when willful ignorant misconduct is as culpable as analogous knowing conduct.

---

[76] United States v. Mendoza-Medina, 346 F.3d 121, 132–33 (5th Cir. 2003) (recognizing "two-pronged test" willful ignorance instruction, requiring that "(1) the defendant was subjectively aware of a high probability of the existence of the illegal conduct; and (2) the defendant purposely contrived to avoid learning of the illegal conduct").

[77] United States v. Geisen, 612 F.3d 471, 485–86 (6th Cir. 2010) ("a deliberate ignorance instruction is warranted to 'prevent[] a criminal defendant from escaping conviction merely by deliberately closing his eyes to the obvious risk that he is engaging in unlawful conduct'").

[78] United States v. Tanner, 628 F.3d 890, 904 (7th Cir. 2010) ("ostrich instruction" warranted "when (1) a defendant claims a lack of guilty knowledge and (2) the government presents evidence that suggests that the defendant deliberately avoided the truth") (quotation marks omitted); United States v. Ramsey, 785 F.2d 184, 190 (7th Cir. 1986) (Easterbrook, J.) (rejecting motive-to-avoid-liability element and adopting unrestricted approach instead).

[79] *Compare* United States v. Anthony, 545 F.3d 60, 64 (1st Cir. 2008) (endorsing two-pronged unrestricted approach), *with* United States v. Brandon, 17 F.3d 409, 452 (1st Cir. 1994) (adopting motive prong for willful ignorance instructions). *Compare* United States v. Jinwright, 683 F.3d 471, 479 (4th Cir. 2012) (adopting unrestricted approach), *with* United States v. Ebert, 178 F.3d 1287 *opinion amended on denial of reh'g*, 188 F.3d 504 (4th Cir. 1999) (adopting motive prong).

[80] United States v. Yi, 704 F.3d 800, 804–05 (9th Cir. 2013) (endorsing two-pronged, unrestricted approach to willful ignorance, citing *Global-Tech*, 131 S. Ct. at 2070).

This inquiry, in turn, requires understanding the nature of criminal culpability. To explain when willfully ignorant defendants are as culpable as their knowing counterparts, a theory of culpability is needed. But what concept of culpability does the criminal law employ? Is it just the moral concept of culpability? Or is it a simplified version of the moral concept? Is it something entirely different? Chapter 2 develops a theory of criminal culpability, which grounds the rest of the arguments in this book.

Broader questions about the criminal law lurk nearby. The willful ignorance doctrine is a mens rea imputation principle,[81] which allows willful ignorance to stand in for knowledge. What justifies such imputation? Doesn't this amount to allowing defendants to be convicted of knowledge crimes although they don't literally satisfy all the required elements—that is, don't possess the knowledge these crimes actually require? Such imputation principles may seem to conflict with the *principle of legality*, under which defendants cannot be legitimately convicted unless it's proven beyond a reasonable doubt (following applicable procedures) that they satisfy all elements of the crime charged. Given the centrality of this principle to the rule of law, one might reject the willful ignorance doctrine as an intolerable threat to rule of law norms.

However, this would be a mistake. Chapter 5 discusses several arguments courts have used to defend the legality of the willful ignorance doctrine, and where they fall short, statutory reforms can preserve the willful ignorance doctrine. Nonetheless, this leaves an important normative question: When, if ever, would such statutory reforms codifying the willful ignorance doctrine be normatively justified? This is a serious challenge that extends beyond the willful ignorance doctrine. It can arise for any equal culpability imputation principle. When is the legislature justified in codifying any particular equal culpability imputation principle into the criminal law?

To answer this challenge, Chapter 5 defends a general theory of equal culpability imputation. The theory explains why it is justified for courts to impute missing elements to a defendant simply on the ground that she is as culpable as if she had literally satisfied those elements. Such substitution, I contend, is justified when, but only when, the defendant's culpability is identical in type and degree to the culpability the legislature sought to defend against when specifying the core elements of the relevant crime. This theory of equal culpability imputation not only vindicates a restricted version of the willful ignorance doctrine, but justifies other equal culpability substitution principles like the transferred intent rule and some applications of the infamous Pinkerton doctrine. But it also shows other controversial doctrines—like the felony murder rule—to be unjustifiable on equal culpability grounds.

By doing all this—explaining why and to what extent willful ignorance is culpable, outlining the proper scope of the willful ignorance doctrine, and explaining how the

---

[81] Gideon Yaffe, *Intoxication, Recklessness, and Negligence*, 9 OHIO ST. J. CRIM. L. 545, 551 (2012) (describing willful ignorance doctrine as a "mens rea substitution principle"); Robinson, *supra* note 46.

willful ignorance doctrine and related rules can be justified as legitimate equal culpability imputation—I aim to provide a more solid theoretical basis for imputation rules like the willful ignorance doctrine than the literature currently provides. In addition, this inquiry offers a window into further questions about criminal law. Some views of willful ignorance assume one's motives for remaining ignorant affect culpability. However, we'll see that this conflicts with the default rule in the criminal law that motives don't matter for culpability. Who is right? Those who assert that motives impact the culpability of the willfully ignorant, or those who support substantive criminal law doctrine's general disinterest in motives? My theory of culpability in Chapter 2 sheds light on the issue. While *capable* of capturing either side of this debate, the theory favors the view that motives shouldn't matter to the notion of culpability that is relevant at the guilt stage of criminal proceedings (as opposed, perhaps, to sentencing).

Lastly, I go on in later chapters to argue that my theory of equal culpability imputation, which provides the normative foundation for the willful ignorance doctrine, also supports going *beyond willful ignorance* to cover other forms of culpable, but nonwillful ignorance. I argue courts should recognize additional *nonwillful ignorance substitution principles* for the same reasons they recognize the existing willful ignorance doctrine. Zooming out and appreciating the full sweep of the equal culpability rationale behind the willful ignorance doctrine gives reason to adopt new equal culpability imputation principles. First, I argue in Chapter 6 that we should allow egregious recklessly preserved ignorance to substitute for knowledge. However, I also explain in Chapter 7 why no form of culpable ignorance should by itself substitute for purpose. Still, I contend that legitimate equal culpability imputation extends further in other ways. Chapter 8 argues that equal culpability licenses treating certain egregious forms of blanket unawareness of risks as a basis for imputing *recklessness*, while Chapter 9 argues that some kinds of culpable ignorance in corporate settings ground the attribution of knowledge to corporations themselves.

In all these ways, investigating the foundations of the willful ignorance doctrine prove a fertile endeavor. It not only helps sharpen our understanding of existing doctrinal tools and the normative considerations they are based on, but it also helps us improve those doctrinal tools and fashion new ones to fill the gaps where the current options fall short.

2 What Is Criminal Culpability?

THIS CHAPTER AIMS to elucidate the concept of criminal culpability. Since the project of the book is to analyze, evaluate, and ultimately defend certain criminal law doctrines that impute mental states on the basis of equal culpability, I need to explain what criminal culpability *is*. As seen earlier, courts expressly base the willful ignorance doctrine on the equal culpability thesis, according to which acting in willful ignorance is just as culpable as the analogous knowing misconduct. To determine when this thesis holds—and thus what the correct scope of the willful ignorance doctrine should be—we need to understand how culpable defendants are for their conduct. Thus, my present aim is to unpack the theory of criminal culpability that will figure into the main arguments of this book. In later chapters, I will home in on the conditions where the equal culpability thesis holds by applying the theory to evaluate willfully ignorant misconduct—specifically, the decision not to investigate one's suspicions before doing the actus reus of a crime. The present chapter does not undertake a full defense of my theory of culpability, as this would require a book unto itself. Still, I aim to show why the theory offers a particularly attractive way to conceive of culpability.

The notion of criminal culpability I'm concerned with, figuring as it does into the express grounds for the willful ignorance doctrine, is a distinctively legal notion. As such, it might come apart from moral blameworthiness.[1] Roughly put, the former is what makes one an apt target of reactive emotions like resentment and indignation, while culpability is the primary determinant of how much one's conduct merits condemnation by the law.[2] All else equal, criminally culpable act tokens warrant punishment and act types that comprise solely such tokens are aptly criminalized (perhaps on the condition that it's not bad policy). The notion of culpability I'm concerned with is legal in nature,[3] and so should be descriptively adequate in the sense of capturing at least the broad contours of the law in the jurisdictions being scrutinized—for me, Anglo-American systems. But culpability is not *merely* descriptive. As I'll explain, it also has a normative dimension, which allows it to be used to critique posited law. Ultimately, an account of culpability should succeed both with respect to descriptive fit and normative defensibility.

The animating idea behind my theory is not novel. My view falls squarely within the dominant approach to understanding criminal culpability. On this approach, one is culpable for an action to the extent it manifests insufficient regard (or more simply, disrespect) for the legally protected interests of others or for protected values more generally. Insufficient regard is a species of ill will—more precisely, making mistakes in the way one recognizes, weighs, and responds to the reasons that bear on how to act.[4] If one attaches so little weight to others' interests that one burns down a building for the insurance despite knowing someone is inside, one acts from insufficient regard.

---

[1] While my theory does not *require* seeing moral blameworthiness as distinct from criminal culpability, I explain in Section IV why I think it is better to distinguish them.

[2] Some might think the degree of condemnation one's offense merits can be impacted not only by culpability but also by how much harm one causes—even if due in part to luck. (Thanks to Massimo Renzo for this worry.) This may be right, though on my view, determining the severity of one's offense should *start* with criminal culpability, and can then be tweaked by pragmatic considerations or reasons of political morality, of which harm caused may be one. I briefly discuss the issue of luck below. *See infra* note 128. I suggest the amount of harm caused does not impact culpability, but can legitimately affect the severity of one's offense for pragmatic and normative reasons.

[3] In talking about culpability, I don't mean "narrow culpability," which refers to the mens rea requirement of crimes. *See* Douglas Husak, *"Broad" Culpability and the Retributivist Dream*, 9 OHIO ST. J. CRIM. L. 449, 456 (2012). Rather, I have something like "broad culpability" in mind. *Id.* at 456–57 ("[T]he broad sense of [culpability] refers to 'a general notion of moral blameworthiness, that is, that the defendant committed the actus reus of an offense with a morally blameworthy state of mind.'" (citation omitted)). While closely tied to moral blameworthiness, I argue in Section IV that criminal culpability should not be identified with the moral notion.

[4] GIDEON YAFFE, ATTEMPTS 38 (2011) (an action is culpable to the degree that "it is a product of a faulty mode of recognition or response to reasons for action").

Larry Alexander and Kim Ferzan endorse such a view,[5] as do Victor Tadros,[6] Peter Westen,[7] Gideon Yaffe,[8] and others.[9]

One attraction of this view is that it preserves a connection to moral blameworthiness while accounting for the ways the law is plausibly seen as different. This is because the insufficient regard theory is itself structurally similar to an increasingly popular theory of moral blameworthiness: the quality of will theory. On this view, acts are morally blameworthy to the extent they manifest ill will, which may be understood as attaching insufficient weight to the relevant *moral reasons*.[10] Likewise, the insufficient regard theory takes criminal culpability to consist in manifesting insufficient regard for the applicable *legally recognized* reasons. Thus, criminal culpability on my account can plausibly be seen as a simplified analog of moral blameworthiness, with the former sensitive to only some considerations that impact the latter.

Despite its attractions, the insufficient regard theory of criminal culpability also faces challenges. Crucially, it is far from clear what it means for an action to *manifest* insufficient regard. The view's proponents are rarely precise about how to determine the *amount* of insufficient regard an act manifests. But the theory cannot do without an account of this key notion. Without understanding manifestation, the insufficient regard theory does not yield determinate results about how culpable various bits of misconduct are. A primary aim of this chapter is to answer this challenge for the insufficient regard theory, thus removing an important impediment to adopting the view.

What's more, I'll argue that a good account of manifestation substantially increases the explanatory power of the insufficient regard theory. Indeed, the principal job of an account of manifestation is to enable our theory of culpability to provide a principled explanation of a range of criminal law doctrines that treat mental states as irrelevant to criminal liability unless they're displayed in action in the right way. What are these doctrines? For one, a "basic premise of Anglo-American criminal law is that no crime

---

[5] Larry Alexander & Kimberly Ferzan, Crime and Culpability 67–68 (2009) ("insufficient concern [is] the essence of culpability").

[6] Victor Tadros, Criminal Responsibility 250 (2005) ("if [a defendant] is convicted of a serious offence, the state communicates . . . that [his] behaviour manifested an inappropriate regard for other citizens and their interests").

[7] Peter Westen, *An Attitudinal Theory of Excuse*, 25 Law & Phil. 289, 373–74 (2006) ("a person is normatively blameworthy for engaging in conduct that a statute prohibits if he was motivated by an attitude of disrespect for the interests that the statute seeks to protect").

[8] *See* Yaffe, *supra* note 4; Gideon Yaffe, *Intoxication, Recklessness, and Negligence*, 9 Ohio St. J. Crim. L. 545, 552–53 (2012). *See also* Yaffe *infra* notes 22 and 50.

[9] Kenneth Simons, *Does Punishment for "Culpable Indifference" Simply Punish for "Bad Character"? Examining the Requisite Connection Between Mens Rea and Actus Reus*, 6 Buff. Crim. L. Rev. 219, 249–50 (2002); Alex Sarch, *Who Cares What You Think? Criminal Culpability and the Irrelevance of Unmanifested Mental States*, 36 L. & Phil. 707 (2018) (presenting earlier version of material in this chapter).

[10] *See* Julia Markovitz, *Acting for the Right Reasons*, 119 Phil. Rev. 201 (2010); Nomy Arpaly & Tim Schroeder, In Praise of Desire 170 (2014).

can be committed by bad thoughts alone."[11] Nor do we enhance punishments merely because we know one was willing to offend in worse ways. If I want to kill my enemy but am bribed to only beat him up instead, I'm not guilty of murder simply because I was willing to go that far. As Ken Simons notes, "we are . . . properly[] reluctant to impose punishment on a person simply for [attitudes or characteristics] unless and until [they] are expressed in action."[12] Similar thinking lies behind the concurrence requirement between mens rea and actus reus: the former must be expressed in (i.e., cause) the latter in the right way for there to be a proper basis for guilt.[13]

Furthermore, one's *motives* for breaking the law generally don't matter.[14] A thief is not guilty of a more serious offense because he is motivated by hatred of the victim rather than wanting to be able to afford a better school for his child. In determining guilt, such motives don't count as manifested. The affirmative defenses function similarly: "when an individual finds himself in a position where the law grants him the right to kill another in his own defense, it makes no difference whether his dominant motive is other than self-preservation."[15] An executioner authorized to execute a death sentence commits no crime even if his actual motivation is the desire to see the prisoner die gruesomely.[16] However, there are exceptions to substantive criminal law's general indifference to motives. A few offenses—like treason,[17] kidnapping,[18] and hate crimes[19]—include bad motives as an element. Motives may also affect sentencing.[20]

---

[11] Wayne LaFave, 1 Subst. Crim. L. § 6.1 (2d ed. 2016). *See also* Michelson v. United States, 335 U.S. 469, 489 (1948) (Rutledge, J., dissenting) ("Our whole tradition is that a man can be punished . . . only for specific acts defined beforehand to be criminal, not for general misconduct or bearing a reputation for such misconduct."); Simons, *supra* note 9, at 234 ("the criminal law should not be brought to bear on individuals who have not yet done anything wrong, but who merely have disreputable—or even dangerous—character traits").

[12] *Id.*

[13] Under this rule, guilt requires not only possessing the required mens rea while doing the actus reus, but also that "the defendant's mental state actuate[] the physical conduct." Wayne LaFave, 1 Subst. Crim. L. § 6.3 (2d ed. 2016). *See also* Joshua Dressler, Understanding Criminal Law 199 (6th ed.) ("[t]he defendant's conduct that caused the social harm must have been *set into motion or impelled by* the thought process that constituted the *mens rea* of the offense"); Alex Sarch, *Knowledge, Recklessness and the Connection Requirement Between Actus Reus and Mens Rea*, 120 Penn. State L. Rev. 1 (2015).

[14] Wayne LaFave, 1 Subst. Crim. L. § 5.3 (2d ed. 2016) ("[M]otive, if narrowly defined to exclude recognized defenses and the 'specific intent' requirements of some crimes, is not relevant on the substantive side of the criminal law.").

[15] *Id.*

[16] *Id.*

[17] Treason requires purpose to aid an enemy of the state, and mere knowledge that this will result does not suffice. Haupt v. United States, 330 U.S. 631, 641–42 (1947); Wayne LaFave, 1 Subst. Crim. L. § 5.2 (2d ed. 2016) (ftn. 9).

[18] Kidnapping often requires a prohibited purpose like obtaining a ransom or terrorizing the victim. *See, e.g.*, Model Penal Code § 212.1 (requiring specified purposes for being guilty of kidnapping).

[19] Hate crimes carry harsher punishments if one acted "because of the actual or perceived race, color, religion, or national origin of any person." 18. U.S.C. § 249.

[20] *See* Carissa Byrne Hessick, *Motive's Role in Criminal Punishment*, 80 S. Cal. L. Rev. 89, 90 (2006).

One of my primary aims here is to explain this jumble of doctrines concerning unmanifested mental states. I won't do so by offering a general theory of what it is for an action to manifest a *mental state*. Rather, I defend a theory of *criminal culpability* that explains why culpability is not impacted by mental states that criminal law doctrine treats as unmanifested.

Of course, it might be tempting to explain these doctrines as merely a function of our epistemic and practical limitations. It will often be complicated and costly to determine or evaluate the attitudes the defendant had while acting. So perhaps it is prudent for the law to ignore unmanifested bad attitudes.[21] However, this pragmatic explanation does not capture the full strength of the principles the law is committed to. Suppose our practical limitations are temporarily alleviated. Most simply, the defendant might just *admit* (credibly) that he had very bad attitudes while acting. Even then, however, it is doubtful that we should punish him merely for his bad attitudes or do so more harshly for his willingness to commit worse crimes. Still, in such a case, our practical limitations provide no bar to doing so.

Thus, my aim is to offer a *principled* explanation of when and why criminal law doctrine is not concerned with unmanifested mental states. I'll offer an account of what it means to manifest a particular *level of insufficient regard*, which explains (i) why one is not culpable for bad attitudes one merely possesses but does not act on, and (ii) why one is not more culpable for breaking (or complying with) the law for bad rather than good motives. In this way, answering the main challenge for the insufficient regard theory endows it with significant explanatory power. The resulting theory, I'll argue, is highly normatively attractive as well.

This chapter proceeds in two stages. The first is a project of inclusion. I want to show that when properly worked out, the insufficient regard theory not only provides principled explanations of the criminal law's core rules related to unmanifested mental states in jurisdictions like ours, but also that it can accommodate a range of substantive views on contested doctrinal questions. The first part thus aims to bring as many into the broad church of the insufficient regard theory as possible by showcasing its explanatory power. Section I explains why the theory must appeal to manifestation at all, while Section II argues against the two most natural ways to understand manifesting a given level of insufficient regard: the *purely causal account*, and the *epistemic account*. Section III presents

[21] This position has recent defenders. *See* David Lefkowitz, *Blame and the Criminal Law*, 6 JURISPRUDENCE 451, 462–65 (2015). Lefkowitz argues it's for practical reasons that we shouldn't punish unmanifested insufficient regard although in principle we could. He mentions several practical limitations—including the challenge of detecting mere bad attitudes in the absence of harm being caused, and the state's limited resources, which may prevent it from "investigating your bad attitude crimes, let alone prosecuting them." *Id.* at 465. *See also* Martin R. Gardner, *The Mens Rea Enigma: Observations on the Role of Motive in the Criminal Law Past and Present*, 1993 UTAH L. REV. 635, 685–86 (1993) (providing practical arguments why the law shouldn't require proof of "evil motive": "[a]ctual motives are often hidden . . . in the subconscious" and "are difficult to evaluate"; and "[s]erious . . . motivational analysis would require trial courts to consider detailed case histories of each defendant," which often are "unavailable to prosecutors at the time necessary to charge the crime").

my fully worked out theory. It is partly causal, but also draws on what Gideon Yaffe dubs a "principle of lenity."[22] The aim is to give a *descriptively adequate* framework that captures core features of the criminal law.

While the first part of the chapter is ecumenical and descriptive, the second is normative. To get as many on board with my insufficient regard framework as possible, Section III stays neutral on key substantive questions. But the second half of the chapter seeks to answer them. Section IV articulates my view of how criminal culpability relates to moral blameworthiness. Section V gives normative arguments for the most distinctive component of my theory: the principle of lenity used to calculate the level of insufficient regard manifested. Finally, Section VI argues that motives *should not* matter to criminal culpability. Thus, while I start by avoiding fights, in later sections I seek them out. This allows readers to disagree with my views on more controversial questions while still buying into the broad framework I'm most concerned to build support for.

I. Why Manifestation Is Essential

As noted, one thing we want from a theory of criminal culpability is *descriptive adequacy*. This is what I'll be most concerned with in this and the following two sections: making sure the theory is a sufficiently good fit with core features of the law in the jurisdictions one cares about. My focus is Anglo-American criminal law. I argue in this section that to capture its basic features, the insufficient regard theory must peg culpability to the insufficient regard manifested, not the amount possessed. Otherwise, the theory does not properly capture the law's commitment to not punishing merely for bad attitudes. As we'll see, this simple idea has many doctrinal expressions. Building in the notion of manifestation helps the theory account for them.

Admittedly, the insufficient regard theory might be able to accommodate *some* doctrinal expressions of this idea even without appealing to manifestation. First, there is the principle that we don't punish without voluntary conduct.[23] If one unconsciously lashes out while asleep, one is not guilty of assaulting one's partner. One has no criminal culpability. Similarly, the criminal law will not regard one as culpable unless one's voluntary conduct violates a legal prohibition. Even if I have an utterly deplorable character and am willing to commit egregious crimes, if the only voluntary action I perform—say, painting my fence—is not criminally prohibited in my jurisdiction, then the law will attribute no culpability to me. We do not punish for a mere *willingness* to offend if no offense is committed.

---

[22] Gideon Yaffe, *The Point of Mens Rea: The Case of Willful Ignorance*, 12 CRIM. L. & PHIL. 19, 26–27 (2018).

[23] *See* MODEL PENAL CODE § 2.01(1) (guilt requires "conduct that includes a voluntary act or the omission to perform an act of which he is physically capable"); LAFAVE, *supra* note 11 (criminal liability requires "an act, or an omission to act where there is a legal duty to act," and that a "bodily movement, to qualify as an act forming the basis of criminal liability, must be voluntary").

One might try to capture these data points with this rudimentary formulation of the theory:

Possession Approach: D's action A is criminally culpable to degree *n* if and only if (1) A is a voluntary action that violates a criminal prohibition, and (2) A was done while D possessed a level of insufficient regard that equals *n*.

Perhaps this goes some way toward capturing the "basic premise of Anglo-American criminal law . . . that no crime can be committed by bad thoughts alone."[24] At least it makes prohibited action a precondition of culpability.

Nonetheless, this account fails. One complication, which I return to later, is that it entails that actions can't be criminally culpable without violating *existing* criminal prohibitions. But some act types may not yet have been criminalized. So this possession approach can at best only capture jurisdiction-specific culpability attributions, not the underlying notion of culpability that the law *should* be tracking. Our theory should make room for both (as will mine).

More basically, culpability cannot be equated with the insufficient regard *possessed* while breaking the law. The trouble is that the possession approach attributes enhanced culpability to defendants who are willing to behave in worse ways than they actually did. Consider:

TED THE WOULD-BE TERRORIST: Ted hates people he perceives as "foreigners," and he resolves to bomb a mosque. But he can't get ahold of any explosives at present. If he had the means to do so, he would carry out the bombing without hesitation. But since he currently is unable to, he does the greatest amount of damage he can under the circumstances, which is to spray-paint anti-Muslim slurs on a public building—a criminal offense where he lives.

The possession approach entails that Ted is highly culpable. He engaged in voluntary conduct that violates a criminal prohibition while possessing seriously deficient regard for others. Under the possession approach, Ted's culpability is pegged to what he is willing to do (i.e., attempt a bombing) and thus is far greater than that of someone who paints racist slurs *without* being willing to bomb a mosque. But this is implausible. Just as we do not punish for a bare willingness to offend, we also refrain from punishing merely for a willingness to behave in worse ways than one actually did. As Simons notes, "we are . . . properly[] reluctant to impose punishment on a person simply for [attitudes or characteristics] unless and until [they] are expressed in action."[25] The full level of

---

[24] LAFAVE, *supra* note 11.

[25] Simons, *supra* 9 note, at 234; ALAN BRUDNER, PUNISHMENT AND FREEDOM: A LIBERAL THEORY OF PENAL LAW 43 (2009) (noting the general agreement on the proposition "that judicial punishment ought not to be inflicted for private thoughts, wishes, inclinations, or states of character where these have not manifested themselves in conduct").

insufficient regard Ted *possesses* is not fully manifested in this case. Thus, he seems less culpable than the possession approach entails.

To avoid the problems in Ted's case, we need a manifestation requirement. The theory should be formulated to say that D's action A is criminally culpable to degree *n* if the degree to which A *manifests* insufficient regard equals *n* (regardless of how much D happened to possess when doing A). This matches legal theorists' canonical statements of the theory,[26] and helps explain why we don't enhance punishments merely because one was willing to offend in worse ways than one actually did. Without actually doing the worse offense, one's willingness is not manifested. But what, in turn, explains *this*? The theory remains incomplete because we still need to know what it *is* to manifest insufficient regard to a particular degree.

II. Explaining Manifestation Is Harder than You Might Think

Explaining how much insufficient regard an action manifests is the big challenge for theories in this family. This section argues against the two most natural proposals.[27] I don't claim to conclusively refute them, but merely seek to motivate my own account, offered in Section III.

A. THE PURE CAUSAL APPROACH

The most natural account takes it that an action manifests a given amount of insufficient regard just in case possessing this amount is what *causes* one to do that act. This approach is naturally suggested by the *concurrence requirement*, which requires that the mens rea of the offense must "actuate" the requisite actus reus.[28] This requirement embodies a theory of mental state expression: an action expresses a mental state, intention, or attitude just in case the former causes the latter (in the right way). However, what we want is an account of manifesting a given *level of insufficient regard*, which depends on one's whole configuration of attitudes and reflects how one weighs the relevant reasons. Thus, the causal theory we're interested in is this:

> **Pure Causal Approach**: An action A manifests a level of insufficient regard *n* if and only if (and because) A is caused by a configuration of mental states that constitutes level *n* of insufficient regard toward legally protected interests or other protected values.

I call this the *pure* causal approach, since it might just be one component of a more sophisticated theory of manifestation. In fact, this is true of my account, which is a *partly* causal view.

---

[26] *See supra* notes 5–8.

[27] I've argued against another attempted solution to this problem as it arises for moral blameworthiness. Alex Sarch, *Review: N. Arpaly & T. Schroeder, In Praise of Desire (Oxford 2014)*, 31 ECON. & PHIL. 320, 324–27 (2015).

[28] *See supra* note 13.

This approach is attractive, since it captures the insight behind the concurrence requirement. Unless this requirement is satisfied (e.g., if one only acquires the mens rea of the crime *after* doing the actus reus), the pure causal approach does not permit the level of insufficient regard inherent in the full crime to be manifested in one's conduct.

However, the pure causal approach has problems. Simply put, causation is not *sufficient* for manifestation. As many cases show, the amount of insufficient regard that causes an action does not always correspond to the amount the action manifests. Recall the following chestnut:[29]

> KILL YOUR UNCLE: Dennis and Charlie intend to kill their respective uncles today. They both have exactly the same motivations and attitudes. Both take a drive to clear their heads and think further about when to do the killing. While driving, Dennis happens to see his uncle on the street and shoots him then and there. Since Dennis intentionally kills, he is a murderer. By contrast, Charlie, while lost in thought and driving carelessly, hits a pedestrian, who turns out to be his uncle—his intended victim. Charlie, unlike Dennis, did not commit murder. He caused his uncle's death, but only negligently.

Dennis and Charlie are stipulated to have exactly the same motivations and attitudes.[30] They both intend to kill. They have equally deplorable characters and levels of regard. On some views, they would be equally morally blameworthy.[31] Still, there is an intuitive sense in which what Charlie *did* is less culpable. Dennis is a murderer, but we wouldn't affix that label to Charlie.

The insufficient regard theory would try to capture this by maintaining that Charlie's conduct did not *manifest* as much insufficient regard as Dennis's did, such that Charlie's conduct is less culpable. But it's unclear whether the pure causal approach to manifestation can deliver this result. Charlie's high level of insufficient regard—that is, the configuration of attitudes that includes his intention to kill—does seem *somewhat* causally active in producing the conduct that resulted in his uncle's death. It caused him to take the drive. This suggests that the amount of insufficient regard manifested is not identical to that which is causally active in producing one's conduct. (There are answers a proponent of the pure causal approach may try, but I doubt they succeed.[32])

---

29 I've adapted this example from Simons's discussion of the case, which he culls from Searle. *See* Simons, *supra* note 9, at 232; JOHN SEARLE, INTENTIONALITY: AN ESSAY IN THE PHILOSOPHY OF MIND 82 (1983).

30 We must suppose neither Charlie's nor Dennis's plan includes a conditional intention to kill their uncle through careless driving if the opportunity presents itself. This might also make Charlie guilty of murder.

31 P. Graham, *A Sketch of a Theory of Blameworthiness*, 88 PHIL. & PHENOMENOLOGICAL AFF. 388, 396–99 (2014).

32 A proponent of the pure causal approach might respond that Charlie's killing his uncle was caused only by his mental state of *negligence*, not the further mental state of intent to kill. Perhaps Charlie's intention to kill was merely free-floating—not causally active in producing the conduct that led to the death. However, this response requires the questionable assumption that Charlie's configuration of mental states at the time

As noted later in this sub-section, this case might be handled by other theories (like Alexander and Ferzan's). Still, the present problem goes deeper. Other cases show that an action might not manifest all the insufficient regard that caused it. Consider a legal version of a case of Arpaly and Schroeder's:[33]

> TRIVIAL WRONGS: Jack and Jill each obtain software that removes fractions of cents from others' bank accounts and transfers the money to the software operator. Jack decides to use the software to enrich himself because he naively sees it as a practically harmless prank. He would not be willing to impose greater harms even if he could. By contrast, Jill harbors profound hatred toward the members of her community (whom she takes to be sinful and unclean). She wants to impose as much pain and suffering on them as possible. It just so happens this is the greatest harm she is currently able to inflict since she is in a remote location and very sick. Given her bottomless ill will, she would jump at the chance to cause vastly more harm (even death) if she could. Indeed, she hopes to use the money obtained with this software to some day purchase the means to wreaking more havoc (though she hasn't decided how). Jack and Jill's conduct is otherwise the same: they each use the software to remove a total of $500 from a large number of bank accounts.

Jill's conduct is caused by vastly more insufficient regard than that which caused Jack to act the same way. Thus, the pure causal account entails that Jill's conduct is vastly more culpable than Jack's. But I submit this is doubtful. Both impose the same small harms on their victims and neither actor has any justification. Instead, their acts seem roughly equally culpable: they would be convicted of equally serious offenses and face the same sentencing range.[34] Accordingly, the full degree of insufficient regard that caused Jill's conduct does not seem to be *manifested* in her offense. What cases like this show, as

---

can be carved up into different components, one of which—his negligence—was causally active, and another of which—his intent to kill—was not. However, it is not clear that mental states can be separated so neatly. Wasn't Charlie's intent *somewhat* causally active? He went for a drive to plan the killing, so he was driving in part because of his intention. Perhaps, then, the intention didn't play *enough* of a causal role in causing the act. Still, it is extremely hard to specify how much of a causal role a mental state must play for it to impact the insufficient regard an action manifests.

[33] *Cf.* ARPALY & SCHROEDER, *supra* note 10, at 188–89 (discussing a praiseworthiness analog about a lost motorist).

[34] One might object that even if Jack and Jill face the same sentencing range, perhaps Jill should be sentenced at the high end of the range and Jack at the low end. Still, the pure causal approach is in trouble for taking Jill to be *vastly* more culpable than Jack. Moreover, even if Jack and Jill should be sentenced slightly differently, I suspect that this is due to the broader range of considerations that legitimately impact sentencing—for example, deterrence and rehabilitation. It does not obviously show a difference in culpability of the sort that matters at the guilt stage of a case. Furthermore, I'm open to the idea that sentencing can consider more fine-grained differences in moral blameworthiness than typically should matter at the guilt stage. (I discuss this at length in Section III.C.)

Arpaly and Schroeder note, is that the amount of "ill will that an action manifests is not the same as the amount of . . . ill will that exists and is being acted on"[35]—a point the pure causal approach fails to capture.[36]

A final, related problem is that the pure causal approach has trouble capturing the default rule that motives (one's aims in acting) generally are "not relevant on the substantive side of the criminal law."[37] This rule is familiar, for example, from the law's approach to defenses. Consider:

> EVIL TROLLEY TURNER: Darryl finds himself in the classic trolley scenario. A trolley is careening toward five people tied to the tracks. It will kill them unless Darryl pulls the switch and diverts the trolley onto another track to which just one person, Vicky, is tied. If Darryl pulls the switch, only one will die, rather than five. Darryl knows all this and decides to divert the trolley onto the other track. However, his sole reason for doing so is that he hates Vicky and wants her dead. He doesn't care one whit for the five on the other track, and he wouldn't bother pulling the lever unless it would allow him to accomplish his aim of killing Vicky.

Darryl is highly morally blameworthy. He has a horrible character, harbors deplorable attitudes, and is willing to act on them. Nonetheless, in many jurisdictions, Darryl would get the benefit of a necessity defense. As LaFave notes, when "the law grants [a person] the right to kill another in his own [or someone else's] defense, it makes no difference whether his dominant motive is other than self-preservation."[38] "[T]he law is not concerned with motive once facts supporting the defense have been established."[39] Many legal scholars endorse this view.[40]

Nonetheless, the purely causal approach cannot deliver this result. Darryl was caused to act as he did by a configuration of attitudes that constitute an extremely high level of disregard for the protected interests of others. Thus, this approach entails Darryl is highly criminally culpable.

Of course, some might challenge the criminal law's position on this issue by trying to individuate actions more finely. One might claim that (i) switching to kill Vicky is a different action from (ii) switching the trolley to save the five. If acts can be individuated

---

[35] *Id.*

[36] Arpaly and Schroeder suggest that only some acts provide *occasion* to manifest extreme ill will, but I've argued this reply fails. Sarch, *supra* note at 27, at 324–27.

[37] WAYNE LAFAVE, 1 SUBST. CRIM. L. § 5.3 (2d ed. 2016).

[38] *Id.*

[39] *Id.*

[40] Larry Alexander, *The Means Principle*, *in* LEGAL, MORAL, AND METAPHYSICAL TRUTHS: THE PHILOSOPHY OF MICHAEL MOORE 28 (K.K. Ferzan & S.J. Morse eds., 2014) ("if the switcher believes switching will save the five, then his switching the trolley is nonculpable *even if his only reason for doing so is to kill the one on the siding*"). *See also* ALEXANDER & FERZAN, *supra* note 5, at 60–61 (defending a similar view).

this finely, then we might say that what Darryl did was the highly culpable act of doing *(i) rather than (ii)*. Of course, this strategy faces difficult questions about how to describe and individuate actions.

While I take this response to be a live option (it has well-known defenders),[41] I am trying to offer a theory of criminal culpability that at least is *able* to capture the criminal law's approach from above, which is maximally generous to criminal defendants. I want to be able to explain why it at least *makes sense* for defendants to get the benefit of all the defenses available to them based on the facts they were aware of when acting. The view I defend in this chapter can do this by taking it that Darryl's bad attitudes do not count as *manifested*.

Notice that the default rule that motives don't matter is not just a feature of the way the law treats defenses. An analogous point applies with respect to the elements of a crime. Consider:

> GOOD THIEF, BAD THIEF: Mary's child is having a hard time at public school, so she steals $5,000 from an ATM to be able to send her child to a better private school. By contrast, Barry is bored and wants to go to Vegas. He steals $5,000 from an ATM to be able to afford the trip.

The pure causal approach says that because Barry's action was caused by a configuration of mental states constituting a much more deficient level of regard than that which caused Mary's act, Barry's is more criminally culpable. But this fits poorly with legal practice. In most jurisdictions, Barry would not be treated as more criminally culpable and convicted of a worse offense just because he had worse motives for breaking the law.[42] Neither Mary nor Barry has a recognized justification for their conduct.[43] Granted, Barry's worse motives might matter at sentencing, but at least when it comes to the offense he is to be convicted of—that is, the level of culpability imputed to him at the guilt stage of the trial, which fixes the applicable sentencing range—Barry's worse motives are irrelevant. Thus, we want our theory to explain why motives do not matter to the sort of criminal culpability that is central to substantive criminal law doctrine applicable at the guilt stage. The pure causal theory isn't up to the job.[44]

---

41 *See* VICTOR TADROS, THE ENDS OF HARM 156 (2011) (endorsing this response to the present case).

42 *See* WAYNE LAFAVE, 1 SUBST. CRIM. L. § 1.2 (2d ed. 2016) ("a good motive will not normally prevent what is otherwise criminal from being a crime. Thus it is nonetheless . . . larceny that one stole a rich man's money to give his impoverished family a better life"). *See also* U.S. v. Badolato, 701 F.2d 915, 921 (11th Cir. 1983) (for crimes aimed at financial gain, "a person would be just as guilty if the motive were . . . to obtain money for a worthy cause").

43 WAYNE LAFAVE, 1 SUBST. CRIM. L. § 5.3 (2d ed. 2016) ("there are numerous . . . cases where a person has been found guilty of a crime in spite of what might be viewed as a good motive in committing it").

44 Perhaps the pure causal approach could be modified to say that an act is criminally culpable to degree *n* if it is *proximately* caused by a degree of insufficient regard equal to *n*. If proximate cause is understood in terms of directness, I don't think this will help. In TRIVIAL WRONGS, Jill's minor misconduct is directly caused by a *tremendous*

To further motivate my account, note that other insufficient regard theories that also are causal in nature encounter difficulties as well. Consider Alexander and Ferzan, who take culpability to be a function of (i) the magnitude of risk one perceives one unleashes on others, and (ii) the reasons that impelled one to do so.[45] Keeping the one factor fixed, one is more culpable the worse one is with respect to the other—that is, the greater the perceived risks one unleashes or the worse the reasons for which one did so. Their view is causal because it makes culpability depend in part on the reasons that caused one to act, which reflect one's level of regard.

Alexander and Ferzan can capture KILL YOUR UNCLE, since they think an actor is not culpable "until he engages in conduct that he believes unleashes a risk of harm over which he no longer has complete control."[46] Charlie does not irrevocably unleash as great a risk of death as Dennis, so Charlie is less culpable than Dennis, although they acted for equally bad reasons.

Nonetheless, their view does not sit comfortably with the default rule, seen previously, that motives generally don't matter in substantive criminal law doctrine. It is at least a point in favor of a theory if it gives a principled explanation of how this default rule can be sensible. In TRIVIAL WRONGS, Jack and Jill irrevocably unleash the same magnitude of perceived risk on others. Because Jill does so for vastly worse reasons than Jack, on natural assumptions it follows from Alexander and Ferzan's view that Jill's act is vastly more culpable than Jack's.[47] Nonetheless, it fits better with legal practice to take the two to be roughly equally culpable. Both were aware they unleashed the same harms, and the simple fact is that neither had any (even partial) legally cognizable justification for doing so. Thus, Alexander and Ferzan's view has trouble with this case. The view seems to place no limit on how culpable one can be for even a minor offense, provided only that one did it for bad enough reasons. (For similar reasons, their view also is an awkward fit with the case of TED THE TERRORIST.[48])[49]

---

degree of insufficient regard. Nonetheless, her act doesn't seem tremendously culpable. It is only roughly as culpable as Jack's. Thus, it might be better to understand proximate cause in terms of normative considerations designed to limit the implausible implications of the view. However, in that case, the theory starts to look indistinguishable from the normatively constrained causal theory I defend below in Section III. On my theory, the amount of insufficient regard manifested is determined using normative assumptions like the principle of lenity. Thus, my theory is partly normative just like the best understanding of the proximate cause approach. Still, my theory is more illuminating because it specifies exactly *how* the relevant normative considerations operate, rather than letting them be diffusely applied through intuitions about what suffices for proximate causation.

45 *See* ALEXANDER & FERZAN *supra* note 5, at 18.

46 *Id.* at 19. *See also id.* at 50.

47 *See id.* at 27 (claiming that "even very tiny risk impositions can be culpable if imposed for insufficient or misanthropic reasons").

48 Ted's violation was caused by a huge amount of ill will. Still, his culpability for his fairly minor offense is not as massive as would be suggested by the exceptionally criticizeable reasons for which he acted.

49 Their view also faces internal tension. On the one hand, they acknowledge motives don't matter when one's action is justified (as in EVIL TROLLEY TURNER). *See* ALEXANDER & FERZAN, *supra* note 5, at 60–61. On the other, they also allow one's reasons (motives) to affect culpability where the act is an unjustified violation

B. THE EPISTEMIC APPROACH

An altogether different approach to manifestation is *epistemic*. It focuses on the level of insufficient regard we would *infer* the actor possesses:

> **Epistemic Approach**: An action A manifests a level of insufficient regard *n* if and only if (and because) a rational, unbiased observer would infer from the relevant evidence that the defendant who did A possessed a level of insufficient regard equal to *n* when doing A.

What does "the relevant evidence" mean here? It can't mean *all the facts*. Then the theory would say an action manifests as much insufficient regard as a *fully informed* observer would infer the actor possessed. But the fully informed observer would of course know what level of insufficient regard the actor actually possessed. Thus, she would recognize that negligent Charlie had just as little regard for others as his murdering counterpart Dennis. So the theory gets KILL YOUR UNCLE wrong. Instead, "the relevant evidence" more plausibly means *the available evidence*—that is, the reasonably obtainable evidence that can be introduced at trial. Typically, the available evidence would not allow us to infer that Charlie had any mens rea but negligence. After all, were Charlie called to answer for his uncle's death, he likely would disavow any intent to kill.

This view can be strengthened further. Gideon Yaffe defends a more sophisticated version of the epistemic approach, which is similar in spirit to the theory I develop in Section III. He postulates a *principle of lenity*, which "requires us to determine what the defendant's conduct says about his [level of insufficient regard] under the assumption that he is as little different from the law-abiding citizen as possible, given his behavior."[50] This principle, *ceteris paribus*, "bars us from being neutral between the hypothesis that the defendant is bad and the hypothesis that he is *very* bad."[51] Thus, there is a *rebuttable presumption* that Charlie only acted with the insufficient regard of negligence, not that of murder.

---

of the law. *See id.* at 50 (discussing the case of Frankie). So in GOOD THIEF, BAD THIEF, they would allow that Barry's bad motives can make his theft more culpable than Mary's similar act done for more sympathetic reasons—although this sits uncomfortably with posited law. I don't claim that this combination of views is *normatively* implausible. Indeed, my theory leaves room for this as a possible normative position (while also explaining as sensible the default irrelevance of motives in posited law). My point instead is that it seems unstable to maintain both that motives do not impact the culpability calculus for justified actions as in EVIL TROLLEY TURNER, but that motives do affect the culpability of unjustified acts as in GOOD THIEF, BAD THIEF. (*Compare id.* at 50 *with id.* at 59–60.) This may not be a decisive objection, but there are benefits to seeking a unified account that makes motives impact culpability the same way in all cases. My view aims to do this.

[50] GIDEON YAFFE, AGE OF CULPABILITY: CHILDREN AND THE NATURE OF CRIMINAL RESPONSIBILITY 89 (2018).

[51] *Id.* at 90.

However, I doubt that these refinements—without more—are sufficient to render the epistemic approach defensible. In particular, one wonders about the case where the available evidence conclusively shows that Charlie in fact had the intention to kill, and thus a correspondingly higher level of insufficient regard. The prosecution might call a psychologist to testify, based on in-depth interviews (or brain scans), that Charlie actually intended to kill. More simply, perhaps Charlie is now overwhelmed by guilt and just *admits* on the stand that he did in fact intend to kill his uncle. Such scenarios are possible. In such a case, a reasonable observer would justifiably infer from the available evidence—even given Yaffe's principle of lenity—that Charlie was not just negligent, but intended to kill. Accordingly, the epistemic approach, even with these refinements, entails that Charlie's action manifests the level of insufficient regard associated with murder—not just negligent homicide.[52]

The difficulty here is that the *available evidence* is highly changeable. Often, the available evidence will only allow us to infer that defendants like Charlie are negligent. But sometimes it would show them to be willing to behave in far worse ways than they actually did. The epistemic approach does not fully preclude fixing their culpability by reference to the far worse acts we know their low levels of regard would make them *willing* to do.[53] That, however, conflicts with fundamental commitments of the criminal law.[54]

The epistemic approach likewise has trouble capturing the rule that motives generally don't matter to culpability. Suppose in EVIL TROLLEY TURNER, we're quite sure Darryl's actual motivation for turning the trolley was just to kill Vicky. Perhaps he admits it on the stand. The epistemic approach then entails that Darryl would not get the benefit of a necessity defense. But this conflicts with a widespread view in the law. Similarly for GOOD

---

[52] Yaffe recently responded to such worries, claiming that brain scans or other psychological evidence about the defendant's motives, and how she'd be willing to act, cannot be considered in determining how much insufficient regard is manifested. *Id.* at 94. Yaffe says such evidence does not concern the defendant's *act*, and so does not affect the level of regard *the act* manifests. Worries remain, however. First, Yaffe's view still seems to allow admissions by the defendant (e.g., about her motivations in acting) to affect the level of regard manifested. Moreover, if the psychological evidence in question concerns the motives or mental states that produced the defendant's action, then more explanation is needed about why this psychological evidence is not *about the act itself* (which would allow it to affect the regard the act manifests). This seems particularly true given that Yaffe allows facts about how one became intoxicated to bear on the level of regard the defendant's conduct manifests. *Id.* at 95. If such evidence about the act's etiology can bear on the level of regard it manifests, then a more principled explanation is needed of why *psychological evidence* about how that act was produced shouldn't similarly matter. In explaining why the one counts, but not the other, Yaffe will have to appeal to an account of how the act is to be described, as well as the difference between *the act* and the mental states producing it. This task isn't insurmountable, but more is needed. (I address similar questions about how the act is to be described, and explain why the regard manifested by the act is not affected by psychological evidence or admissions about motives, in Section III and more fully in Section VI. *See also* Chapter 3, Section III—especially the text accompanying footnotes 50–52.)

[53] Similarly, one might worry that some versions of the epistemic approach might allow one to be criminally culpable merely for one's attitudes even if they have not yet generated any action.

[54] *See supra* notes 11–12.

Thief, Bad Thief. Suppose Barry admits he stole money just because he was bored and wanted to gamble. The epistemic approach entails that Barry is more culpable than others who steal for more sensible reasons. But, again, that is not the law's view. It does not take worse motives to be the basis for convicting one of a worse offense. Moreover, even if one thinks the law's view here is mistaken, our theory should at least be *able* to capture such a widespread aspect of the law.

Of course, it is always open to defenders of the epistemic approach to say that motives generally don't matter only for practical reasons—that is, only because it is usually hard to identify and evaluate defendants' actual motives for breaking the law. Nonetheless, this pragmatic explanation is unsatisfying. It does not capture the full strength of the principles to which the criminal law is committed. After all, in some cases our practical limitations will be alleviated—that is, where we know the defendant's motives and have no trouble evaluating them. In such cases, the epistemic approach gives no reason not to punish Darryl and Barry to the full and much harsher level that their bad motives seem to call for. But the law does not change its view on this point when our practical limitations are temporarily alleviated. Even when we know with certainty what Darryl's and Barry's motives are and how seriously deficient their regard for others is, the law does not depart from its stance that Darryl gets the defense and Barry is not to be convicted of a more serious offense.

Accordingly, I remain skeptical about the prospects for the epistemic approach—though I have not decisively refuted it. More work may yield better answers.[55] But we at least have reason to continue looking for alternative ways to understand manifesting insufficient regard.

III. Toward a Better Theory of Criminal Culpability

This section aims to formulate a better insufficient regard theory by providing the sought-after account of manifestation. Thus far, several partly overlapping datapoints have emerged. These should preferably be given a *principled explanation*, which applies even in isolated cases where our practical limitations are alleviated. Two are fairly basic:

---

[55] Perhaps we could adopt certain presumptions—based on principles of political morality—to constrain the evidence from which we may draw inferences about the defendant's level of regard. If we can block the evidence suggesting that Charlie actually possessed a worse mental state than negligence—like psychiatric testimony or brain scans that reveal his intention to kill—perhaps the observer could be blocked from inferring that Charlie possessed more insufficient regard than the amount seen in negligence.

However, I'm skeptical about this strategy. What guarantee is there that the problems won't just re-emerge in isolated cases where the available evidence clearly rebuts the presumptions? Moreover, I think it will be hard to specify *ex ante* all the forms of evidence from which we might infer that the defendant was willing to act in worse ways than she actually did. It seems especially difficult to rule out evidence stemming from *admissions* by the defendant about her act, such as that she acted with worse mental states or was willing or trying to do worse things than was initially apparent.

(i) *Act Requirement*: Only voluntary conduct can be criminally culpable. Merely possessing bad attitudes that one does not act on cannot be criminally culpable.

(ii) *No punishment without prohibited conduct*: A legal system will not attribute culpability to you unless you've violated one of that system's prohibitions (though in principle these prohibitions could be normatively mistaken). One is not criminally culpable if one complies with the law—even if it is for very bad reasons.

Moreover, we have seen several datapoints relating to the idea that one should not be punished for bad attitudes, or a willingness to offend, unless it's manifested in action:

(iii) *Punishment only for actual conduct, not for willingness to behave in worse ways*: The criminal law should not attribute greater culpability merely because one would be willing to act in worse ways than what one actually did. Examples include TED THE WOULD-BE TERRORIST and KILL YOUR UNCLE.

(iv) *Concurrence Requirement*: To be guilty of a crime, the defendant's mens rea must concur with (i.e., actuate) the actus reus.[56] This means one cannot be punished merely on the basis of mental states acquired *after* doing the actus reus. Rather, some causal-explanatory nexus is needed between mens rea and actus reus.

However, (iv) must be tempered by the following datapoint, which posed a problem for the pure causal approach to manifestation:

(v) *The amount of "ill will . . . an action manifests is not the same as the amount . . . that exists and is being acted on."*[57] Thus, one's act may not manifest the full amount of insufficient regard or animosity that actually impelled one to act—as when very bad attitudes cause one to act in ways that are only slightly criticizeable. An illustration is TRIVIAL WRONGS.

Finally, our theory must explain the complexities of the role of motives in the criminal law:

(vi) *Motives generally don't matter*: Substantive criminal law doctrine usually is not concerned with one's motives for acting. First, as (i) suggests, one is not criminally culpable for acting lawfully even for bad reasons. An example is

---

[56] *See supra* note 13.

[57] ARPALY & SCHROEDER, *supra* note 10, at 188.

> EVIL TROLLEY TURNER. Second, substantive criminal law doctrine usually is not concerned with one's reasons for violating the law. An illustration is GOOD THIEF, BAD THIEF. But, third, there are exceptions to the default irrelevance of motives—as with (a) crimes of which bad motives are an element and (b) the role of motive in sentencing—which must also be explained.

I will defend a theory that captures these datapoints. It has two components: (a) a necessary condition on culpability, that is, a Manifestation Requirement, and (b) an account of *how much* insufficient regard is manifested. Under (a), culpability requires that insufficient regard is a cause of one's act. Under (b), how much the act manifests is largely independent of how much one possesses. I explain each component in turn. But first, the notion of culpability must be clarified.

A. TWO NOTIONS OF CRIMINAL CULPABILITY

Thus far, I have gestured at but mostly ignored an important distinction. We must distinguish between the amount of culpability a jurisdiction actually attributes and the amount it ideally should. Call the jurisdiction-specific notion *posited culpability*. Suppose a jurisdiction recognizes no distinction between starting a fire in a building while knowing it is occupied and doing so without such knowledge. Suppose both types of arsonist are to be convicted of the same crime and subject to the same sentencing range. This jurisdiction *attributes* the same amount of culpability for both forms of arson. They have the same amount of posited culpability.

However, there is also a sense in which this is normatively implausible. The same amount of culpability plausibly should not be attributed to these two forms of arson. The one arsonist disrespects the value of human life far more than the other. This suggests a *normative notion of criminal culpability*, which is what the law ideally should track. Normative criminal culpability is especially important for critical purposes. We can meaningfully ask how much normative culpability an action possesses even if it has not yet been criminalized. Or we might ask whether the posited culpability a jurisdiction attributes for an offense matches its normative culpability.

The insufficient regard theory neatly captures this distinction. This theory, recall, claims that an action is criminally culpable to the extent it manifests insufficient regard for legally protected interests or values—that is, the legally recognized reasons that bear on whether to do the act.[58] To see how the theory accounts for the distinction between posited and normative culpability, it will help to clarify what's meant by "legally recognized reasons." This phrase is supposed to denote the considerations that the law

[58] This idea of legally recognized reasons is also used by Gideon Yaffe. *See* Yaffe, *supra* notes 22 and 50.

recognizes as bearing on how an individual actor should behave in particular cases. These reasons roughly fall in two groups: the reasons in virtue of which an action is criminalized (i.e., the features which make it likely to threaten certain interests or values the law cares to safeguard) and those in virtue of which an action might count as justified or at least permitted (e.g., that the action prevents harm to others or furthers socially valuable activities or relationships). Faced with the choice of whether to perform a given action in a given case, there will be numerous considerations about the action's benefits and burdens, which can support it or count against it in the eyes of the law. These are the legally recognized reasons, as I use the term. These reasons bear an important relationship to the aims of the legislature in prohibiting certain acts. In criminalizing a given type of action (and in recognizing certain justifications), the legislature seeks to protect, promote, or acknowledge certain interests and values. The fact that a given type of action threatens these interests or values is among the basic considerations in virtue of which this type of action is criminalized. Thus, these considerations form the most important category of legally recognized reasons—that is, category of considerations the law takes it that one should not display insufficient concern for when acting.

Having clarified the notion of legally recognized reasons, we can now see how the insufficient regard theory captures the distinction above between posited and normative culpability. Specifically, it does so by distinguishing between (i) the interests, values, or reasons that the law *actually* recognizes as bearing on whether to do a particular act, and (ii) the ones the law *should* recognize as doing so. Manifesting insufficient regard for the reasons the law actually recognizes as bearing on whether to do an act is what posited culpability consists in, while manifesting insufficient regard for the reasons the law should recognize lies at the core of normative culpability.

A helpful guide to identifying the interests, values, or reasons that the criminal law recognizes in a given jurisdiction is to look at how harshly the jurisdiction punishes different types of conduct. The more harshly punished a particular type of conduct is, the more weighty the reasons are that we can infer the law sees as counting against this type of action. By looking at the elements of a crime, we can often discern what interests or values it threatens, which the legislature sought to protect by criminalizing such conduct. The fact that *this* sort of action threatens *these* kinds of interests or values is a paradigm example of legally recognized reasons, which the law regards as bearing on how individuals should behave. By contrast, when it comes to the second group of reasons—the ones the law *should* (not merely does) recognize as bearing on how to act—these can be discerned through normative theorizing and policy assessment. This exercise can also plausibly be furthered by critical reflection on the legitimacy of existing criminal prohibitions in jurisdictions like ours.

With this distinction between posited and normative culpability in hand, we can begin to account for datapoint (ii) from earlier. For an action to possess *posited culpability*, it clearly must violate an existing criminal prohibition. After all, no well-functioning legal system that respects the principle of legality would permit punishment for an action that does not violate an existing prohibition. But this is not required for an action to be *normatively* criminally culpable. The law in a given jurisdiction might fail to protect certain interests or values (i.e., recognize certain reasons) that it ought to. One can manifest insufficient regard for interests or values the law *should* protect without violating an existing prohibition. Therefore, datapoint (ii) is only a necessary condition on posited culpability, not normative culpability.[59]

While the theory I sketch in Section III is primarily designed to capture posited culpability, the same framework accounts for normative culpability. To do so, we simply need to ask how much insufficient regard an action manifests not for the interests and values that the law *actually* seeks to protect (the reasons it actually recognizes), but rather for the ones it *should*. To be clear, in later chapters I will be mainly concerned with normative culpability. A plausible account of this notion should provide an optimal balance of both descriptive fit with the law around here and normative defensibility. Thus, the notion of normative culpability I employ to critique the law in later chapters can be seen as a normatively cleaned-up version of the concept at work in jurisdictions like ours.

B. NECESSARY CONDITION: INADEQUATE REPULSION FROM CRIMINALITY MUST BE A CAUSE OF YOUR ACT

Focusing on posited culpability for now, we reach the core question. On the present view, the criminal law's basic demand is not to avoid *possessing* insufficient regard, but to avoid *manifesting* it in conduct. What does this mean? The causal approach offers promising start: to manifest insufficient regard, an action must be caused by it. But as seen in Section II, the pure causal approach fails because our actions do not necessarily manifest the full amount of insufficient regard that caused them. Thus, causation by insufficient regard is only a *necessary condition* for culpability. The *amount* manifested is a separate issue, discussed later (in III.C).

This idea of causation by insufficient regard requires clarification. Importantly, it is not the same as being caused by overt animus. Actions can be culpable without such a cause. Instead, we can profitably understand this idea as failing to be sufficiently *repelled* by criminality. This happens when the legally recognized reasons against the action (i.e., the protected interests or values it threatens) fail to motivate one to avoid doing it. Causation by lack of contrary motivation[60] thus lies at the heart of an action's being caused by insufficient regard.

This does not mean the law requires one to be motivated *by* the legally recognized reasons to comply. Its demand is only that one have some motivations or other that prevent one from breaking the law. A convenient way to encapsulate this is to say that the law requires us to have some kind of *repulsion mechanism* whose job it is to repel us from

---

[59] Still, it plausibly is a condition on normative culpability that one's action violate a prohibition the relevant jurisdiction *should* recognize, even if the jurisdiction doesn't yet do so. *See infra* notes 62 and 65.

[60] Arpaly and Schroeder convincingly defend this sort of causation as scientifically respectable. *See supra* note 10 at 82–85.

criminality and to see to it that we are motivated to always act in legally justifiable ways. By "legally justifiable action," I mean an action such that, under the facts *as you believe them to be*, the legally recognized reasons in its favor outweigh those counting against it. Thus, the repulsion mechanism is supposed to be responsive to the balance of available legal reasons that bear on your actions, and its task is to ensure that you always are motivated (in some way or other) to behave in ways that are supported by the balance of legal reasons. (I include the limitation to the facts as you believe them to be because criminal culpability is supposed to be largely a subjective notion, not just an assessment of whether one lives up to an objective standard—as in tort law.)

Crucially, the law is indifferent to the content of one's repulsion mechanism. Any motivations can in principle do the job.[61] Regardless of whether you are motivated to comply with the law for self-interested reasons, out of respect for law, to be seen as respectable, or for a hodge-podge of different reasons, the criminal law has no complaint against you. Its basic demand is only that some motivational failsafe kicks in to repel you from criminality when necessary. This begins to capture the law's default indifference to motives. To summarize:

> **Insufficient Regard as Repulsion Failure**: An action, A, that violates a legal prohibition[62] (i.e., satisfies the elements of a crime and is not otherwise justified) *manifests insufficient regard* for legally protected interests or values (i.e., the legally recognized reasons) only if the actor's repulsion mechanism is part of what *caused* A.

What, then, is involved in causation by repulsion failure? Two requirements must be met:

> **Causation by repulsion failure**: Your action A was caused in part by a failure of your repulsion mechanism if:
> (a) Your repulsion mechanism was *actually called upon to do some work* under the circumstances—that is, called on to provide motivation against doing A, since it would be an unjustifiable violation of the law under the facts as you believe them to be—and
> (b) Your repulsion mechanism failed to do the job it was called on to do (i.e., provide enough motivation to behave as required), such that you actually went on to perform A.

Only when the failure of your repulsion mechanism helps *cause* your conduct in this sense[63] is it *manifested* in that conduct. After all, even if the safeguard mechanism whose job it is

61 And when it fails to keep you within the bounds of legally justifiable conduct, it has the secondary job of motivating you to commit only the least bad violation possible (i.e., the one least disfavored by the legal reasons).

62 To get an account of normative culpability, just replace this with "a prohibition the law *should* recognize."

63 On this account, the repulsion failure is usually going to be a but-for cause of the action. However, one could imagine Frankfurt-style overdetermination cases where the repulsion failure (i.e., one's insufficient regard)

to keep you within the bounds of legally justifiable conduct is faulty, this failure won't be *manifested* until the mechanism is actually called on to do its job, but doesn't. Before that, the failure of the mechanism is just a latent defect that has not yet been manifested.

What, then, does it mean for one's repulsion mechanism to be *called on* to do work in motivating one not to act unjustifiably? For posited culpability, it is fixed by the prohibitions in the jurisdiction. In passing a criminal code, the legislature takes a stand on the normative question of when citizens' repulsion mechanisms should be called on. Of course, the legislature may get this *wrong*. Its laws might call on the repulsion mechanism to motivate one in ways that it should not. Criticizing the law in this way moves us into the realm of normative culpability.

Indeed, there are intuitive limits on when it would be fair to expect the repulsion mechanism to do work. It would be a blatant mistake to call on us to be motivated to avoid that which is impossible to resist. If someone pushes you off a bridge, your repulsion mechanism cannot be called on to motivate you not to fall. Similarly, it seems unfair for your repulsion mechanism to be called on to do work when you are neither engaged in any (relevant) conduct nor have any duty to act. When you are neither acting nor failing to discharge a duty, you are having no relevant effect on anyone else. In such cases, it would be odd and unfair for your repulsion mechanism to be called on to do any work. If that's right, the repulsion mechanism should not be called on to avoid bad attitudes that are in no way revealed in action. As a result, one cannot be *normatively* culpable merely for possessing bad attitudes. (Section IV further argues for this.)

Putting all this together, we get the following necessary condition on criminal culpability:

> **Manifestation Requirement**: The conduct of a competent, practically rational actor[64] who violates a legal prohibition[65] is criminally culpable *only if* a failure in her repulsion mechanism is part of the *cause* of that conduct (in the above sense).

One might question whether all of criminal law really involves such a requirement. What about crimes that require specific bad purposes or desires? Do they also involve only the failure to be repelled by criminality? Treason, we saw, requires the overt *purpose* of

---

actually led one to do the act, but where the repulsion failure was not a but-for cause. Perhaps other forces would have intervened to get one to do the action if the repulsion mechanism hadn't failed. Thus, I think repulsion failure strictly speaking needn't be a but-for cause of the action. Rather, it just has to be an *actual* cause of the act—on whatever the best account of causation turns out to be. (Thanks to an anonymous reviewer for pressing me on this point.)

[64] This claim is meant to apply only where the actor is at least minimally competent or practically rational. One who doesn't weigh the reasons incorrectly but violates a statutory prohibition only due to, say, a psychotic episode should not be deemed to have manifested insufficient regard. Thus, actors without normal practical reasoning capacities are are excluded from the present claim.

[65] Again, for normative culpability, just replace this with "a prohibition the law *should* recognize."

aiding the enemy; hate crimes require the *desire* to harm those with certain racial, gender, or other protected characteristics—not just failure to be repelled by this result.[66] So don't these crimes involve an overt attraction to evil, not insufficient repulsion therefrom?

The main answer is that to be affirmatively attracted to a bad state of affairs is to *overvalue* the reasons in favor of bringing it about, which is equivalent to proportionally undervaluing the reasons against doing so. In my view, culpability depends on whether one attaches weight to the relevant reasons in the right *proportion*—not the absolute amount of weight one gives them.[67] Thus, when one overvalues the reasons in favor of a crime and doesn't attach correspondingly greater weight to the reasons against, one can be described as *undervaluing the reasons against the crime in the proportional sense* (i.e., compared to the weight attached to the reasons in favor of the act). Hence, treason and hate crimes involve *proportionally undervaluing* the reasons not to act with attitudes like racial animus or a desire to aid the enemy—a form of insufficient regard. (This worry also admits of other answers.[68])

Introducing this Manifestation Requirement already goes quite a ways to capturing the data from above. It explains datapoints (i), and parts of (iv) and (vi). First, it captures the voluntary act requirement in (i) and the related idea that one cannot be criminally culpable merely for possessing bad attitudes. After all, you do not count as *manifesting* insufficient regard when you merely possess bad attitudes that don't produce any action. This, in turn, is because the above-mentioned necessary condition is not satisfied. Under existing law (and any plausible set of normative assumptions), the repulsion mechanism would not be called on to do any work in such cases. It is only called on to ensure that you don't act in ways that cross the line into unjustifiable conduct (i.e., that are not supported by the balance of legal reasons that exist given the facts as you believe them to be). When you merely possess a bad attitude and don't act on it, there is nothing for your repulsion mechanism to kick in to correct. So no failure of this mechanism is manifested.[69]

---

[66] *See supra* notes 17–19.

[67] *See* Sarch, *supra* note 9; Sarch *infra* note 68. I doubt the notion of the absolute weight given to a reason is even intelligible.

[68] In addition, the basic duty not to manifest insufficient regard can give rise to subsidiary duties—perhaps to prevent oneself from allowing certain proscribed attitudes from influencing one's conduct (i.e., to be so repelled by them that one keeps them in check). In this way, affirmative attractions to bad states of affairs can be culpability aggravators, which come *in addition* to the culpability of direct failures to be repulsed by bad states of affairs in their own right. *Cf.* Alex Sarch, *Double Effect and the Criminal Law*, 11 CRIM. L. & PHIL. 453 (2015) (especially section 3).

[69] One might worry that my theory *could* in principle allow punishing merely for bad attitudes. (Thanks to Gideon Yaffe for this worry.) If the legislature criminalizes a particular attitude (e.g., disliking the supreme leader), then our repulsion mechanisms may be called on to motivate us to prevent ourselves from developing this attitude. Failing to properly manage one's own mental states to block this attitude from taking root might thus be a repulsion failure.

While it's true that my theory thus has the resources to explain what is happening in such cases, that is a feature not a bug. For it's also true that my theory explains what has gone *wrong* in such cases: The legislature has endorsed a view about what work the repulsion mechanism is called on to do *that is obviously unjustifiable on normative grounds*. There are a range of moral, policy, and practical reasons that explain why, in any

Second, the necessary condition helps explain some aspects of the concurrence requirement in datapoint (iv). It shows why you cannot be criminally culpable if you form the mens rea of the crime *after* doing the actus reus. There, too, no repulsion failure *actually helped cause your conduct*. For a failure of your repulsion mechanism to help cause your conduct, you at least had to possess the mens rea of the crime either *before or during* your performance of the actus reus.

Finally, the necessary condition helps explain part of datapoint (vi)—that is, why motives don't matter to whether one possesses a defense. (Other explanations are available too, as noted in the next subsection.) In EVIL TROLLEY TURNER, Darryl turns the trolley not in order to save the five but to kill the one on the other track. Why might this actor—despite clearly having insufficient regard—still get the benefit of the justification available to him based on the facts he was aware of? After all, he wasn't *actually* motivated by the facts that justify his conduct. One answer is that, although he possessed insufficient regard, it wasn't *manifested* in his conduct. Plausibly, his repulsion mechanism was not called on to do any work in this case. Since his conduct (turning the trolley) was justified on the facts as he knew them to be, no *failure* of his repulsion mechanism was part of what actually caused his conduct. Even though his repulsion mechanism was clearly *faulty* at the time, the fault remained latent. So no failure of the mechanism helped produce his conduct.[70]

C. HOW MUCH INSUFFICIENT REGARD IS MANIFESTED?

The theory is not yet complete. We still must answer the question of *how much* insufficient regard an act manifests to know how culpable it is. As we saw, an action's being caused by a given amount of insufficient regard is not sufficient for manifesting that amount. My answer to this question employs a version of Yaffe's principle of lenity.[71] But

world similar to ours, we should never punish merely for bad attitudes. (Section IV also mounts a *principled* argument for this claim.) This explains why the repulsion mechanism should never be called on to provide motivation to block the development of bad attitudes alone (as opposed to motivating us to prevent them from *impacting* our conduct, which can be legitimately required). Thus, although my theory does not render punishment for mere attitudes conceptually impossible, it does explain why this would be prohibited under any *minimally plausible set of normative assumptions*—which I go on to justify directly in Section IV.

[70] Does my view thus mistakenly entail that we shouldn't punish "factually impossible" attempts? Factual impossibility traditionally was not a defense to attempt charges. *See* Yaffe *supra* note 4, at 112. But perhaps my view entails the opposite? When Jane tries to kill Victor by sticking pins into a voodoo doll replica of him, my view might suggest she doesn't merit punishment because her repulsion mechanism wasn't called on to get her to avoid this act. If no repulsion failure caused her act, she isn't culpable. (Thanks to Kim Ferzan for this worry.)

However, my view can avoid this result. The question of what the repulsion mechanism is called on to do is a normative question for the legislature in each jurisdiction to resolve. Quite plausibly, though, the best normative view is that one's repulsion mechanism *is* called on to halt one's attempted misconduct even in cases of factual impossibility. On the facts as Jane believes them to be, putting pins in the doll will kill Victor. Thus, it's very plausible that the law *should* call on her repulsion mechanism to motivate her not to stick pins in the doll. Hence, Jane *would* be culpable for attempting to kill Victor in this case. In this way, my view can capture the result that factual impossibility is not a defense to an attempt charge.

[71] Yaffe, *supra* note 22.

while Yaffe's is epistemic, and constrains what we may infer from the available evidence, my principle is nonepistemic:

> **Principle of Lenity**: D's action, A, only manifests *the least amount* of insufficient regard for legally protected interests or values (i.e., the least amount of error in weighing the legally recognized reasons) that is needed to explain why a rational and otherwise well-motivated person would do A (i.e., what D did under the relevant description[72]) in the circumstances as D believed them to be.

The motivation for this principle is that the state, given its superior power, should resolve any ambiguity in its punishment practices in favor of accused citizens. This is a principled way to resolve difficult normative questions: when in doubt, benefit the defendant. I've discussed other justifications for this principle,[73] and Section V gives further normative arguments for it.

Of course, the devil is in the details. How do we determine what this "least amount of insufficient regard" is? To start, I follow Yaffe in understanding insufficient regard for legally protected interests and values as *committing an error in how one weighs the legally recognized reasons* that bear on how to act.[74] Next, distinguish the insufficient regard *possessed* when acting from the amount the action *manifests*. Culpability is pegged to the latter, not the former. My view uses an idealized procedure to determine the magnitude of the error in weighing the relevant legal reasons that a given action manifests. This procedure compares the motivations (i.e., weighing of reasons) of (a) the rational, perfectly law-abiding citizen and (b) the citizen who does the crime but represents the *smallest possible departure* from the law-abiding person.

To flesh out the idea, let's use a model of the ideal case—that is, the motivations of the perfectly law-abiding citizen (PC). PC weighs the reasons for and against any putatively criminal action, A, she could perform the *correct way*. That is, she assigns weight to the legally recognized reasons for or against A exactly in line with the law's view of how they should be weighed.

To be more precise, assume first that the facts as the defendant, D, in the actual case believes them to be *are true*. (After all, this is a subjective culpability inquiry we're

---

72 As discussed below, it is an important question how this action, A, is to be described. When determining the culpability of an action that already counts as a crime in the relevant jurisdiction—that is, when calculating posited culpability—the salient description of the act is given by the elements of the applicable statute. So it will typically include not just the relevant body movements but also any required mens rea or attendant circumstances. However, when there is no statute on point prohibiting the conduct—as when we're concerned with normative culpability—it will be up for debate what the most apt description is. Different contexts plausibly call for different descriptions.

73 *See* Sarch, *supra* note 13, at 32 (ftn. 97), and Sarch, *supra* note 68, at 23 (ftn. 74).

74 Yaffe, *supra* note 22.

engaged in.[75]) Given the facts as D believes them to be, suppose there is a set of legally recognized reasons *against* A.[76] Call this set of reasons R–. These reasons will usually involve the legislature's reasons for criminalizing acts of type A (i.e., the interests or values this conduct was criminalized to protect).[77] Suppose there is a certain amount of weight that, according to the law, *should* be attached to these considerations. Let "X" denote this amount, the correct weight. For PC, R– = X.

For completeness, suppose there also are some legally recognized reasons *in favor* of A. Perhaps A would promote some legitimate interests or prevent unjustified harms to others. Call this set of reasons R+. Suppose there is a certain amount of weight that, according to the law, an actor *should* attach to these considerations. Let "Y" denote this amount, the correct weight. For PC, R+ = Y. Of course, because A is assumed to be unjustified, it must be the case that X > Y.

PC's key characteristic, then, is that she is motivated by all and only the legally recognized reasons bearing on A, and she weighs them correctly. Thus, she does not actually perform A. Now, the core question to determine how much culpability a criminal action manifests is this:

> **Core Question:** What is the *smallest possible departure* from the motivations of the perfectly law-abiding citizen (PC) that would get an otherwise well-motivated person to do the criminal action A under the circumstances as the actual defendant believes them to be?

That is, what is the *smallest amount of incorrectness* in the weights attached to the legally recognized reasons for and against A that is needed to get an otherwise well-motivated person to do the criminal action A under the facts as the actual defendant, D, believes them to be? This is going to be our measure of *how much* insufficient regard is manifested in D's performance of A.

The Core Question admits of a general answer, indicating how culpable D's actual action is.

> **Answer to Core Question:** The smallest amount of incorrectness in the weights attached to the legally recognized reasons bearing on criminal action A that would lead an otherwise well-motivated person to do A given the facts as the actual defendant believes them to be = *an amount just infinitesimally larger than* $X - Y$ (i.e.,

---

[75] *Cf.* Alexander, *supra* note 40, at 24 ("Moral permissibility turns on how things really are, not on what an actor believes. (...) Culpability, on the other hand, is a matter of the actor's beliefs.").

[76] To turn this into an account of *normative* culpability, rather than *posited* culpability, we would focus not on the reasons that the law actually recognizes but rather the reasons that the law should recognize (whatever they are).

[77] Note that this is just a *hypothesis* about what the real reasons are. The law can get this wrong.

the correct weight to be attached to the legally recognized reasons against A, or R–, minus the correct weight to be attached to the legally recognized reasons in favor of A, or R+).

Why is that? Call the otherwise well-motivated citizen OC. This person represents the smallest departure from the motivations of PC that would be needed to get someone to do A under the circumstances as D believes them to be. To get someone to do A, more weight must be attached to R+ than to R–. This means that the *least possible amount* that OC's valuation of the weights of the reasons for and against A must be off the mark by in order to get her to do A is just *slightly more* than X – Y. If R+ = R–, the actor's valuation of the reasons bearing on A would be in equipoise and no action would result. So what's needed is an amount slightly greater than this.

But what is the proof? How do we *know* the least amount of incorrectness in weighing reasons that would be needed to get OC to do A is just slightly greater than X – Y? To see why, note that there are three ways OC might attach more weight to R+ than to R–, and thus do A:

(1) OC attaches the right amount of weight to R+ (i.e., Y) but undervalues the reasons in R– so the total weight of R– dips down from X to a point below Y.
(2) OC attaches the right amount of weight to R– (i.e., X), but overvalues the reasons in R+ so the total weight of R+ rises from Y to a point above X.[78]
(3) OC both undervalues R– somewhat (so it's below X) and overvalues R+ (so it's above Y), and these mistakes together are big enough to make it the case that R+ > R–.

In all three cases, the *least* amount of error in weighing reasons that's required to get R– to be lower than R+ is the same: it's just slightly more than the difference between the correct weights for these two sets of reasons, viz. X and Y, respectively. Think of it like the levers on a sound mixing board, with one lever for R+ and another for R–. Ideally, the R– level should be at X, and the R+ level should be at Y (where X > Y). The smallest total distance that the two levers would have to traverse so that R+ > R– is just infinitesimally greater than X – Y. If they in total traversed a distance exactly equal to X – Y, then the two levers would not cross; at most they could end up at the same place, so that R+ = R–. Thus, for the R+ lever to *pass* the R– lever, such that R+ > R–, the smallest distance the two levers must traverse—the smallest error in weighing reasons that's needed—is an

[78] Note this could happen either by overvaluing some legally recognized reasons that belong in R+, or by erroneously including reasons in R+ which aren't legally recognized as counting in favor of A at all.

amount just slightly greater than X – Y. Using this model, we can now characterize *how much* insufficient regard an unjustified action manifests:

> **Level of Manifestation:** The amount of insufficient regard manifested in defendant D's unjustified action (assuming D is at least minimally competent and practically rational) directly corresponds to the *least amount of error* in weighing reasons that is needed to get an otherwise well-motivated person (OC) to do A under the circumstances as D actually believed them to be. That is, action A *manifests* an amount of insufficient regard that is just slightly greater than X – Y (as defined above).

A manifests an amount of insufficient regard just slightly in excess of X – Y because that is the smallest amount of error in weighing reasons needed to transform PC into OC. This is a principled approach. The amount manifested is not just a matter of how offended or harmed the victim is. Nor is it a matter of how bad we can infer the actor's response to reasons is given the available evidence, as Yaffe frames his view.[79] This approach would be unreliable because the evidence might be incomplete or inaccurate. My approach sidesteps such evidential problems.

By adding this second component to the theory, we can explain the remaining datapoints: (iii), (iv), (v), and (vi). Datapoint (iii) was that the law should not attribute greater culpability merely because one was willing to act in worse ways than one actually did. Recall TED THE WOULD-BE TERRORIST. The salient description of what he did is given by the violation he committed: defacing public buildings with racist slogans. Thus, his culpability corresponds to the least amount of insufficient regard for legally protected interests and values that it would take to get OC, an otherwise law-abiding citizen, to behave as Ted did. Suppose the perfectly law-abiding citizen, PC, would recognize no reasons in favor of this action (as with a great many crimes). Moreover, given the interests and rights of the victims, PC would attach five units of weight to the reasons against this action. Thus, the smallest amount of error in weighing reasons that could get OC to behave as Ted did is an amount that is slightly greater than five units. (The size of the units doesn't matter, so long as they're consistent across cases.) Granted, Ted wanted and was *willing* to behave in far worse ways. And Ted might have *actually* assigned, say, 10 units to the reasons in favor of this act and just 0.1 units against. But this is neither here nor there. The full amount of insufficient regard he possessed and acted from is not manifested. It reflects only a character flaw of the sort the law ignores. In this way, my theory explains

---

[79] *See generally* Yaffe, *supra* note 22 (discussing the "inferences" we may draw about culpability from the defendant's conduct); *see also, e.g., id.* at 9 (observing that "[i]nformation about the agent's psychological state at the time of action gives us information about the" factors that bear on culpability, and "[t]he principle of lenity mandates that we assign [culpability levels that are] as low as possible, consistent with the evidence").

why he is not more culpable just because his bad attitudes make him willing to behave worse than he actually did.

For similar reasons, the theory explains the concurrence requirement in datapoint (iv). It states that a mens rea you possess when acting is appropriately connected to the actus reus only if the former *caused* (actuated) the latter. Recall KILL YOUR UNCLE, where Charlie negligently killed someone who turned out to be the person he intended to murder. Charlie is not guilty of murder, only negligent homicide. To account for this under the concurrence requirement, one might argue that Charlie's intent did not cause his action in the right way—though specifying what this causal role is appears difficult. But my theory offers a simpler explanation of this case. The amount of insufficient regard manifested in an action equals the least amount of error in weighing reasons that's needed to get OC to do the same conduct under the circumstances. The least amount of insufficient regard needed to get OC to perform Charlie's actual conduct—that is, cause a death through carelessness—is the amount seen in negligence, not the far greater level associated with intentional killing. PC will appreciate and be motivated by the legally recognized reasons to pay adequate attention to the road while driving. Thus, the smallest error in attaching weight to legal reasons needed to get OC to behave as Charlie did is the amount involved in not attaching enough weight *to the reasons to pay attention to the road*—that is, the amount in negligent unawareness of the risks he imposed.[80] So this is all the insufficient regard Charlie's actual conduct manifests. Even if he was willing to act worse than he did, his conduct does not *manifest* this fact about him.[81]

For similar reasons, the theory also captures the additional wrinkle in datapoint (v). This was Arpaly and Schroeder's point that one is not always culpable to the full extent of the bad attitudes "that existed and were acted on"—even if these attitudes *were* causally active in producing the act in question. Recall TRIVIAL WRONGS. There, the

---

[80] One might object that my view does not explain Charlie's sort of inadvertent negligence, which does not involve the deliberate choice not to pay attention to the road. However, my view does not require a choice or the conscious weighing of reasons in order for an action to be culpable. Rather, all it requires is that the applicable legal reasons were accessible to one but failed to motivate one to abstain from the prohibited conduct. (Failing to pay attention to the road does not have to stem from a decision to attend to something else.) Nonetheless, on my view, negligent act A, done while being distracted in ways one ought not to be, can be culpable if A is caused in part by the failure to be sufficiently motivated to pay attention to the road. The insufficient regard A manifests lies in the failure to attach sufficient weight—whether consciously or unconsciously—to the legal reasons that exist to get oneself to pay attention to the road and thus avoid A. Of course, this is just a sketch of how my account might explain inadvertent negligence. Much more must be said to adequately address this difficult topic. *See also infra* notes 98–100.

[81] We could also get this result from the Manifestation Requirement. The only repulsion failure that was causally active in producing Charlie's conduct was the failure to be motivated to pay sufficient attention to the road. Had Charlie gone on to commence an intentional killing, his repulsion mechanism would have been called on to motivate him to cease it. But he never got to that point. So this more egregious repulsion failure wasn't any cause of his actual conduct. In fact, his repulsion mechanism was only called on to motivate him to pay sufficient attention to the road, which it failed to do. Thus, only this smaller repulsion failure was actually causally active.

actual cause of Jill's decision to use the software to skim small amounts of money from her victims' accounts was bottomless ill will. Nonetheless, the insufficient regard Jill's act *manifests* seemed rather small. The reason, on my view, is that the minimum amount of error in weighing the relevant legal reasons needed to get OC to do Jill's action under the circumstances as she believed them to be is *far less* than the amount she actually possessed and acted on. Thus, here too, although she has a deplorable character and is willing to behave in far worse ways than she actually did, the full extent of the bottomless ill will that she acted on was not manifested in what she did.

Finally, my theory can account for the complex role of motives in the criminal law. However, to do so, we need to attend to an issue I've glossed over thus far: How are we to describe *what the defendant did* when assessing culpability? Where the relevant description does not mention the defendant's specific motives for breaking the law (only the actus reus he did and the mens rea that caused him to do it), my theory straightforwardly explains why one's subjective motives or aims do not impact the amount of insufficient regard manifested in one's action. After all, on my view, it would equal the minimum amount of insufficient regard (i.e., the smallest amount of error in attaching weight to reasons) needed to get OC to do the same conduct so described.

This gives a straightforward way to capture cases that illustrate the default rule. In Evil Trolley Turner, if what Darryl did is described without mentioning motives—that is, turning the trolley while aware that this will save five lives—it would not take any insufficient regard to get an otherwise well-motivated person, OC, to behave the same way. After all, the act is justified. Accordingly, even though Darryl was actually motivated by bad attitudes, the amount of insufficient regard his conduct manifests, thus described, is zero. Hence, my view is perfectly able to explain the law's position that the defendant gets the benefit of the defenses that exist on the facts he is aware of—even if these justifying circumstances did not actually motivate him.

Good Thief, Bad Thief can be handled the same way. If we use a motive-free description, Mary and Barry did the same thing: stealing something of value while aware that it did not belong to them. And neither was aware of facts that amounted to a defense. (In the circumstances as they believed them to be, the theft was not necessary to prevent imminent bodily injury or death, etc.) Thus, it would take the same amount of insufficient regard to get OC to do what they both did. Thus, Barry (who stole for bad reasons) would not merit greater condemnation than Mary (who stole for not quite as bad but still insufficient reasons).

Of course, some might reject the standard legal view on these issues. One might think it is normatively mistaken to ignore motives in such cases. Isn't Darryl worse than someone who turns the trolley to save the five? Isn't Barry worse than Mary, since she was motivated at least somewhat by altruistic considerations? It is a virtue of my account that it also can capture this view—if that's what one prefers. To do so, we simply need to adopt a thicker, motive-laden description of what was done. We get a harsher result in Evil Trolley Turner by describing what Darryl did as *turning the trolley for the sole purpose of killing one person and not at all in order to save the five.*[82] The least amount of insufficient regard needed to get OC to do this more richly described action would be quite high. So it would be very culpable. Likewise, it plausibly would take more insufficient regard to get OC to do the act of *stealing to afford gambling in Vegas* than *stealing to afford a fancier school for one's child*. Thus, Barry's act would be more culpable than Mary's. In this way, my theory can capture either intuition one has about these cases, which attests to its explanatory power.

Ultimately, it will be up to the legislature to decide what description to use. To benefit defendants in such cases and not attribute greater culpability to actors like Darryl and Barry, the legislature should define the applicable crimes in a motive-free way. By contrast, to prevent badly motivated actors like Darryl from having a defense, and to impose harsher penalties on badly motivated actors like Barry, the legislature should adopt a motive-laden description. Indeed, I think this is precisely what occurs for crimes like treason, kidnapping, and hate crimes, where a specific bad purpose or motive is included as an element. For these crimes, the legislature decided that some kinds of bad aims or motives are especially worthy of condemnation (perhaps because there is a special duty to avoid being motivated by, for example, racial animus, disloyalty to country, or the desire to terrorize victims). Thus, my theory also explains what's going on with exceptions to the default rule that motives don't matter.

Still, this is only enough to account for posited culpability. What about normative culpability—that which the law *should* attribute? This notion is important for critiquing existing law and deciding whether to adopt new offenses or defenses. There, theorists must take a stand on how to describe the defendant's conduct and can't simply defer to the legislature's view.

Although I will take sides on this issue in Section VI, for now, I am most concerned to highlight the descriptive adequacy of my theory and show that it has the resources to capture most any plausible substantive view on such questions. Nonetheless, this issue needs to be resolved for the theory to be complete, so to tip my hand, I will argue in Section VI that a coarse-grained, motive-free description will generally be more appropriate for substantive criminal law doctrine, that is, the rules applicable at the guilt stage. Specifically, I will argue that allowing motives to impact the notion of culpability tracked by criminal liability would render the law too indeterminate to effectively serve as a publically available guide to action for most adults.[83] Moreover, I will contend that at least when the law is normatively ideal, determining culpability using a coarse-grained, motive-free description of the defendant's conduct benefits and helps protect citizens accused of crimes.[84] However, these are normative arguments that I defer until later.

---

[82] This is Tadros's view about the case example. *See supra* note 41.

[83] *See infra* notes 118–120 and accompanying text.

[84] *See infra* Section VI.B.

In closing, note that I am also open to the idea that a more fine-grained, motive-laden description may be more appropriate at the sentencing stage, after the defendant has been convicted. Many get accused of crimes, but before a conviction is reached, it is not yet clear if it's warranted for the court to spend time and effort in closely examining all the details of the case. Prior to conviction, the question is simply which coarse-grained box to place the defendant into—that is, which offense to convict him of, if any, or whether he qualifies for one of the narrowly defined affirmative defenses. For this question, the defendant's mens rea (or what he was aware of) will be relevant, but typically not his motives. By contrast, once a verdict has been reached regarding what coarse-grained category the defendant belongs in, we can be confident that there is a basis for more closely considering the details of the case. Thus, at sentencing, a fine-grained, motive-laden description begins to seem more appropriate.[85]

Accordingly, my theory accounts well for the complex role of motives in the criminal law. Usually, they don't matter because legislatures (reasonably) take the coarse-grained, motive-free description to be the most suitable way to define the act types to be criminalized. But sometimes legislatures take the opposite view—as we see with hate crimes or treason. Moreover, once the defendant is convicted, the prerequisites are met for taking a closer look at what the defendant did. So motives might matter to the more fine-grained assessments in sentencing. (Of course, motives may also be relevant to sentencing because culpability is not the only relevant sentencing factor.[86] A defendant's motives in doing the crime, and subsequent attitudes like remorse, might help show what sentence is needed for specific deterrence and rehabilitation. So this provides a supplementary, or perhaps an alternative, explanation of why motives affect sentencing.)

D. OBJECTIONS

Two objections demand a response. First, doesn't my theory impute culpability not just on the basis of the defendant's actual conduct—even though I've said this is something we generally shouldn't do? Two points in response. First, I grant that my theory relies on an idealized inquiry to determine how much culpability an action manifests. But this inquiry will never be relevant *unless* the failure of the defendant's repulsion mechanism *actually* helped cause her criminal action. Thus, my theory does not impute culpability merely for counterfactual attitudes or conduct. Instead, culpability is only imputed for actual conduct, and it is just the *amount* of culpability imputed that gets calculated using an idealized procedure. Second, any remaining aspects of my theory that might seem "counterfactual" in nature all redound to the benefit of the accused. On my view, the defendant will never be punished *more harshly* using the idealized calculation I advocate

---

[85] *Cf.* 18 U.S.C. § 3553(a)(1) (including "the nature and circumstances of the offense and the history and characteristics of the defendant" as one of the factors to be considered in sentencing).

[86] *See, e.g.*, 18 U.S.C. § 3553 (listing factors to be considered in sentencing).

than her actual mental states merit (i.e., the level of insufficient regard she possessed at the time). The idealized calculation in my theory only helps defendants, but doesn't hurt them. This should make us more comfortable with this idealized calculation.[87]

A second objection is this. Perhaps you think it's not a problem to *overvalue* something that really is valuable—say, your children's interests. How can it be bad, one might wonder, to care *too much* about something good? David Shoemaker recently raised such an objection to theories like mine: I "could 'take extremely seriously your interests in doing what you want with your property but still steal from you because I weigh my [children's interests] as slightly more important than yours.' "[88] Here I seem to have sufficient regard, but am still criminally culpable.

Granted, overvaluing something good (like one's children's interests) may not be bad in itself. But it *is* a problem when it leads you to attach too much weight to your kids' interests as a reason to do a criminal act *compared to* the weight you attach to the other legally recognized reasons against doing that act. In that case, you do manifest insufficient regard for legally protected interests. On my view, an important aspect of criminal culpability is the *proportional relationship* between the weights you attach to R+ and R–. After all, this is what determines if your repulsion mechanism has failed. If overvaluing your children's interests leads you to attach a *disproportionally* large amount of weight to R+ (the reasons in favor of A) *compared to* the weight you attach to R– (the reasons against A), then your repulsion mechanism should kick in to get you to attach correspondingly greater weight to R–. If it doesn't, and you end up overvaluing R+ without increasing the weight attached to R– sufficiently to get you to avoid doing A, then your repulsion mechanism has failed. That is, you end up *proportionately undervaluing* R–, and that is just what having insufficient regard for the reasons not to do A consists in. When

[87] One might object to this on the basis of things I say below about regretful knowing wrongdoers. *See infra* note 95 and accompanying text. Doesn't my ideal calculation impute more culpability to a character I later dub D2, a knowing killer who has great regret, than the amount of insufficient regard she actually possesses at the time of acting? Suppose regretful D2 weighs the reasons against the killing at +10, which is the correct amount, and the reasons in favor at +11, which is well above the correct amount of only +1. It might seem that D2 possesses a fairly small amount of insufficient regard. Doesn't my ideal calculation impute more culpability to her than the amount she possesses?

No, the idealized calculation still imputes less culpability than the amount of insufficient regard she actually possesses. Here's why. Suppose that the weight D2 should have attached to the reasons in favor of the act was only +1. She thus overvalued R+ by a factor 11. This means her repulsion mechanism was called on to create a correspondingly large increase in the weight attached to the reasons against. After all, that's what's needed to preserve the proportional relationship between the actual weight of reasons (i.e., 10 against versus 1 in favor). But the mechanism didn't do its job, and this helped cause her criminal act. Thus, my theory says we impute the most lenient possible amount of culpability to her for her action—that is, slightly more than 10 – 1 = 9 units. Although D2 in fact dramatically undervalued the reasons against the act (i.e., she assigned +10 to the reasons against when she should have assigned 11 times as much), she is treated far more leniently. In fact only +9 units of culpability are imputed to her. Thus, on my idealized calculation, she is in fact held to be less culpable than the full amount of insufficient regard she actually possessed at the time.

[88] David Shoemaker, *Blame and Punishment*, *in* BLAME: ITS NATURE AND NORMS 110 (D. Justin Coates & Neal A. Tognazzini eds., 2012).

such a repulsion failure ends up causing a prohibited act, that is the essence of criminal culpability.[89,90]

E. FURTHER BENEFITS: DEFENDING THE CULPABILITY HIERARCHY

There are further explanatory benefits to my insufficient regard theory. My principle of lenity helps defend the familiar mens rea culpability hierarchy from well-known objections.

The thought behind the culpability hierarchy is that the four traditional mens rea—purpose, knowledge, recklessness, and negligence[91]—are ordered such that it's worse to perform a bit of misconduct with a mens rea that is higher in the hierarchy. More precisely:

> **Culpability Hierarchy**: All else equal, it is more culpable to do a wrongful act, A, with a higher mens rea than to do an act, B, that is identical in every relevant respect except that it was done with a lower mens rea.

This immediately raises the question of what it means for all else to be equal. At the very least, the harmfulness of A and B, and the justifications in their favor (i.e., benefits the actors believe they provide), must be held fixed. Knowingly causing a bruised shoulder is far less culpable than recklessly killing. So the harms toward which the actors have mens rea must be kept constant. Likewise for the anticipated benefits of (justifications for) the actions.[92] Plausibly, it's less culpable to intentionally kill one of your group trapped in a mine while genuinely believing (even if falsely) that this is necessary for the group to survive than recklessly causing death by imposing "high risks of death on others *for the mere*

---

[89] That's why overvaluing the reasons in favor of a crime can be aptly described as *insufficient regard*. It's insufficient regard for the reasons against the crime as *compared to* the weight you happen to attach to the reasons you see in favor of doing it. (Nonetheless, as I've argued elsewhere, an overt attraction to the reasons in favor of a crime where no such reasons exist can still be a source of *heightened* culpability. *See* Sarch, *supra* note 68.)

[90] One might also object that my view does not explain why strict liability crimes are legitimate. One could be convicted of a strict liability crime even when my view says one has no criminal culpability—for example, if one has no insufficient regard and does a strict liability crime purely by accident. The least amount of insufficient regard needed to get an otherwise well-motivated citizen to commit such a violation is zero. I accept this implication. My view does not entail that those convicted of strict liability crimes are culpable—and it's a good thing too. This is precisely what makes strict liability crimes troubling. Thus, on my view, if such crimes can be justified at all, it will likely have to be for consequentialist reasons pursuant to some hybrid theory of punishment.

[91] *See* Dannye Holley, *Culpability Evaluations in the State Supreme Courts from 1977 to 1999: A "Model" Assessment*, 34 AKRON L. REV. 401, 410 (2001) (discussing which states adopt the MPC's "hierarchical interrelationship"); Kenneth Simons, *Rethinking Mental States*, 72 B.U. L. REV. 463, 464 (1992) (discussing "the hierarchical ordering of states of mind in contemporary law").

[92] Probably these anticipated harms and benefits should be probability weighted as well.

thrill of it but [where death is not the] conscious object."[93] This also is no counterexample because all else is not equal. The former action should admit of a justification (even if only partial), while the latter should not. There may be other things that also must be held fixed between the actions.[94] In the end, perhaps all we can say is that a higher mens rea is *one respect in which* the wrongful action is more culpable than the analogous act with a lower mens rea (i.e., is a pro tanto contributor to making the former all things considered more culpable).

Even this sophisticated version of the culpability hierarchy faces interesting objections. Consider the following objection to the ceteris paribus greater culpability of knowing over reckless misconduct.[95] Suppose D1 disregards a substantial and unjustified *risk* of death (say, a 30 percent chance) but is thoroughly callous about it. He cares not at all for his victims. By contrast, D2's case is the same as D1's except that D2 *knowingly* causes death (i.e., is aware of a practical certainty it will result) and has great regret and hesitation about doing it. Suppose the two cases are otherwise identical: neither D1 nor D2 has any justification for their lethal acts. Isn't D1, given his callousness, worse than D2? Why can D2 be convicted of a more serious offense than D1? Is this a counterexample to the culpability hierarchy? Note that analogous cases afflict the other levels of the hierarchy. Is D3 who only knowingly but callously causes death more culpable than D4 who kills on purpose but with great remorse? Is D5, who is unaware of the grave risks her negligent driving imposes, but who wouldn't care or do anything differently if she realized it, more culpable than D6, who is aware that her driving is risky but feels terrible about it? If the answer is "yes" to these questions, the culpability hierarchy is in trouble.

A cheap reply is that all is not equal as between these cases. However, this can't be the answer to *every* proffered counterexample. We need to know what differences are relevant and why. Instead, I offer a more principled answer: the picture of manifestation presented above defuses the counterexamples.

Take the knowledge versus recklessness example. The response to this case is that while D1 may be a worse person, this fact is not *manifested* in his conduct. D1's act does not manifest the full amount of insufficient regard he *possessed* when acting. Rather, it manifests the least amount of insufficient regard—the smallest error in weighing reasons—needed to get OC (an otherwise law-abiding citizen) to do this reckless act

---

93 Larry Alexander, *Insufficient Concern: A Unified Conception of Criminal Culpability*, 88 CAL. L. REV. 931, 943 (2000) (purposeful criminal acts are not "always more culpable than [that same conduct performed with] knowledge or recklessness").

94 In addition, when comparing purposeful to knowing, reckless, or negligent misconduct, we must keep fixed the actors' beliefs about likelihoods. (Thanks to Ken Simons for this point.) Here's why. If you do an act *in order to* cause death but while believing the act only has a 5 percent chance of succeeding, while I do the same act not intending to cause death but believing it has a 55 percent chance of the same, then I may be more culpable even though I'm reckless as to death and you are purposeful toward it. Again, this is no counterexample since all else is not equal.

95 *See* Kenneth Simons, *Punishment and Blame for Culpable Indifference*, 52 INQUIRY 143, 146 (2015).

under the circumstances as D1 believed them to be—that is, to get such a person to impose a perceived 30 percent chance of death without justification. But this is *less* than the amount of insufficient regard that D2's act manifests—that is, the least amount needed to get OC to *knowingly* (or with practical certainty) cause death without justification. This defuses the counterexample. It explains why, despite appearances, reckless D1 is actually less culpable than knowing D2.[96] D1 is surely a worse person, but that is irrelevant to his criminal culpability—and my theory explains why.

Similar responses are available to the other counterexamples. Even if knowing but callous D3 is a worse person than purposeful but regretful D4 (indeed, even if we know D3 is willing to do far worse things than D4), D3's additional badness is not manifested here. Instead, holding fixed the anticipated harms, benefits, and beliefs about the likelihood of each, D3's conduct manifests less insufficient regard than D4's. Under the circumstances, it takes a smaller error in weighing reasons to get an otherwise law-abiding citizen to behave like D3 than like D4. Perhaps D3 gets lucky in this respect, but luck is pervasive in the law.[97]

Finally, the same response applies as between D5's negligent callous conduct and D6's reckless regretful conduct. Again, all else equal, the former manifests less insufficient regard and is less culpable than the latter. On my view, the culpability of negligent misconduct equals the least amount of insufficient regard it would take to get an otherwise law-abiding citizen to behave as D5—that is, fail to recognize the risks her conduct imposes.[98] Under natural assumptions (i.e., setting aside cases of pure lapse and

---

[96] Note one limitation. If there were facts about D2 that, for legal purposes, *partially* but not fully justified her conduct (e.g., if causing the death would prevent her friend from being injured), though these facts are not present in D1's case (i.e., D1 has no partial justifiers), then my view would not entail that D2 is more culpable than D1. All else is not equal between these two cases. It might well take less insufficient regard to get someone like D1 to recklessly cause death without any justification than it does to get someone like D2 to knowingly cause death that is *nearly but not quite justified*.

Of course, the law of actual jurisdictions may not recognize all the partial justifiers it *should*. Perhaps Mary in GOOD THIEF, BAD THIEF should have a partial justifier, which Barry lacks. But this is at most a problem for the jurisdiction in question, not my view. Were the law changed to give Mary a partial justifier, so she's guilty of a lesser offense, then my view could capture that result too. My view makes posited criminal culpability a function of whatever the legally recognized reasons are. To determine normative culpability, we need to take a position on what reasons the law *should* recognize.

[97] For more on this kind of defense of the greater culpability of intentional wrongdoing over knowing wrongdoing, *see* Sarch, *supra* note 68.

[98] Consider texting while driving during rush hour. In saying the negligent driver should have been aware of the risks he was imposing, what we mean is that he has information that *should* have motivated him to pay more attention to the road, and thus recognize the risks he's creating. He knows that looking away from the road risks collisions, and that flashing screens create strong temptations to look away from the road. Together, these two pieces of knowledge should trigger sufficient motivation to get him to take steps to ensure he doesn't look at his phone instead of the road. But it doesn't. Thus, his repulsion mechanism has failed. The failure—assuming it's not a pure lapse, that is, a breakdown of his cognitive faculties—consists in not being motivated to exert sufficient effort to get himself to pay attention to the road. Thus, to figure out how much insufficient regard his conduct manifests the question is: *What is the least amount of insufficient regard for others (error in weighing*

breakdowns of one's cognitive faculties), this is less than the insufficient regard it would take to get an otherwise law-abiding citizen to behave the same way while *aware* that one is imposing this level of risk (i.e., the same as D6).[99] Thus, at least in this important subset of negligence cases, the culpability hierarchy is correct that acting recklessly as to a harm is more culpable than the analogous action done while negligent as to that harm and holding fixed the magnitude of risk and justifying reasons (if any). (Pure lapse cases are much harder, and I can't solve that problem here.[100])

In providing this defense of the traditional culpability hierarchy, my insufficient regard theory of culpability provides further explanatory benefits.

F. CONCLUDING REMARKS

I have not argued for my picture of culpability by conclusively refuting other theories or showing that only my view can account for this or that aspect of the law. Indeed, I want my view to be compatible, at least in outline, with other leading theories. I take this broad compatibility to further support my way of thinking about criminal culpability.

Instead, I have been trying to show that my picture of culpability is attractive because of all it can explain. I've shown how the view explains the distinction between posited

---

reasons) it would take to get an otherwise law-abiding citizen to look at the phone rather than pay attention to the road, under the circumstances the driver was aware of?

[99] Why, in the standard case, does failing to be aware of a risk of harm one is imposing, which one should have noticed, manifest less insufficient regard than acting while *aware* that one's action imposes that same risk of harm (i.e., is reckless as to that risk)? When texting while driving, one is looking at the phone rather than paying attention to the road. Not paying attention to the road risks preventing one from noticing the risks of harm that one's dangerous driving imposes. If the risk of harm is, say, a 30 percent chance of +10 units of harm, then recognizing that one is imposing this risk should trigger a motivating reason against driving dangerously that has a weight (let's say) of +3 units. But if, by looking at one's phone in traffic, one is merely *running the risk* that one will not recognize the underlying risk that one's dangerous driving imposes, then the motivating reason against looking at the phone in traffic that should be triggered by your beliefs is going to be *less* than +3. Assume that looking at the phone creates a 50 percent chance that one won't realize the risks of harm one's dangerous driving imposes. Thus, given the driver's (at least latent) beliefs that looking at the phone might prevent him from noticing the risks he's running, a motivating reason against looking at the phone should have been triggered with a weight of 0.5 * 0.3 * + 10 = 1.5 units.

Thus, in the standard case, negligently causing this harm manifests less culpability than recklessly causing it. It takes *less* insufficient regard to get someone to look at the phone in traffic, and thereby run a 50 percent chance of not noticing the 30 percent chance of +10 units of harm from one's dangerous driving, than the amount of insufficient regard it takes to get one to recklessly impose that same risk of harm, that is, drive while aware that one is creating a 30 percent risk of causing +10 units of harm. Of course, this analysis doesn't cover pure lapse cases. See next footnote.

[100] *See* GEORGE SHER, WHO KNEW: RESPONSIBILITY WITHOUT AWARENESS, ch. 1 (2009) (discussing cases like Hot Dog, where through a pure lapse the dog owner forgets her beloved pet in a hot car and, tragically, it perishes). Pure lapse cases involve forgetting or inadvertence despite not having any insufficient concern for the victim. My analysis does not apply to such cases. All I've argued is that, in paradigmatic cases, negligently causing harm H by failing to recognize that one was imposing a risk of H is less culpable than recklessly causing H by acting while aware that one was imposing the same risk of H.

culpability in a given jurisdiction and the notion of normative culpability used to critically assess the law. I've shown how my picture captures the complex role played by motives in the criminal law, and how it explains the tangle of doctrines pertaining to unmanifested mental states. Furthermore, I suggested that my account provides a promising defense of the criminal law's culpability hierarchy. In Section IV, I will emphasize another explanatory benefit of the view: namely, that it neatly preserves continuity between moral blameworthiness and criminal culpability, while also respecting the differences between them. On my view, criminal culpability can be seen as a stripped down analog of moral blameworthiness, with the former tracking a less fine-grained set of reasons than the latter.

Finally, I will put my insufficient regard theory to a range of further uses in subsequent chapters—including using it to explain and constrain the equal culpability thesis behind the willful ignorance doctrine (Chapter 4), defend a general theory of mens rea imputation (Chapter 5), and show how to make sense of corporate culpability (Chapter 9). Thus, the strongest argument for my account comes from the wide range of questions the account illuminates.

IV. Moving to Normative Culpability: Culpability vs. Moral Blameworthiness

To this point, I've been mainly concerned with posited culpability. I've been highlighting my theory's explanatory benefits by showing how it captures the culpability attributions made in jurisdictions like ours. But another explanatory benefit deserves mention. The theory preserves a tight connection between criminal culpability and moral blameworthiness, while also respecting their differences. This stems from the structural similarity between my theory and an increasingly popular view of moral blameworthiness: the quality of will theory. On this view, an act is *morally blameworthy* to the extent it manifests insufficient regard for the moral reasons bearing on whether to do that act.[101] These moral reasons can in principle be as detailed and case-specific as you like. By contrast, my theory takes it that an act is *criminally culpable* to the extent it manifests insufficient regard for the relevant legal reasons.

Some think criminal culpability *just is* moral blameworthiness, such that legitimate punishment requires being morally to blame.[102] Others see differences between the two notions, which stem from institutional design constraints on culpability that the moral notion is not subject to.[103] The explanatory power of the insufficient regard theory is further attested to by the fact that it can easily capture both views. Each one corresponds to a different picture of what reasons the law demands we not manifest insufficient regard

---

[101] Markovitz, *supra* note 10; ARPALY & SCHROEDER, *supra* note 10, at 170.

[102] *Cf.* Michael Moore, *Choice, Character, and Excuse*, 7 SOC. PHIL. & POL'Y 29, 30–31 (1990).

[103] Mark Dsouza, *Criminal Culpability after the Act*, 26 KING'S L.J. 440, 453 (2015).

for. On the one hand, criminal culpability collapses into moral blameworthiness if the reasons the law recognizes simply *are* the moral reasons bearing on how to act. By contrast, criminal culpability comes apart from moral blameworthiness if the law should recognize a different—perhaps narrower, less fine-grained or differently weighted—set of reasons that one's conduct shouldn't display insufficient regard for. Thus, criminal culpability would be a stripped-down analog of moral blameworthiness, with the legal notion tracking a different set of reasons than the moral notion.

Few would deny that the latter view is correct as to *posited* culpability. Given the law's imperfections, the reasons for action it actually recognizes clearly won't perfectly track the moral reasons. But what about normative culpability? *Should* the law recognize, for culpability purposes, all the perhaps very fine-grained reasons for action that apply in morality? So far in the chapter, I've remained ecumenical. But in moving to normative culpability, I now start taking a stand.[104] Although I cannot say exactly what reasons the law should recognize (a matter for the legislature to decide), my view is that the legislature should not automatically include all moral reasons within the set of legally recognized reasons that the law demands we not disrespect.

Here is why. The notion of culpability I'm concerned with is a distinctively *legal* notion. To take a central example, it's what courts appeal to when basing the willful ignorance doctrine on the (perhaps overbroad) claim that willfully ignorant misconduct is as culpable as the analogous knowing misconduct.[105] As a legal notion, criminal culpability is properly subject to a range of institutional design constraints and concessions to widespread practical limitations that the moral notion is not. One is plausibly less morally blameworthy for theft if the motive behind it is to help one's child afford school supplies, but the legislature may reasonably decline to recognize this as a consideration that justifies theft even partially. Why? It might be due to design constraints like the need for easy-to-apply, bright-line rules. Or perhaps it is grounded in the epistemic limitations that can make it difficult (or at least costly) to assess the veracity of requests for exemptions based on claims of need. Or perhaps the explanation is something more principled like the need for the law to be simple and stable enough to serve as a publically available guide to action. As discussed further in Section VI, we cannot (at least not routinely) be given carte blanche to determine for ourselves what interests are sufficiently weighty to exempt us from the otherwise applicable criminal prohibitions. Because of such legal design constraints, the landscape of legally recognized reasons that determine criminal culpability properly will be more anemic than the richer landscape of moral reasons that affect blameworthiness.

For present purposes I needn't settle exactly what relation the moral reasons bear to the narrower set of reasons the law should recognize and demand we not manifest insufficient

---

[104] Admittedly, the view that criminal culpability just is moral blameworthiness is more plausible as a claim about *normative* culpability (and for charity, this is how such views should be interpreted).

[105] Global-Tech Appliances, Inc. v. SEB S.A., 131 S. Ct. 2060, 2070 (2011).

regard for. Plausibly, there are moral reasons the law would properly decline to recognize, or at least assign different weight. Perhaps the law should recognize reasons that map onto no corresponding moral reason (e.g., for mala prohibita offenses)—though this is more contentious. I will not settle this detailed question here. All I contend is that, due to institutional design constraints, the legal reasons legitimately can diverge from the moral reasons for action.[106]

Thus, a further explanatory benefit of my account is that it preserves a structural analogy between criminal culpability and moral blameworthiness, while also respecting the differences that legitimately arise as between the two. Simply put, the former tracks one's responses to a different, thinner set of reasons than the latter. Criminal culpability—even its normative variety—is plausibly seen as a stripped-down analog of moral blameworthiness, with the legal notion tracking a different, less fine-grained set of reasons than the moral notion. This is the view I presuppose in the rest of book—though in

---

[106] Two main pictures are live options concerning the relation between the legal and moral reasons. On either picture, only criminal culpability (in the normative sense) is a prerequisite for deserved punishment—not moral blameworthiness.

First, the *Venn Diagram View* takes there to be (i) some reasons that both the law and morality recognize, but also (ii) some reasons that the law recognizes which morality doesn't, and (iii) some reasons that morality recognizes which the law doesn't. To illustrate, assume there are three applicable legal reasons: L1, L2, and L3. Suppose L1 and L2 are identical to two applicable moral reasons, M1 and M2. But L3 has no moral analogue: there is no "M3." However, there is an additional moral reason, M4. This gives us the Venn Diagram picture. Now suppose your action manifests sufficient regard for all the moral reasons: M1, M2, and M4. Thus, you are not morally blameworthy. As a result, your action also respects L1 and L2. However, suppose your action manifests *insufficient regard* for L3. Thus, you would be legally culpable without being morally blameworthy.

A second, perhaps more normatively attractive view—the *Subset View*—takes the legal reasons to be a subset of the moral reasons. Does this view entail that moral blameworthiness is always necessary for criminal culpability and legitimate punishment? No. Here's why. Suppose now there are three applicable moral reasons, M1, M2, and M3, but only two legal reasons: L1 and L2. Suppose M1 = L1 and M2 = L2. Assume M1 and M2, like L1 and L2, count against action X, while M3 supports X. However, M3 is not recognized in law. There is no "L3." How could this happen? Perhaps X is stealing to feed your hungry children, rather than going to a soup kitchen. M1 is respect for property rights, while M2 is respect for law and order, while M3 is the fact that stealing would help your children and the alternative (going to a soup kitchen) is burdensome. Suppose there is no L3, however, because the scenario does not satisfy the elements of the narrow necessity defense, as there is a possible alternative to stealing (trekking to the soup kitchen). Now attach weights to these reasons, corresponding to how much support they provide for X. Positive numbers support X, and negative numbers count against X. Thus, suppose M1 = −5, M2 = −5, and M3 = +10. On one simplistic way of doing the math, this means that if you do X, your moral blameworthiness is 0. But matters are different in the law's view. Assume the law assigns the following weights: L1 = −5 and L2 = −5. Since there is no legally recognized reason supporting X (no legal analog to M3), this means that if you go ahead and steal, you are culpable to degree −10. (These numbers are just meant as a toy example.)

What follows is that even on the Subset View, you can be criminally culpable despite having no moral blameworthiness. One might object that this is unfair, since the law should not assign weights to the applicable reasons in this way. (I'm inclined to think the necessity defense should be widened substantially.) Nonetheless, it is at least an *intelligible* way for the law to assign weights to these reasons in this manner. Indeed, I think it plausibly could be legitimate given the institutional design reasons to keep the law simple enough to publically guide conduct and resolve difficult normative questions. For more on this, see Section VI.

most places it will make little difference if one prefers to think that there is substantial overlap (or even a one-to-one mapping) between the moral reasons and the reasons the law should recognize as relevant to criminal culpability.

V. Normative Arguments for a Lenity Approach to Manifestation

Section III showed that my insufficient regard theory neatly accounts for a range of data points about existing criminal law's reluctance to attribute culpability for mere bad attitudes or a willingness to offend in worse ways. But I said little about why culpability attributions *should* be this way. Even if the theory reflects *posited* culpability in Anglo-American systems, why think this matches the correct attributions of *normative* culpability? To fill this gap, this section argues that our view of culpability should include a Manifestation Requirement and Principle of Lenity of the sort I defended in Section III, and thus deliver results roughly in line with existing law on this point. Moreover, my Principle of Lenity is likely to be the most surprising component of my account and needs additional buttressing.

The considerations I adduce to justify my lenity-based approach to manifestation of insufficient regard can be loosely grouped into two categories: those focusing on legislatures that pass criminal laws, and those focusing on benefits to citizens. The former face limitations and are not fully satisfying. Thus, the second group is more important. Still, these considerations are compatible, and together provide a weighty case in favor of a lenity-based approach.

A. LEGISLATURE-FACING CONSIDERATIONS

Some considerations that support my Manifestation Requirement and Principle of Lenity concern benefits to the legislature itself when promulgating criminal laws. The most simplistic concerns political prudence. Plausibly, the state would be wise to punish citizens only as much as it practically *must* in order to be seen as credible and effective. It might be prudent for the state not to punish citizens more harshly than is demanded by the minimum amount of culpability required to explain their actual behavior, as the Principle of Lenity mandates. Such restraint might help the state avoid resentment and retain popular support. If so, the state may have prudential reasons to withhold punishment until citizens perform observable conduct that manifests their bad attitudes, and when the state does go ahead and punish, it would have a reason to do so as little as it plausibly can.

Nonetheless, this argument doesn't cut it. First, it relies on highly variable factual circumstances. It applies only where particular attitudes prevail in the community. In some communities, the legislature might gain more from overpunishing and seeming "tough on crime" than from seeking to impose the most lenient punishments it realistically can. Thus, in some political climates, prudential considerations may militate in the opposite direction—that is, favoring harsher criminal law responses. Second, and more fundamentally, the present argument does not normatively justify the legislature in adopting a lenient stance in attributing culpability as the Principle of Lenity favors. Even when it serves the political interests of legislators to pass laws that don't attribute enhanced culpability based on deplorable attitudes that are not fully manifested, this is the wrong kind of reason to show the practice to be normatively justified—that is, show it to serve justice or other important values.

A better argument, therefore, appeals to virtues that we want the state, acting on behalf of the community, to display—like generosity, kindness, or mercy. If these virtues are to be cultivated by our institutions and displayed in our laws, then this gives a reason to interpret and judge the actions of fellow citizens charitably.[107] This line of thinking would support the legislature in adopting the Principle of Lenity and Manifestation Requirement in passing laws attributing culpability.

Still, one might worry that this argument from virtue is not weighty enough to fully ground the Principle of Lenity. While it might be desirable for our institutions to cultivate the virtues, this might also go beyond what we can *demand* of it. That is, citizens may not have a *complaint* against the legislature if it fails to display such virtues. Still, perhaps citizens would have a complaint against the legislature if it acted in ways that are outright merciless or vicious. Perhaps there is affirmative *unkindness* in not adopting a policy of lenity, which mandates treating citizens as the least bad version of themselves that is consistent with the actions they actually performed in the public sphere (as opposed to what they were willing to do). Whether this would generate a true complaint, however, remains an open question requiring additional work.[108]

B. CITIZEN-FACING CONSIDERATIONS

A more promising kind of argument concerns the value *to citizens* in adopting my Principle of Lenity and a Manifestation Requirement in the law's attributions of culpability. I suggest two considerations of this sort. There may be others (e.g., related to preventing abuses by the state).[109]

---

[107] Aquinas endorsed this view. He claimed: "unless we have evident indications of a person's wickedness, we ought to deem him good, by interpreting for the best whatever is doubtful about him." *Summa Theologica* II-II 60, 4. This rests on the argument that "from the very fact that a man thinks ill of another without sufficient cause, he injures and despises him," and "no man ought to despise or in any way injure another man without urgent cause." *Id.* (Note this may only support an epistemic version of the Principle of Lenity, which I criticized in Section II.C.)

[108] Elsewhere, I explore such arguments from mercy for the legislature to adopt a lenient approach to criminalization in more depth. Further refinements may be available. *See* Alex Sarch, *Don't Be an Asshole: Building the Case for Moral Luck in the Law* (manuscript).

[109] Perhaps the Principle of Lenity and Manifestation Requirement help offset the danger of governmental abuse. The state enjoys great power over individual citizens, and it can be abused. Thus, it's a familiar point that defendants need certain benefits and protections to make up for this power differential. While commonly used to support procedural safeguards, perhaps this idea also should inform substantive criminal law. The Principle of Lenity and Manifestation Requirement might help provide such protection for defendants. *Cf.*

First, the criminal law, I maintain, should strive to ensure that those subject to it remain able to preserve their self-conception as good, law-abiding citizens—to continue to see themselves as insiders, rather than outsiders in the social project. The benefits this carries in terms of social cohesion and allegiance to the state should be obvious.[110] Thus, the criminal law should make it feasible for citizens who genuinely *want* to follow the rules, and remain committed to the collective project of serving all citizens, to do so by avoiding criminal condemnation as much as possible. Many desire to see themselves as upstanding members of society. But criminal sanctions heavily burden precisely this self-conception. That, in turn, likely would undermine convicted persons' feelings of civic belonging. Accordingly, the criminal law should be especially concerned to protect our self-conception as upstanding citizens as much as possible (especially since this is precisely what punishment repudiates).

One familiar step the criminal law should take toward this end, of course, is to provide ex ante notice of what conduct is prohibited, so that citizens can avoid punishment.[111] But this is not all the law should do. Similar thinking provides a weighty reason for legal attributions of culpability to follow the Principle of Lenity. Not attributing more culpability to the defendant than the least amount needed to explain why an otherwise law-abiding citizen would do what the defendant did is a principled way to ensure that citizens are viewed, as much as possible, as upstanding, law-abiding members of the community. To treat everyone—even those who misbehave—as the least bad version of themselves consistent with what they actually did (as opposed to what they were willing to do) serves valuable functions: it promotes social solidarity, prevents alienation from the community, and protects our dearly held identity as upstanding citizens.

This is a weighty consideration that supports the Principle of Lenity. While a stricter criminal law that rejects lenity could conceivably carry other benefits in isolated cases, I submit that these are almost certainly outweighed by the substantial and widespread

---

A.P. Simester, *Is Strict Liability Always Wrong?*, *in* APPRAISING STRICT LIABILITY 47 (A.P. Simester ed. 2005) (suggesting in a different context that reducing our overall exposure to criminal liability by making harm a condition of conviction, even if it's on a strict liability basis, could have "rule of law benefits, since it confines what otherwise might be wide-ranging discretionary powers of arrest and prosecution"). Still, this idea may be too general to support the precise version of the Principle of Lenity and Manifestation Requirement my theory relies on. One might wonder why the protections defendants should get against the greater power of the state should take precisely this form.

[110] Tadros explores the idea that one thing the criminal law should aim at is promoting social solidarity, and he suggests this supports the principle of fair labeling. *See* Victor Tadros, *Fair Labelling and Social Solidarity*, *in* PRINCIPLES AND VALUES IN CRIMINAL LAW AND CRIMINAL JUSTICE: ESSAYS IN HONOUR OF ANDREW ASHWORTH 67–80 (Lucia Zedner & Julian Roberts eds., 2012). I'm suggesting something similar. The importance of protecting our self-conception as upstanding citizens, which fosters social solidarity, provides a reason to punish as leniently as we can, other things equal—that is, it's a reason for the criminal law to repudiate this valuable self-conception as little as possible. The Principle of Lenity in my theory embodies this idea and derives support from it.

[111] H.L.A. HART, PUNISHMENT AND RESPONSIBILITY 22–24 (2d ed. 2008) (offering a similar argument for the importance of fair notice as a way to ensure that we can avoid punishment).

benefits that the lenity approach confers in helping preserve many citizens' identity as upstanding members of society, thereby promoting solidarity and reducing alienation. This is one promising way to argue that the Principle of Lenity should be part of *normative* culpability.

Second, I'll bolster this argument by sketching a harm-prevention argument I've defended in detail elsewhere.[112] The thought is that because there is so little extra harm to others involved in bad mental states that are not manifested in conduct, there is little call, on preventive grounds, to increase criminal liability based on unmanifested mental states. More precisely, consider three possible regimes. The *maximalist regime* doles out punishments according to the full amount of insufficient regard one possesses, regardless of whether it is manifested in action. In the *minimalist regime*, one is only punished for insufficient regard manifested in conduct, and the amount manifested is determined by the Principle of Lenity as my theory suggests. Third, the *intermediary regime* includes a rudimentary manifestation-like requirement but no lenity principle. Thus, one's culpability equals the level of insufficient regard that actually *causes* one's actions, even if it's not *fully* manifested under the lenity principle.

I contend that the minimalist regime offers us the best deal. To see why, consider cases where the regimes differ, which involve not fully manifested mental states:

(a) Charlie drives off intending to kill his uncle, and in his distracted state hits and kills a pedestrian who just happens to be his uncle.
(b) Alan burns down an unoccupied building for $5,000, though we know he'd be willing to burn it down for the same sum even if he knew a person was inside.

The maximalist and intermediary regimes regard Charlie as just as culpable as a murderer and Alan as just as culpable as an extreme arsonist who knows the building is occupied. After all, Charlie and Alan *possess* levels of insufficient regard associated, respectively, with murder and this extreme form of arson, and their conduct was *caused* by these high levels insufficient regard. In the minimalist regime, Charlie is as culpable only as someone who commits negligent homicide, and Alan as culpable as a less-extreme arsonist who thought the building unoccupied.

The minimalist regime is less burdensome than the other regimes, while providing comparable harm prevention benefits. To see why, start with this most lenient system and ask whether there is reason to move to a harsher one. Suppose for now that all three regimes are implemented so as to adequately deter harms that are wrongfully imposed. That is, none of them noticeably *underdeter*. (I return to this assumption in a moment.)

---

112 *See* Sarch, *supra* note 9 (defending a version of this argument in contractualist terms).

First, moving from the minimalist regime to either of the others entails significant costs. Making actors punishable for the full level of hateful thoughts, uncaring attitudes or willingness to harm that happen to play a causal role in getting them to act, as mandated by the maximalist or intermediary regime, entails significant enforcement-related costs compared to the minimalist regime. Enforcing the rules of the maximalist or intermediary regimes would be highly invasive. It requires allowing the state to investigate and concern itself with evidence of whether one possesses or was even partly motivated by insufficiently respectful attitudes. This evidence includes utterances, writings, and communications. But that undermines the substantial benefits we get from privacy and unencumbered speech—such as getting to consider dubious hypotheticals and mull over a range of plans (some perhaps quite bad) before deciding how to act, not to mention the feeling of safety we get from having a private, protected mental space. Giving law enforcement the control over us required to implement the maximalist or intermediary regimes would involve heavy costs to values like privacy and autonomy that the minimalist regime avoids.[113]

Could there nonetheless be sufficient added benefits of the maximalist or intermediary regimes to overcome their greater costs? It seems unlikely. When others harbor hateful thoughts or disrespectful attitudes toward us, but don't act in ways that bring the full badness of these attitudes to light, the extra harm we suffer from the unmanifested badness of these attitudes is extremely limited—if there is any extra injury at all. When Charlie or Alan are merely willing to act in worse ways than they did, but don't manifest it, I maintain there is little or no extra injury from the mere willingness. That means there is little or no additional harm to be *prevented* in cases of unmanifested mental states—the only cases where the regimes differ—by imposing the greater punishments of the maximalist or intermediary regimes. The overall level of harm to be prevented is roughly the same whether we focus on (a) defendants' actions plus the full amount of insufficient regard they possessed or acted on at the time, or (b) their actions plus the insufficient regard these actions *manifest* (understood according to the Principle of Lenity). Thus, there is little call, on protective grounds, for preferring the maximalist or intermediary regime to the minimalist regime. Assuming the three regimes already provide adequate harm prevention (i.e., a sufficient baseline level of deterrence), there will be no harm-prevention-based reason to move beyond the minimalist regime to the maximalist or intermediary version.

However, this presupposes that the minimalist regime sets punishment levels so as to already provide adequate, cost-justified deterrence of harmful wrongs. What if we relax

[113] A further cost of the maximalist or intermediary regime compared to the minimalist regime is, of course, that the former entail greater punishments should we ever find ourselves in the position of Charlie or Alan by acting criminally without fully manifesting all our insufficient regard. These greater harms also affect the calculus.

this assumption? Is there *then* a call on harm-prevention grounds to move to a harsher regime?

The maximalist and intermediary regimes admittedly provide more *general deterrence*. But if the minimalist regime really did underdeter wrongful harms, the fix would not be to start criminalizing nonharmful character traits or unmanifested attitudes, which don't add much extra injury. If the minimalist regime is found to underdeter theft and fraud, for example, the solution is not to criminalize unrelated harmless mischief like enjoying Justin Bieber music or letting one's hair grow long. This would not be a narrowly tailored response to the problem and amounts to unfairly punishing those with such innocuous traits (which don't independently merit a criminal law response) merely as a means. The same problem arises if, upon finding the minimalist regime to underdeter wrongful harms, we move to the maximalist or intermediary regime to obtain the greater general deterrence these systems provide. This would likewise not be a narrowly tailored, fair response to underdeterrence in the minimalist regime.

Thus, those who would go beyond the minimalist regime face a dilemma. Either this regime provides adequate deterrence or it doesn't. If the former, there is no call on preventive grounds to move to the maximalist or intermediary regimes—and this is further blocked by the heavy added costs of the latter regimes. But if the minimalist regime does underdeter, then for the fairness reasons just sketched this problem ought not be fixed by moving to a regime that condemns and penalizes the possession of not-fully-manifested attitudes, which carry only trivial harms at most.

Accordingly, if I'm right that we are not significantly harmed by people harboring bad attitudes that are not fully manifested, I conclude that the bargain offered by the maximalist or intermediary regimes is just not worth it. The bargain offered by the minimalist regime, by contrast, with its Manifestation Requirement and Principle of Lenity, is a better deal. It is doubtful, for instance, that those negotiating behind the veil of ignorance would agree to be punishable for the full extent of the insufficient regard they only possess or that merely helps cause their actions—as with Charlie and Alan. The benefits we, as potential victims, get from extracting such concessions from the Charlies and Alans of the world are not great—certainly not substantial enough to justify the steep costs of punishing unmanifested bad attitudes.

VI. Clarifying the Theory: The Proper Role of Motives

When presenting my theory in Section III, I was noncommittal about the role motives should play in assessing culpability. However, the theory remains indeterminate until this question is settled. After all, the theory can accommodate either the view that actual motives impact culpability, the *motive matters approach*, or the view that they don't, the *motive-free approach*. On my account, the defendant's criminal culpability equals the least amount of insufficient regard it would take to get an otherwise law-abiding citizen to do what she did under the facts she was aware of. If "what the defendant did" is described in a fine-grained way that includes motives (i.e., the goals she sought to obtain thereby), then my theory becomes the motive matters approach.[114] But if "what one did" is described in a coarse-grained way that does not mention motives, then it becomes the motive-free approach.[115] For the account to be complete, I need to answer this crucial question about how to describe what the defendant did.

Where posited culpability is concerned, this question is answered by the legislature. The motive-free approach is the default rule in Anglo-American jurisdictions. Motives generally don't figure in the descriptions of the act types criminalized by statute (although exceptions exist). So in assessing posited culpability, we can assume that what the defendant did generally is to be described in a coarse-grained way that does not mention motives. Still, the question remains wide open for *normative* culpability—that is, the culpability the law should attribute. Here, we can't solely defer to the legislature on how best to describe the defendant's conduct (even if that is a useful stating point). Thus, I still need to answer this question for my theory to be complete. That's the task of this final section.

I offer two arguments for the motive-free approach to normative culpability.[116] But before that, I must defuse a possible confusion. Some might object that positive law's endorsement of the motive-free approach is surely mistaken since it overlooks crucial normative distinctions. In Good Thief, Bad Thief, Mary stole from an ATM to send her child to a better school, while Barry did it because he wanted to gamble in Vegas. The motive-free approach might seem to entail that the law must necessarily regard Mary and Barry as equally culpable. But surely Mary's better motives should make her less culpable than Barry?

The motive-free approach does not entail that the law *must* see Mary and Barry as equally culpable. This approach can also make room for case-specific circumstances that help justify one's conduct. In principle, the law could recognize a partial justification in Mary-style cases. If the legislature were to accept that Mary has a legally recognized reason that *partially* supports her conduct (perhaps by reducing it to a lesser offense), then also the motive-free view could generate the result that Mary is less criminally culpable than Barry.

Thus, the motive-free approach doesn't *necessarily* overlook any normative distinction that might exist between Mary and Barry. To capture it, one just has to claim the law *should* recognize different reasons as applying to Mary and Barry. Even if the motive-free approach regards them as doing the same thing, it does not require that Mary's legally recognized reasons are identical to Barry's. Culpability, on the motive-free approach, is a function not of *why* one acted, but of the support that *exists* for what one did on the facts

---

[114] This was Tadros's approach to Evil Trolley Turner. *See supra* note 41.

[115] Alexander and Ferzan endorse this approach to Evil Trolley Turner. *See supra* note 40.

[116] Note this is mainly in service of injecting greater clarity into the theory. If one prefers the motives matter approach, the few arguments later in the book where this makes a difference can be reformulated using the motives matter view without too much loss.

one is aware of.[117] Thus, any normative difference that may exist between Mary and Barry can still show up in the justifying facts these actors are aware of that the law recognizes as helping support their conduct.

A. INSTITUTIONAL DESIGN ARGUMENTS FOR THE MOTIVE-FREE APPROACH

Having defused this worry, I'll now offer reasons to favor the motive-free approach to normative culpability. To start, several institutional design considerations support this view.

One is grounded in how our epistemic limitations filter down to the judicial system. It will often be difficult for courts to determine defendants' real motives in acting. We often do not know ourselves what considerations pull us to act in this way or that. We rationalize our conduct after the fact, and are often deceived about the real reasons why we did what we did. Moreover, rationally self-interested defendants can be expected to not always be truthful about their motives. Accordingly, it might seem preferable to have courts only ask *what factors supported D's conduct* on the facts as she believed them to be, not what her actual motives were. This is a practical argument for why criminal culpability in particular—the legal concept—should not generally concern itself with a description of the defendant's conduct that references actual motives.

However, this argument does not ground a complete prohibition on considering motives in worlds like ours. Sometimes our epistemic limitations will be temporarily alleviated—for example, because the available evidence happens to be especially good or because the defendant credibly admits on the stand how bad his motives actually were. In those cases, our epistemic limitations don't block us from mentioning motives when describing the conduct to be evaluated.

Here, then, is a better institutional design argument for the motive-free approach. The idea is that the proper description of what the defendant did is constrained by the fact that the law must be *publically available* as a guide to action if it is to do its job. Statutes defining crimes should be capable of guiding the actions of, if not all citizens, then at least the vast majority of normal adults. This places limits on how fine-grained the description of the conduct in question can be. Accordingly, the argument goes, the law *should* (even where normative culpability is concerned) adopt a description of the relevant conduct that is at least somewhat coarse-grained.

Does this mean *motives* in particular should generally be left out of the description? I think so. Granted, many actors are perfectly able to appreciate—provided the issue is put to them and they have time to think about it—the normative difference between eating breakfast with the motive of fortifying oneself to commit an act of terrorism and eating breakfast with the motive of fortifying oneself for a difficult business meeting.

[117] The relevant facts here are chiefly the harms and benefits, weighted by perceived likelihood, that would flow from one's action (though other considerations might matter too).

Still, actors often will not have the benefit of sufficient reflection. Accordingly, it is less reasonable to expect actors in the moment to be generally able to appreciate and correctly apply the distinction between (i) doing an otherwise criminally prohibited type of action with a sufficiently good motive to justify it, and (ii) doing a prohibited action with an insufficiently good motive. This is a conceptually complex distinction. Furthermore, the difficulty is compounded by the fact that this distinction rests on a contested normative question on which reasonable minds might differ—namely, what motives can justify otherwise criminal actions. Such normative questions introduce serious uncertainty into the law.[118] The problem cannot be remedied by listing all the sufficiently good motives with any reasonable degree of specificity in advance. Thus, an effective way to keep the law determinate and publically available as a guide to action for most adults is to adopt motive-free descriptions of the actions whose culpability is to be assessed.

Admittedly, this argument may not apply in all cases—particularly where the motives in question are sufficiently bad to be condemned on a nearly universal basis. For example, a law prohibiting any act done for the purpose of facilitating terrorism might perhaps be capable of serving as an effective, publically available guide to action for most people.[119] Still, the present argument does *in general* support a preference for the motive-free approach. The need to keep the law determinate enough to be a publically available guide to action gives good reason for *usually* not mentioning motives when describing the conduct to be evaluated.[120]

B. THE PRO-DEFENDANT ARGUMENT

Let me end by offering a more principled normative argument.[121] The idea is that the motive-free approach gives a structural advantage for defendants that offsets the significantly greater power of the state and attendant risks of abuse. The state enjoys major advantages

---

[118] Rebecca Stone offers a related argument, deriving from the idea that the private law is akin to self-defense, to the effect that the private law must provide publically accessible and determinate standards. My argument is similar in spirit to hers. *See* Rebecca Stone, *Private Law as Self-Defense* 3 (manuscript) ("there may be uncertainty about whether [another person's] conduct has or will wrong another . . . because [of] uncertainty about the relevant standard of wrongdoing[.] Because of this uncertainty, it is important that the use of force by one private actor against another be limited by standards that are reasonably accessible to both parties. And this means[, assuming the private law is akin to a system of defensive force,] that the boundaries of legal liability may exceed or fall short of the boundaries of moral liability from which they are ultimately derived.").

[119] *Cf.* U.K. Terrorism Act 2000 § 16(2).

[120] As briefly noted in Section IV, this shows one way legal culpability differs from moral blameworthiness. Insofar as moral blameworthiness is merely supposed to involve ex post evaluation of conduct from the perspective of a fully informed neutral observer, this concept needn't be able to provide publically available guidance of conduct ex ante. Thus, the descriptions used for evaluating moral blameworthiness can in principle be as fine-grained as you like, taking any facts that might impact the evaluation into account. Legal culpability, by contrast, is constrained by considerations of public availability, determinacy, and the capacity to guide action. This favors a coarse-grained description of the conduct to be evaluated in terms of legal culpability.

[121] Thanks to Ira Lindsay for helpful conversations about how to frame this argument.

vis-à-vis putative defendants given its investigative powers, prosecutory discretion, and leverage in negotiating plea deals. In the criminal law, our weightiest of interests are at stake—up to and including life and liberty. This suggests we should take reasonable steps to even the playing field by building in protections for would-be defendants—not only where the procedural and evidential rules that govern trials are concerned (as with the "beyond a reasonable doubt" standard)[122] but also with in the criminal law's substantive liability rules.[123]

Thus, the present argument starts from the premise that when choosing between competing approaches to criminal law doctrine that are roughly on a par normatively, we should prefer the one that provides greater protections for defendants. All else equal, the law should employ a concept of criminal culpability that is more protective of citizens who may be accused of crimes.

Given this premise, the core claim of the argument is that the motive-free approach to describing "what the defendant did" is the more lenient approach, offering greater protections for would-be defendants, than the motives matter approach. However, as we'll see, this conclusion applies only if the criminal law is normatively ideal in a certain sense.

1. Setting Up the Argument: Where the Two Views Come Apart

The motive-free and motives matter approaches deliver the same results when the defendant was motivated by all and only the legally recognized reasons that exist on the facts she is aware of. Take the classic trolley case, where a necessity defense plausibly applies:

> GOOD TROLLEY TURNER: A trolley is careening toward five people who are tied to the tracks. It will kill them unless Jocelyn pulls the switch, and diverts the trolley onto another track to which just one person, Vicky, is tied. This will kill Vicky but will save five other lives. Jocelyn pulls the switch because she wants to save the five.

---

[122] WILLIAM BLACKSTONE, COMMENTARIES ON THE LAWS OF ENGLAND (1765), Book 4, Chapter 27 (famously observing that it is "better that ten guilty persons escape, than that one innocent suffer"). In re Winship, 397 U.S. 358, 364 (1970) (expressly adopting the beyond a reasonable doubt standard); *id.* at 374 (Harlan, J. concurring) ("I view the requirement of proof beyond a reasonable doubt in a criminal case as bottomed on a fundamental value determination . . . that it is far worse to convict an innocent man than to let a guilty man go free"). Another procedural rule with such motivations, employed in US federal courts, is that convicted parties enjoy an appeal of right, while the government cannot appeal an acquittal. Dworkin suggests that similar reasoning underlies the rule that the accused may not be compelled to testify. RONALD DWORKIN, *Principle, Policy, Procedure*, *in* A MATTER OF PRINCIPLE 89 (1985).

[123] Others agree such considerations should influence substantive liability rules—such as through canons of statutory interpretation like the interpretive rule of lenity. *See* Zachary Price, *The Rule of Lenity as a Rule of Structure*, 72 FORDHAM L. REV. 885, 887 (2004) (because legislative dynamics tend to push criminal law toward overbreadth, the lenity canon of interpretation is justified because of its ability to promote accountability: it forces the "legislature to detail the breadth of prohibitions in advance of their enforcement" and "[w]ithout the rule, politicians might prefer to choose broad language that obscures the extent to which criminal laws encompass unremarkable conduct").

Regardless of whether Jocelyn's action is described in a motive-laden way or a motive-free way, it takes the same amount of insufficient regard to get someone to do what she did under these circumstances: zero. On either approach, Jocelyn is not culpable.

The two views come apart when one is motivated by *other* considerations—whether better or worse—than the ones that are legally recognized as existing on the facts one is aware of. There are two types of case where this happens: (1) one is motivated by *worse* reasons than the best available set of legally recognized reasons that support one's conduct on the facts one is aware of, and (2) one is motivated by *better* reasons than the best available set of legally recognized reasons that support one's conduct on the facts one is aware of. Call these *Type (1) Cases* and *Type (2) Cases*.

In Type (1) Cases, the motive-free approach is better for defendants. Recall EVIL TROLLEY TURNER, where Darryl knows facts that would justify turning the trolley, but his real motive for doing so is that he wants to kill the one victim on the other track. On the motive-free approach, Jocelyn and Darryl did the same thing and would have the same culpability. But on the motive matters approach, Darryl did something much more culpable than Jocelyn. Thus, actors like Darryl fare better on the former approach to describing "what the defendant did" than the latter.

Type (1) Cases need not involve affirmative defenses. Compare the following two cases:

> CRAZY DRIVER 1 (D IS AWARE OF AND MOTIVATED BY THE JUSTIFYING CIRCUMSTANCES): Lisa's mother has become seriously ill. Lisa puts her in the car and drives as fast as she can to the hospital. She runs all the red lights, speeds at 90 mph on the highway, and weaves in and out of traffic in dangerous ways. Lisa is aware this poses a substantial risk of harm to others, but (correctly) believes it to be justified. Her driving is motivated by this consideration.

Lisa is not guilty of reckless endangerment supposing the risk she creates is justified. Now compare the following case akin to EVIL TROLLEY TURNER:

> CRAZY DRIVER 2 (D IS AWARE OF BUT NOT MOTIVATED BY THE JUSTIFYING CIRCUMSTANCES): Maggie loves racing on the highway: it's exhilarating and makes her feel alive. Maggie's mother has become seriously ill, and Maggie realizes this is her chance to do some crazy driving without getting in trouble. She puts her mother in the car and drives as fast as she can to the hospital. She runs all the red lights, speeds at 90 mph on the highway, and weaves in and out of traffic in dangerous ways. She doesn't care at all about saving her mother (whom she hates). Maggie, too, is aware this poses a substantial risk of harm to others, but her crazy driving is not motivated at all by any concern for getting her mother to the hospital.

The motive-free approach entails that Lisa and Maggie are equally culpable, since on this view they did the same thing. Since they are aware of the same factual circumstances, their actions do not manifest any insufficient regard. But on the motives matter approach, Maggie and Lisa did not do the same thing. Maggie's act manifests far more insufficient regard on this view. The motive-free view thus is much better for people like Maggie.

Now consider Type (2) Cases, where one is motivated by *better* reasons than the best legally recognized reasons that exist on the facts one is aware of. In such cases, the motives matter approach is better for defendants. Recall Mary and Barry from GOOD THIEF, BAD THIEF. If their conduct is described in a motive-laden way, they did not do the same thing. Mary's act of stealing to help her child manifests less insufficient regard than Barry's act of stealing to afford a trip to Vegas. But on the motive-free approach, their acts manifest the same insufficient regard—assuming the jurisdiction does not (as is plausible) give Mary a partial justification based on her need to help her child go to a better school. In such jurisdictions, Mary and Barry did do the same thing and both equally lack justification. Thus, their actions are equally culpable. The upshot is that actors like Mary, who are motivated by reasons that are better than the best legally recognized reasons they're aware of, do better under the motives matter approach.

2. Clinching the Argument

Now the key to the argument becomes clear: *there are no Type (2) Cases if the law is normatively ideal.* Suppose the law is normatively ideal in the sense that it recognizes all and only the justifying reasons it should (whether partial or full). If so, the legally recognized reasons that exist in favor of the defendant's conduct given the facts she's aware of will always be *the best possible legal case that can be provided in favor of her conduct on the facts as she sees them.* So if the law is ideal, the defendant cannot be motivated by better reasons than the ones the law recognizes on the facts she's aware of. Thus, there would be no Type (2) Cases.

Take the two trolley cases above. Holding actors' beliefs fixed and taking them as true, there is no stronger normative case to be had in favor of turning the trolley than the reasons that stem from saving the five—that is, the reasons for which GOOD TROLLEY TURNER acted and that EVIL TROLLEY TURNER knew to exist. Even if the trolley turner acted with unbounded sympathy and love toward all the people involved, the strongest normative case in favor of turning the trolley would still be the same: *it saves five lives.*[124] An analogous point holds for CRAZY DRIVER 1 and

[124] Of course, if the actor possessed *different* beliefs—perhaps she also believed that turning the trolley would save a sixth person held hostage nearby—then there might be an even stronger normative case for turning the trolley. But that's neither here nor there. This difference can be accounted for by the motive-free approach.

2. The best normative case for driving as the actors did is that it's needed to save the mother.[125]

This also applies in more contestable cases like GOOD THIEF, BAD THIEF. I don't know if the need to assist one's child should provide even a small, partial justification for Mary's theft, but suppose it does. If so, then to be normatively ideal, the law would have to recognize it. If so, then there would be no benefit Mary could get from an approach to culpability that considers her actual motives. For if the law is ideal, and assuming (maybe counterfactually) that the law should recognize the need to help one's child as a partial justifier of minor thefts, then there are no better motives for which one can do this act under the circumstances than the legal reasons Mary is already aware of. So no Type (2) Case can arise.

Maybe it's a mistake to think that Mary should have a partial justification. So consider one last example. Suppose one intentionally steals $1,000 where it's absolutely necessary to save one's beloved pet from an otherwise easily avoidable death. Plausibly, this gives *some* support for the theft, but it is outweighed by the legally recognized reasons against that action. This is far from a sufficient justification, but it is also not *nothing*. The law, of course, does not take saving a beloved pet to be a defense, nor would it provide the basis for convicting the actor of a lesser grade of theft. But if the law were truly normatively ideal, it plausibly should allow even weak reasons like saving one's pet to provide *some* perhaps small mitigation of culpability for doing this action.[126] Nonetheless, even if one has sympathetic motives, this does not strengthen the case in favor of the theft beyond that which the law already recognizes as existing on the facts one is aware of here, assuming the law is ideal. The best normative case that can be given in favor of the theft, given the actor's beliefs, is still just that it's necessary to save the pet.

Thus, if the law is normatively ideal, there are no Type (2) Cases. The defendant cannot be motivated by *better* considerations than the strongest legal case (if any) that exists in support of her conduct given the facts she's aware of. So the motives matter approach provides no benefit to defendants, assuming the law is ideal, compared to the motive-free approach. By contrast, even when the law is ideal, there *are* going to Type (1) Cases, such as EVIL TROLLEY TURNER and CRAZY DRIVER 2, where the motive-free approach is better for defendants. Thus, *ideally* the law should use the motive-free approach for normative culpability.

---

125 I don't claim to know what reasons the law *should* recognize as existing. Perhaps irrational beliefs should not be held to provide legally recognized reasons. I remain neutral on this question.

126 Following the determinacy argument in Section VI.A, perhaps the law should not recognize all such partly justifying reasons because it would make the law more difficult to apply. Perhaps the law should opt to recognize only the justifying reasons that are above some threshold of weight. I leave this open. Regardless, we're now concerned with the normative ideal.

3. What about the Real World?

Of course, in the real world, the law is not normatively ideal: it does not recognize all and only the reasons for action that it should. Accordingly, in reality one *can* be motivated by a better set of considerations than the strongest set of legal reasons, as recognized by the law around here, in favor of one's conduct on the facts one is aware of.

Thus, in the real world, it's an empirical question whether defendants are benefited more by the motives matter approach or the motive-free approach. It depends on whether Type (1) Cases (like EVIL TROLLEY TURNER and CRAZY DRIVER 2), where the motive-free approach is better for defendants, are more frequent than Type (2) Cases, where the motive matters approach benefits defendants more. I have no way to establish which is more frequent.

Nonetheless, the previous discussion suggests a *dialectical strategy* for defending the motive-free approach to normative culpability even in the real world: whenever the motives matter approach seems better for defendants, I can respond that this is because the law *is not normatively ideal*. Suppose you object that the motives matter approach is better for defendants in cases like the stealing to save a pet example, given that our law does not recognize any culpability difference between stealing for fun and stealing because it's necessary to save a beloved pet. Since we're talking about normative culpability, I can just respond that this is a problem *with the law*, not with the motive-free approach. Were the law reformed to recognize at least a small partial justification for those who steal when necessary to save a pet, the motive-free approach, too, would entail that doing so is less culpable than stealing for fun. In this way, I can fend off counterexamples to the motive-free approach to normative culpability. Is that satisfying? Maybe not, but it shows the motive-free approach will be hard to refute with isolated counterexamples.

C. SUMMING UP

In Section VI, I've tried to make my theory more determinate by arguing that the motive-free approach to normative culpability is preferable. This is supported by institutional design constraints of the sort I think it's legitimate for the legislature to employ. Moreover, I argued that to resolve normatively close calls on substantive legal questions—such as whether to prefer a motive-free or motive-laden description of what the defendant did for assessing culpability—we may justifiably select the approach that is best for citizens accused of crimes. This will be the motive-free description, I argued, at least when the law is normatively ideal.

I remain open to thinking that in the real world, we could perhaps move our posited culpability attributions closer to the actor's normative culpability by switching to a motives matter approach. This depends on empirical questions. However, be this as it may, when the law is normatively ideal in the sense of recognizing all the reasons for action it should, defendants would receive greater protections under the motive-free approach than the motive matters approach. Thus, I'll adopt the motive-free approach for the remainder of the book.[127,128]

[127] However, with the exception of a few places noted in the next few chapters, adopting the motive matters approach would not alter most of the arguments in the book.

[128] One might think my theory gives an easy way to account for moral luck in the law, but this is a mistake. The classic case of luck in the law is where A and B both attempt murder by shooting at their victim. A succeeds and thus commits murder, while B fails, but only because a bird unforeseeably flies in front of the bullet and saves the victim. *See* DAVID LEWIS, *The Punishment that Leaves Something to Chance*, *in* PAPERS IN ETHICS AND SOCIAL PHILOSOPHY 227 (2000) (discussing Dee and Dum). Why punish A more harshly than B given that they differ only in the consequences their actions by luck happened to have? A tempting answer is that when their actions are properly described, A did not do the same thing as B. A pulled the trigger with intent to kill and succeeded, while B pulled the trigger with the intent to kill and failed through luck.

However, this response fails. It does not show that A's conduct is any more culpable than B's. The reason is that although their conduct is plausibly described differently (mentioning their different results), if everything is identical between A and B except that one succeeds and the other fails *only due to luck*, then it takes the *same amount of insufficient regard* to get an otherwise law-abiding citizen to do what either A or B did. Doing either of their actions—even if differently described—would require the same departure from how the perfectly law-abiding citizen weighs the applicable reasons. Thus, A's and B's conduct manifests exactly the same amount of insufficient regard, and so are equally culpable on my theory. It takes the same degree of error in weighing reasons to get someone to (a) pull the trigger with the intent to kill and succeed as it does to (b) pull the trigger with the intent to kill but fail solely due to luck.

Thus, my theory does not entail that A and B differ in normative culpability. I think this is correct. There is no *culpability-based* reason to punish A and B differently. Nonetheless, I think the legislature has good reasons to ratchet down the punishment it imposes on actors like B compared to actors like A. These are victim-centered rather than agent-centered. If the legislature is forced to choose which victims' rights to reaffirm, as I think it must, then it's more important to reaffirm the rights that were violated harmfully than the ones violated nonharmfully (or less harmfully). The reason the legislature must choose is that not ratcheting down some permissible punishments at least sometimes would be *cruel. See* Alex Sarch, *Don't Be an Asshole: Building the Case for Moral Luck in the Law* (manuscript) (developing this argument in detail).

II From Willful Ignorance to a Theory of Equal Culpability Imputation

THIS PART EXAMINES the normative foundations of the willful ignorance doctrine and extracts from it a general theory of equal culpability mental state imputation, which underlies the willful ignorance doctrine and grounds a range of other imputation principles. Chapter 3 critiques existing attempts to specify when willfully ignorant misconduct is as culpable as knowing misconduct—that is, when the so-called equal culpability thesis holds. Chapter 4 then defends my own attempt to properly restrict the equal culpability thesis. This constrains when willful ignorance should be allowed to substitute for knowledge. On my account, willful ignorance involves breaching a duty to reasonably inform oneself, and the equal culpability thesis holds when one breaches it in a sufficiently serious way before doing the actus reus. If correct, this shows the need to reform the willful ignorance doctrine. Jury instructions that capture a normatively improved version of the doctrine are also articulated. Finally, Chapter 5 uses the foregoing discussion to defend a general theory of equal-culpability-based imputation of mental states in the criminal law. Why should we take equal culpability to be a legitimate basis for imputing missing mental states? Answering this challenge requires a general theory of equal culpability imputation, which Chapter 5 seeks to provide. This theory grounds a range of other imputation principles as well as the willful ignorance doctrine, and it also establishes clear limitations on when equal culpability imputation may legitimately be used.

3 The Scope of the Willful Ignorance Doctrine (I)

HAVING EXPLICATED THE notion of criminal culpability, let's now return to willful ignorance. As seen earlier, the normative basis for the willful ignorance doctrine—its "traditional rationale," as the Supreme Court put it—is the *equal culpability thesis*. This is the claim that acting in willful ignorance is just as culpable as the analogous knowing action. Is it true across the board or only sometimes? If the latter, then when? Answering these questions is the task of this and the next chapter. Determining when the equal culpability thesis holds sets the proper scope of the willful ignorance doctrine. After all, there are normative grounds for allowing willful ignorance to substitute for knowledge—and instructing juries accordingly—*when but only when* the equal culpability thesis holds.

This chapter considers the best existing attempts to specify the conditions in which the equal culpability thesis holds, but argues that none succeeds. Still, each failure is instructive. First, I argue against the unrestricted equal culpability thesis, introduced in Chapter 1. Not all willful ignorance, it turns out, is as culpable as the analogous knowing misconduct.

Then I consider three leading attempts to restrict the thesis. Section II argues that the most common restriction among federal courts is too narrow. Its failure raises questions about the relevance of motives to criminal culpability, and shows that deciding to remain ignorant can be highly culpable even when it's not the means to avoiding liability.

Section III considers a counterfactual restriction, according to which willful ignorance is as culpable as knowing misconduct when one *would* do the actus reus with knowledge.

Criminally Ignorant. Alexander Sarch.

This approach was suggested separately by Alan Michaels[1] and David Luban.[2] However, the lesson of Section III (as Chapter 2 also argued) is that culpability does not depend on the counterfactual conduct one would be willing to perform.

Finally, Section IV discusses a third restriction, offered by Deborah Hellman.[3] This approach asks whether the decision to remain in ignorance was itself justified. This version of the thesis is on the right track. But it, too, requires refinement in important ways.

Employing the lessons of this chapter, Chapter 4 will present my own account of the culpability of willful ignorance. This forms the basis for a more defensible version of the equal culpability thesis, which reveals the proper scope of the willful ignorance doctrine.

Two clarifications before proceeding. First, the notion of culpability I'll be concerned with throughout is normative criminal culpability. Chapter 2 distinguished between posited culpability, which is what a given jurisdiction actually attributes for a particular offense, and normative culpability, which is what the jurisdiction ideally *should* attribute. In the present context, I am interested in critically evaluating the law and determining what scope the willful ignorance doctrine *should* have. Thus, it won't do to simply appeal to the amount of culpability this or that jurisdiction actually attributes. These attributions may be flawed. Instead, my project is squarely within the realm of normative culpability. Since my aim is to home in on a normatively defensible version of the willful ignorance doctrine, I argue in part from intuitive claims about how much culpability should be attributed. But at the same time, to ensure that the notion of culpability I'm employing is genuinely *legal*, I also aim to respect at least the broad, well-settled principles of criminal law in jurisdictions like ours. Thus, the concept of culpability I appeal to is not merely descriptive; it is a normatively cleaned-up version of the concept at work in jurisdictions like ours.

Second, given the arguments of Chapter 2, I assume the sort of normative culpability that is relevant to substantive criminal law doctrine, and thus at the guilt stage of criminal proceedings, should be largely unconcerned with the defendant's motives. I take it that the best description of the defendant's conduct to use in assessing culpability does not mention her motives for what she did. If it turns out motives should be taken into account for assessing normative culpability, then the arguments of this section would have to be somewhat revised. Nonetheless, the same broad conclusions would follow.[4]

---

[1] Alan Michaels, *Acceptance: The Missing Mental State*, 71 S. Cal. L. Rev. 953 (1998).

[2] David Luban, *Contrived Ignorance*, 87 Geo. L.J. 957 (1999).

[3] Deborah Hellman, *Willfully Blind for Good Reason*, 3 Crim. L. & Phil. 301 (2009).

[4] *Cf.* Alex Sarch, *Willful Ignorance, Culpability and the Criminal Law*, 88 St. John's L. Rev. 1023 (2014). There I argued against restricted versions of the equal culpability thesis on similar grounds while assuming that motives affect culpability. Since writing that paper, I've changed my mind on the relevance of motives to culpability.

I. The Unrestricted Equal Culpability Thesis

Chapter 1 formulated the simplest equal culpability thesis that is still plausible:

> **Unrestricted Equal Culpability Thesis (UECT):** Suppose A1 and A2 each perform the actus reus of a given crime that requires knowledge of an inculpatory proposition, p. A1 and A2, and their respective actions, are identical in every respect except one: while A1's action is performed with knowledge of p, A2's action is performed in willful ignorance of p (in the basic sense). On these suppositions, A2 is (at least) as culpable for her action as A1 is for his.

If true, this claim would support treating all defendants who are willfully ignorant (in the basic sense) of the inculpatory proposition as if they knew it. Many courts endorse this view—most notably, the Ninth Circuit in *United States v. Heredia*.[5] Other circuits do too.[6] Moreover, the Supreme Court in *Global-Tech* arguably favored the unrestricted approach, since it adopted only the two-pronged basic account when defining willful ignorance.[7] Of course, *Global-Tech* did not squarely decide whether additional restrictions to the willful ignorance doctrine are warranted.

Despite its widespread acceptance, UECT is false. As several legal scholars argue, some willfully ignorant individuals are less culpable than their knowing counterparts.[8] While the falsity of UECT is perhaps unsurprising, considering its problems reveals the challenge in defending the equal culpability thesis. I start by explaining this challenge and then I argue that the only apparent answer to this challenge fails.

A. THE CHALLENGE FOR THE EQUAL CULPABILITY THESIS

The criminal law embodies the idea that the more confidence one has in the truth of the inculpatory proposition, all else equal, the more culpable one is when one does the actus reus.[9]

---

[5] 483 F.3d 913, 920 (9th Cir. 2007) (en banc).

[6] United States v. Svoboda, 347 F.3d 471, 480 (2d Cir. 2003); United States v. Stadtmauer, 620 F.3d 238, 257 (3d Cir. 2010); United States v. Mendoza-Medina, 346 F.3d 121, 132–33 (5th Cir. 2003); United States v. Mitchell, 681 F.3d 867, 876 (6th Cir. 2012); United States v. Tanner, 628 F.3d 890, 904 (7th Cir. 2010).

[7] *Global–Tech*, 131 S. Ct. at 2070; *see also* United States v. Yi, 704 F.3d 800, 804–05 (9th Cir. 2013) (following *Global–Tech*'s two-pronged definition of willful ignorance).

[8] *See* Hellman, *supra* note 3, at 305–12; *infra* notes 18–25 and accompanying text; Michaels, *supra* note 1, at 986.

[9] Alexander and Ferzan adopt roughly this principle. They "are inclined to say that culpability does vary with the actor's estimate of the probability" of the relevant risks. Larry Alexander & Kimberly Ferzan, Crime and Culpability 38 (2009). Charlow suggests the criminal law endorses something similar: "the more certain [the defendant] is that some significant fact exists that will make his conduct criminal, (. . .) the more blameworthy he is if he goes ahead and acts despite his awareness of that fact." Robin Charlow, *Wilful Ignorance and Criminal Culpability*, 70 Tex. L. Rev. 1351, 1394–95 (1992).

> **Comparative Confidence Principle (CCP):** For any two people who commit the actus reus of a crime, if they are identical in all respects except that one is more confident in the truth of the inculpatory proposition, p, than the other, then—assuming there are no relevant excuses or justifications, and all else is equal—the person with the greater degree of confidence in p is more culpable than the one with the lesser degree of confidence in p.[10]

CCP captures the intuition that lighting a building on fire while aware of a substantial risk that someone is inside (a reckless act) is less culpable—maybe just a bit—than doing so while practically certain (knowing) someone is inside.[11] The latter, after all, manifests more disregard.

This raises a question about how acting in willful ignorance could possibly be as culpable as knowing misconduct. Setting aside problems of proof, defendants for whom willful ignorance jury instructions are actually needed will fall short of having knowledge of the inculpatory proposition, p. After all, were the defendant certain enough of p to qualify as having knowledge, there would be no need to prosecute her on a willful ignorance theory. Accordingly, when willful ignorance jury instructions are genuinely needed (and it's not just due to evidentiary shortcomings), the defendant will have a lower confidence in p than a similarly situated actor with knowledge. Thus, by CCP, this defendant would be less culpable than her knowing counterpart (all else equal).

What, then, could the general feature of willful ignorance be that always makes up the culpability difference that CCP entails between actors with a subknowledge degree of belief in p and those who know p? Let "C_R" be the culpability of doing the actus reus while aware of a substantial risk (i.e., suspecting) that p is true, and let "C_K" be the higher culpability of doing it while knowing (i.e., practically certain) that p is true. Unless something is present *in all cases* of willful ignorance that fills this gap between C_R and C_K—"ΔC"—we cannot maintain, with UECT, that willfully ignorant misconduct is always as culpable as knowing misconduct.

The obvious answer to this question is that willfully ignorant actors all *deliberately* preserve their ignorance about p. However, it's doubtful that this always confers enough extra culpability to fill the gap, ΔC. UECT is true only if the extra culpability of deliberately preventing oneself from learning whether one's suspicions about p are correct—call it "C_{WI}"—is always at least as large as ΔC. But what *guarantee* is there that C_{WI} is always be greater than or equal to ΔC? None that I can see. This is the first worry about UECT.

This worry is especially pressing when ΔC is large. If I just barely count as suspecting, say, that someone is in the building I plan to burn down, then ΔC is especially great.

---

10 To be clear, this principle concerns subjective confidence.

11 *Cf.* N.Y. Penal Law § 150.15.

Assume the cutoff for *suspecting*—that is, being aware of a substantial risk[12]—that p is a 0.1 credence.[13] Any lower degree of belief than this and I'm not aptly described as suspecting that p. (Perhaps I just have a feeling that p.) If my credence in p is exactly 0.1, then by CCP, ΔC is especially large. Here, C_R is the culpability of lighting the building on fire with a 0.1 credence that someone is inside, provided I'm in conditions where I can't investigate and thus am not willfully ignorant. C_K is the culpability of doing the same while practically certain that someone is inside. Since C_R is as low as it can be here, CCP entails that the difference between C_R and C_K is about as large as it can be.

What *guarantee* is there, then, that, when I *can* investigate my suspicion that someone is in the building but decide not to, the culpability I incur for this decision, C_{WI}, necessarily is at least as great as ΔC? However much culpability one incurs for deliberately preserving one's ignorance in a given case, I'm unsure why it would *always* be enough to fill the gap between C_K and C_R. Thus, it's unclear how to mount an affirmative argument for UECT.

B. POSITIVE ARGUMENTS AGAINST UECT

Of course, this is merely to raise doubts about the case in favor of UECT. Still, we can leverage these considerations into a positive argument against UECT by focusing on several factors that impact the culpability of deliberately preserving one's ignorance.

1. First Argument: Burdensome Investigation

One factor that impacts the culpability of deliberately remaining ignorant is the burdens of learning whether one's suspicions are true. The more burdensome, dangerous or costly it would be to learn the truth about them, the less culpable one intuitively is, all else equal, for not doing so. In principle, it could be so burdensome or dangerous to learn whether one's suspicions are correct that it would be *unreasonable* to expect one to investigate at all. If investigating would cause the death of 1,000 people, say, then one would not be reasonably expected to investigate. Of course, in that case, one may not count as truly willfully ignorant. Recall the basic definition of willful ignorance requires deliberately declining to take *reasonably* available steps to learning whether p is true before acting. Nonetheless, it remains true that, within the realm of reasonably available investigative steps, the costs of investigating can affect the culpability of deliberately preserving one's ignorance. Thus, some of the most culpable cases of willful ignorance, all else equal, will be the ones where it would be entirely costless to learn whether p—perhaps because someone was about to tell

---

[12] If you have misgivings about this way of using "suspicion," just think of it as a stipulative definition. I have to stipulate that *one suspects that p if one is aware of a substantial risk that p* to get the definition of willful ignorance—in terms of suspicions—to link up with the definition of recklessness—in terms of awareness of substantial risks. I adopt this stipulation for simplicity. Little of substance turns on it.

[13] In fact, I think the threshold for counting as suspecting that p likely is context-sensitive. But set that aside for now.

you whether your suspicions were correct, and you had to take affirmative protective steps (like plugging your ears and running away) to prevent yourself from hearing what they say.

This first culpability factor is by itself enough to show that UECT is false. Take a case where ΔC is large since the defendant just barely counts as suspecting that p. If investigating is so costly that I'm not very culpable for deliberately preserving my ignorance, then we can be quite certain my extra culpability for not investigating, C_{WI}, is less than ΔC. Consider:

> ***Dangerous Investigation***: Cory rents a house to Dora, and suspects Dora might be manufacturing drugs in the basement. (In fact she is.) Cory could investigate by sneaking into the basement. However, he knows the basement contains a fungus that he and his children are dangerously allergic to (though the allergy is rare in the general population). If Cory comes home with some of the fungus on his clothes, his kids could also suffer a severe allergic reaction. So Cory concludes it is too dangerous to investigate (and there is no one else to do it for him). Accordingly, he decides to preserve his ignorance and avoids going into the house altogether.

If Cory *knew* the house he was renting to Dora was being used for manufacturing drugs, he could be convicted of aiding and abetting Dora's drug operation.[14] But Cory does not know this. Nor does his willful ignorance seem to render him as culpable as a knowing wrongdoer. Investigating would risk a serious and painful (though not deadly) allergic reaction for himself and his kids. This seems to at least partially justify his decision to remain ignorant. If investigating entailed no burdens whatsoever, then plausibly his decision to remain ignorant would get his culpability up from C_R up to C_K. But here, there are good reasons for him to remain ignorant, which plausibly make him less culpable than the analogous knowing wrongdoer.

One might object that Cory cannot be truly willfully ignorant if investigating is not practically possible.[15] However, this objection is unconvincing. Granted, if the only way Cory could investigate his suspicions would get him *killed*, then perhaps we could say investigating is not practically possible or a reasonably available option. But that's not

---

[14] United States v. Verners, 53 F.3d 291, 295 (10th Cir. 1995) (affirming aiding and abetting conviction where defendant was aware of drug operation being operated out of her home).

[15] The defendant in *Heredia* argued that she should not be convicted on willful ignorance grounds because she declined to investigate whether her car contained drugs only for safety reasons, as she was driving on the highway. 483 F.3d at 920. The Ninth Circuit rejected this argument, noting that "[a] decision influenced by coercion, exigent circumstances or lack of meaningful choice is, perforce, not deliberate. A defendant who fails to investigate for these reasons has not deliberately chosen to avoid learning the truth." *Id.* However, this view can only be taken so far. Clearly, it can't be the case that *whenever* investigating entails risks or costs, that precludes the decision to remain ignorant from being willful. After all, almost any decision not to investigate will be due to perceived costs of investigating. But this cannot mean that hardly anyone is ever willfully ignorant. Instead, only truly extreme circumstances or coercion, etc., could make deciding not to investigate count as nonwillful.

what we have here. Here, the costs of investigating are not so severe as to make investigating not reasonably possible. It's more accurate to say that Cory has an *available* method of investigation—one that he on balance should use—but it entails risks of pain for himself and his kids. It's doubtful that these risks *fully* justify his decision to remain ignorant, but they plausibly do justify it *partially*. Thus, he still counts as genuinely willful ignorant. Accordingly, we have a counterexample to UECT. If $C_K - C_R$ is large, then having reasons that help justify the decision to remain ignorant can prevent a willfully ignorant defendant from being as culpable as her knowing counterpart.[16]

2. Other Considerations that Can Help Justify One's Ignorance

Other circumstances can help justify the decision to remain in ignorance (even if not fully). As Deborah Hellman argued, professional obligations might function this way.[17] On her view, criminal defense lawyers, and doctors treating patients who claim to suffer from chronic pain, can sometimes have a justification, in virtue of their professional roles, for remaining ignorant.[18] The defense lawyer might suspect her client is not telling the truth, thus making the lawyer's arguments to the court potentially perjurious. Nonetheless, the lawyer's duties of loyalty and zealous representation might help justify her decision not to investigate her doubts about her client's claims.[19] Thus, the lawyer plausibly is less culpable than the analogous actor who knows the client is lying and repeats these falsehoods to the court. Similarly, the doctor might suspect her patient is illegally reselling the prescribed medication, but because of the doctor's duties to the patient, she might be somewhat justified in not investigating these suspicions and prescribing the pain medication anyway.[20] Such a doctor might not seem as culpable as her knowing counterpart who prescribes medication *knowing* it will be illegally resold. These are further counterexamples to UECT.[21] Such cases show there can be *ethical costs* to investigating, which lessens the culpability of deciding to remain in ignorance.[22]

---

[16] To make the argument as watertight as possible, suppose investigating my suspicions is so dangerous and costly that I am only *a tiny bit culpable* for deciding not to investigate. Let's say $C_{WI} = 0.00001$. Now assume ΔC is large because I just barely count as suspecting that p. If so, we can be quite confident that $C_{WI} < \Delta C$. Thus if I proceed to do the actus reus in my state of willful ignorance, my total culpability ($C_R + C_{WI}$) will be less than C_K. Such cases are plausible. So UECT must be false.

[17] *See* Hellman, *supra* note 3, at 305–12.

[18] *Id.*

[19] *Id.* at 305–06.

[20] *Id.* at 308–09.

[21] Hellman thinks these justifications are supposed to be "objective," meaning they apply regardless of whether they actually motivated the actor to remain in ignorance. *See id.* at 307. I discuss this feature of Hellman's view in Section IV.

[22] One might object here that Hellman's doctors and lawyers are not genuinely willfully ignorant because there is no reasonably available way to investigate—no way to do so without breaching their ethical obligations. As before, I'm not sure this objection works since investigative steps do not obviously become *unavailable* simply because there are good reasons not to take them. Nonetheless, to fully avoid this worry, we should construe Hellman's cases as instances not of fully justified ignorance (which may perhaps render it not truly willful

I think some nonprofessional relationships can function analogously.[23] Special obligations to family and loved ones likewise give rise to cases where willfully ignorant actors seem less culpable than their knowing counterparts. Some burdens that investigating one's suspicions of wrongdoing might impose on valuable relationships can partially justify (even if not fully) the decision to remain ignorant. Consider:

> ***Overly Trusting Parent***: Patty and her adult child, Charles, had gone through a long period of estrangement due to Charles's trouble with the law, and they were only recently reconciled. Thus, Patty is very concerned to rebuild trust with her son. When Charles asks Patty to drive a sealed crate across town to a friend of his, Patty decides not to look inside. She realizes there's a risk the crate might contain some kind of contraband. She has a slight suspicion that this is the case, but she strongly desires not to take part in any illegal activity. But after much agonizing, she deliberately chooses not to open the crate or ask Charles to do so because this sign of mistrust would irrevocably damage their recently repaired relationship. It is her conscious object to remain in ignorance because this is the means to preserving her relationship with Charles. So she sets off across town with the crate in the trunk. On the way, the police stop her, and it turns out the crate contains drugs.

Patty is willfully ignorant about whether the crate contains drugs. She has slight suspicions it does, but deliberately prevents herself from acquiring more information about the matter. Nonetheless, the circumstances Patty is aware of help justify, at least somewhat, her decision to remain ignorant. Thus, she seems less culpable than someone who acts the same way knowingly. The person who is credibly told, and thus *knows*, that the crate contains drugs, but decides to deliver the package anyway, would display greater disregard than Patty did for society's legitimate interest in combating the proliferation of drugs. She seems not to have acted with *as much* disregard for the legitimate interests of others as an analogous knowing actor. Although she is willfully ignorant[24] and very likely somewhat culpable, I submit that Patty intuitively is *less* culpable than her knowing counterpart. This is especially clear since she only barely counts as suspecting that the

---

ignorance for the above reason), but as *nearly justified willful ignorance*. The latter also reduces the culpability of the decision to remain ignorant, and so also generate counterexamples to UECT.

[23] *See* Sarch, *supra* note 4. Hellman also is open to this possibility. *See* Hellman, *supra* note 3, at 316.

[24] One might object that Patty does not *purposefully* remain ignorant, since she does not *want* this. So she's not truly willfully ignorant. Two responses. First, she at least *knows* her conduct will preserve her ignorance. Chapter 1 argued that knowingly remaining in ignorance suffices for willful ignorance. We saw some courts accept this view. Second, even assuming *arguendo* that willful ignorance requires *purpose* to remain ignorant, Patty still is willfully ignorant. She *deliberately* chooses not to investigate whether the crate contained illicit items. Remaining ignorant is her conscious objective, as she aims at ignorance *as the means* to achieving her other ends. One need not aim at ignorance as an end in itself to count as remaining ignorant purposefully. If I kill you as the means to getting the inheritance, I still count as purposefully killing you even if I regret your death and aim at it only as a means. Patty consciously aims at ignorance as the means to preserving her relationship with her son. So it's clear she remains ignorant purposefully.

inculpatory proposition is true, thus making ΔC quite large. It is doubtful that the culpability of her willful ignorance suffices to fill this gap. Accordingly, we have another case that shows UECT to be false. An actor can sometimes have good reasons—deserving of legal recognition—that help justify the decision not to acquire full-on knowledge.[25]

II. First Restriction: Husak and Callender's Restricted-Motive Approach

The obvious response to the failure of UECT is to restrict the thesis. Technically, the restrictions might take one of two forms. First, they might be expressly built into the thesis, so it claims that *provided certain conditions obtain*, acting with willful ignorance in the basic sense is at least as culpable as acting knowingly. Second, one might replace the basic account of willful ignorance with a narrower technical definition, which is then used to formulate the thesis. While either approach could work, I prefer the first for reasons of transparency and to keep the question of what willful ignorance *is* distinct from evaluative questions about how culpable it is.

As it happens, courts and commentators largely have taken the second route. Husak and Callender adopt a narrower conception of willful ignorance. Besides being willfully ignorant in the basic sense, their account also requires that one's ignorance-preserving behavior was motivated by "a conscious desire to remain ignorant of p in order to avoid blame or liability in the event that [one] is detected."[26] They dub this the "motivational condition."[27] The Eighth, Tenth, and Eleventh Circuits likewise take it that this particular reason for remaining ignorant is a necessary part of willful ignorance.[28] The charitable way to understand this view is that it restricts the notion of willful ignorance to get a definition that, if satisfied, makes the defendant especially culpable—plausibly as culpable as a knowing actor. For transparency, I stick with the basic definition of willful ignorance, but plug the suggested restriction into the equal culpability thesis directly, as follows:

> **Restricted Equal Culpability Thesis 1 (RECT1)**: Suppose A1 and A2 each perform the actus reus of a crime requiring knowledge of an inculpatory proposition, p. A1

[25] I mean for this phrase—"have good reasons that help justify the decision to remain in ignorance"—to be neutral between Hellman's objectivist view and the subjectivist view that actual motives matter to criminal culpability, a legal notion. Perhaps having such reasons requires only being aware of circumstances that help justify remaining ignorant, or perhaps it requires that the justifying considerations actually are one's motive for not investigating. Either one is covered by this phrase. *See* Section IV for more discussion.

[26] Douglas N. Husak & Craig A. Callender, *Wilful Ignorance, Knowledge, and the "Equal Culpability" Thesis: A Study of the Deeper Significance of the Principle of Legality*, 1994 WIS. L. REV. 29, 40 (1994) (emphasis added).

[27] *Id.*

[28] United States v. Willis, 277 F.3d 1026, 1032 (8th Cir. 2002) (requiring that the defendant, to be willfully blind, had to have "purposely contrived to avoid learning all of the facts in order to have a defense against subsequent prosecution"); United States v. Delreal-Ordones, 213 F.3d 1263, 1268 (10th Cir. 2000) (same); United States v. Puche, 350 F.3d 1137, 1149 (11th Cir. 2003) (same).

and A2, and their respective actions, are identical in every respect except one: while A1's action is performed with knowledge of p, A2's action is performed in a state of willful ignorance *the motive for which was to avoid liability in the event of prosecution*. On these suppositions, A2 is (at least) as culpable for her action as A1 is for his.

However, RECT1 faces problems. Hellman rejects it because she thinks the criminal law should not concern itself with motives.[29] Thus, she thinks not only that doctors who decide not to investigate their suspicions due to justifiable concerns for their ethical duties to patients should not face enhanced penalties, but the same should be true for doctors in similar circumstances who decide not to investigate for worse reasons (like wanting to avoid liability).[30] Both actors occupy a professional role that can help justify their ignorance at times. As argued in Chapter 2, I think this view is correct particularly for the legal concept of criminal culpability—both posited culpability and, I argued, normative culpability. Plausibly, when it comes to the notion of culpability that substantive criminal law doctrine should track (for use at the guilt stage of proceedings), one's motives for breaching the law should not matter.

This, then, is one reason to be skeptical of RECT1. But the problems don't end there. RECT1 faces other problems, which even those who think motives *do* matter can accept. First, the desire to preserve a defense against liability does not always seem disqualifying, since sometimes the defendant's circumstances help justify the desire to preserve a defense *and* the overall decision to remain ignorant. Consider a variation of *Dangerous Investigation*. Suppose Cory not only realizes that investigating would be risky for himself and his kids, but he also wants to preserve a defense against liability should the authorities discover Dora's (possible) criminal scheme. This, in turn, is because Cory is the sole caretaker for his children, and if he gets in trouble for aiding Dora's (possible) drug operation, his kids will be gravely harmed by the appalling foster care system in the city. Accordingly, given the facts Cory is aware of, deciding not to investigate is supported by two considerations: (1) it would prevent his kids from suffering a severe allergic reaction, and (2) by preserving a defense for himself (he thinks), it makes his kids less likely to suffer at the hands of the broken foster care system. These considerations plausibly provide at least some justification for his desire to avoid liability and the decision to remain in ignorance. Accordingly, although Cory was motivated in part by a desire to preserve a defense, he does not seem as culpable as the analogous wrongdoer who rents the house to Dora *knowing* she is running a drug operation. Thus, being motivated to remain ignorant by a desire to preserve a defense seems not to *necessarily* make one as culpable as the analogous knowing wrongdoer. The desire to preserve a defense can itself be justified at times. Hellman and the motives matter approach would offer different explanations of why this is, but they can both agree RECT1 gets this case wrong.

---

[29] Hellman, *supra* note 3, at 310–11.

[30] *Id.*

Furthermore, RECT1 is too narrow. Sometimes remaining in ignorance is not a means to avoiding liability, but it is still is highly unjustified. Thus, some cases fall outside the scope of RECT1, although the actor seems just as culpable as his knowing counterpart. Consider:

> ***Don't Rock the Boat***: Fred works the night shift at a warehouse and has heard rumors that the boxes he spends his nights loading and unloading contain drugs. His suspicions are strengthened when the boss starts giving him a weekly bonus for "doing a good job and minding his own business." Fred realizes he could check whether the contents of the boxes are improper by lifting up the box flaps, but not so much that the packing tape rips. However, this would still stretch the packing tape, and Fred thinks there is a chance that investigating in this way might tip off the boss to his snooping. If the boss thinks Fred knows too much, the bonuses will stop and he might lose his job. Fred wants the bonuses, though, so he doesn't investigate. He doesn't think that remaining ignorant would have any benefits in terms of preserving a defense to liability. (Even if his boss were running a drug operation, Fred knows the cops are not skillful enough to uncover it, and even if they did, the authorities would never prosecute.) Instead, the only expected benefit of preserving his ignorance is that it will help him continue to get paid. As it happens, Fred is right: the boss is engaged in transporting drugs and stolen goods, and the weekly bonuses stem from the fruits of this operation.

Fred is willfully ignorant in the basic sense, but his reason for not investigating is not that he hopes it will help him avoid liability. He thus falls outside of the scope of RECT1. Instead, the only benefit he sees in not investigating is that it will let him continue to get paid. Intuitively, Fred's decision not to investigate is highly unjustified, and he plausibly is just as culpable as a similarly situated actor who knows what's in the boxes. Choosing not to investigate for fear of no longer getting paid seems to demonstrate just as much disregard for legally protected interests as knowingly committing the crime. Some courts have recognized as much.[31] Since RECT1 does not support willful ignorance instructions for defendants like Fred, RECT1 is too narrow.[32,33]

---

[31] *See* Jandro v. Ohio Edison Co., 167 F.3d 309, 316 (6th Cir. 1999) ("employer [wa]s virtually certain that harm [wa]s about to occur but cho[se] to 'look the other way' in the interest of continuing the job"); Fiore v. C.I.R., 105 T.C.M. (CCH) 1141, at *30 (Tax Court 2013) (holding that defendant committed tax fraud because he was willfully blind "for the purpose of getting and keeping clients").

[32] One might try to save RECT1 from this problem by recasting it just as sufficient condition for equal culpability. But then it would no longer be a comprehensive account of when willful ignorant conduct is as culpable as knowing misconduct. Moreover, it would still suffer from my first objection.

[33] One might also object that the mere fact that RECT1 is underinclusive is not a problem. Perhaps it's unobjectionable to sometimes decline to punish on a willful ignorance theory where it might have been permissible. How is this unfair? The reason is that it gives defendants who were convicted on a willful ignorance

III. Second Restriction: The Counterfactual Approach of Luban and Michaels

A better—but still problematic—restriction of the equal culpability thesis is the counterfactual approach suggested separately by David Luban and Alan Michaels. The idea is that a willfully ignorant actor is as culpable as an analogous knowing wrongdoer just in case she would perform the actus reus even with full knowledge of the inculpatory proposition.

This is most explicitly defended by Michaels.[34] He begins by defining a mental state he dubs acceptance: "The accepting actor is someone who, aware of a substantial risk that a particular circumstance is present or that a particular result might ensue, is so determined to act that he would do so even if he *knew* the circumstance was present or that the result would ensue."[35] Michaels then contends that "those who act with [the mental state of] acceptance are as culpable as those who act with knowledge. Those who act without acceptance are less culpable than those who act with knowledge. Therefore, acceptance is neither underinclusive nor overinclusive."[36] Michaels's view corresponds to this version of the equal culpability thesis:

> **Restricted Equal Culpability Thesis 2 (RECT2)**: Suppose A1 and A2 each perform the actus reus of a crime requiring knowledge of an inculpatory proposition, p. A1 and A2, and their respective actions, are identical in every respect except that A1's action is performed with actual knowledge of p, while A2's action is performed in a state of willful ignorance, *and A2 is such that if she were given actual knowledge of p, she would still perform the actus reus*. On these suppositions, A2 is (at least) as culpable for her action as A1 is for his.

David Luban can also be read as endorsing the counterfactual test in RECT2.[37] He claims the concept of willful ignorance encompasses three prototypical cases. First, there is the *fox*, who "aims to do wrong and structures his own ignorance merely to prepare a defense."[38] Second is the *unrighteous ostrich* who "doesn't want to know she is doing

theory, having possessed the motive of wanting to avoid liability, a *complaint of arbitrariness* against the state. These defendants can legitimately ask why *they* were singled out for conviction, while other willfully ignorant defendants who were just as culpable, but simply had other motives for remaining ignorant, were exempted. There is no obvious rationale in the offing for why *this* particular motive for remaining in ignorance (wanting to preserve a defense) should be treated more harshly than other equally deplorable motives.

34 Michaels, *supra* note 1.

35 *Id.* at 957.

36 *Id.* at 995.

37 Luban, *supra* note 2, at 968–69.

38 *Id.* at 969.

wrong, but would do it even if she knew."[39] Third, the *half-righteous ostrich* "shields herself from guilty knowledge, but would actually do the right thing if the shield were to fail."[40] She, too, does not want to know she is doing is wrong, but would not do it if given knowledge that it is wrong.

Luban contends the fox is as culpable as the purposeful actor, the unrighteous ostrich as culpable as the knowing actor, and the half-righteous ostrich as culpable as a reckless actor.[41] Unlike the fox who "aims to do wrong" and is most culpable,[42] the unrighteous ostrich does not affirmatively desire the crime, but also would do it if given knowledge. Thus, Luban claims the unrighteous ostrich is "precisely fitted for the commonlaw equation of willful ignorance with knowledge," since "her guilt is unchanged whether she knows or not, because her behavior would be unchanged."[43] However, the half-righteous ostrich, "who won't do wrong if she knows, but would prefer not to know, [imposes] a substantial and unjustifiable risk of wrongdoing—precisely the [MPC's] definition of recklessness."[44]

Thus, Luban's discussion suggests that defendants akin to either the fox or the unrighteous ostrich are at least as culpable as analogous knowing wrongdoers. Accordingly, the equal culpability thesis holds of them. By contrast, the half-righteous ostrich is only as culpable as a *reckless* wrongdoer. What separates the fox and the unrighteous ostrich from the half-righteous ostrich is that the latter would *not* do the actus reus with knowledge, while the fox and the unrighteous ostrich *would*. Thus, Luban also endorses the counterfactual test in RECT2.

RECT2, however, suffers from fatal flaws. The problem it faces is an instance of the general criticism that Ken Simons has leveled against the counterfactual nature of Michaels's "acceptance" criterion.[45] Simons points out that punishing based on the counterfactual mens rea that one would have acted with, but actually didn't, amounts to punishing merely for character.[46] This problem afflicts RECT2 because this thesis lets

---

[39] *Id.*

[40] *Id.*

[41] *Id.*

[42] *Id.* at 969 (the fox "has the same level of culpability as any other willful wrongdoer—the highest level, in the [MPC] schema.").

[43] *Id.*

[44] *Id.*

[45] Kenneth W. Simons, *Does Punishment for "Culpable Indifference" Simply Punish for "Bad Character"? Examining the Requisite Connection Between Mens Rea and Actus Reus*, 6 Buff. Crim. L. Rev. 219, 267–75 (2002).

[46] Simons thinks appealing to "counterfactual culpability is highly problematic." *Id.* at 269. He illustrates with a version of Alexander's case of Deborah. *Id.* at 269–70. She drives within the speed limit but is so callous that "even if she [came] to believe that the risks imposed by her Sunday driving were much higher than she actually believes them to be, she would continue to drive notwithstanding (. . .). Deborah is not acting recklessly at this moment and is therefore not culpable. She has an undesirable character trait, one that might dispose her to act recklessly . . . but her counterfactual culpability does not translate into present culpability." *Id.*

us take willfully ignorant defendants who actually lacked knowledge to be just as culpable as knowing wrongdoers solely based on how the former *would have* behaved under nonactual circumstances. RECT2 thus ties the willfully ignorant defendant's culpability not to the mental state she *actually* acted with, but rather to what she was *willing* to do.

This conflicts with a fundamental principle of criminal law.[47] The criminal law takes it that culpability attributions must be tied to the nature of one's *actual* conduct and mental states—not how one would behave under nonactual circumstances. As Simons explains, "the harsh sanctions of the criminal law should not be brought to bear on individuals who have not yet done anything wrong, but who merely have disreputable—or even dangerous—character traits. (. . .) We are similarly, and properly, reluctant to impose punishment on a person simply for [attitudes or characteristics] unless and until [they] are expressed in action."[48] This is the reason, for example, that when Bill drives off intending to kill his uncle but carelessly hits and kills a pedestrian who just happens to be his uncle, we do not say Bill is guilty of murder.[49] Granted, we know his *character* is as deplorable as a murderer's, given that he *would have* killed his uncle intentionally had he gotten the chance. But, as argued in Chapter 2, Bill's culpability *for the act at issue*—his driving—is not as great as the culpability of intentionally killing. In general, it's not true that doing A with mental state M is just as culpable as doing A with a worse mental state M* simply because the actor *would have* done A with M*.

This makes trouble for RECT2. Take a revised version of *Overly Trusting Parent*, where Patty decided not to look in her son's crate to avoid harming their relationship. I claimed Patty's act was less culpable than the analogous action done while knowing the crate contained drugs. Now add one detail: Patty is so concerned not to damage her recently rebuilt relationship with her son that she *would have* agreed to drive the package across town even if her son had confessed to her that it contained drugs. In fact, however, her son does *not* tell her this. So she proceeds to drive the crate across town without looking inside. Thus, Patty in the revised case—"Patty 2"—performs exactly the same action as Patty in the original version—"Patty 1." We know Patty 2 would have acted the same with full-fledged knowledge of the crate's contents, but this is not *actually* the mental state she acted with. Thus, the culpability manifested in Patty 2's *actual* conduct in the revised case is exactly the same as the amount manifested in Patty 1's conduct. If Patty 1's culpability for her conduct in the original case is less than that of the analogous

---

[47] Although I am primarily concerned with a normative notion of culpability (not a purely descriptive one), I still take it to be appropriate to appeal to such settled principles of the criminal law. Even the normative notion of culpability I employ is supposed to be a *legal* concept. It's meant to be a normatively cleaned-up version of the concept at work in jurisdictions like ours. Thus, we can presume that widely accepted, well-settled features of the criminal law are good indications of how the law should operate, normatively speaking.

[48] Simons, *supra* note 45, at 233–34.

[49] *Id.* at 232.

knowing wrongdoer, then the same must be true of Patty 2. Hence, Patty 2 is less culpable than a knowing actor too.

Of course, Patty 2's character is as deplorable as the analogous knowing wrongdoer. But it does not follow from this that her conduct *manifests* as much insufficient regard as the analogous knowing misconduct. It is essential not to allow intuitions about the defects in Patty 2's character, or what she's willing to do, to infect our judgment of her culpability *for her actual conduct*. The additional badness in Patty 2's character compared to Patty 1's is not manifested in what she did, since on any natural description, they behaved the same way while aware of exactly the same circumstances. Accordingly, we seem to have a counterexample to RECT2. Patty 2 is a willfully ignorant actor who would do the actus reus with knowledge, but her conduct still is not as culpable as analogous knowing misconduct.

However, there is a natural response to this problem. Some theorists insist that the counterfactuals in RECT2—that is, considerations about what the defendant would do with knowledge—are not *constitutive* of culpability. Rather, they are evidence of (explained by) the underlying attitudes one actually acts with. And these attitudes—that is, the level of regard for others one possesses—are what really determine culpability, they say.[50] Perhaps this blocks the objection. It would mean the counterfactual test in RECT2 wouldn't attribute culpability based on counterfactual behavior, but rather the *actual* mental states that produced one's behavior (of which the counterfactuals are merely evidence).

I think this reply might be plausible where moral blameworthiness is concerned. But I don't think it succeeds for normative criminal culpability, as a legal notion.[51] Chapter 2 argued that the criminal law should peg culpability not to the amount of insufficient regard one *possesses* when acting, but rather the level of insufficient regard one's conduct *manifests*. This, in turn, is understood as the least amount of insufficient regard needed to get an otherwise law-abiding citizen to behave the same way as the defendant—even if the defendant actually possessed more insufficient regard than this. This was illustrated by cases like TRIVIAL WRONGS and TED THE TERRORIST and backed by several normative considerations supporting the lenity-based approach to culpability.

This means RECT2 still faces two problems. First, consider Diana, who has a partial justification for deciding not to investigate her suspicions that her intended action, x, of rolling a boulder down a hill might cause grievous bodily harm. She realizes investigating would be dangerous (it would require her to climb a tall tree), so she decides not to investigate. Given her partial justification for not investigating, Diana's doing x manifests less insufficient regard, and is less criminally culpable, than the analogous conduct of

---

50 *See* Jan Willem Wieland, *Responsibility for Strategic Ignorance*, 194 SYNTHESE 4477, 4492–93 (2017) (offering this sort of response to similar worries about the counterfactual test).

51 Still, I agree that such counterfactuals, when we know them, might be useful evidence of the normative culpability of one's conduct (i.e., the insufficient regard manifested).

someone who *knows* the boulder will hit someone. However, suppose Diana also happens to satisfy the counterfactual test: she *would* do x even with knowledge. Diana actually *possesses* so much insufficient regard that she'd do x while knowing it would injure someone. Nonetheless, her actual conduct does not does fully *manifest* all the insufficient regard she possesses. What she actually did, after all, was to roll the boulder down the hill while aware of a *risk* that it would harm someone—having decided not to investigate this suspicion for somewhat good (if not completely justifying) reasons. Thus, what she actually did manifests less insufficient regard than the analogous knowing misconduct. And this seems true even though she also satisfies the counterfactual test. Of course, because she would do the actus reus with knowledge, we know her attitudes and character are as bad as a knowing wrongdoer's. But this fact about her is not manifested in what she actually did. So the present response does not save RECT2.[52]

A second, simpler problem is this. If we say, with RECT2, that willfully ignorant misconduct is as culpable as knowing misconduct when the actor would act the same with full knowledge, then why not make the same claim about negligent actors (or merely reckless ones)? The thinking behind RECT2 implies that someone who did the actus reus while negligently unaware of its risks, but who we know *would* do the actus reus with knowledge, should similarly be deemed as culpable as a knowing actor. Thus, if RECT2 is correct, why not say that actors who are unaware of the risk that their conduct will be harmful *also* are as culpable as knowing actors provided they would act the same if they knew these harms would result? This would allow the law to punish even some negligent actors as much as knowing wrongdoers.

However, this implication is too radical to accept. It would largely erase the boundaries between the criminal law's traditional mental state categories, and significantly depart from the principle that punishment should be doled out for what one actually did, not what one was willing to do. Routinely convicting negligent actors of knowledge crimes because of how they would behave counterfactually would be too much to bear. If nothing else, the potential for abuses would significantly increase.[53]

---

[52] To this, one might respond that it's a different action to (a) do the actus reus in willful ignorance when one also would have done it knowingly than to (b) do it in willful ignorance when one would not do it knowingly. Perhaps it takes more insufficient regard to do (a) than (b). However, this response is unconvincing. Not only does it seem ad hoc, but to distinguish between (a) and (b) is to cut the relevant conduct much more finely than criminal statutes in systems like ours do or plausibly should. Chapter 2 argued that the relevant description of one's conduct is to be fixed by reference to the definition of the crime one committed. But it would require a large departure from existing practice to rewrite the criminal law to distinguish between acts like (a) and (b). I don't think cutting the conduct this finely is a feasible or desirable approach to legislative drafting. So I doubt the counterfactual view of criminal culpability can be saved by distinguishing (a) from (b). Moreover, even if it is *possible* to overhaul our criminal law to punish on the basis of the conduct one would be willing to perform, I suspect this would make for bad policy. Further, it would be too serious a departure from existing practice to be acceptable here. My project, after all, is to defend a normatively cleaned-up version of our existing practice without it ceasing to be *our practice*.

[53] Note that it's no help here to insist that RECT2 attributes culpability not on the basis of counterfactual conduct, but rather the actual attitudes one acts with, which merely explain the truth of the relevant counterfactuals. Even on this view, the reasoning behind RECT2 still implies that purely reckless or negligent

In closing, note that we cannot save RECT2 by taking it to merely provide a necessary condition on equal culpability. First, this would prevent RECT2 from settling the proper scope of the willful ignorance doctrine, which is our primary question. Second, satisfying the counterfactual test is also not *necessary* for willfully ignorant misconduct to be as culpable as analogous knowing misconduct. Sometimes willfully ignorant conduct can be as culpable as knowing misconduct even though the actor would *not* do the actus reus in full knowledge. Suppose Jeff is hired to burn down a Catholic school. Jeff went to Catholic school himself, and became conditioned to be constitutionally unable to knowingly harm any member of the clergy. As Jeff is about to light the fire, he notices a car of the sort that priests drive parked outside. Thus, he comes to suspect a priest is in the building. However, Jeff is aware that he will not be able to go through with the arson if he investigates and learns a priest is inside. Therefore, wanting to still get paid for the job, he decides not to investigate whether anyone is inside and he proceeds to light the fire.[54]

It is plausible that Jeff's act, although willfully ignorant as to the presence of a person in the building, is just as culpable as the analogous act performed with full knowledge that someone is in the building. After all, Jeff's decision not to investigate—which he knows is the necessary means to being able to go through with the crime under the circumstances and get paid—is highly unjustified. Indeed, his willfully ignorant conduct seems just as culpable as the analogous knowing misconduct *even though* it was stipulated that Jeff would not light the fire with knowledge. Accordingly, being willing to perform the actus reus even with knowledge also is not a *necessary* condition for equal culpability.

IV. Third Restriction: Hellman's Unjustified Ignorance Approach

Deborah Hellman offers a different approach to restricting the equal culpability thesis, which is similar in spirit to the view I defend. She focuses on whether the willfully ignorant actor's decision to remain ignorant itself is justified. While I think her proposal is on the right track, I argue that it, too, is overinclusive and requires refinement.

Hellman "propose[s] that contrived ignorance [is blameworthy] when the actor's blindness about the relevant fact is not justified."[55] Rather than focus on whether the risks imposed by the actus reus are justified (which bears on recklessness), Hellman "brings this burden of justification to bear on . . . the decision to remain blind."[56] She

actors who would do the same actus reus with full knowledge—in particular, because they actually act with attitudes bad enough to make this counterfactual true—should be convicted of knowledge crimes. But, as noted, that would be an unacceptably radical departure from settled criminal law. A concept of culpability that countenanced this would be too alien to count as a normatively cleaned-up version of the concept our system actually employs.

[54] In Luban's terms, Jeff is akin to a fox who simply would not be able to do the actus reus with full knowledge.

[55] *See* Hellman, *supra* note 3, at 312.

[56] *Id.* at 313.

"rejects Husak & Callender's 'motivation' criterion" and claims "we ought instead to ask whether there *are* good reasons for the actor to choose blindness rather than focus on what reasons actually motivated the actor in choosing blindness."[57] What matters for her is whether there actually is a justification for remaining ignorant, not the actor's motives. Formulated as a version of the equal culpability thesis, Hellman's view is:

> **Restricted Equal Culpability Thesis 3 (RECT3)**: Suppose A1 and A2 each perform the actus reus of a crime requiring knowledge of an inculpatory proposition, p. A1 and A2, and their respective actions, are identical in every respect except that A1's action is performed with actual knowledge of p, while A2's action is performed in a state of willful ignorance toward p *and A2's decision to remain ignorant is unjustified*. On these suppositions, A2 is (at least) as culpable for her action as A1 is for his.

A. MAIN PROBLEM: OVERINCLUSIVENESS

The main difficulty for RECT3 is overinclusiveness. While any instance of unjustified willful ignorance plausibly is *somewhat* culpable, there is no guarantee that it will always provide *enough* additional culpability to get the willfully ignorant actor up to the level of the analogous knowing wrongdoer. An unjustified decision to remain ignorant does not always suffice to make one's action as culpable as knowing misconduct. Consider:

> ***Product Manager***: Karen is in charge of developing a drug that cures Alzheimer's if taken early enough. She is aware there is some risk that the drug will have harmful side effects for people with gene X, who constitute a small portion of the population. She believes there is roughly a 10 percent chance the drug will be harmful to this group. If she releases the drug in awareness of this risk, she would be reckless. Karen knows she *could* conduct an additional lengthy and expensive study to determine whether the drug really will be harmful to those with gene X or not. But this would delay the release of the drug, thereby preventing the cure from reaching many early-stage Alzheimer's patients in time to cure them. In light of what she sees (based on her evidence) as the small risk that the drug will harm those with gene X, she decides *not* to conduct the study and goes ahead and releases it. However, suppose her decision not to investigate further *in fact* is unjustified—though just barely. In fact, the all things considered better decision would have been to conduct the study.

[57] *Id.* (emphasis added).

Karen is willfully ignorant. Her decision to remain in ignorance is unjustified, but only slightly. Hers is a case of *nearly justified willful ignorance*. I submit that Karen intuitively is less culpable than the analogous actor who *knows* the drug will be harmful to those with gene X, but releases it anyway. Thus, the mere fact that one's decision not to further investigate the risks of the drug is on balance unjustified given one's evidence does not *guarantee* that one will be as culpable as the analogous knowing wrongdoer. Intuitively, Karen's nearly justified willful ignorance does not make her as culpable as the analogous knowing product manager. Hence, RECT3 is false. It does not identify a sufficient condition equal culpability.[58]

To avoid this overinclusiveness, the equal culpability thesis must be refined further. It should be restricted to precisely those cases where the decision to remain in ignorance really does add enough extra culpability to get the willfully ignorant actor up from the level of a merely reckless actor to that of a knowing actor. The account I develop in the next chapter does just this.

B. SECOND PROBLEM: OBJECTIVE JUSTIFICATION OR JUSTIFYING CIRCUMSTANCES ONE IS AWARE OF?

A second worry for Hellman's view stems from its "objectivist" flavor. Hellman is explicit that the justifications that the doctor and lawyer in her examples possess are supposed to be "objective" in the sense that they apply regardless of the actor's *actual* motivations for remaining ignorant. On her view, "it doesn't matter whether the lawyer is motivated to avoid discipline, to serve her clients zealously, or to strike a balance between competing ethical demands"; rather "[w]hat matters is that professional obligations of loyalty and confidentiality constrain the lawyer's actions. . . ."[59] Later, she claims "we ought . . . to ask whether there *are* good reasons for the actor to choose blindness rather than focus on what reasons actually motivated the actor in choosing blindness."[60]

Having argued for a motive-free approach to culpability in Chapter 2, I'm sympathetic to Hellman's attempt to reduce the importance of the actor's actual reasons for acting. Nonetheless, her view as she presents it may be *overly objectivist*. On the view I defended, the culpability of an action is determined by the reasons the law should recognize as existing given the circumstances as one saw them. Your culpability equals the least bad configuration of these available reasons that could get an otherwise law-abiding person to behave as you did (described in a motive-free way) under the perceived circumstances.

[58] In fairness, Hellman might be read as aiming only to lay out the conditions in which willful ignorance is culpable at all—not to specify when willful ignorance followed by a subsequent reckless act is as culpable as knowing misconduct, which is my focus. Hellman plausibly has identified a necessary condition for the equal culpability thesis to be true—namely, that one's decision to remain in ignorance is unjustified—but it is not sufficient.

[59] *Id.* at 307.

[60] *Id.* at 313 (emphasis added).

Thus, to get the benefit of an actually existing reason for remaining ignorant, you must at least be aware of the facts constituting it.

However, for all Hellman says, it remains possible that one could get the benefit of justifying circumstances that objectively exist even if one is not aware of those circumstances. Her own presentation of her view is at best ambiguous on this point. As she puts it, "[a]n actor is culpably blind if his blindness is unjustified. Blindness is justified when *the reasons to remain ignorant* outweigh the reasons to investigate, all things considered. (...) If *there are no* good reasons for [remaining ignorant], this blindness is culpable."[61] Thus, for all Hellman says, it is possible that anyone who simply *occupies* the right kind of professional role would get the benefit of the reasons this role provides in favor of remaining ignorant, even without being aware of the facts that explain why it is justified for people occupying those professional roles to remain ignorant. Hellman's own discussion does not rule out this possibility. But it should.

Recall Karen. She is in circumstances that provide some but not full justification for deciding against doing the additional study. She is a bit culpable for deciding to remain in ignorance, but not very. Now compare Lauren, who is just like Karen, except that she is entirely unaware of the burdens that the study would entail for the patients who will go untreated because of the delay in releasing the drug. This thought does not cross Lauren's mind. Accordingly, Lauren seems more culpable for deciding to remain ignorant than Karen. Still, on the strongly objectivist interpretation of Hellman's view, Karen and Lauren would both have the same level of culpability, since they both are in the same external circumstances.

Hellman's view would be strengthened by clearly ruling out this possibility. In my view, we should take it that one is culpable to the extent that one's decision to remain in ignorance is unjustified on the facts as one believes them to be.[62] This would let us say that Lauren is more culpable than Karen. Lauren, after all, is aware of fewer considerations that help justify her ignorance than Karen is.[63]

---

[61] Hellman, *supra* note 3, at 315 (emphasis added). *See also id*. at 313 ("we ought... to ask whether there are good reasons for the actor to choose blindness...").

[62] I do not take a stand here on whether what matters is the beliefs *one actually possesses* about the facts, or the beliefs one *should possess* about the facts given one's evidence. That is too tricky a normative question for me to resolve in this book. I'll leave the issue open in what follows.

[63] More specifically, my view is that culpability depends on the justifying reasons the law should recognize as existing on the perceived facts. Culpability is pegged to the smallest error in weighing the applicable legal reasons that is needed to get an otherwise law-abiding citizen to make the defendant's same decision to remain ignorant under the circumstances as the defendant believed them to be. This means, however, that any two actors with the same beliefs about the facts will get evaluated the same in terms of culpability—even if they were actually motivated by different reasons. Thus, I take normative culpability to be pegged to the strongest available case in favor of one's conduct that the circumstances one is aware of can plausibly provide.

Thus, I join Hellman in rejecting the fully subjectivist approach, which lets actual motives impact culpability. But I also reject the extreme objectivist approach that Hellman's discussion leaves open, which allows culpability to be impacted by the justifying circumstances that exist even if one is unaware of them. Rather,

To avoid the above-mentioned problems for RECT3, the equal culpability thesis must be further refined. It should be restricted to cases where the decision to remain ignorant really is sufficiently culpable to get one up to the culpability level of one's knowing counterpart. Moreover, it should avoid the strongly objectivist interpretation of Hellman's position.

C. ANOTHER WORRY: EXCUSED IGNORANCE?

A third worry about Hellman's view is that it does not account for cases where the decision to remain ignorant is unjustified but excused. However, as we'll see, it remains a nondecisive problem because one might reject the problem by seeking to recast excuses as justifications.

An excuse involves a disability (whether internal, as with insanity, or external, for duress) that causes an excusing condition or attribute—that is, that lowers the responsibility or blame the defendant should be deemed to bear for her act.[64] Excusing conditions can apply also when one's conduct is unjustified. Hellman's account does not make room for cases where the decision to remain ignorant is unjustified but excused. Consider this version of *Dangerous Investigation*:

> ***Trauma-Triggering Investigation***: When Ryan was deployed in Iraq, he got seriously injured in an attack. He is now back in the United States but suffers from PTSD. Ryan has inherited a factory, and agrees to lease it to his brother, Steve, at a discount. Ryan has begun to suspect Steve might be using the factory to manufacture and distribute meth. Ryan feels he should investigate, but the only available way to do so is to go into the factory to look around. (Ryan is aware that if he asks anyone else to investigate for him, his trigger-happy brother will shoot them as an intruder. Ryan knows he must go in himself to investigate.) However, the prospect of going into the factory, with its loud machinery and flashing lights, suddenly seems extremely daunting to Ryan. As he imagines going inside, with the deafening machinery crashing continuously, Ryan starts to hyperventilate, and the trauma from the explosions he experienced in battle comes flooding back. He suddenly feels paralyzed. He knows he must investigate, but every time he thinks about going into the factory, his trauma is triggered and he relents. (In fact, his trauma leads him

I endorse the moderately objectivist position that culpability is a function of the strongest normative case for one's conduct (described in a motive-free way) that exists on the perceived facts.

[64] *See* Paul Robinson, *Criminal Law Defenses: A Systematic Analysis*, 82 COLUM. L. REV. 199, 221–22 (1982) ("Excuses admit that the deed may be wrong, but [insist] the actor is not responsible for his deed. (. . .) [E]xcuse defenses ha[ve] the following internal structure: a disability causing an excusing condition. The disability is the abnormal condition of the actor at the time of the offense. (. . .) The requirement of an excusing condition [demands] the actor's disability cause . . . a particular exculpating mental condition in relation to the conduct," which fully or partially exempts the actor from blame.)

to exaggerate what it would be like to go inside. Ryan knows consciously that were he to go into the factory, it wouldn't actually be that painful for him. But he suffers from a psychological disorder that leads him to be overcome with anxiety when contemplating entering the factory.) Accordingly, he chooses to remain in ignorance. He decides to avoid the factory at all cost—even though he is well aware this will keep him in the dark about the suspected drug operation. Ryan continues to rent the factory to Steve to continue getting the rental payments (his only income) despite his suspicions about what Steve is up to.

Although Ryan decides to remain in ignorance about whether Steve is manufacturing drugs, Ryan plausibly is not as culpable as an analogous actor who continues to rent to Steve while knowing what Steve is up to. This is not because Ryan's decision to remain in ignorance is justified. Very plausibly, it's not. Ryan consciously believes that if he walked into the factory, it would not be very uncomfortable or painful, and it's only his psychological ailment that makes him experience crippling anxiety upon contemplating going near the factory. Thus, let's suppose the costs of investigating (not only for an objectively reasonable person, but for Ryan himself) are not enough to justify the decision to remain in ignorance. Since Ryan's ignorance is unjustified, RECT3 entails that he is as culpable as the analogous knowing wrongdoer.

Nonetheless, this result seems implausible. Given the Ryan's psychological disability, he seems less worthy of criticism than someone who rents to Steve while knowing about the drug operation. Granted Ryan is somewhat culpable for continuing to rent to Steve, given Ryan's suspicions. But specifically his *decision to remain in ignorance* still seems substantially excused. Ryan experienced severe trauma that we should have sympathy for and that should make us less inclined to blame Ryan than if he had no such disability. On my account of culpability, we would capture this by saying that the amount of insufficient regard Ryan's conduct manifests should be pegged to the amount it would take an otherwise law-abiding citizen to behave as Ryan did *while possessing the specific disability Ryan labors under*.[65]

If I'm right that Ryan's PTSD substantially excuses his decision to remain ignorant, he plausibly is less culpable than the analogous knowing wrongdoer although this decision is unjustified. Because Ryan's remaining ignorant is largely excused, his willful ignorance plausibly does not add enough culpability to get him up to the level of the analogous knowing wrongdoer. Since RECT3 considers only whether remaining in ignorance is justified, and here it is not, RECT3 implies the opposite. So it seems to be in trouble.

---

[65] More specifically, here is how my account of culpability would handle excuses. Generally, where no excusing disabilities are at issue, we would figure out how much culpability an act manifests just by looking at the justifications that exists given the actor's beliefs. But to consider excuses in the culpability calculation, we'd ask how much insufficient regard is needed to get an otherwise law-abiding citizen, OC, to do what the defendant did *while possessing the specific disability that the defendant labors under*. This is a more precise description of "what the defendant did" than we usually ask in the culpability inquiry, where no excusatory conditions are in play.

However, I'm unsure whether this objection to RECT3 is a distinct problem, or whether it can simply be recast as a version of the first objection, involving partially justified willful ignorance. Suppose one shares the intuition that Ryan is less culpable than the analogous knowing wrongdoer. Still, one might reply that this is not because Ryan's decision to remain ignorant is excused; rather, it's because the psychological burdens he expects to suffer from investigating is a *partial justification*, which reduces his culpability. Thus, any time we face a putative excusatory condition that seems to lessen the culpability of deciding not to investigate, one might try to recast it as a partially justifying circumstance. If so, then *Trauma-Triggering Investigation* would simply become another instance of the objection leveled at RECT3 in subsection A—the problem of partially justified willful ignorance.

I doubt that reading *Trauma-Triggering Investigation* as involving justifications is the best construal of the case. I told the story of Ryan so that he himself—at least consciously—believed he would not experience much pain or anxiety were he to go into the factory. Thus, I suggested that any pain he would experience from investigating would not be weighty enough to provide any justification for remaining in ignorance. Nonetheless, I can't fully rule out this reading of the case, which recasts potential excusatory conditions as partial justifiers. That is, I can't rule out that Ryan seems less culpable than a knowing wrongdoer only because he has a partial justifier, not an excuse. Thus, I remain unsure whether *Trauma-Triggering Investigation* is a distinct problem for RECT3.

Accordingly, I offer this only as a *potential* problem for RECT3, which merits further scrutiny. If there are cases where deciding to remain ignorant is excused despite being unjustified, then this would pose another distinct problem for RECT3. It would also require amending the equal culpability thesis to take such cases into account. But I am not able to conclusively settle the issue here.

In the next chapter, I defend my own account of the culpability of willful ignorance. It seeks to avoid the above-mentioned worries about Hellman's view—as well as the problems for the other accounts this chapter criticized. But due to my lingering doubts about cases of excused willful ignorance,[66] I don't build excuses into my account. Instead, I focus only on factors that help *justify* deciding to remain ignorant (even if only partially). Still, if one prefers, my account can easily be extended—as sketched here—to also cover internal or external conditions that excuse the decision to remain ignorant. Having provided enough hints about and motivations for my own account, let me now go on to articulate and defend it.

---

[66] Furthermore, one might think only justifying considerations, not excuses, properly bear on whether one's conduct should count as a wrong of a given type—here, a knowledge crime. One might think excuses, by contrast, should be considered only later, after it's been determined that the conduct counts as a particular wrong—that is, conduct that satisfies the prima facie case and lacks justification. This may be another reason not to let excuses impact the culpability attributed in determining whether one committed a wrong that requires knowledge.

4 The Scope of the Willful Ignorance Doctrine (II)

THE DUTY TO REASONABLY INFORM ONESELF

THIS CHAPTER DEFENDS my own approach to restricting the equal culpability thesis. Refining the account I've offered elsewhere,[1] I argue that willful ignorance involves breaching a *duty to reasonably inform oneself*, and the equal culpability thesis holds when one breaches it in a *sufficiently serious way* before doing the actus reus. This chapter thus offers a limited defense of the equal culpability thesis. If I'm right, the willful ignorance doctrine requires reform. To remain faithful to the courts' "traditional rationale," knowledge should not be imputed in just *any* case of willful ignorance (as many courts allow[2]), but only when one's willful ignorance rendered one's conduct as culpable as the analogous knowing wrong. Identifying a defensible version of the equal culpability thesis thus places constraints on the proper application of the willful ignorance doctrine. After defending my account in the first four sections, I discuss how to formulate workable willful ignorance jury instructions that lower the risk of unfairness.

[1] *See* Alex Sarch, *Willful Ignorance Culpability and the Criminal Law*, 88 St. John's L. Rev. 1023, 1077–90 (2014); Alex Sarch, *Equal Culpability and the Scope of the Willful Ignorance Doctrine*, 22 Legal Theory 276 (2016).

[2] *See* United States v. Heredia, 483 F.3d 913, 920 (9th Cir. 2007) (en banc) (construing the willful ignorance doctrine to require only willful ignorance in what I call the "basic" sense); United States v. Ferrarini, 219 F.3d 145, 154 (2d Cir. 2000); United States v. Flores, 454 F.3d 149, 155 (3d Cir. 2006); United States v. Geisen, 612 F.3d 471, 485–86 (6th Cir. 2010); United States v. Tanner, 628 F.3d 890, 904 (7th Cir. 2010).

Criminally Ignorant. Alexander Sarch.

I. How to Properly Restrict ECT

In Chapter 3, we saw the Unrestricted Equal Culpability Thesis fail because deciding to remain ignorant can be at least partially justified. This can prevent the decision to remain ignorant from adding enough culpability to get one up from a subknowledge level of culpability to the level of a knowing wrongdoer. My account is premised on the idea that sometimes this decision *can* fill the gap. I will argue that willful ignorance involves breaching a narrow *duty to inform oneself*, and willfully ignorant conduct is as culpable as the analogous knowing misconduct when this duty is breached in sufficiently serious ways. Thus, I defend:

> **Restricted Equal Culpability Thesis 4 (RECT4):** Suppose A1 and A2 each perform the actus reus of a crime requiring knowledge of an inculpatory proposition, p. A1 and A2, and their respective actions, are identical in every respect except one: while A1's action is performed with knowledge of p, A2's action is performed *with a form of willful ignorance toward p that involves a sufficiently culpable breach of the duty to reasonably inform oneself.* On these suppositions, A2 is (at least) as culpable for her action as A1 is for his.

Defending RECT4 requires establishing three main claims: (1) there is a duty to reasonably inform oneself,[3] (2) breaching it renders one's conduct more culpable than if no investigation had been feasible (what I call the *Added Culpability Thesis*), and (3) this added culpability can sometimes suffice to make one's conduct as culpable as the analogous knowing misconduct.

I defend (1) and (2) in Sections II and III. But already we can see that (3) is plausible if we grant (1) and (2). If there is a duty to reasonably inform oneself, and if breaching it confers added culpability beyond that of doing the actus reus when unable to acquire more information about the suspected inculpatory proposition, then it's easy to see how RECT4 would be true.

As argued in a moment, willful ignorance in the criminal law sense always involves breaching the duty to reasonably inform oneself—DRI. That is because what triggers DRI is that one suspects the inculpatory proposition, p, and on the facts one is aware

---

[3] Why postulate such a duty at all? Why not simply apply one's preferred theory of criminal culpability directly to see if particular willfully ignorant actions are as culpable as analogous knowing wrongs? It's because formulating an affirmative duty to inform oneself is more illuminating than leaving it to readers to apply a theory of culpability themselves. I aim to provide more concrete guidance by showing what factors enhance or mitigate culpability. A helpful way to do this is to posit an affirmative duty to inform oneself. Still, the substantive implications are not meant to differ from those of directly applying my theory of culpability to willful ignorance.

of there are reasonably available ways to acquire more information about whether one's suspicions are correct. As seen in Chapter 1, this is also what's required for willful ignorance in the basic sense:[4] one must suspect p and reasonably be able to get more information about whether p (thus triggering DRI), but then consciously decide not to learn whether p (thus breaching DRI) before doing the actus reus. I'll argue below that this breach confers additional culpability beyond what the actor would have had if he merely did the actus reus recklessly—that is, without being able to obtain more information. Let C_{WI} stand for the extra culpability incurred from deciding not to obtain more information before doing the actus reus.

Supposing the willfully ignorant actor does not actually know p, he'll have a subknowledge degree of confidence in p. Let C_R stand for the culpability of acting with this subknowledge level of confidence in p. This is the amount he'd incur if he did the actus reus purely recklessly—that is, without being reasonably able to obtain more information about p.

Moreover, let C_K stand for the culpability of a similarly situated actor who does the actus reus with enough certainty in p to count as knowing it in the legal sense. C_R is assumed to be less than C_K. Because of CCP from Chapter 3, as we increase the willfully ignorant actor's confidence in p, his conduct becomes more culpable and approaches C_K.

This supports RECT4 because at least sometimes C_{WI} will be equal to or greater than $C_K - C_R$. Sometimes the decision not to inform oneself will confer enough extra culpability to get one up to the culpability level of doing the actus reus with knowledge of p. If we restrict the equal culpability thesis to these cases—as RECT4 does—we can be confident that it holds.

Of course, RECT4 is nonvacuously true only if there really are cases of this sort. Still, given the wide range of actors in the real world, we can be confident that there are some. The easiest way to drive this home is to note that some defendants will have a degree of confidence in p just short of knowledge. In such cases, $C_K - C_R$ is very small. Thus, it wouldn't take a very serious breach of DRI (i.e., a very large C_{WI}) to get one's willfully ignorant conduct to be as culpable as the analogous knowing misconduct. Since some breaches of DRI are more culpable than others, we can be quite sure that sometimes C_{WI} will be large enough to fill the gap.

Admittedly, RECT4 by itself is underwhelming. It just abstractly describes the conditions in which willfully ignorant misconduct is as culpable as the analogous knowing misconduct. However, this chapter fleshes out RECT4 by providing a substantive account of the culpability of willful ignorance.[5] It shows what factors determine

---

[4] *See* Chapter 1, Section III. *See also Global-Tech*, 131 S. Ct. at 2070.

[5] This is the main way my account is substantively superior to Hellman's, captured in RECT3. In addition, RECT4 also has two technical advantages. First, it only posits equal culpability between willfully ignorant and knowing misconduct when the decision to remain in ignorance is *sufficiently unjustified*—not when it's unjustified *simpliciter*, as RECT3 said. Second, by employing my theory of culpability, I also avoid the worry that Hellman's view might be overly objectivist. My view pegs culpability to the justifying circumstances one is aware

whether particular instances of willfully ignorant misconduct are as culpable as knowing misconduct. This helps us zero in on the cases in which the equal culpability thesis holds, and it reveals what kind of inquiry is needed to decide if a specific willfully ignorant defendant deserves treatment as a knowing wrongdoer.

Note one limitation of my account: it only seeks to explain what makes willfully ignorant defendants with a *subknowledge* level of confidence in p as culpable as a knowing wrongdoer. Although some suggest one can be willfully ignorant despite knowing p (a claim I doubt),[6] a defendant who possesses knowledge can be straightforwardly convicted of the knowledge crime in question (provided the trial evidence suffices). It is only when the defendant has a subknowledge level of certainty in p that any puzzle arises about how willfully ignorant misconduct can be as culpable as knowing misconduct.

I'll now proceed to unpack the culpability of willful ignorance. I first make the case for assumption (1): why there is a duty to reasonably inform oneself of suspected risks before acting. Then I argue for assumption (2): breaching this duty renders one more culpable.

II. There Is a Duty to Reasonably Inform Oneself

The first order of business is to explain the duty to reasonably inform oneself. What kind of duty is it? It is the sort of moral duty that is appropriately codified in the criminal law—one it would make sense for the law to attribute criminal culpability for breaching. It is not an epistemic, rational, or prudential duty. Of course, obtaining more information may well be epistemically required *as well.* Alternatively, ignorance might serve one's self-interest (as when the perceived benefits of ignorance outweigh the expected costs of acquiring more information).[7] While self-interest surely explains why so many people actually opt to remain in ignorance (with lamentable consequences for important political issues like global climate change), none of this is my concern here. Instead, I contend we have an obligation—morally and sometimes legally—not to preserve our ignorance about important matters that affect the rights and interests of others. The scope and justification of the duty the *law should recognize* is my concern.[8]

---

of, not the external facts of one's situation. Still, these technical improvements are a less important contribution than the substantive account of the culpability of willful ignorance I offer.

[6] *See* Douglas N. Husak & Craig A. Callender, *Wilful Ignorance, Knowledge, and the "Equal Culpability" Thesis: A Study of the Deeper Significance of the Principle of Legality*, 1994 Wis. L. Rev. 29, 48 (1994). I'm not persuaded, because if one has enough certainty in the inculpatory proposition to count as knowing it, it's odd to describe one as *ignorant* of it.

[7] *See* Michael Huemer, *Why People Are Irrational About Politics*, http://www.owl232.net/irrationality.htm ("people often choose—rationally—to remain ignorant because the costs of collecting information are greater than the expected value of the information," and noting "[t]his is very often true of political information"). *See also* Jan Willem Wieland, *Responsibility for Strategic Ignorance*, Synthese (2016).

[8] Throughout this book, my concern is not to map out the investigative duties the law in the United States or other jurisdictions actually recognizes. Rather, my question is what duty of this sort the law *should recognize* if it is to be as normatively defensible as it can be (within practicable limits).

The duty to inform oneself belongs to a broader group of informational duties. One plausibly is responsible not just for informing *oneself* in certain cases (e.g., when occupying certain professional roles or in exigent circumstances). Additionally, one also plausibly has duties to *inform others* when important interests or values are at stake. This duty to inform others might require, for instance, affirmatively disclosing information to proper authorities when harm is imminent or one's ethical or legal duties require it. Moreover, it plausibly requires one not to block others from becoming appropriately informed—as with the obligation not to cover up wrongdoing, or the duty not to obstruct law enforcement investigations.[9] I return to duties concerning *others' information* in Chapter 9. Here, my focus is the duty to inform *oneself*. It, too, requires both taking certain affirmative steps to investigate or dig up more information, *and* not preventing oneself from obtaining pertinent information that otherwise would have reached one. My formulation of the duty will cover both.

Some are skeptical of such investigative obligations.[10] Arpaly and Schroeder argue we do not plausibly have a duty to "become informed about morally important matters, to double check our morally relevant beliefs and do our best to make sure that they are true."[11] Their concern is that "we cannot in general know which of our beliefs need checking."[12] After all, "it is not the case that [we are] under a moral obligation to scrutinize all of [our] beliefs regarding" morally important matters.[13]

I think this worry is correct, as far as it goes. But my account avoids the concern because the duty I postulate is limited to a narrow, especially charged context. All I claim is that being aware that one's intended conduct will create risks of harm or illegality generates a duty to inform oneself in reasonable ways. I do not claim that all morally important beliefs require checking. Only one specific kind triggers the need to inform

---

[9] *See* Chapter 9, Section I; 18 U.S.C. § 4 (misprision of felony); 18 U.S.C. §§ 1503, 1512–13 (obstruction).

[10] Holly Smith offers a different objection, at least where duties to inform oneself are "subjective duties" arising out of what one believes. Holly Smith, *The Subjective Moral Duty to Inform Oneself before Acting*, 125 Ethics 11, 23–31 (2014). She argues it can't be the case that we subjectively ought to investigate solely because this would enable one to subsequently do what has most "deontic value." Even though keeping a weightier promise has more deontic value than keeping a less weighty promise, it doesn't follow that one has an obligation to go around making additional promises. Likewise, one doesn't have a duty to go around investigating things just so one will be able to do actions with more deontic value.

My view avoids this worry. The trouble with the investigative duty she considers is that it takes the duty to investigate to be purely derivative of the deontic values of the subsequent acts which investigating would enable one to perform. However, as we'll see, my view makes the duty to investigate *nonderivative* in Smith's sense. I argue there is an *independently existing reason* to inform oneself: namely, that not doing so can manifest insufficient regard for the interests others. On my view, there is something in itself good (or at least culpability-avoiding) about informing oneself in reasonable ways. It shows a kind of seriousness, conscientiousness, and respect toward others.

[11] Nomy Arpaly & Tim Schroeder, In Praise of Desire 237 (2014).

[12] *Id.*

[13] *Id.*

oneself: the belief that an action one plans to perform would pose substantial risks to the interests or rights of others.[14]

When one possesses such a belief, one's primary duty is, of course, to refrain from performing the underlying risky action. However, this is not the only duty one incurs. The primary duty not to act in certain ways can generate secondary duties—as when breaking a promise or wrongfully injuring someone triggers duties to apologize or offer compensation.[15] In addition to secondary duties that arise *after* the breach of a primary duty, there are also secondary duties that arise *before* such a breach. This would be the case if one plans to break a promise and there are preemptive steps one should take to mitigate the inconvenience it will cause the promisee. The duty to reasonably investigate is likewise a secondary duty that arises in anticipation of subsequent wrongdoing.

Let's be more precise about when this duty arises. Suppose one plans or intends[16] to perform an action that one is aware would pose substantial and unjustified risks of harm to interests that are legitimately protected by law. This would be the case whenever one has suspicions about the inculpatory proposition of a crime (assuming the law is just) and there is no justification or excuse. In that case, I submit, one has a distinct secondary duty, which derives from one's primary duty not to perform the underlying action, to make reasonable investigations before doing that action[17] (provided one remains intent on performing it). To summarize:

---

[14] Others mention duties to investigate, but have not developed them as systematically as I do here. Holly Smith mentions the case of a driver who "should have checked his mirror earlier, but given that he did not, he should check it now rather than back down the driveway." Holly Smith, *Culpable Ignorance*, 92 PHIL. REV. 543, 546 (1983). *See also* GEORGE SHER, WHO KNEW? RESPONSIBILITY WITHOUT AWARENESS 111–12 (2009) (discussing idea that one's moral obligations can give rise to secondary epistemic duties to be or become aware of morally relevant features of one's situation). William K. Clifford, *The Ethics of Belief*, *in* THE ETHICS OF BELIEF AND OTHER ESSAYS, 70–96 (T. Madigan ed., 1999) (famously defending—in 1877—a broad moral "duty of inquiry").

Tadros also posits a duty to investigate, and like me, he thinks it is reduced in stringency where investigating is dangerous or difficult. VICTOR TADROS, CRIMINAL RESPONSIBILITY 246–47 (2005). However, Tadros's duty to investigate is much broader than mine, covering not only actors who *actually* have suspicions of the risks to be investigated but also actors who do not. Thus, his duty to investigate also covers some instances of negligent unawareness of the risk (what UK courts call "objective recklessness"). By contrast, my duty to investigate applies only where one already suspects the risk (has "subjective recklessness"). Thus, my focus is the more serious investigative failures that plausibly provide a basis for treating one as a knowing wrongdoer. *See also infra* note 38.

[15] *See, e.g.*, Gregory Keating, *The Priority of Respect over Repair*, 18 LEGAL THEORY 293, 309 (2012) ("[r]emedial responsibilities arise out of the breach of antecedent primary duties"); John Gardner, *What Is Tort Law For? Part 1: The Place of Corrective Justice*, 30 LAW & PHIL. 1, 33–35 (2011).

[16] One might think the duty to investigate arises not just when one intends or plans to perform the underlying risky action, but even when one merely seriously *considers* performing it. I leave open whether some lesser degree of commitment, short of intention, also triggers the duty to investigate.

[17] My discussion presupposes the law is *just*. The duty to reasonably investigate, to be normatively defensible, ideally should not be triggered if the relevant criminal statute is substantively unjust. Admittedly, the law often is unjust. But this does not mean courts must evaluate whether the law is just before applying the willful ignorance doctrine. That would be inappropriate, since a court's primary task is to apply, and adjudicate disputes

Duty to Reasonably Inform Oneself (DRI):

(a) If a person
  (i) is intending or planning to perform the actus reus of a crime,
  (ii) possesses substantial confidence (short of knowledge) that the associated inculpatory proposition, p, is true (but lacks reason to think the risk of p's truth is somehow justified), and
  (iii) believes or reasonably should believe (based on one's evidence) that there are available ways to acquire more information about whether p is true that are not unduly burdensome,

then this person has a *pro tanto* obligation, conditional on continuing to hold the relevant intention, to (at least try to) acquire more information about whether p is true or false (i.e., learn whether p), in the reasonably available ways (if any), before performing the actus reus.[18] Any act that breaches this obligation is said to help "preserve one's ignorance about p."

(b) Moreover, if one breaches the obligation in (a), one has a further *pro tanto* obligation to breach it with the least bad mens rea that one can. That is, it is a less serious breach of the obligation in (a) to negligently as opposed to recklessly preserve one's ignorance about p (i.e., fail to acquire the required information); to do so recklessly rather than knowingly; and to do so knowingly rather than purposefully.

Thus, suppose Brad plans to set fire to a building despite recognizing a substantial risk someone is inside. Having settled on this less-than-ideal course of action, DRI entails Brad has a conditional duty to investigate in reasonably feasible ways before proceeding—say, by looking inside the building. The duty is *conditional* in the sense that were Brad to abandon his plan, his duty to inform himself would evaporate.[19,20] Moreover, the duty is

under, the law as given. The issues courts confront are different from my question as a theorist. Since I'm concerned with normative culpability (i.e., what the law *should* attribute), all I claim is that there *should* (from the theorist's perspective) be a legal duty to investigate only where the law actually is just (again, as evaluated from the theorist's vantage point).

[18] I remain agnostic on whether this duty should be read as having wide or narrow scope. *Cf.* Mark Schroeder, *The Scope of Instrumental Reason*, 18 PHIL. PERSPECTIVES 337 (2004).

[19] One might worry this allows Brad to sidestep his investigatory duties: perhaps he could withdraw his intention to burn down the building until the last moment, and thereby avoid incurring any secondary duty to investigate before starting the fire. However, on closer inspection, this strategy cannot succeed. Were Brad to adopt this scheme, he would not *genuinely* be abandoning his intention to burn down the building. He would merely be executing a plan to burn it down that involves much self-deception. The intention that triggers the duty to investigate remains in place.

[20] Because DRI is triggered only when the defendant believes his planned act would pose a substantial and *unjustified* risk of the inculpatory proposition being true, DRI accommodates cases where some exigency intuitively prevents the need to investigate from arising at all. Suppose Laura knows the building must be burned down to halt a fire that is rapidly spreading toward town, but she realizes there is little time to check if someone is inside. Investigating is not impossible, but it would leave less time for other important precautions (like warning

pro tanto in the sense that it can be outweighed by weightier considerations, for example, if complying with the duty would make it too hard to comply with the primary duty not to do the actus reus, or if investigating otherwise is unduly harmful or costly. The required steps to inform oneself can involve either *external* actions aimed at acquiring further information, or *internal* measures like further processing of information one already has. Moreover, the duty to inform oneself covers not only actively acquiring new information but also not *blocking* information one would have received. The duty to inform oneself about the truth of p entails that one should not act in ways that prevent one from learning whether p. One minimal form of keeping oneself informed, after all, is *refraining* from taking steps to avoid learning the truth.

How do one's beliefs about whether one can investigate impact this *pro tanto* duty? Although the main arguments of this book don't depend on it, I favor the following view (and have formulated DRI accordingly). First, if unbeknownst to one, one actually *can* feasibly investigate, but cannot be expected to know it given one's evidence, then the *pro tanto* obligation to investigate in this way is not triggered.[21] By contrast, if one (reasonably) believes one can feasibly investigate, but is mistaken, then I take it one has a *pro tanto* obligation at least to attempt to investigate. After all, it arguably shows some insufficient regard for others to fail to even *try* to investigate in ways that plausibly seem available.[22]

Note finally that in *complying* with DRI, what one learns can impact the stringency of one's primary duty not to do the actus reus. Recall Brad. If he investigates as DRI requires, there are three possibilities. First, he might learn there is a greater chance than he believed that someone is in the building. This would strengthen his primary duty not to set fire to it. (By CCP, from Chapter 3, he would be more culpable were he to start the fire with this increased certainty that someone is inside.) Second, he might learn there is a smaller chance than expected that someone is inside. In that case, his duty not to start the fire would be slightly weakened (though it would remain in force thanks to the independent reasons not to set fire even to an unoccupied building). Third, the strength of his duty not to start the fire would remain unchanged if investigating did not alter the correct estimate of the likelihood that someone is inside.

---

the town authorities). The best way to describe this case might not be to say that Laura is justified in *breaching* DRI, but rather that the duty to investigate does not arise at all. It is to leave room for this possibility that DRI says investigations are required only if the risk one is aware of is *unjustified*.

21 What if one does not know one can investigate, but even if one did know, one would not? DRI says if it's reasonable to expect one to know of available investigatory steps, then one has a *pro tanto* duty to take them, but if it's not reasonable to expect one to know one can investigate, the duty does not arise. The counterfactual truth that one *would not* investigate even if one knew one could does not directly impact one's culpability—for the reasons that led me to reject the counterfactual test in RECT2.

22 One might doubt this is true where one only *unreasonably* believes one can investigate. I can't settle this here. I formulated DRI so the *pro tanto* obligation to investigate is triggered even by unreasonable beliefs that investigation is feasible, but this may be controversial. Still, my main argument doesn't require it.

III. How the Duty to Reasonably Inform Oneself Affects Culpability

A. BREACHING DRI ENHANCES CULPABILITY

To explain why willfully ignorant conduct is sometimes as culpable as acting knowingly, I need to argue that breaching DRI can be an independent source of culpability. The claim to be shown is that breaching DRI before doing the underlying risky action is *more culpable* (provided one has no excuse or justification) than doing the action when investigating is not an option (in which case DRI would not be breached and the action is merely reckless). More precisely:

> **Added Culpability Thesis:** For any person, A, to whom DRI applies, if A breaches DRI and proceeds to perform the underlying actus reus that DRI requires A to investigate the risks of, then in virtue of this breach, A is at least *a little bit more culpable* for his conduct (provided he has no justification or excuse) than a similarly situated person, B, who performs the same actus reus but had no reasonable way to investigate the risks of that action, would be for her conduct.

This claim has intuitive support, but I'll also give an argument for it. I then offer a more general account of how complying with or breaching DRI impacts culpability.

The argument for the Added Culpability Thesis is that—from the perspective of the actor—doing the underlying risky action having breached DRI involves *two* missed chances to assure oneself that conduct one intends will not be wrongful, while doing the risky action when investigating is not an option involves only *one*. Suppose I intend to do an action at *t1* that I'm aware will be risky. Moreover, I realize I can feasibly investigate at *t0* whether this risk really will materialize after I act. My first chance to assure myself that my intended conduct will not be wrongful comes at *t0*. As things seem to me then, if I investigate, I might learn that the risk in question will not materialize. But if I fail to investigate, while retaining my intention to perform the risky action (and I have no justification or excuse), I manifest a lack of due regard for others that makes me culpable. However, my culpability level is not yet fixed at *t0* because I have a second chance to assure myself that my intended conduct will not be wrongful—that is, during the period up to *t1*. After all, until *t1*, I can simply abandon my intention to perform the underlying risky action at *t1*. Going ahead with that action is another manifestation of insufficient regard. Thus, breaching DRI and doing the risky action involves two missed chances (one epistemic and the other practical) to rule out the possibility that conduct that I intend is wrongful. By contrast, when I have no feasible way to investigate (such that DRI is not breached), doing the underlying risky action only involves one such missed opportunity, and thus only one manifestation of insufficient regard. Accordingly, breaching DRI and doing the risky action is more culpable than doing that action when investigating is not an option—just as the Added Culpability Thesis says.

One might think there is something odd about my claim that breaching DRI is an independent source of culpability. Arpaly and Schroeder object to investigative duties on the ground that complying with them would "not absolve one of moral blame."[23] After all, even if one investigates as DRI requires, one might still proceed to behave culpably. If one learns the inculpatory proposition is true, but performs the actus reus anyway, then one would be a knowing wrongdoer and display a correspondingly high level of culpability. Thus, even if one complies with DRI, one might display more on-balance culpability than others who breach DRI by not investigating—for example, those who don't investigate but then have a change of heart and don't do the actus reus. Accordingly, there is no guarantee that someone who breaches DRI will be on balance more culpable than someone who complies with it. So in what sense can failing to investigate be independently culpable?[24]

These considerations actually are consistent with my account of how DRI impacts culpability. I do not claim that informing oneself as DRI requires fully absolves one of blame. Nor do I claim that it always renders one *on balance* less culpable than someone who breaches DRI. Rather, I contend only that, in virtue of breaching DRI, there is *one respect* in which one is more culpable than someone who does not breach DRI. This leaves it open that someone who complies with DRI might still be *on balance* more culpable than someone who breaches it. Thus, my basic claim about the culpability of breaching versus complying with DRI is this:

> **Culpability for Breach vs. Compliance (CBC):** For any two similarly situated individuals, A and B, if A breaches DRI while B does not breach DRI (either by complying with it or its not applying), then (in virtue of A's breach) there is at least *one respect* in which A is more culpable than B—even if B (in virtue of other features of her behavior) ultimately is on balance more culpable than A.

CBC is consistent with cases where complying with DRI seems on balance more culpable than breaching it—for example, where the person who investigates learns that the inculpatory proposition is true but does the actus reus anyway, while another who breaches DRI decides not to do the actus reus after all.

Moreover, the Added Culpability Thesis flows naturally from CBC. The Added Culpability Thesis compares the culpability of two similarly situated people, A and B, who do the actus reus with suspicions about the inculpatory proposition, but where A breaches DRI and B has no opportunity to investigate such that DRI does not apply and is not breached. According to CBC, there is *one respect* in which A is more culpable

[23] *Supra* note 11, at 238.

[24] A related worry is discussed below. *See infra* note 41.

than B. Since all else is assumed to be equal, A is also *on balance* a bit more culpable than B—just as the Added Culpability Thesis claims.[25]

To further flesh out CBC, the culpability of complying with or breaching DRI can be mapped out as follows. In scenarios where DRI applies, there are three main variables: (1) whether the actor informs herself at *t0* as DRI requires; (2) whether the inculpatory proposition, p, is true (such that informing herself would raise the actor's credence in p) or false (such that informing herself would lower her credence in p);[26] and (3) whether the actor proceeds to perform the actus reus at *t1*. Given these three variables, there are eight cases in which DRI applies. Table 4.1 summarizes CBC's implications.

Some comments about these cases are in order. Case 1 is the scenario that worried Arpaly and Schroeder. But, as seen, it is consistent with CBC. The paradigm case of acting in willful ignorance is Case 5, and A's culpability here conforms to the Added Culpability Thesis. In Case 6, I take it A's culpability is the same as an analogous instance of Case 5, but because p is not true in Case 6, A generally will not face criminal liability. Suppose Brad intends to light a building on fire believing someone is inside, but is mistaken. If Brad decides not to investigate, then although he breaches DRI, he would not be convicted of a higher grade of arson that requires the presence of a person inside the building. After all, the inculpatory proposition *someone is inside the building* actually is false. Thus, Brad benefits from a sort of moral luck that is prevalent in existing criminal

[25] This also answers an objection Gideon Yaffe has raised against my account. *See* Gideon Yaffe, *The Point of Mens Rea: The Case of Willful Ignorance*, 12 CRIM. L. & PHIL. 19 (2018). He contends that breaching a duty of inquiry is not *necessary* for the willfully ignorant defendant to be as culpable as his knowing counterpart, although my account claims it is. Yaffe claims "a case of [willful ignorance] can be core," such that we can be sure the defendant is as culpable as a knowing wrongdoer, "without the defendant having any duty to inquire." *Id.* at 37 (ftn. 17).

However, Yaffe's objection does not threaten my account. *See* Alex Sarch, *A Reply to Yaffe on the Culpability of Willful Ignorance*, 12 CRIM. L. & PHIL. 107 (2018). All I claim is that deliberately breaching DRI, as required for willful ignorance, *is a pro tanto contributor to one's culpability*. This doesn't mean breaching it always makes one on balance more culpable, or that not inquiring would always be wrong. I don't claim there is a duty to inquire in any such strong sense. Rather, my claim is that breaching DRI pro tanto contributes to culpability. This means there is a duty to inquire only in a very weak sense of "duty."

With this clarification, I think Yaffe and I largely agree on the role of "duties" of inquiry in this weak sense. Both he and I think not inquiring when one should can render one more culpable, and I simply add the further claim that there's a sense in which one, all else equal, should—that is, has a weak pro tanto "duty"—to avoid that source of extra culpability. I don't see any cases where (1) one would be more culpable for failing to inquire, but (2) there is no "duty" in the weak pro tanto sense to inquire (i.e., where inquiring isn't something one all else equal should do to avoid extra culpability). If so, then at least this kind of weak pro tanto duty to inquire really *is* necessary for willfully ignorant conduct to be as culpable as the analogous knowing misconduct.

[26] It is a simplifying assumption of my model that when inculpatory proposition p is true, investigating would lead one to acquire greater certainty that p, while when p is false, investigating would lower one's certainty that p. However, this will not always be accurate. It is possible that p is, say, false, but investigating under the circumstances would yield evidence that should raise one's credence in p. However, I set aside this complication to keep the model simple. The model can easily be expanded to capture this additional wrinkle if need be.

TABLE 4.1

The Impact of DRI on Culpability

	A informs herself at *to*; does actus reus at *t1*	**A informs herself at *to*; does not do actus reus at *t1***	**A does not inform herself at *to*; does actus reus at *t1* (Willful Ignorance)**	**A does not inform herself at *to*; does not do actus reus at *t1***
P is true; A would learn that p is more likely than initially believed	*Case 1*: A manifests no insufficient regard at *to*, but manifests extreme insufficient regard at *t1* (as much as a knowing actor).	*Case 3*: A manifests no insufficient regard at *to* or at *t1*.	*Case 5*: A manifests some insufficient regard at *to*, and manifests substantial insufficient regard at *t1*. A's total culpability is the sum of the culpability displayed at *to* and at *t1*.	*Case 7*: A manifests some insufficient regard at *to*, but manifests no insufficient regard at *t1*. A's total culpability level likely is far less than the amount needed to be criminally liable.
P is false; A would learn that p is *less* likely than initially believed	*Case 2*: A manifests no insufficient regard at *to*, and manifests less insufficient regard at *t1* than if her initial credence in P had not been lowered.	*Case 4*: A manifests no insufficient regard at *to* or at *t1*.	*Case 6*: Same as Case 5, except that A will not face criminal liability because P is false. (A is as culpable as in Case 5, but gets lucky since P is false.)	*Case 8*: Same as Case 7.

law.[27] Finally, in Cases 7 and 8, CBC entails that A displays at least a little bit of insufficient regard in virtue of breaching DRI, even though A in fact ends up avoiding the wrong involved in the actus reus. One might quibble with this result on the ground that if A does not do the actus reus, then since there is "no harm," there can be "no foul" (i.e., no culpability). Nonetheless, I think it is plausible in this case that breaching DRI can itself be a manifestation of insufficient regard, even if one goes on to see the error of one's

[27] *Cf.* Larry Alexander & Kimberly Ferzan, Crime and Culpability 171 (2009) (under current law, "resulting harm makes an actor" subject to greater punishment, but arguing this is problematic).

ways and abandons the intention to do the actus reus. However, this is of little practical concern, since whatever culpability A incurs just by breaching DRI is likely to be well below the amount needed to make criminal liability warranted.

Fully defending all the claims in this table isn't necessary to vindicate the basic claim I need for my argument—namely, that breaching DRI is an independent source of culpability beyond what's displayed in doing the actus reus purely recklessly (i.e., the Added Culpability Thesis). Still, this detour was useful because seeing how complying with or breaching DRI systematically impacts culpability supports seeing DRI as a genuine, theoretically well-behaved *pro tanto* duty.

B. HOW MUCH CULPABILITY DOES BREACHING DRI CONFER?

Suppose I'm right that breaching DRI entails one respect in which one is more culpable than if one had not breached it (either because one complied or it did not apply). We then need to know *how much* additional culpability breaching DRI confers. The way to answer this question is to apply the best going theory of culpability to that breach.[28] Having defended such a theory in Chapter 2, that is what I'll apply here. (However, the factors in my analysis can be translated over to other theories of culpability one might prefer.)

On my theory, the culpability of a given breach of DRI equals the insufficient regard it manifests for the interests, rights, or values that are properly protected by law. That is, its culpability is pegged to the least amount of insufficient regard for these interests, rights, or values (i.e., the smallest error in weighing the applicable legal reasons) that is needed to get an otherwise law-abiding citizen to act as the defendant did under the circumstances.

I am here interested in the sort of *normative* culpability that is relevant to evaluating the law—not the *posited* culpability attributions involved in judgments of particular jurisdictions. Thus, to determine the defendant's culpability, we need to focus on the reasons the law *should* recognize as bearing on whether to do the ignorance-preserving conduct in question (not merely the ones the law does recognize). This set of reasons, in turn, is a function of the interests, rights, and values the criminal law properly aims to protect. (I leave this latter concept unanalyzed, and only make fairly uncontroversial assumptions about which reasons belong in this set.)

There are several factors that impact how much insufficient regard ignorance-preserving conduct manifests. These can be collected into three main groups. At bottom, these factors help identify (i) the kinds of *benefits* of acquiring information the law should recognize as

[28] Gideon Yaffe has recently defended a theory of culpability and applied it to willful ignorance with interesting results. Most importantly, he offers a compelling proof that what he calls *Core Cases* of willful ignorance (involving costless inquiry) are just as culpable as the analogous knowing misconduct. *See* Yaffe, *supra* note 25. Yaffe's account is illuminating and dovetails well with mine. However, in other work, I've raised some objections to several aspects of his analysis. *See* Sarch, *supra* note 25.

reasons for behaving as DRI requires, and (ii) the kinds of *costs* of acquiring information the law should recognize as reasons against complying with DRI (i.e., justifying reasons for not learning more). Additionally, (iii) one's mens rea in breaching DRI matters.

1. One's Mens Rea in Breaching DRI

As clause (b) in DRI indicates, the duty in clause (a) can itself be breached with different mens rea. If, before committing the actus reus, defendant D does an act (or course of conduct), A, that constitutes a breach of DRI, D would be a culpably ignorant actor, and A is an act of ignorance preservation.[29] To figure out how much insufficient regard A manifests, we need to know D's mens rea toward the fact that A will help preserve his ignorance of p. That is, the question is whether D did A:

- *in order to* preserve D's ignorance of p (a purposeful breach of DRI);
- while *practically certain* that A will preserve D's ignorance of p (a knowing breach);
- while *aware of a substantial and unjustified risk* that A will preserve D's ignorance of p (a reckless breach); or
- while *unaware* of a substantial risk that A will preserve D's ignorance of p, even though D *should* have been aware of this risk (a negligent breach).

All these could amount to culpable ignorance. For the reasons given in Section III.E in Chapter 2, I take it that, *all else equal* (i.e., holding fixed the harm or wrong involved in the inculpatory proposition, etc.), it is more culpable to breach DRI with a higher mens rea toward the fact that one's conduct will preserve one's ignorance of p than doing so with a lower mens rea toward that fact. This is because the legal reasons against breaching DRI with a higher mens rea are fairly seen as weightier than the legal reasons against breaching DRI with a lower mens rea.

For example, one might negligently fail to investigate if one, say, forgets or is distracted. One would then not be as culpable for the breach (all else equal) as if one *consciously* decided not to investigate in reasonable ways. Similarly, breaching DRI because one fails to realize that some method of investigation exists or that one should investigate (either one of which could be negligence) seems less culpable than if one failed to investigate while *knowing* it's possible to investigate and that one should.

In Chapter 6, I'll discuss the culpability of breaching DRI with lower mens rea like recklessness or negligence. However, this chapter is about *willful ignorance*, which typically involves breaching DRI with *purpose* to remain in ignorance. In addition—given some courts' use of terms like "conscious avoidance" or "conscious ignorance" (discussed

[29] *Cf.* Smith, *supra* note 14, at 547 (dubbing this the "benighting action").

in Chapter 1, Section III)—breaching DRI *knowingly* plausibly also suffices for willful ignorance. As such, willful ignorance is going to involve a more culpable breach of DRI, all else equal, than merely *reckless* or *negligent* breaches thereof.

Besides mens rea, we must also consider the legally recognized benefits that give reason to inform oneself as DRI requires and the legally recognized costs that count against doing so (i.e., the justifications for not informing oneself). The amount of insufficient regard manifested in breaching DRI is a function of how much the former outweigh the latter. This balance of legal reasons determines the smallest error in weighing reasons needed to get otherwise law-abiding citizens to behave as the DRI-breaching defendant did. Let's take each group of reasons in turn.

2. Legally Cognizable Benefits of Acquiring More Information: Seriousness of the Suspected Risks of One's Conduct

The main legal reasons *in favor* of acquiring more information as DRI requires stem from the perceived risks of the actus reus one intends. The culpability of breaching DRI varies with how grievous the harm or illegality is that the subsequent actus reus one intends or contemplates would risk. The greater the harm or illegality one suspects one's subsequent conduct may produce, the stronger one's reason to inform oneself about whether this harm or illegality will result if one does the act (provided one remains committed to it).

Suppose someone will pay me $20 to push a button. I want the money but am unsure what the button does, though I can investigate. If I believe there's a 30 percent chance it would erase the valuable contents of Bryan's hard drive, this provides some reason for me to inform myself about whether this suspected risk will materialize if I act as I want to. Failing to do so when I easily could manifests some disrespect toward Bryan, and his right to control his property. But compare this to the situation where I believe there is a 30 percent chance the button is wired to a bomb that might go off in a shopping center. I now have a much, much stronger reason to acquire more information about whether the harm will ensue if I press the button. Not investigating in feasible ways here manifests far more insufficient regard than in the first case.

A similar point applies if we focus not on harm, but on illegality involved in the actus reus if the inculpatory proposition turns out to be true. There is greater reason to acquire more information about the suspected inculpatory proposition if the proposition is (a) a fact that would make one's intended conduct treasonous than (b) the fact that one's individual tax return contains misstatements. Breaching DRI in (a), all else equal, is more culpable than in (b).

While the seriousness of the suspected risks of one's conduct is key in determining how culpable a particular breach of DRI is, notice that this factor is not likely to be crucial for homing in on the conditions where the equal culpability thesis is true. After all, to find out when this thesis holds, what we need to know is which willfully ignorant defendants are as culpable as the *similarly situated* knowing wrongdoers. For this, the risks involved must be held fixed.[30]

3. Legally Cognizable Costs of Acquiring More Information: Justifying Reasons for Preserving One's Ignorance

The other group of factors affecting the culpability of breaching DRI concerns the *costs*—to oneself or others—of acquiring more information. Such costs, assuming the law should recognize them, provide support (i.e., justifying reasons) for not acquiring more information and thus lessen one's culpability for breaching DRI. Recall, however, that my theory of culpability does not consider *actual* motives—that is, the goals one sought to obtain (the costs one sought to avoid) by breaching DRI. Rather, my theory looks at the facts the defendant was aware of, and asks what legal reasons against acquiring more information (i.e., what legally cognizable justifying reasons[31] for breaching DRI) can reasonably be assumed to exist on those facts.[32]

This group of factors could cover many considerations. Acquiring more information about the inculpatory proposition might be *difficult* and require expertise that is costly to obtain. It might be dangerous or entail risks to self or others—for example, if bad actors threaten to harm oneself or third parties should one's snooping be detected. Acquiring more information about one's suspicions might be time-consuming or cripplingly expensive. It might conflict with valuable projects or commitments, or it may be emotionally burdensome should it require confronting past traumas. It could also burden relationships with loved ones—as in *Overly Trusting Parent* from Chapter 3.

Furthermore, obtaining more information could require compromising one's ethical commitments—for example, if one can get more information only through threats or coercion (not to mention torture). This, too, would be a cost of conforming to DRI. Similarly, learning more might conflict with one's professional or other role-based obligations—as with Deborah Hellman's cases of doctors and lawyers from Chapter 3 whose investigations were constrained by duties of loyalty to patients or clients. Such costs in the ethics or professional responsibility realm are also legally cognizable costs that could help justify preserving one's ignorance.

Recall, however, that DRI only requires obtaining information in reasonably *available ways*. At the extreme, if informing oneself about one's suspicions becomes too costly, the investigatory steps may cease to qualify as reasonably available. Thus, when DRI requires acquiring more information at all, we will be within the realm of investigatory steps are

---

[30] We saw the reasons for this in Chapter 1, Section IV, when formulating the equal culpability thesis.

[31] I use "legally cognizable" reasons, or costs, because I'm concerned with normative culpability. Posited culpability tracks the reasons the law *actually* recognizes. Legally cognizable reasons, which help determine normative culpability, are the ones it is legitimate for the law to recognize—or more simply, the ones it should.

[32] Actual motives, if known, for declining to inform oneself as DRI requires could be *evidence* of what reasons exist in favor of breaching DRI—on the facts one is aware of.

available—that is, where acquiring more information is not too costly to be reasonable to expect. Nonetheless, even within this realm, there can be costs to acquiring information that partially (if not fully) justify one's failure to do so. These are the justifying considerations I'm mapping here.

Recall also that DRI's demands are not limited to gathering new information; it also requires not blocking information otherwise easily coming one's way. Not only is breaching DRI more culpable, all else equal, the less costly it would be to go out and investigate one's suspicions, but the same is true the more costs one incurs to *avoid* pertinent information one naturally would acquire. Exerting effort to wall oneself off from freely available information—say, by taking a detour on the way to work to avoid seeing the bad thing one suspects one might—can be an especially egregious investigatory failure. This likely explains why some courts require that the defendant take affirmative steps to avoid knowledge in order for a willful ignorance jury instruction to be appropriate.[33] Taking steps to insulate oneself from information otherwise freely coming one's way is likely to be more costly than declining to go dig up new information. In the former case, one shows oneself willing to pay something of value to avoid information one could have gotten at no cost. By contrast, in the latter case, one only displays an unwillingness to *incur* costs to obtain information it would be costly to acquire. The former is akin to saying "I'll give you $100 to put this blindfold on me," while the latter is like saying, upon finding out that getting more information would cost $100, "No thanks, I'd rather not pay that." If it's information one ought to have, the former is worse than the latter, all else equal.

Finally, bear in mind that the law does not, and *should* not, recognize all the possible burdens of acquiring more information as fully or partially justifying reasons for not doing so. On my theory, the normative culpability of breaching DRI is a function of the balance of reasons the law *should* recognize for or against the breach. It's important to determine what these are. For instance, if acquiring more information likely would cause harm to others—especially physical or emotional, but perhaps also financial (if imposed on others)—it's plausible that the law should recognize these costs as helping to justify breaching DRI. If great enough, these costs might even fully justify not acquiring any more information. Likewise, if acquiring more information would infringe one's ethical or professional duties (as in Hellman's doctor or lawyer cases), the law plausibly should recognize these as reasons for not acquiring more information. By contrast, other everyday costs seem less worth recognizing in law: such as when investigating requires a (not disproportionate) amount of effort, or if it costs some money one would rather use on

---

33 *See, e.g.*, United States v. Giovannetti, 919 F.2d 1223, 1228 (7th Cir. 1990). *See also Global-Tech*, 131 S. Ct. at 2071 (criticizing willful ignorance instructions that did "not require active efforts by an inducer to avoid knowing about the infringing nature of the activities," though ultimately approving the jury instructions).

luxury items. These are not the sorts of considerations the law should recognize as providing support for remaining ignorant.[34]

This is merely a preliminary discussion of the costs the law should recognize as helping to justify not acquiring the information DRI requires one to. I have not given a comprehensive list. The inquiry will necessarily be case-specific. For normative culpability, the question in each case is this: Given the facts the defendant was aware of when failing to acquire more information about his suspicions, what are the plausibly available reasons that could have led a law-abiding citizen to decide not to acquire more information? What legally cognizable aims might acquiring more information frustrate in the defendant's situation? The normative culpability of breaching DRI depends on this very fact-specific inquiry.[35]

4. Putting the Pieces Together: Applying the Insufficient Regard Theory to the Breach of DRI

Let me conclude by putting these factors together into a general account of how the culpability of breaching DRI is determined on my theory of culpability. Let ϕ be a course of conduct by defendant D that breaches DRI. D suspects inculpatory proposition p and is aware he can easily acquire more information about p by doing something besides ϕ. But D does ϕ *knowing* and *intending* that it will preserve his ignorance of p. This information was freely coming his way at little cost. By doing ϕ, he blocked it from reaching him.

On my theory, a threshold question is whether ϕ was caused at least in part by a failure of D's repulsion mechanism. Given DRI's recognition in law, the law calls on D's repulsion mechanism to motivate D (in some way or other) to inform himself about p. When he nonetheless does ϕ, his lack of contrary motivation is part of the cause of his ϕ-ing.

The next, harder question is *how much* insufficient regard for the relevant legally protected interests or values ϕ manifests. It directly corresponds to *the least amount of insufficient regard* (the smallest error in weighing the relevant legal reasons) it takes to get an otherwise law-abiding citizen to do ϕ on the facts D is aware of. How do we figure out

---

[34] Monetary costs likely must be above some substantial threshold—perhaps above a certain percentage of income or net wealth—to be a legally cognizable cost that could help justify the decision to remain in ignorance.

[35] One might think other factors are relevant to the culpability of breaching DRI. Consider two: whether one is aware one *can* investigate and whether one knows one *should*. Regarding the former, not investigating may seem more culpable when one didn't recognize the available methods of investigation. However, this is already taken into account on my view because culpability is a function of the costs and benefits of investigating. If on the facts as one (reasonably) believes them to be, there is nothing one plausibly can do to investigate, then the perceived costs to investigating would be extremely high—even if, unbeknownst to you, you easily could have investigated.

Alternatively, one might think culpability for not investigating is lessened if one honestly didn't believe one *should*. I think being culpable for preserving one's ignorance doesn't *require* believing one should investigate; one can breach DRI without that belief. (However, precisely how mistaken beliefs about normative matters impact culpability, and whether they lessen the culpability of not investigating, is a difficult issue that I cannot fully resolve here. For helpful discussion of related issues, *see* Doug Husak, Ignorance of Law (2016).)

this amount? There are two sets of reasons applicable to whether to ϕ: the legal reasons *against* ϕ on the facts D is aware of, R–, and the legal reasons (if any) in favor of ϕ on the facts D is aware of, R+.

Consider R– first. Since ϕ violates DRI and D knows ϕ will preserve his ignorance of p (e.g., his employees are defrauding customers), we know there are reasons in this group. They derive mainly from the harm or wrong that the truth of p would entail. The greater the harm or wrong involved in p—that is, the worse it would be to do the actus reus if p is true—the weightier the reasons in R–. That means there is a stronger case for not doing ϕ and instead obtaining more information about one's suspicions before doing the actus reus.

R– includes further costs as well. It also includes the costs to D (or others) that doing ϕ would entail. Here, more information about p was coming D's way with little effort had D not done ϕ. Thus, by doing ϕ, D incurred affirmative costs to prevent it from reaching him. Incurring these costs to create the barrier to obtaining otherwise freely available information is another reason against ϕ, which goes into the R– column.

Putting this together, the total weight of the legal reasons in R– (which count against doing ϕ and in favor of acquiring more information) is substantial. For simplicity, suppose R– = +10.

Now consider R+. These are the legally cognizable costs—to self or others—of acquiring more information about p. These are the justifying reasons for ϕ. There is greater reason in favor ϕ the more difficult, dangerous, harmful, or wrongful it would be to acquire more information about p. If there are significant burdens associated with investigating (e.g., if it may get one shot or harm one's children), then this adds reasons to R+. As we're concerned with paradigmatic willful ignorance, let's suppose there are only small costs in obtaining more information. Thus, the weight of the legal reasons in R+ is small. For simplicity, suppose it's +1.

The law must take a stand on what reasons go in R– and R+. Moreover, it must take a stand on how weighty the reasons are in each. The law can get this wrong. But we are concerned with normative culpability here, so let's assume the law attaches appropriate weights to the reasons in R– and R+. Since ϕ violates DRI, R– should substantially outweigh R+. Thus, ϕ is culpable.

Once we know the weight the law should attribute to the reasons in R– and R+, which bear on whether to ϕ, we can determine how much insufficient regard ϕ manifests. It equals the smallest error in weighing the applicable reasons that is needed to get an otherwise well-motivated citizen to do ϕ under the circumstances D is aware of. This corresponds to an amount of insufficient regard that is just slightly greater than the difference between the weights of the legal reasons in R– and R+. We're assuming that R– = 10 and R+ = 1. So D's ϕ-ing *manifests* slightly more than 9 units.[36] That is the smallest amount

[36] The absolute magnitude of these units doesn't matter as long as they stay constant across cases.

of error in weighing reasons needed to get the otherwise correctly motivated, law-abiding citizen to do ϕ.

This, then, shows how culpable it is for D to do ϕ in violation of DRI. It equals the insufficient regard ϕ manifests. To see whether this breach of DRI renders D as culpable as the analogous knowing wrongdoer, we have to add[37] (i) the culpability of doing ϕ to (ii) D's culpability for doing the actus reus with suspicions about the risks he remained willfully ignorant of by doing ϕ. If (i) + (ii) is as great as the culpability of the analogous knowing misconduct, it is not unfair to impute knowledge of the inculpatory proposition to D.[38]

IV. The Problem of Additivity: Preliminary Considerations

My account may face objections. One might question its implications in specific cases.[39,40] Or one might worry that DRI does not fit with traditional accounts of conditional

[37] In principle, this aggregation could employ more complex mathematical operations instead should it prove more normatively plausible. I needn't take a stand on this here, so in what follows I stick with addition for simplicity.

[38] It should be apparent how my account of willful ignorance is different from Tadros's, although he also posits a duty to investigate. *Cf.* TADROS, *supra* note 14, at 246–47, 258–61. My account, premised on the narrow duty DRI, is designed to answer a specific puzzle about how some reckless actors could be treated *as if* they possessed knowledge. My account singles out a particularly egregious kind of (subjective) recklessness that can substitute for knowledge—as needed to vindicate the willful ignorance doctrine. By contrast, Tadros is interested in whether willful blindness ever "manifests the degree and kind of vice for which the attribution of criminal responsibility is appropriate," and he argues it can. *Id.* at 258. I don't take issue with this claim. But Tadros is not concerned, as I am, to home in on the worst cases of willful ignorance, which surpass mere recklessness and are as culpable as knowing misconduct. He seeks to distinguish cases that are not appropriate for punishment from those that are. My account, by contrast, focuses on cases that are already within the proper scope of criminal liability, and I defend a claim about precisely how culpable they are. (This difference is also apparent from the fact that Tadros's investigative duty applies not just to those with suspicions of p, but even to actors who were unaware of the relevant risks but objectively should have investigated. *See id.* at 246–47.)

[39] Perhaps my account implausibly entails that Patty in *Overly Trusting Parent* is as culpable as an analogous knowing wrongdoer. Chapter 3 used this case to refute the unrestricted equal culpability thesis as overinclusive. Nonetheless, my account easily explains why Patty is less culpable than her knowing counterpart—at least where normative culpability is concerned. Because Patty desired not to break the law and only opted to transport her son's crate because she knew investigating would utterly destroy their fragile relationship, it's doubtful that whatever additional culpability she incurs from breaching DRI is enough to make her as culpable as a knowing wrongdoer. While her conduct displays at least as much insufficient regard as is displayed by recklessly transporting contraband having had no opportunity to investigate, it is doubtful that Patty is as culpable as a knowing wrongdoer because protecting this valuable relationship plausibly deserves some legal recognition as a partially justifying reason.

[40] Alternatively, perhaps my account gives the wrong result about Alexander and Ferzan's case of the hundred drug mules. Each is paid to transport a suitcase without looking inside, but only one of the hundred suitcases actually contains drugs. *See* ALEXANDER & FERZAN, *supra* note 27, at 34. Because each drug mule took only a 1/100 risk of transporting drugs, Alexander and Ferzan suggest it would be implausible to treat the one mule whose suitcase actually contains drugs as a knowing wrongdoer "merely because one disapproves of the reasons

obligation.[41] Nonetheless, these admit of answers. Instead, consider the largest worry for my view. One might wonder why it is legitimate to aggregate (I assume through addition[42]) the culpability of the two components of willful ignorance: breaching DRI and recklessly performing the actus reus while suspecting p. If these two quantities of culpability can be added together, why can't we supplement the reckless actor's culpability with the culpability of other bits of misconduct he does—say, cheating on his taxes?[43]

Properly answering this worry requires a theory of equal culpability imputation of mental states, which tells us when other bits of conduct, which in aggregate are as culpable as doing the actus reus with a missing mental state, M (like knowledge), is a justifiable basis for imputing M to the defendant. Defending such a theory is the task of Chapter 5. I'll argue that adding up the culpability of different bits of conduct, if sufficiently culpable in aggregate, can justify the imputation of M *only if* they all manifest insufficient regard for the same protected interests and values as doing the actus reus with M does.

This is a complex theory that requires unpacking. So while my full answer to the present objection must wait until the next chapter, let me offer some intuitive considerations

---

for undertaking" the risks in question. *Id.* Still, because the drug mules all unjustifiably declined to investigate, perhaps my account seems to have the implication that worries Alexander and Ferzan.

This worry is mistaken. Each drug mule has a very low credence in the inculpatory proposition. By CCP (from Chapter 3), this means there is a large culpability gap to be filled for the drug mule who does carry drugs to become as culpable as someone who knowingly does so. Thus, my account delivers Alexander and Ferzan's preferred result: the drug mule whose suitcase contains drugs is less culpable than his knowing counterpart.

41 On the standard account of conditional obligation, A has an obligation to ϕ conditional on C if all of the best possible worlds, according to the relevant standard of evaluation, where C is true are also ones in which A does ϕ. *See, e.g.*, Frank Jackson, *On the Semantics and Logic of Obligation*, 94 MIND 177 (1985) (discussing the "standard approach"). However, this seems not to hold for DRI. Some worlds in which the antecedent conditions of DRI are met and A fails to investigate still might be *better* in respect of culpability than some worlds in which the antecedent of DRI is met but A *does* investigate. Suppose A intends the actus reus, breaches DRI by not investigating, but then decides not to do the actus reus. This scenario seems better than the one where A complies with DRI, learns the inculpatory proposition is true, but then does the actus reus knowingly anyway.

This objection admits of several answers. One might reject the standard account of conditional obligation, as some philosophers have done. *See* Jackson, *id.* at 179–80. Alternatively, we might back off the claim that there is a conditional *duty* to investigate, asserting instead only that one has a weighty moral *reason* to investigate in virtue of intending the actus reus. However, this might seem weaker and less deontic than the claim I want to defend.

Thus, my preferred response is this: breaching the *pro tanto* obligation in DRI entails only that there is *one respect* in which one is more culpable than if one had complied. This allows that a person who fails to investigate still might be *on balance* less culpable for his conduct than the person who does investigate. (After all, DRI is a *pro tanto* obligation.) This amounts to claiming the standard analysis of conditional obligation does not apply to DRI. The standard analysis seems to apply only to claims about *on-balance* culpability, not contributors to (or *pro tanto*) culpability. This is why CBC was formulated as it is.

42 *Supra* note 37.

43 Thanks to Jake Ross, Steve Schaus, and Gideon Yaffe for pressing me on this point.

regarding willful ignorance to motivate the idea that the addition posited by my theory is legitimate.

The culpability of the components of willful ignorance—(i) breaching DRI and (ii) doing the actus reus while suspecting p (recklessly)—are fairly added together because they form one *unified course of conduct*. The full explanation of why this is so comes in Chapter 5, but already we can see this claim is intuitive. Both components are tightly connected in that (i) is an integral part of the deliberative process that gives rise to (ii). Part of the motivational process that issues in the willfully ignorant defendant's doing the actus reus is the information and apparent reasons he possessed while deliberating about how to act. What information he deliberates from, in turn, is a function of (i), that is, his failure to investigate the suspected risks of the actus reus. Thus, the failure to investigate is a part of the genesis of the willfully ignorant actor's performance of the actus reus and is legitimately considered together with it. Of course, there are line-drawing questions about where to say the process that generates some bit of behavior begins. But in general, the motivational and deliberative process that issues in a course of conduct is a proper basis for deciding how culpable that conduct is—as is clear from the fact that we decide, say, whether a homicide constitutes first-degree murder by asking whether it was premeditated.

Accordingly, there are intuitive grounds for thinking the culpability of breaching DRI can be added to that of doing the actus reus with suspicions. To fully vindicate this claim, we need a principled explanation for why (i) and (ii) are fairly seen as a unified course of conduct, such that the culpability of (i) can be added to that of (ii), as needed to justify imputing knowledge to the willfully ignorant. Explaining this key move is the task of the general theory of equal culpability imputation articulated in the next chapter. That will complete my defense of the willful ignorance doctrine, plus ground other related imputation principles in later chapters.

V. Getting Practical: Formulating Better Willful Ignorance Jury Instructions

Before offering my general theory of equal culpability imputation in the next chapter, I want to address some practical issues regarding the willful ignorance doctrine. My aim thus far has been to home in on the conditions where the equal culpability thesis holds. The importance of this task lies in the courts' traditional rationale for willful ignorance jury instructions. To remain faithful to this rationale, such instructions should permit the jury to convict a willfully ignorant defendant of a knowledge crime only when the trial evidence shows he acted with a form of willful ignorance that rendered his conduct as culpable as the analogous knowing wrong.[44] That is, it should be permitted only when the evidence shows RECT4 to be satisfied.

[44] Federal courts agree that willful ignorance instructions may be given only if it can reasonably be inferred from the evidence that the defendant was willfully ignorant. *See* United States v. Anthony, 545 F.3d 60, 64 (1st Cir.

But how do we implement this view in practice? Ideally, the approach should avoid both *overbreadth*—allowing willful ignorance to substitute for knowledge without equal culpability—and *underbreadth*—preventing it from substituting for knowledge although equal culpability is present. Both are unfair. Overbreadth is unjust to willfully ignorant defendants convicted of knowledge crimes despite this exceeding their desert. Underbreadth is also unfair, though perhaps less so. It would mean the law arbitrarily stops short of convicting defendants of knowledge crimes although it's deserved, but without a good rationale. The willful ignorance doctrine is on firmest normative footing when it minimizes these kinds of unfairness (though perhaps we should be more concerned to avoid overbreadth).

The question confronted in this section is how to manage this in practice. How do we formulate workable willful ignorance jury instructions that accurately track the conditions of equal culpability, thus minimizing overbreadth and underbreadth?[45] This task is particularly important because some might object that the restricted willful ignorance doctrine I've argued for is unworkable and will confuse juries. Jury confusion is a common worry in debates about the willful ignorance doctrine.[46] To combat this worry, this section shows how to formulate workable willful ignorance jury instructions that are nonetheless more normatively defensible.

An overly simple way to formulate normatively ideal willful ignorance instructions is to directly ask the jury to answer the question posed by RECT4: Was *this* defendant's decision to remain ignorant in breach of DRI sufficiently serious to make his conduct as culpable as the analogous knowing misconduct? It might initially seem that directly putting this question to the jury would be a way to perfectly track the conditions of equal culpability that RECT4 picks out.

However, this normatively ideal approach clearly is nonideal in practice. It is much too complex to be workable. Although the substance of this rule perfectly tracks the conditions of equal culpability, it is doubtful that actual juries could reliably apply it. Instead, substantial arbitrariness in application would likely result. The complexity of this rule is due in part to the many normative factors that affect the culpability of willful

---

2008); United States v. Reyes, 302 F.3d 48, 55 (2d Cir. 2002); United States v. Abbas, 74 F.3d 506, 513 (4th Cir. 1996).

45 A different approach might be to use broad, simple willful ignorance instructions, but restrict when they are given. Courts already do something similar, however, since they will not issue a particular instruction unless the jury could rationally infer from the trial evidence that the rule expressed in the instruction is satisfied. *See supra* note 44. (This prevents juries from being misled by irrelevant distractions.) Thus, existing practice already restricts giving willful ignorance jury instructions to cases where the defendant could at least *plausibly* be convicted on willful ignorance grounds, given the trial evidence. Hence, my focus is what willful ignorance jury instructions *should say*.

46 Jessica A. Kozlov-Davis, *A Hybrid Approach to the Use of Deliberate Ignorance in Conspiracy Cases*, 100 MICH. L. REV. 473, 486–87 (2001) (discussing whether willful ignorance instructions might be overly confusing to juries).

ignorance. Moreover, the normatively ideal approach requires the jury to answer the difficult counterfactual question of how culpable the analogous knowing actor is, and then determine if the actual defendant's culpability rises to this level. Courts should be reluctant to ask juries to engage in such a difficult and speculative task.

Instead, what's needed is an implementable *approximation* of the normatively ideal rule. We need willful ignorance jury instructions that can feasibly be applied by actual fact-finders while also doing better than existing approaches—particularly the unrestricted approach used by most courts—at tracking the conditions of equal culpability. We want our jury instructions to minimize the risk of overbreadth and underbreadth while remaining workable.

There are two main approaches to striking this balance. First, courts might be most concerned to maximize workability, while still improving the normative accuracy of the test the jury is to apply. Because simplicity is its main aim, I call this the Simple Approach. Second, courts might be more concerned to avoid what's plausibly seen as the comparatively greater injustice of overbreadth. Thus, courts might tolerate some degree of underbreadth to minimize overbreadth. This approach focuses on the worst forms of willful ignorance and makes sure to treat only these as a substitute for knowledge. I call this the Safe Approach. Consider each in turn.

A. THE SIMPLE APPROACH

This section sketches a normatively second-best approach that prioritizes workability while still increasing normative defensibility compared to existing doctrine. In pursuit of workability, simplifications and normative compromises are necessary. But this approach remains superior to the unrestricted approach (UECT), used by most circuits, and the restricted motive approach (RECT1), favored by the Eighth, Tenth, and Eleventh Circuits.

To formulate a normatively better rule, we must consider the factors bearing on the culpability of remaining ignorant. To reach a sufficiently simple approximation of the ideal, I set aside several of those seen previously in this Chapter and focus on the single most important factor that impacts the culpability of willful ignorance: whether the defendant was aware of legally cognizable circumstances[47] that help *justify* his decision to remain in ignorance. Thus, I set aside two other factors: one's level of confidence in the inculpatory proposition (which affects culpability via CCP), and incurring affirmative costs to avoid information about the inculpatory proposition. (These matter in the next section, though.)

Because I favor the view that motives do not impact the amount of insufficient regard an action manifests (as argued in Chapter 2), I do not claim the culpability of preserving one's ignorance is aggravated by acting with bad motives. Rather, I assume deciding to remain ignorant is culpable *unless* one is aware of circumstances that help justify this

[47] Because I'm concerned with normative culpability, I use "legally cognizable reasons" rather than "legally recognized reasons." The latter is more apt when discussing posited culpability.

decision. One incurs more culpability, all else equal, the less of a legally cognizable justification one is aware of for remaining ignorant. The fewer justifying factors one is aware of, and the less weighty they are, the more culpable one's decision to remain in ignorance is, all else equal—up to the point where one is aware of no legally cognizable justifications at all for remaining ignorant.

Of course, it will be difficult *ex ante* to specify all possible justifying factors in whose absence the decision to remain ignorant remains culpable. Thus, I think this should largely be left for the jury to determine. Still, this would be the only substantive normative question the jury would be asked to take a stand on. The present proposal does not ask the jury to reach an *all things considered judgment* about culpability.

That said, courts may decide that, in certain cases where remaining ignorant likely is justified, willful ignorance instructions should be withheld. Perhaps, following Deborah Hellman,[48] courts might hold that when a lawyer suspects her client is lying to her, deciding not to investigate these suspicions should not trigger willful ignorance jury instructions in perjury cases. Plausibly, the ethical costs of investigating all such suspicions would largely justify remaining in ignorance. Thus, courts might hold that willful ignorance instructions should be withheld in such cases. This would limit the willful ignorance doctrine through precedent.

Still, it normally should be for the jury to decide whether the defendant was aware of factors that help justify the decision to remain in ignorance. We can further increase workability by distinguishing different levels of justification for the decision to remain ignorant. This decision is *highly unjustified* when the defendant is aware of no justifying factors—as when the only explanation for remaining ignorant is the desire to preserve a defense against liability or to continue to get paid out of a conspiracy. This decision is *partially justified* when one is aware of factors that help justify ignorance but don't obviously do so fully—as when deciding not to investigate helps protect one's family from crippling financial hardship. Lastly, the decision is *fully justified* in cases where, for example, remaining ignorant is necessary to avoid the dangers of provoking an abusive spouse, or to avoid exposing others to serious risks of physical harm. The jury's job is easier if all it has to do is decide which of a small number of categories the present case of willful ignorance falls into.

Still, sorting cases into three such categories is harder than two. So to get the simplest rule, we should only ask juries to determine whether, on the facts the defendant was aware of, there were any *substantial justifying reasons* for the decision to remain ignorant. The jury should not be asked whether these factors strictly speaking are weighty enough to *fully* outweigh the reasons to investigate one's suspicions. Rather, on my proposed simplification, being aware of substantial justifications for not investigating would prevent the defendant's willful ignorance from satisfying the knowledge element of the crime.

[48] Deborah Hellman, *Willfully Blind for Good Reason*, 3 CRIM. L. & PHIL. 301, 308–11 (2009).

This would be true even if there might be reasonable disagreement as to whether these justifying circumstances are enough to *fully* justify the decision to remain ignorant. As long as remaining ignorant is *nearly justified*, the defendant would get the benefit of the doubt and not be deemed to satisfy the crime's knowledge element.

The practical benefit of this simplification is that juries would not be called on to make the fine-grained evaluation of whether the available justifications strictly speaking are enough to outweigh the reasons against preserving one's ignorance. Instead, if substantial justifying factors exist on the facts the defendant was aware of, this warrants presuming that his decision to remain ignorant does not confer enough extra culpability to make him as culpable as a knowing wrongdoer. Thus, the proposal adopts an *evidentiary presumption* to simplify the jury's task.

Putting all this together yields the following test:

Simple Rule: A defendant, D, who lacks actual knowledge of the inculpatory proposition, p, as required for crime C may nonetheless be deemed to know that p if and only if:

(1) D satisfies the basic definition of willful ignorance (i.e., suspects p and has reasonably available methods for informing himself whether p is true, but deliberately fails to use them); and

(2) The circumstances D is aware of do not include any *substantial justifying* factors (e.g., professional or ethical obligations, risks of harm to others, etc.) that provide significant support for D's decision not to inform himself about whether p is true.[49]

This makes it unnecessary for the jury to decide whether remaining in ignorance really is on balance justified. Instead, if it's a close call, D gets the benefit of the doubt and his willful ignorance may not substitute for knowledge. Thus, any substantial partial justifications for preserving one's ignorance are presumed to be enough to prevent the defendant's conduct from being as culpable as the analogous knowing wrong.

---

[49] This proposal is underinclusive. To further guard against this, we can add another condition to the Simple Rule. Recall one is more culpable if one has more serious suspicions, approaching knowledge, of the inculpatory proposition. There then is a smaller culpability gap to fill to become as culpable as a knowing actor. Thus, the decision to remain ignorant plausibly doesn't have to be a *highly unjustified*, devoid of *any* justifying factors, to make the defendant's conduct as culpable as a knowing wrong. Rather, in this case, even *slightly unjustified* decisions to remain ignorant would be enough. Thus, the further condition is this:

(3) But if willfully ignorant D has *high confidence* in p (i.e., falls just a little bit short of practical certainty), then any *even slightly unjustified* decision to remain ignorant is enough for treating him as knowing that p.

Thus, D's willful ignorance could substitute for knowledge even if the jury finds some *substantial* justification under the circumstances for not investigating—provided it also finds that this justifying factor is not weighty enough to *fully* justify the decision to remain ignorant. I omitted this from the Simple Approach for (wait for it) simplicity.

Unlike the normatively ideal rule, the Simple Approach approximates this ideal in an implementable way. It can be captured in the following jury instructions:[50]

> **Simple jury instructions:** You may find that the defendant acted knowingly if you find beyond a reasonable doubt that (a) the defendant suspected [the inculpatory proposition was true], but (b) he deliberately refrained from obtaining more information about whether his suspicions were correct, although (c) it was possible for him to do so, and (d) he was not aware of anything that helped justify the decision not to learn the truth (such as serious difficulty or danger to self or others in investigating, or conflicts with important obligations).
>
> However, the mere desire not to spend effort or money in investigating is *not* a justifying factor. Nor is the desire to preserve a defense against liability, or the desire to get paid from suspected criminal conduct. Factors such as these do not provide any legal justification for the decision not to inform oneself. [This paragraph can be edited to highlight the justifying circumstances relevant to the case at hand.]
>
> Finally, it is important to remember that, as stated in (a), you may not find that the defendant acted knowingly under this rule if you find that he did not actually suspect that [the inculpatory proposition was true].

These jury instructions are a practically feasible way to place the willful ignorance doctrine on a more secure normative footing than existing approaches. First, it solves the major problem of the Unrestricted Approach, championed by the Ninth Circuit. As seen in Chapter 3, allowing just any willful ignorance to substitute for knowledge is overbroad. Some willfully ignorant actors are not as culpable as the analogous knowing wrongdoers. The Simple Approach largely avoids this problem by ruling out cases of willful ignorance where there is at least a substantial (even if not full) justification for remaining ignorant. By contrast, the Restricted Motive Approach of the Eighth, Tenth, and Eleventh Circuits was flawed not only because it allowed motives to impact culpability but because it arbitrarily singled out certain bad motives—which might themselves be justified under the circumstances—as necessarily inculpatory. The Simple Approach avoids these problems as well. Accordingly, the Simple Approach is a major improvement over the status quo, while remaining workable.

B. THE SAFE APPROACH

Even with this normative improvement over the status quo, courts might still be concerned about overbreadth—that is, convicting willfully ignorant defendants of knowledge crimes even when less culpable than knowing wrongdoers. This section sketches

[50] These are loosely modeled on the instruction discussed in *Heredia*, 483 F.3d at 917.

two restrictions that can easily be added to the Simple Approach to further reduce the risk of overbreadth. Although these restrictions make the rule underinclusive, this might reasonably seem an acceptable trade-off—particularly if one sees greater injustice in overbreadth than underbreadth. Thus, this section aims to articulate the "safest" version of the willful ignorance doctrine.[51] The idea is to focus on the worst cases of willful ignorance by adding further conditions to the Simple Approach. By allowing only the most culpable willfully ignorant actors to be convicted of knowledge crimes we can further reduce the risk of punishing defendants in excess of their culpability.

Toward this end, recall the two culpability-enhancing factors set aside in pursuit of maximum simplicity. One was the strength of one's suspicions about the inculpatory proposition. If these suspicions are strong, then by CCP there will be a smaller gap to fill to get the willfully ignorant actor up from the level of the purely reckless actor to that of the analogous knowing actor. Thus, to home in on the worst cases of willful ignorance, we should require that *the defendant has a level of suspicion in p that comes close to knowledge*.

Another culpability-enhancing feature, seen previously, was to incur affirmative costs to prevent oneself from learning the truth about one's suspicions. This likewise enhances the culpability of the decision to remain ignorant. After all, if one is willing to *pay* to wall oneself off from information one would otherwise get for free, this shows that unjustifiably remaining in ignorance is *even* more important to one, thus enhancing one's culpability.

Thus, to home in on the worst cases of willful ignorance, we need to add two more conditions to the Simple Approach: (a) that the defendant had *serious* suspicions about the inculpatory proposition, approaching (if not quite reaching) knowledge, and (b) that she incurred affirmative costs to block herself from receiving relevant information that was otherwise coming her way. Both enhance culpability, all else equal.

Consider more carefully how these additional restrictions might be implemented. Regarding the first, my suggestion is again to ask juries to distinguish between two categories of willfully ignorant actors: (a) those who believe the inculpatory proposition is *quite likely* to be true, while still falling short of practical certainty, and (b) those who merely have *slight suspicions*. There is a smaller culpability gap to fill in the former case. Thus, we can home in on the more culpable willfully ignorant actors by insisting that the defendant must have the former type of *serious suspicions* (just short of knowledge) that p is true for the willful ignorance doctrine to apply. How serious must these suspicions be? I suggest using a cutoff that is familiar from the civil context: the *more-likely-than-not* standard. Thus, the present proposal is that to further reduce the risk of injustice, courts should replace prong (1) of the Simple Rule with this:

---

[51] The thought is similar to the intuition behind "J. Ross's Principle." *See* LARRY TEMKIN, RETHINKING THE GOOD 40 (2011) (discussing several claims reflecting the idea that it can be "rational to follow certain theories for the purposes of practical reasoning; acting *as if* they were true, even if one has most reason to *believe* that another theory is, in fact, more likely to *be* true").

(1*) D acts with a "serious form of willful ignorance," which is present when D not only satisfies the basic definition of willful ignorance (i.e., suspects p and has reasonably available methods for informing himself whether p is true, but deliberately fails to use them), but also believes it is more likely than not that p is true, and . . .

The second additional restriction concerns affirmative steps to block information otherwise coming one's way. Such steps enhance culpability when costly. Being willing to *pay* something to wall yourself off from information you could and should have obtained for free manifests even more insufficient regard for the relevant interests and values, all else equal. Thus, cautious courts might want to make incurring such affirmative costs a further requirement. Some have done just this.[52] This suggests adding a third condition to the Simple Rule:

(3) D also must go further and take affirmative steps that are *costly* to himself—either financially or in terms of time commitment or other things he cares about—to prevent himself from receiving further information about p that he otherwise would have received.

When all three requirements are satisfied, we'd have a case that is fairly deemed one of the worst cases of willful ignorance (absent justifications or excuses). Willfully ignorant defendants who satisfy (1*), (2), and (3) are (all else equal) the most culpable of the bunch. The risk of unjustly punishing them under the willful ignorance doctrine—that is, convicting them of knowledge crimes despite their being less culpable than analogous knowing wrongdoers—will be as low as we can realistically achieve. Particularly cautious courts concerned to avoid injustice can reasonably take the safe option and add these further restrictions to the Simple Approach.

Can these additional restrictions on the willful ignorance doctrine also be implemented in workable jury instructions? Consider:

Proposed Safe Jury Instructions: You may find that the defendant acted knowingly if you find beyond a reasonable doubt that all of the following are true:

(a) The defendant believed it was more likely than not that [the inculpatory proposition was true], *but*

(b) He deliberately refrained from obtaining more information about whether his suspicions were correct, *although*

(c) It was possible for him to do so, *and*

[52] *See, e.g., Giovannetti*, 919 F.2d at 1228.

(d) He was not aware of anything that helps justify the decision not to learn the truth of his suspicions (such as serious difficulty or danger to himself or others in investigating, or conflicts with other obligations), *and*

(e) He took steps that were costly to him (either financially or in terms of time commitment or other things he cared about) to prevent himself from receiving further information about [the inculpatory proposition], which he otherwise would have received.

[The last two paragraphs of the instructions would be as before—providing examples of the justifications mentioned in (d), and reminding the jury, per (a), that the defendant had to *actually* suspect the inculpatory proposition.]

I doubt these instructions are that much harder to follow than what juries are routinely called on to apply in other technical cases involving, say, securities fraud, or products liability with complex causal chains. I have faith that most juries will be up to the task most of the time.[53,54]

---

[53] Another way to reduce jury confusion, adopted by some courts, is to give willful ignorance instructions only when the defendant opens the door by denying he had knowledge. Willful ignorance instructions shouldn't be available in every case, but only when the knowledge element is contested. *See* United States v. Reyes, 302 F.3d 48, 55 (2d Cir. 2002) (willful ignorance instructions given "when a defendant *claims to lack some specific aspect of knowledge* necessary to conviction but where the evidence may be construed as deliberate ignorance" (emphasis added)).

[54] It may further increase workability to formulate affirmative investigative duties. Specifying ex ante what investigations must be undertaken in different contexts would help actors guide their conduct and provide fair warning. Affirmative investigative duties could be tethered to different roles. Different investigative duties might attach in virtue of one's (1) professional responsibilities (as doctor, lawyer, manager, accountant, compliance officer, government official, teacher, etc.), (2) personal responsibilities (as parent or caregiver), or (3) role relative to other wrongdoers (i.e., a duty to inform oneself so as to avoid complicity). Formulating specific role-based investigative duties would be valuable, but I can't do so here.

5 Toward a Normative Theory of Equal Culpability Imputation

THE WILLFUL IGNORANCE doctrine is a *mens rea imputation principle*. It says that under certain conditions, a mental state *other* than knowledge—willful ignorance—can satisfy the knowledge element of a crime. Suppose Denise is willfully ignorant about whether the company she is CEO of is disposing of hazardous waste without a permit. This could be a criminal offense if done knowingly.[1] The willful ignorance doctrine allows courts to impute to her the knowledge that the company lacks the right permit. Her willful ignorance can substitute for the knowledge required for guilt—at least in certain conditions. Which ones? Equal culpability. What grounds imputing knowledge to a willfully ignorant actor is that her conduct is as culpable as the analogous knowing conduct. The doctrine thus is an *equal culpability* mens rea imputation principle.

In the last two chapters, I examined the scope of this doctrine. The aim was to say when acting in willful ignorance really is as culpable as acting knowingly. But deeper worries linger. Even if equal culpability is *necessary* for this mode of imputing knowledge to the willfully ignorant, does it provide *sufficient* justification? This chapter confronts two such deeper objections. One is pressing for practitioners within an existing legal framework (courts and litigants), but admits of straightforward answers. The other is a harder

[1] 42 U.S.C. § 6928(d)(2)(A) (imposing penalties on anyone who "knowingly treats, stores, or disposes of any hazardous waste identified or listed under this subchapter without a permit").

normative problem for those who make law. Answering it requires a general theory of equal culpability imputation, which it's the aim of this chapter to provide.

The practitioner's worry concerns the legality of mens rea substitution principles. Doesn't imputing knowledge to Denise, on the ground that her willful ignorance makes her as culpable as the analogous knowing actor, violate the principle that courts must apply the law as written? If the crime charged expressly requires knowledge, how can it be *legal* to convict a defendant of it despite not actually having knowledge?[2] Doesn't that violate the so-called *principle of legality*?[3] Often this principle is rendered *nulla poena sin lege* ("no penalty without a law"). The idea is that it is not legally permitted to penalize someone for an action without a law prohibiting that conduct. Convicting Denise seems in tension with this principle because she did not actually satisfy the knowledge element of the crime. How can her conviction—and the willful ignorance doctrine that underwrites it—be legal?

Courts deploy a range of arguments to deal with this worry when approving willful ignorance jury instructions—from legislative intent to the idea that mens rea terms should be given their common law meanings. If such arguments fail, the legality of the willful ignorance doctrine might be called into question. Nonetheless, as Husak and Callender point out, the fix for any remaining legality problems is to advocate for statutory reforms that redefine knowledge so that willful ignorance is allowed to satisfy the knowledge element of crimes (e.g., by replacing "knowledge" and similar terms with "knowledge or willful ignorance" or the like). Calling for such statutory reforms is always an option for commentators.

However, this is not the end of the matter. It points the way to a deeper question that remains unanswered. We still need to know *why* such statutory reforms would be defensible. Even if lingering legality problems for the willful ignorance doctrine (if any) can be solved through statutory reforms, lawmakers would still want to know why this would be substantively justified. Why is it a normatively defensible reform to adopt? Why *should* the law allow willful ignorance to substitute for knowledge under conditions of equal culpability? Answering this tougher question is the main thing I seek to accomplish in this chapter. To do so, I offer a general theory of equal culpability mental state imputation, which aims to explain when and why equal culpability imputation is justified on normative grounds.

Notice that this issue is not limited to the willful ignorance doctrine. It arises for a range of criminal law doctrines. Many other rules can plausibly be seen as equal culpability imputation principles, which allow the court to treat defendants *as if* they satisfied

---

[2] *See* United States v. Jewell, 532 F.2d 697, 706 (9th Cir. 1976) (en banc) (Kennedy, J. dissenting) ("When a statute specifically requires knowledge as an element of a crime, . . . the substitution of some other state of mind cannot be justified even if the court deems that both are equally blameworthy.").

[3] Douglas N. Husak & Craig A. Callender, *Wilful Ignorance, Knowledge, and the "Equal Culpability" Thesis: A Study of the Deeper Significance of the Principle of Legality*, 1994 Wis. L. Rev. 29 (1994).

some element of the crime although they actually don't. For example, recklessness, knowledge, or purpose can all substitute for negligence, and this rule is plausibly based on the idea that the former are at least as culpable as the latter.[4] Similarly, the *voluntary intoxication doctrine* allows negligence (unawareness of a risk) plus intoxication for which one is responsible to substitute for recklessness (awareness of a risk).[5] This, too, is plausibly seen as an equal culpability mens rea imputation principle.[6] The same might be said for the *doctrine of transferred intent*, which allows the intent to commit one crime, or victimize one person, to transfer to the commission of another crime, or to the victimization of another person.[7] Likewise, while the felony murder and Pinkerton doctrines are not substitution principles involving specifically mens rea elements, one might nonetheless try to justify them as equal culpability imputation principles.[8]

These doctrines, like the willful ignorance doctrine, face questions about their normative legitimacy. One might think some of them sweep too broadly and are not normatively justified as they stand—even if any legality problems they raise can be solved through statutory reforms. Perhaps not all the equal culpability imputation principles currently recognized in law *should* be encoded by statute in their current form. Thus, we want a normative theory of equal culpability imputation to tell us when this is or isn't the case, so we can know which of the many imputation principles in current law should be retained, reformed or rejected.

The main aim of this chapter is to offer such a theory of equal culpability imputation. Section I sets the stage by offering a taxonomy of equal culpability imputation principles. Section II confronts the legality problem as applied to the willful ignorance doctrine, and I sketch the main moves that have been suggested in response. However, I argue that even if these can support the willful ignorance doctrine as a legally valid fixture of US federal law, a deeper question remains about why such imputation principles are normatively defensible. That is the question I'll go on to offer a general theory to answer. Drawing on my theory of culpability from Chapter 2, Section III articulates my account of when and why equal culpability imputation is normatively legitimate. In Section IV, I use this account to argue that some equal culpability imputation principles are justified, while others require substantial revisions. While the transferred intent doctrine involves a justified form of equal culpability imputation, the felony murder rule and Pinkerton doctrine must be heavily restricted if they are to be justified on equal culpability grounds. Finally,

---

4 Model Penal Code (MPC), § 2.02(d)(5).

5 MPC, § 2.08(2) ("When recklessness establishes an element of the offense, if the actor, due to self-induced intoxication, is unaware of a risk of which he would have been aware had he been sober, such unawareness is immaterial."); Wayne LaFave, 2 Subst. Crim. L. § 9.5 (2d ed.) (summarizing intoxication doctrine similarly).

6 Gideon Yaffe, *Intoxication, Recklessness, and Negligence*, 9 Ohio St. J. Crim. L. 545, 551 (2012) (describing the intoxication doctrine as a "mens rea substitution principle").

7 Douglas N. Husak, *Transferred Intent*, 10 Notre Dame J.L. Ethics & Pub. Pol'y 65 (1996).

8 Paul Robinson, *Imputed Criminal Liability*, 93 Yale L.J. 609, 616–20 (1984) (analyzing felony murder and Pinkerton rules as equal culpability imputation principles).

in Section V, I revisit the willful ignorance doctrine and argue that it too is normatively justifiable, thus completing the book's overall defense of this doctrine.

I. The Structure of Equal Culpability Imputation Principles

A. IMPUTATION PRINCIPLES GENERALLY

In his seminal discussion, Paul Robinson observes that equal culpability imputation principles provide that "an element should be imputed because the actor is as culpable as if he had in fact satisfied the element."[9] In general, imputation principles can vary depending on what type of element is imputed and what antecedent conditions trigger the imputation. In their simplest form, they have the following form:

> IMPUTATION SCHEMA: When defendant D satisfies certain conditions, C, then D may be treated as if he satisfied some missing element(s), E, of the crime charged (i.e., E may be imputed) even though D does not actually satisfy E.

When the missing elements are mens rea elements, we have a *mens rea imputation principle.* If actus reus elements are imputed, it's an *actus reus imputation principle.* Where a mens rea imputation principle has triggering conditions that themselves involve mens rea, we have a *mens rea substitution principle*. Such principles allow courts to impute the mens rea of a crime when one has some *other* mens rea, perhaps together with other conditions like equal culpability.[10]

While actus reus imputation principles exist,[11] by far the most interesting imputation principles are the mens rea substitution principles. The willful ignorance doctrine is a clear example. It allows willful ignorance to substitute for knowledge under conditions of equal culpability. The voluntary intoxication doctrine, in allowing negligence to substitute for recklessness in cases of self-caused intoxication, fits here as well.[12] The same is true for the rule that a higher mens rea can substitute for a lower mens rea.[13] The doctrine

---

[9] *Id.* at 620.

[10] In principle, there may be other kinds of imputation principles depending on the element imputed. Robinson discusses circumstance imputation principles, for instance. *See id.* at 614 & n.12. Perhaps the burglary of a store might be grounds for imposing liability for burglary of a dwelling if the actor believed it to be a dwelling. This hypothetical principle would take a particular mens rea (false belief that one is burglarizing a dwelling) as the basis for imputing the attendant circumstance of burglarizing a dwelling—even if one in fact only burglarized a store.

[11] For instance, acts of an innocent person can be imputed to you if you caused her to produce a prohibited result. *See id.* at 614; MPC § 2.06(2); 18 U.S.C. § 2(b).

[12] Robinson, *supra* note 8, at 640 (analyzing the intoxication doctrine as a negligence-for-recklessness substitution principle).

[13] *See supra* note 4.

of transferred intent can be seen as a mens rea substitution principle,[14] as can the felony murder rule.[15] The latter says that if one's felony (or attempted felony) proximately causes an unintended death, this is the antecedent condition for imputing the mens rea of murder (purpose or knowledge as to death).[16]

Some imputation principles don't neatly fit into the above-mentioned categories. The triggering conditions and imputed elements might involve a combination of mens rea and actus reus elements. The Pinkerton doctrine, for example, says a co-conspirator can be held liable for the crimes of co-conspirators within the scope of their criminal agreement and for foreseeable crimes beyond the scope of the agreement.[17] The triggering conditions are membership in the conspiracy plus further crimes by co-conspirators. The rule permits the imputation of an entire crime (a whole set of elements), and so is a hybrid imputation rule.

B. THE ROLE OF EQUAL CULPABILITY

There are two ways to count as an equal culpability imputation principle. Most simply, the notion of equal culpability might be expressly included in the triggering conditions of the imputation rule. However, I am not aware of any examples of this in the law. The second, more realistic route is for the equal culpability rationale to be *implied* from the normative justification that courts offer for the imputation principle. This is what we see with the "traditional rationale" given for the willful ignorance doctrine—namely, that willful ignorance should satisfy the knowledge element of a crime when and because one's willful ignorance makes one as culpable as a knowing actor.[18] Thus, the second way to qualify as an equal culpability imputation principle is for the relevant imputation to be *grounded in* (i.e., justified by) equal culpability. That is, imputing an element can be justified in virtue of the fact that the triggering conditions ensure that one is as culpable as if one had acted with the missing element. Thus, a rule counts as an equal culpability imputation principle only if the courts applying the principle also are committed to the following "because claim":

> EQUAL CULPABILITY GROUNDS IMPUTATION: The relevant missing elements E may be imputed to D in triggering conditions C (even though D does not actually

[14] Robinson, *supra* note 8, at 650 ("The actor is, by normal rules . . . , liable for two offenses: attempted murder of the person he misses and negligent or reckless homicide of the person he hits. Using the notion of cumulative culpability, one may aggregate the culpability of these two offenses to impute to the actor the mental state required for murder.").

[15] Robinson, *supra* note 8, at 616–20 (analyzing felony murder as an imputation principle).

[16] WAYNE LAFAVE, 2 SUBST. CRIM. L. § 14.5 (2d ed.) ("At the early common law one whose conduct brought about an unintended death in the commission or attempted commission of a felony was guilty of murder.").

[17] Pinkerton v. United States, 328 U.S. 640 (1946). *See also infra* note 69.

[18] Global-Tech Appliances, Inc. v. SEB S.A., 131 S. Ct. 2060, 2069 (2011) ("[t]he traditional rationale for this doctrine is that defendants who behave in [a willfully ignorant] manner are just as culpable as those who have actual knowledge."); *see also* Husak & Callender, *supra* note 3.

satisfy E) *because* D's satisfying C makes D at least as culpable as if D had actually satisfied E.

However, this claim requires refinement. The antecedent conditions, C, might permit imputing an element, E, even when being in C does *not* actually render the defendant as culpable as if she had satisfied E. That is, the triggering conditions might be *overbroad* compared to the cases in which imputation is actually justified on equal culpability grounds. This, I argued, is what we see with the Ninth Circuit's unrestricted approach to the willful ignorance doctrine.[19] It was overbroad in letting just any willfully ignorant action be punished as the analogous knowledge crime even where the former isn't as culpable as the latter.

Accordingly, normatively justified imputation principles should not only take equal culpability as the grounds for imputing missing elements but also *limit* this form of imputation to cases where the defendant really is as culpable as if he possessed the missing element. Why should equal culpability also *constrain* imputation? Because it's only when equal culpability is present that the current justification holds. Outside this domain, the present ground for imputation runs out. Thus, if willful ignorance is the antecedent condition that triggers imputing knowledge, say, then the equal culpability rationale entails that this imputation is justified *only when* the former is as culpable as the latter—provided no other affirmative ground for the imputation exists.[20] This limit flows from the internal logic of taking equal culpability to ground imputation generally. EQUAL CULPABILITY GROUNDS IMPUTATION thus should be replaced with:

> EQUAL CULPABILITY GROUNDS AND LIMITS IMPUTATION: The relevant missing elements E may be imputed to D in triggering conditions C (even though D does not actually satisfy E) *when, only when, and because* D's satisfying C makes D at least as culpable as if D had actually satisfied E (at least insofar as imputing E to D is to be justified on equal culpability grounds rather than some other affirmative rationale).

[19] *See* Chapter 3, Section 1 (criticizing the unrestricted equal culpability thesis endorsed by the Ninth Circuit).

[20] Note that the absence of equal culpability need not absolutely bar the desired imputation. Imputation might be justified on grounds other than equal culpability. Robinson discusses several examples—for example, the evidentiary theory that people in the triggering conditions are likely to actually satisfy the imputed element, or the purely consequentialist, deterrence-based theory of imputation. Robinson, *supra* note 8. However, for present purposes I assume we are dealing with imputation principles for which there is no other acceptable affirmative justification besides equal culpability. For the doctrines I discuss in this chapter, equal culpability plausibly provides the best available justification. Nonetheless, I sidestep this complication by talking mainly about the limits only of *equal culpability based imputation*—not on imputation generally.

Thus, defensible equal culpability imputation principles not only conform to IMPUTATION SCHEMA, but entail a commitment to EQUAL CULPABILITY GROUNDS AND LIMITS IMPUTATION.

Together, these two claims entail an aspirational goal. They entail that the triggering conditions of an equal culpability imputation principle should be limited such that being in them really does make one as culpable as if the imputed element had been present. The principle must make sure to limit the triggering conditions to the actual conditions of equal culpability in order to avoid overbreadth. Thus, I take it the *ideal* equal culpability imputation principle would be explicit about its reliance on equal culpability and the limits this carries:

> IDEAL EQUAL CULPABILITY IMPUTATION SCHEMA: Assuming defendant D does not actually satisfy some element(s), E, of the crime charged, E may nonetheless be imputed to D on an equal culpability theory *if and only if, and because* D satisfies triggering conditions C, which include (or obviously entail) the fact that *D is at least as culpable for his conduct as if E had actually obtained.*[21]

C. REACHING EQUAL CULPABILITY THROUGH AGGREGATION

One last wrinkle must be added here. As Robinson notes, some imputation rules allow equal culpability to be reached by aggregating (I assume through addition[22]) the culpability of distinct acts or their features.[23] The voluntary intoxication doctrine arguably fits this pattern.[24] We can see it as being based on an equal culpability rationale that uses aggregation. The thought is that the culpability of (i) negligently imposing a risk while intoxicated can be combined with that of (ii) getting oneself intoxicated while reckless or negligent as to the risk that it might lead one to behave dangerously when intoxicated. It's arguable that this can add up to a total amount of culpability as great as the culpability of (iii) recklessly imposing this same risk of harm.[25]

As seen in earlier chapters, the willful ignorance doctrine also fits this pattern. Willfully ignorant misconduct has two components: (i) deliberately preserving one's ignorance of the inculpatory fact, and (ii) subsequently doing the actus reus recklessly. I argued that

---

[21] It's not enough that D *accidentally* is as culpable as if he satisfied E. Instead, it must be in virtue of D's satisfying triggering conditions C that he is as culpable as if he satisfied E. Only then is there the right kind of basis for imputing E to D. My reasons for this come from the general theory of equal culpability imputation presented below.

[22] Aggregation in principle needn't involve addition. It could be another mathematical operation. However, I needn't settle this question here, so I continue using addition throughout for simplicity.

[23] Robinson, *supra* note 8, at 650 (imputing "the elements of a serious offense can be justified on a finding of equivalent culpability reached by aggregating the actor's culpability for two or more less serious offenses").

[24] *See supra* notes 5–6.

[25] Robinson, *supra* note 8, at 650.

the equal culpability thesis is true, and imputing knowledge is permitted, if and only if the culpability in (i) and (ii) adds up to at least that of the analogous knowing misconduct.

However, two worries must be addressed for it to be legitimate to use aggregation to reach equal culpability as needed to impute missing elements. First, we must avoid double-counting. Felony murder, for example, contains a rule that killing during a felony can be treated as murder only if the felony is sufficiently *independent* of the conduct that causes the killing.[26] Thus, battery will not suffice for the felony murder enhancement. If Reginald unjustifiably punches someone and the victim unforeseeably dies as a result, this will not be felony murder.[27] The felony here, battery, is not sufficiently independent of the lethal conduct to justify the felony murder enhancement. The conduct that constitutes (a) the felony (i.e., the punch) is the same as that which constitutes (b) the lethal action. It would be double-counting to add together the culpability of (a) and (b). There intuitively is only one action here, and its culpability cannot be counted more than once. There is nothing to aggregate.[28]

Determining what is or isn't double-counting is a hard metaphysical question that I cannot solve here. I take it to be a very case-specific issue, which raises difficult questions about how to describe and individuate actions. For present purposes, I'll simply rest easy with the stipulation that aggregation of culpability must avoid double-counting to be legitimate. Courts are likely to be at least as good as any theorist at figuring out what is or isn't double-counting in real cases.

The second worry is more important, and I tackle it head on through the theory I defend in Section III. Specifically, one might wonder whether there are any *limits* on which actions can have their culpability aggregated to reach equal culpability. Some courts worry that aggregation principles in general are "illogical."[29] The concern is that it would be impermissible to aggregate the culpability of *wholly unrelated actions*. Applied to the

---

[26] LaFave, *supra* note 16 ("Some cases have held that the collateral felony must be a felony which is 'independent' of the conduct which kills; it must involve conduct separate from the acts of personal violence which constitute a necessary part of the homicide itself. Thus, although rape, arson, robbery and burglary are sufficiently independent of the homicide, manslaughter and aggravated battery toward the deceased will not do for felony murder."); State v. Jones, 257 Kan. 856, 896 P.2d 1077 (1995) ("the lethal act cannot serve as the independent collateral felony necessary to support a felony-murder conviction").

[27] LaFave, *supra* note 16 ("Suppose *A* commits a battery on *B* with a deadly weapon but not intending to kill, and *B* unforeseeably dies therefrom, for example, *A*, with a knife, cuts *B* in the arm and *B*, a hemophiliac, bleeds to death. This constitutes manslaughter, not murder.").

[28] Robinson, *supra* note 8, at 651 ("cumulative culpability may also help explain felony-murder cases: The culpability for the underlying felony and for the killing . . . are aggregated to support conviction for a higher degree of homicide than would be justifiable otherwise"). The idea is that (a) the culpability of the felony plus (b) the culpability of (negligently? recklessly?) risking death equals (c) the culpability of a higher grade of homicide. But one cannot be convicted of *both* the felony and the higher grade of homicide. This is double-counting.

[29] Commonwealth v. Life Care Centers of America, 926 N.E.2d 206, 213 (Mass. 2010) (discussing the aggregation of different individuals' mental states to impute a collective mens rea to a corporation charged with a crime, and arguing that "aggregation of less culpable behavior to create more culpable behavior" is "illogical"). *See* Chapter 9 for more discussion of mens rea imputation to corporations.

involuntary intoxication doctrine, one might wonder why negligently creating risks while drunk is not too different from the prior act of getting oneself intoxicated to block the aggregation of their culpability. Similarly, why is deciding to remain ignorant of the inculpatory fact not too different from recklessly doing the actus reus for their culpability to be added together, as the willful ignorance doctrine suggests?

In Chapter 4, I offered the preliminary answer that it is legitimate to aggregate the culpability of the two bits of misconduct in willfully ignorant action because they constitute a "unified course of conduct." But why is this true, and why does it solve the problem? The theory I provide in Section III provides an explanation.[30] In so doing, it delineates the limits of using equal culpability as the basis for imputing missing elements to the defendant.

Before that, however, we must distinguish two objections to imputation principles in general. One is more practical and can be largely avoided for purposes of my project. I discuss this kind of worry in the next section before moving on in Section III to tackle the second, deeper question of what the normative basis for equal culpability imputation is.

II. The Practitioner's Problem vs. The Lawmaker's Problem

Recall the two remaining objections to equal culpability imputation principles. One is the *practitioner's worry*: Is there a sufficient legal basis for courts to apply the relevant imputation principle? Second is the *lawmaker's worry*: Would it be normatively sound for the lawmaker (typically legislatures, but perhaps courts where judge-made law is concerned) to adopt the relevant imputation principle?

This section focuses on the practitioner's worry. For a defendant who does not satisfy an element of the crime, practitioners (courts or lawyers) might wonder if can it be legally appropriate to convict her nonetheless because she is as culpable *as if* she had satisfied it? Doesn't this offend the principle of legality? I'll discuss several attempts to address this concern. I start with the most ambitious sort of argument, which rests on legislative intent or purposive theories of statutory construction. This kind of argument aims to provide a legal defense of equal culpability substitution in general. After that, I discuss two textualist arguments that have actually been employed by courts in defending the willful ignorance doctrine. These arguments are less ambitious in that they only aim to justify a specific imputation principle as applied to a specific statute—though they are also more likely to succeed. Nonetheless, they face limitations. So one might prefer to call for statutory reforms to truly lay the practitioner's legality worries to rest. Still, this leaves the core

---

[30] In a nutshell, being a unified course of conduct suggests that the different bits of conduct are sufficiently closely related. That roughly means, I'll argue, manifesting insufficient regard for the *same protected interests and values*.

normative question in the lawmaker's worry unresolved, which the rest of the chapter will aim to answer.

A. DEFENDING EQUAL CULPABILITY IMPUTATION GENERALLY: LEGISLATIVE INTENT AND PURPOSIVE ARGUMENTS

For practitioners seeking to defend equal culpability imputation principles in general, one strategy appeals to the idea that the legislature, in passing a statute setting out the elements of a crime C, *intended* for any defendant who behaved as culpably as if she had done C to have the missing elements imputed to her so she can be convicted of C. This strategy rests on a legislative intent theory of statutory interpretation.[31] This theory holds, roughly, that where a statute is ambiguous—for example, when a plausible question comes up as to the meaning or scope of a term it contains—courts can appeal to evidence of legislative intent (like floor debates or other forms of legislative history) to resolve the ambiguity—perhaps even by making additions or modifications to the semantic meaning of the statutory text.[32] This is a controversial theory, to be sure. But consider how the argument it suggests would go.

The argument envisions the legislature—focus on Congress for now—reasoning as follows. Congress wants to criminalize some general kind of conduct that is harmful or wrongful in a particular way. But knowing that it can't specify ex ante every specific variation of the conduct it wants to prohibit, Congress passes a law prohibiting only the *paradigm case* of this conduct, but it does so with the intent that any other equally culpable conduct (and perhaps that is culpable in the same way) should also fall within the ambit of the statute and be subject to the same penalties. Congress might pass a statute criminalizing, for example, knowing possession of drugs as the paradigm instance of the conduct it wants to prohibit, while also intending that any defendants who engage in similar conduct in ways that are equally culpable—for example, as when the actors are willfully ignorant—should have the missing element(s) imputed to them so they can be convicted of knowing possession as well. Thus, one might try to appeal to congressional intent to support an imputation principle like the willful ignorance doctrine.

---

[31] *See, e.g.*, John F. Manning, *Textualism and Legislative Intent*, 91 VA. L. REV. 419 (2005) (discussing Classical Intentionalism, which covers the sort of legislative intent theory I mean to discuss here). One could perhaps also construe this as a textualist view—that is, that the text of the statute just means whatever the legislature intended it to mean. I discuss other overtly textualist arguments below.

[32] As Manning explains it, "classical intentionalists emphasize that meaning depends on what the speaker actually intends to convey. (. . .) [T]he true meaning of [a] term as used on a particular occasion depends on the meaning intended by the speaker." *See* Manning *supra* note 31, at 428. Thus, "when the words of a statute leave a residue of ambiguity, intentionalists find it appropriate to examine the bill's internal legislative history for further evidence of what members of Congress 'intended.'" *Id.* (To be fair, in Manning's presentation, Classical Intentionalism also covers the bolder sort of purposivism where the text of a statute must be interpreted in light of the overarching purposes of the statute. However, I discuss this later as a separate, more radical theory.)

There are three major problems with this strategy. *First*, Congress may not actually have the required intent. It may not engage in reasoning like the above before passing the law, in which case there would be no basis for courts to adopt the imputation principle in question. *Second*, even if Congress did think through the matter and form the intention that equally culpable conduct should also be criminalized under the statute, there may be little or no evidence to prove it. This argumentative strategy can succeed only if there is enough available evidence to show that Congress really did possess the intent to also criminalize equally culpable conduct.

Third, and most damningly, there is a serious textual objection to this argument: If Congress intended to also criminalize any equally culpable conduct, why didn't it say so in the text of the statute? For example, if Congress really intended to criminalize not just knowing drug possession but also any related conduct that is equally culpable, why not include a provision stating this? Moreover, if Congress did not include language indicating that other conduct that is as culpable as the paradigm case of knowing drug possession also suffices for conviction, the text of the statute would not seem ambiguous in the way that, under this approach to statutory interpretation, is needed to allow looking at legislative history to support the imputation principle in the first place. Thus, I doubt this line of argument is likely to succeed.[33]

To avoid the worry that legislatures might lack the necessary intention to justify such imputation, one might try to defend equal culpability imputation by shifting to a broader *purposive theory* of interpretation.[34] This is roughly the view that courts should interpret a statute in light of the *purposes* for which it was enacted to give effect to those

[33] A possible response is that even if the legislature never considered whether equally culpable conduct should be punished the same as the paradigm case of the crime, courts are still justified in punishing equally culpable conduct the same as the paradigm case provided the legislature *would have intended that this be done* were the question put to them. Although unpopular today, such a hypothetical intent theory of statutory interpretation has received some discussion. Judge Learned Hand argued in a speech to the Massachusetts Bar Association in 1942 that when a statute requires interpretation that "[c]ourts must reconstruct the past solution imaginatively in its setting and project the purposes which inspired it upon the concrete occasions which arise for their decision." *See* Monarch Life Ins. Co. v. Loyal Protective Life Ins. Co., 326 F.2d 841, 845 (2d Cir. 1963) (quoting Judge Hand's speech). *See also* Carlos E. Gonzalez, *Reinterpreting Statutory Interpretation*, 74 N.C. L. Rev. 585, 608 (1996) (discussing the theory of imaginative reconstruction, which posits that "where no clear congressional intent on the issue at hand can be discerned, . . . a judge ought to put himself in the shoes of the enacting Congress and determine what it would have done had it squarely faced the novel issue"). Nonetheless, I take it that this hypothetical legislative intent theory is not ideal—most importantly because it requires so much speculation about what the legislature would intend. Moreover, there are difficult normative questions about why hypothetical intent—as opposed to actual intent—should have binding force at all.

[34] *See* Stephen Breyer, Active Liberty 88 (2005) (describing the "purpose-based approach" as focusing on "the 'reasonable member of Congress'" and asking "how this person (real or fictional), aware of the statute's language, structure, and general objectives (actually or hypothetically), *would have wanted a court to interpret the statute* in light of present circumstances in the particular case" (emphasis added)). *See also* Gonzalez, *supra* note 33, at 611–12 (describing Hart and Sacks's legal process approach as starting from the purposes that "ought to be attributed to the statute and to any subordinate provision of it which may be involved").

purposes. The least controversial version of this theory, I take it, says merely that courts should interpret a statute so as not to frustrate the aims it was passed to accomplish. More precisely:

> **Modest Purposivism:** There is a weighty reason (overridable only by an even more weighty reason like contrary intent explicitly appearing in the text) for courts to interpret and apply the statute in ways that *do not conflict with, frustrate or undermine* the underlying purposes for which the statute was passed—even where this requires expanding or amending the legal definition of certain statutory terms beyond their common-sense, nontechnical meanings.

Here then, in schematic form, is the argument this view would generate in support of equal culpability imputation. Let C designate the paradigm conduct that the statute in question criminalizes, and let C* designate some nearby conduct that is *just as culpable* as C but differs from C only in that someone who does C* fails to satisfy at least one element of the official statutory definition of C. Thus, the argument is this:

> The Argument from Modest Purposivism:
> (1) Modest Purposivism is true.
> (2) The underlying purpose of the statute criminalizing C is to protect a particular set of interests, rights or values, V.
> (3) It would *undermine* this purpose—that is, hinder the protection of V—to *decline* to interpret the statute criminalizing C so that the penalties imposed on C also are to be imposed on C*. That is, it would undermine the statutory purpose for courts *not* to impute the elements missing from C to those who do C*.
> (4) Therefore, the statute criminalizing C should be interpreted to permit imputing the elements missing from C to those who do C* (so that C* can be punished the same as C).

The crux of the argument is premise (3). For the argument to work, it has to be shown that the only way to avoid undermining the protection of V is to punish C* the same as C by imputing the missing elements of C to those who do C*.

A worry remains, however. One might object that it is tricky to prove in particular cases that *declining* to impute the missing elements of C to those who do C* would actually go so far as to *undermine* the purposes of the statute (i.e., to protect V, the relevant rights, interests and values). Granted, going ahead with the imputation and punishing C* the same as C when the two are equally culpable would plausibly protect V *more* than not doing this imputation. But is failing to do more to protect V the same as *undermining* the statute's underlying purpose of protecting V? Unless the answer is "yes," one might object that premise (3) in the argument is unsupported.

With my philosopher's hat on, I am inclined to think the answer to this question is "yes." Not doing more to protect someone or something, strictly speaking, can be described as undermining the protection of that person or thing. But I realize that the practically minded might dig in their heels and contest this—especially if they think there is some intuitive distinction between actively frustrating a purpose and merely failing to promote it. I can't take on the task of refuting this distinction here, however.[35] Accordingly, since many would regard this distinction as a genuine one, I conclude that the purposivist argument for equal culpability imputation in general is unlikely to be widely accepted.

B. NARROWER TEXTUALIST ARGUMENTS

1. Congressional Acquiescence

If we can't give a blanket defense of equal culpability imputation in general, there is more likelihood of success in considering each imputation principle on a statute-by-statute basis. In fact, this is the route that federal courts have generally taken when defending the willful ignorance doctrine. Two related textualist arguments in this vein are common.

The first is based on congressional acquiescence. The Ninth Circuit's 2007 decision in *United States v. Heredia* relied on such an argument in adopting the willful ignorance doctrine.[36] It dealt with a defendant charged with knowingly possessing narcotics in violation of 21 U.S.C. § 841(a)(1)—a classic knowledge crime.[37] In upholding Heredia's conviction of this crime under willful ignorance jury instructions, the court argued:

> Congress has amended section 841 many times since *Jewell* [approving the willful ignorance doctrine] was handed down, but not in a way that would cast doubt on our ruling. Given the widespread acceptance of *Jewell* across the federal judiciary, of which Congress must surely have been aware, we construe Congress's inaction as acquiescence.[38]

---

[35] Those who think there is an important difference between (i) undermining a statutory purpose and (ii) failing to maximally promote it can only get the present argument to succeed if they accept a bolder form of purposivism:

> **Bold Purposivism:** There is a weighty reason (overridable only by an even more weighty reason like a contrary intent explicitly appearing in the text) for courts to interpret and apply the statute in ways that *maximally promote* the underlying purposes for which the statute was passed—even where this requires expanding or amending the legal definition of certain statutory terms beyond their common sense, non-technical meanings.

Adopting this theory would avoid the problem with the argument from Modest Purposivism. However, I expect that Bold Purposivism will be even more controversial than its modest cousin—especially given the premium placed on judicial restraint in legal systems like ours. Accordingly, I doubt the Bold Purposivist line will be popular.

[36] 483 F.3d 913, 918–19 (9th Cir. 2007) (en banc).

[37] *Id.* at 917.

[38] *Id.* at 918–19.

Thus, the court reasoned that since Congress knew courts were interpreting the knowledge element of this crime to also cover cases of willful ignorance and amended the applicable statute *without* rejecting this interpretation, Congress can be taken to have endorsed—or at least acquiesced in—the practice of allowing willful ignorance to substitute for knowledge.

This seems like a fine argument for the Ninth Circuit writing in 2007 to rely on in approving willful ignorance jury instructions (which the Ninth Circuit had already endorsed in 1972 in the seminal case of *U.S. v. Jewell*[39]). However, there are two serious limitations to this argument. First, it is contingent and limited in scope. The acquiescence argument works only as applied to statutes like 21 U.S.C. § 841 that (a) had *already* been interpreted by courts to allow willful ignorance to substitute for knowledge, and (b) were revised numerous times by Congress without rejecting the courts' interpretation. Not all statutes—especially recent ones—will be like this. Second, this argument does not explain why the first instances of courts applying the willful ignorance doctrine were justified. What permitted courts to *start* interpreting statutes to allow the knowledge element to be satisfied by willful ignorance? To answer that question, we need more.

2. Give Statutory Terms Their Common Law Meanings

A second textualist argument appeals to the interpretive rule that technical legal terms in statutes—like mens rea concepts—should be construed in accordance with their traditional legal or common law meanings.[40] As Justice Jackson explained this interpretive canon,

> where Congress borrows terms of art in which are accumulated the legal tradition and meaning of centuries of practice, it presumably knows and adopts the cluster of ideas that were attached to each borrowed word in the body of learning from which it was taken and the meaning its use will convey to the judicial mind unless otherwise instructed. In such a case, absence of contrary direction may be taken as satisfaction with widely accepted definitions, not as departure from them.[41]

Thus, as a more recent Supreme Court case noted,

> where a common law principle is well established, . . . the courts may take it as a given that Congress has legislated with an expectation that the principle will apply except "when a statutory purpose to the contrary is evident."[42]

---

[39] 532 F.2d 697 (9th Cir. 1976).

[40] *See, e.g.*, U.S. v. Gray, 780 F.3d 458, 465 (1st Cir. 2015) (observing, in construing "malice" as an element in the crime of giving false information about a bomb threat, that "where a federal criminal statute uses a common-law term of established meaning without otherwise defining it, the general practice is to give that term its common-law meaning" (internal citations and alterations omitted)).

[41] Morissette v. United States, 342 U.S. 246, 263 (1952).

[42] Astoria Federal Savings & Loan Ass'n v. Solimino, 501 U.S. 104, 108 (1991).

This argument is similar in spirit to the congressional acquiescence argument, but with important differences. The previous argument was that Congress can be assumed to have acquiesced in an interpretation of a statute when it amends the statute numerous times while on notice of how courts are construing it, but Congress does not reject that construal. By contrast, the current argument is not about congressional acquiescence to an interpretation of a statute, but rather about *what Congress intended that statute to mean when first passed*. Congress is assumed to have known the common law or traditional meanings of widely used legal terms, and so absent any indication to the contrary, Congress can be assumed to have intended the common law meanings by its use of these terms. (This is a claim about the textual meaning of statutory terms.) Some courts have used this argument in approving the willful ignorance doctrine—as did *Jewell* itself.[43]

This argument seems more widely applicable than the congressional acquiescence argument. Unlike the acquiescence argument, this argument does not require courts to have already interpreted a term like "knowingly" in a statute to include willful ignorance and for Congress to have revised the statute numerous times without rejecting this interpretation. Rather, all the present argument requires is that when Congress passed the statute containing terms like "knowingly" or "knowledge," it is also the case that these terms were already widely assumed at common law to include willful ignorance (which it plausibly did, as we saw in discussing the history of the willful ignorance doctrine in Chapter 1[44]). Thus, the present argument can be used in the *first* case to interpret a statute that uses terms like "knowledge" or "knowingly."

While the present argument thus seems better than the acquiescence argument, it suffers from related limitations. In particular, what justified common law courts in construing terms like "knowledge" or "knowingly" to cover willful ignorance as well? The present textualist argument just pushes the justificatory question back one stage. It remains an open question why a given legal system was justified in *beginning* the practice of taking willful ignorance to satisfy the knowledge element of particular crimes. Perhaps legislative endorsement of the common law (like acquiescence to prior statutory interpretation) can serve to bless an *existing*, if perhaps questionable, practice of taking willful ignorance to substitute for knowledge, thus turning an interpretive practice that was once unlawful into one with legal support. But we still might wonder why the interpretive

---

[43] *Jewell*, 532 F.2d at 703. The court reasoned that "[n]othing is cited from the legislative history of the Drug Control Act indicating that Congress used the term 'knowingly' in a sense at odds with prior authority. Rather, Congress is presumed to have known and adopted the 'cluster of ideas' attached to such a familiar term of art" as "knowingly" and on this basis the court took willful ignorance to be a legitimate ground for finding knowledge. *Id.*

[44] *See* Chapter 1, Section II.C.

practice was justified to begin with. How could courts ever permissibly *start* treating willful ignorance as a substitute for knowledge?

However, even if we can defend judge-made law in general, and thus explain how courts might have permissibly started treating willful ignorance as a substitute for knowledge, there would still be an open normative question—a question faced by any lawmaker considering whether to adopt some imputation principle. Why would it be a *good idea*—a sensible and normatively defensible practice—for the relevant lawmaker (whether legislature or common law court) to adopt an imputation principle like the willful ignorance doctrine? This normative question remains open and in Section III, I'll offer a theory to help answer it.

C. STATUTORY REFORMS

If one is not satisfied with the above-mentioned responses to the practitioner's worry, one might simply assert that equal culpability imputation principles like the willful ignorance doctrine offend the principle of legality too broadly to be legitimate.[45] If so, one's only fallback option—short of calling for the willful ignorance doctrine and similar principles to be abolished—is to advocate for statutory reforms by the legislature that explicitly codify the imputation doctrine in question.

This is more or less the route taken by Husak and Callender. On their view, the only plausible way to fix the legality problems for the willful ignorance doctrine is through statutory reform. In principle, this might happen through laws that *redefine* knowledge as used in criminal statutes so another mental state like willful ignorance can satisfy the knowledge element of crimes.[46] Thus, we might advocate for a law proclaiming that any instance of "knowledge," "knowingly," or a similar word in criminal statutes is defined as something along the lines of practical certainty *or* willful ignorance. By contrast, Husak and Callender prefer a different sort of reform. They argue that it would be better to formulate specific duties of investigation in different contexts and then define new offenses for the violation thereof.[47] Regardless of the precise form these statutory reforms should take, however, the basic point is that calling for the legislature to address the legality problem through statutory reforms is always on the table as a fallback for commentators who are troubled by the practitioner's worry.

---

[45] *See, e.g.*, Husak & Callender, *supra* note 3, at 58 (arguing that "[a]ttempts to reconcile the principle of legality with the punishment of wilfully ignorant defendants are almost certain to be unsuccessful, since the concept has been created for the sole purpose of circumventing the principle of legality").

[46] *Id.* at 62–63 (discussing several statutory reform proposals along these lines).

[47] Husak & Callender, *supra* note 3, at 68–69 (arguing that "[i]f wilfully ignorant defendants are to be held liable, the proper course is to draft a new statute that imposes reasonable duties of inspection on them").

While this would be a safe and simple response to the legality worries about equal culpability imputation principles, it would not answer all the questions we need to confront. Just as with the second textualist argument above—that is, that mens rea terms should be given their common law meanings—we still face a fundamental normative question: Which equal culpability imputation principles *should* lawmakers adopt? If we want to push for statutory reforms to make the willful ignorance doctrine less problematic from a legality perspective, there is still the question of whether Congress should enact such reforms and if so which ones. Some equal culpability imputation principles might be legitimate, but others might sweep too broadly, or criminalize conduct that is too different from the paradigm instance of the crime, to be defensible for the legislature to codify. Thus, to know which such statutory reforms to endorse and which to oppose, we need *a normative theory of equal culpability imputation*. In the rest of this chapter, I defend such a theory and then show how it helps evaluate a range of equal culpability imputation principles including the willful ignorance doctrine.

III. Answering the Lawmaker's Question: A Normative Theory of Equal Culpability Imputation

In the remainder of this chapter, I confront the lawmaker's question head on. In a sense, what I will offer is a parasitic theory. It uses the normative justification for criminalizing the target offense to construct a justification for an associated imputation principle. Thus, the sort of justification I offer of an imputation principle as applied to a criminal statute will work only if we assume the underlying criminal statute itself is normatively justified. The idea is that *if* we assume the criminal statute in question is legitimate, *then* we can articulate the conditions under which it would be normatively defensible to use a particular equal culpability imputation principle as applied to that statute. If the statute is normatively defensible as a way to protect certain interests, rights, or other values, then particular imputation principles can also be justified as a way to accomplish those same goals.

The theory I offer is inspired by a related account offered by Gideon Yaffe about why equal culpability supports mens rea substitution—that is, why the mental state element of a crime can be satisfied by another mental state when acting with the latter is just as culpable as acting with the former.[48] Using the theory of culpability defended in Chapter 2, I extrapolate from Yaffe's view a *general* theory of equal culpability imputation. That is the main task of this section. Doing so reveals the deeper normative principles on which equal culpability mens rea imputation rests.

[48] Yaffe, *supra* note 6, at 550.

A. YAFFE'S ACCOUNT

Yaffe's view starts with an assumption about the purpose of requiring mental states for crimes *in general*. He thinks "a particular mental state is required for a crime because it makes a contribution to the objectionable nature of the agent's conduct in virtue of which the agent is properly punished; it contributes to making the conduct punishable."[49] Next, Yaffe observes that "another mental state [besides the one required by statute] that is just as bad or worse can make *the same, or a greater contribution of this sort*."[50] When this is the case, he thinks, it would make sense to allow this other mental state to substitute for the mental state expressly required for the crime. More precisely, if mental state M is required for crime C because the presence of M makes a particular kind of contribution to explaining why the conduct designated by C is criminalized in the first place, then if another mental state, M*, makes *exactly that same contribution* (or a greater contribution of the same kind) to explaining why that conduct is criminalizable, then M* should be allowed to substitute for M. It would make sense because punishing [the conduct in C accompanied by M*] would *serve the very same underlying purpose* as punishing [the conduct in C accompanied by M]. As Yaffe puts it, "[t]he conduct in question, when accompanied by the substituting mental state, is just as worthy of punishment (or even more worthy) than it would be were it accompanied by the mental state the law requires."[51]

I think Yaffe is at bottom correct about the basis for allowing one mental state to substitute for another under conditions of equal culpability. However, his idea can be extended beyond mens rea substitution principles, and also cover other kinds of imputation—regardless of whether the elements imputed are mens rea elements, actus reus elements, or some combination thereof. Doing so also requires being clearer about what it is for two bits of conduct to display the same level of culpability, and explain *why* this would be a sufficient basis for imputing missing elements to defendants.

B. A GENERAL BUT PRECISE STATEMENT OF THE SAME RATIONALE RATIONALE

I think Yaffe is on the right track that the ground for imputing missing mental states on equal culpability grounds has to do with the purposes, aims, or reasons that provide the underlying normative justification for the laws criminalizing various actions. However, in this section, I seek to improve Yaffe's account in two ways. First, I want to generalize it beyond mens rea substitution to cover all equal culpability imputation. Second, I want to deepen and clarify it so it can be used to separate legitimate imputation principles from the indefensible ones.

---

[49] *Id.*
[50] *Id.*
[51] *Id.*

To generalize the view beyond mental state imputation, we can summarize the underlying insight as follows:

> Same Rationale Rationale: When the defendant who lacks a given element, E, which is required for a given crime, X, is in conditions, Y, that make her display the same *type* and *degree* of culpability that justified the legislature in criminalizing conduct of type X in the first place, then it would be *justified on the basis of that same rationale* to impute E to the defendant.

This idea remains imprecise, however. We need to know not only what it means for two bits of conduct to display the same type and degree of culpability, but also (and more importantly) why this means that imposing the same criminal sanctions on both bits of conduct would be *supported by the same legislative rationale.*

To explicate the Same Rationale Rationale while keeping it general, let me introduce some terminology. Consider a statute criminalizing act type X. Suppose X* is some nearby conduct that differs from X only in that someone who does X* fails to satisfy at least one element of the official statutory definition of X. To keep the discussion general, I won't specify what kind of element of X is missing in someone who does X*: it could be a mens rea element, an actus reus element, an attendant circumstance, or a combination thereof. The question, then, is what might justify imputing to a defendant who does X* the missing elements needed to get her to count as doing X. The Same Rationale Rationale holds that this particular imputation is justified when it is supported by the same legislative considerations that support criminalizing X—that is, when it serves the same legislative aims that X was legitimately criminalized to accomplish. When these aims themselves provide a solid normative basis for criminalizing X, then the same justification would carry over to X*, thus ensuring that the imputation in question will be justified as well. It is in this sense that the theory is a parasitic theory. Given this way of setting up the problem, the two questions we must answer are:

> (Q1) What does it mean for criminalizing two bits of misconduct to be justified by the same *legislative rationale*?
> (Q2) Why would criminalizing X* the same way as X (i.e., imposing the same criminal label and penalties on both) be supported by the same legislative rationale when X and X* are *equally culpable*?

On (Q1), I think Yaffe is right in supposing that the *broad* rationale for criminalizing some type of misconduct is to target behavior the legislature deems culpable and impose penalties on it. (Again, I'll be supposing the legislature is correct in this assessment.) This, in turn, can be for many reasons: consequentialist, retributivist, expressive, etc. I won't take a stand on the deeper question of *why* we should punish culpable conduct. Any of the main theories could be used for my purposes.

However, this isn't the end of the story. Beyond the general aim of targeting culpable conduct, legislatures usually have more fine-grained purposes in mind that they take to support the criminalization of particular types of action. They do not just aim to punish particular *amounts* of culpability, but rather to punish particular *kinds* of culpability. It seems plausible that the culpability involved in theft is *different in kind* than the culpability involved in homicide. Offenses of the former sort manifest disrespect for property rights, while offenses of the latter sort disrespect our rights to bodily integrity and life. Thus, the legislature's *rationale* for criminalizing theft offenses seems importantly different than for criminalizing assault or homicide. For the former offense, the rationale that supports legislature's decision to criminalize it is plausibly the aim of protecting the interests that underlie property rights, but for the latter, the legislature aims to protect the interests that underlie our rights to bodily integrity and life.

We can use this picture to answer (Q1). I take it that when the legislature criminalizes act type X, the aim that justifies it in doing so (whether explicit or implicit, conscious or unconscious) is to protect a particular set of interests, rights, or other values that are usually infringed, violated, threatened, or set back in some way by people who do X.[52] Criminalizing X offers some level and manner of protection for these interests, rights, and values.[53] Now suppose we were to criminalize some distinct act type X* in the same way as X—that is, by including X* under the same offense as X and imposing the same penalties on X* as on X. When criminalizing X* in the same way as X would provide the same level and manner of protection for the same set of interests, rights, and values, then we can say that *punishing X and X* the same would be justified by the same legislative rationale*. Assuming the rationale for criminalizing X is sound, this means that the imputation of missing elements needed to treat someone who does X* as if he did X would also be normatively justified.

This, in turn, gives us our answer to (Q2). *When*, substantively speaking, is punishing X and X* the same way supported by the same legislative rationale? My theory is that this is the case when doing X and doing X* possesses the same *degree* and *type* of culpability. And this, in turn, applying my theory of culpability from Chapter 2, just means that doing X* manifests the same *level* of insufficient regard *toward the very same* protected interests, rights, or values as doing X would. Thus, we can put the view as follows:

> SAME SUPPORT CRITERION: When doing X* manifests the same level of insufficient regard toward the very same set of interests, rights, or values that X was legitimately criminalized in order to protect (which just is to say, when X and X* possess the same degree and type of culpability), then punishing X* the same as X would be supported by the same legislative rationale.

---

[52] This seems true also for *mala prohibita*. They too should seek to protect our interests or other important values.

[53] Note that these considerations are paradigmatic examples of the legally recognized reasons that bear on how to act, as I explained that concept in Chapter 2, Section III.A.

Thus, when this test is satisfied, it would be justified under the Same Rationale Rationale to impute to a person who does X* the missing elements needed to get him to count as doing X. After all, when the Same Support Criterion is satisfied, imputing these missing elements just is what's necessary to punish X* the same as X, and punishing X* the same as X would be supported by the same legislative rationale as the statute criminalizing X. Assuming the rationale for punishing X is normatively legitimate, this would generate a strong normative argument for courts to impute these missing elements to someone who does X* as well.

Let me summarize by formulating a recipe for determining whether a particular instance of imputation is justified on equal culpability grounds under the Same Rationale Rationale. As before, let "E" stand for the element(s) that are missing from act type X* but if added would amount to crime X. To see if E can be imputed to defendant D who does X*, follow these steps:

Recipe for assessing the normative soundness of imputing missing elements:

(1) Find the set of interests, rights, or values that the statute criminalizing X aims to protect by way of imposing the applicable criminal label and penalties on X. (Of course, this may require some charitable reconstruction of the aims of the statute.) Let P_{IRV} stand for this set of protected interests, rights, and values.

(2) Determine whether the aim of protecting P_{IRV} is a normatively adequate justification for criminalizing X in the first place. If it's not, then stop; but if it is, then continue to step (3).

(3) Determine how much insufficient regard toward P_{IRV} D manifested in doing X*. Call this amount α.

- According to my theory, α equals the least amount of insufficient regard for P_{IRV} that it would take to get an otherwise law-abiding citizen to do X* under the circumstances as D believed them to be.
- This, in turn, equals the least amount of error in attaching weight to the legally recognized reasons *in favor* of doing X* (if any) and the legally recognized reasons *against* doing X*, the latter of which will necessarily include the reasons not to do X* that are provided by the interests, rights or values (P_{IRV}) that the statute in question aims to protect by criminalizing X. (Specifically, α = an amount just slightly greater than the legally recognized weight to be given to the reasons against X* minus the legally recognized weight to be given to the reasons in favor of X*.)

(4) Determine how much insufficient regard would be manifested toward P_{IRV} by the exactly analogous person who does X (not X*) in the same circumstances as D believed he was in. Call this amount β.

- Again, β equals the least amount of insufficient regard for P_{IRV} that it would take to get an otherwise law-abiding citizen to do X (not X*) under the very same circumstances as the actual D in fact believed he was in.

(5) If, and only if, α is equal to or greater than β, then the Same Support Criterion would be satisfied—that is, punishing X* the same as X would be justified by the same legislative rationale. Then, but only then, would it be justified on equal culpability grounds (under the Same Rationale Rationale) to impute E to D, such that D can be convicted and punished as if he had done X.

This is my theory of when it's justified on equal culpability grounds to impute E such that X* may be punished the same as X. If X* manifests the same degree and type of culpability—the same level of insufficient regard for the same interests, rights or values as X is criminalized to protect—then someone who does X* can be convicted and punished as if he did X, even if he doesn't literally satisfy all the elements of X. And that's because the defendant's conduct has all the properties that the legislature intended X's penalties to attach in virtue of.

Finally, notice that this theory entails clear limits about when equal culpability provides the basis for imputing criminal liability. In particular, on my theory, if two actors happen to possess the same amount of culpability in total, but don't manifest the same degree of insufficient regard *toward the same interests, rights, or values*, then their actions will be too different for them to be punished the same under an equal culpability theory. For instance, even if someone who commits tax fraud happens to possess the very same *amount* of culpability in general as someone who steals a purse, it would not be permitted to impute liability for stealing a purse to the tax fraudster. After all, the tax fraudster would not have manifested the same amount of insufficient regard *toward the same interests, rights, and values* as the purse-snatcher. The Same Support Criterion is not satisfied as between these two act types. For ease of reference, call this idea the *Content Restriction on Equal Culpability Imputation.*

For the same reason, my theory also explains the limits of aggregating the culpability of different acts in order to reach the sort of equal culpability that could justify imputation. The culpability of acts that are entirely unrelated to the interests, rights, or values protected by the statute in question, of course, cannot be added together to reach the culpability level needed for substituting or imputing elements. For example, suppose X* consists of a string of actions. The culpability of all these actions can be added together to justify imputing the missing elements and punishing X* the same as X *only if* the string of acts X* consists of all manifest insufficient regard *toward the same set of protected interests, rights, and values* as X was criminalized to protect (viz., P_{IRV}). That explains why it would be crazy to add together an act of tax fraud, cheating on your spouse, and mistreating your dog in order to reach the level of culpability involved in, say, negligent homicide. The statute criminalizing negligent homicide aims to protect interests, rights, and values that are unrelated to those that tax fraud, cheating on one's spouse, and mistreating one's dog manifest insufficient regard for. (Some of the latter interests, rights, and values—especially regarding marital fidelity—are not even protected by law.)

In this way, my theory provides clear limits on when equal culpability legitimately supports imputing liability to a defendant who doesn't literally satisfy the elements of the crime at issue. This is a normative theory that directly answers the lawmaker's question (which remained even after dealing with the practitioner's worry). As a normative theory, it has the resources to tell us which imputation principles the legislature *should* codify through statutory reforms. Moreover, it explains why common law courts might be on solid normative footing in *starting* to apply an imputation principle like the willful ignorance doctrine. To see how the theory generates concrete normative results about particular equal culpability imputation doctrines, let us go on to consider a range of examples before returning to the willful ignorance doctrine in Section V.

IV. Applications

The normative theory of equal culpability imputation I articulated previously can be used to evaluate particular imputation principles. My theory plausibly vindicates some of them, but recommends the rejection or reformation of others. This section discusses some examples. My view supports the doctrine of transferred intent, while recommending that the felony murder rule and the Pinkerton doctrine should be rejected—or at least heavily restricted. In the final section, I go on to discuss the willful ignorance doctrine, which my theory also ends up vindicating.

A. JUSTIFYING SOME IMPUTATION DOCTRINES: TRANSFERRED INTENT

My theory supports the doctrine of transferred intent insofar as it is construed as an equal culpability imputation principle. Focus on homicide for simplicity. Under this doctrine, the defendant's intent to kill "transfers" from intended victim to actual victim. Suppose Mac shoots at Abe intending to kill him, but misses and hits Boris instead. Courts generally agree that Mac is guilty of Boris's murder.[54] In this way, Mac's killing with the intention to kill Abe can be used as the basis for treating Mac as though he intended to kill Boris.

The rule is easy to apply but harder to explain. After all, Mac didn't actually possess the intention to kill his actual victim, Boris, and he only killed Boris accidentally. So why is Mac guilty of murder? Doug Husak nicely encapsulates the problem with the following argument:

(1) Murder is the intentional killing of a human being.

[54] *See* Glanville Williams, The General Part 101–02 (1953).

(2) [Mac] is guilty of murder only if there is some human being whom she has killed intentionally.
(3) [Mac] did not kill [Abe].
(4) [Mac] did not kill [Boris] intentionally.
(5) Therefore, there is no human being whom [Mac] killed intentionally.
(6) Therefore, [Mac] is not guilty of murder.[55]

One might try to respond to this argument in several ways, but the strategy I am concerned with here is that the transferred intent doctrine can be justified *on equal culpability grounds*.[56] I don't claim this is the *only* way to justify it. But it is a promising candidate. Thus, all I want to argue here is that *if* the transferred intent doctrine is to be justified as an equal culpability substitution principle, then my theory from Section III has a plausible explanation of why it holds.

The basic idea is that Mac's conduct has two culpability-relevant features. It consists of (a) the attempt to kill Abe (which involves acting on the intention to kill Abe), and (b) imposing some risk of death on Boris (perhaps merely negligently), which materializes such that Boris dies. Mac's conduct can be described as the combination of an attempt to kill Abe and behavior that kills Boris (perhaps only negligently).[57] Even if one thinks (a) necessarily is less culpable than the completed murder (a claim I doubt),[58] there still is an equal culpability rationale in the offing for convicting Mac of murder. Even if the culpability of (a) alone is less than (c) succeeding in intentionally killing Abe, the culpability of (a) plus (b) plausibly is as great as that of (c).

---

[55] Doug Husak, *Transferred Intent*, 10 Notre Dame J. L. Ethics & Pub. Pol'y 65, 66 (2012).

[56] Another promising strategy is to claim that the mens rea required for murder just is the intention to kill some human being or other (i.e., one whose identity is not necessarily specified). This amounts to denying line (2) and replacing it with the claim that Mac is guilty of murder only if (i) there is some human being Mac killed and (ii) that person's death was the proximate result of Mac's acting on an intention to kill some human being or other. Nonetheless, even if this is the right way to unpack the doctrine, we still need an explanation of why this expansion—this departure from the way the doctrine is usually stated (i.e., as requiring the intent to kill *the victim*)—is warranted. Plausibly, this is because of equal culpability considerations: because Mac is just as culpable for his actual conduct as he would have been had he intended to kill Boris and succeeded in doing so. Thus, even this strategy plausibly rests on an equal culpability theory.

[57] It's doubtful that (b)—the risk of death to the actual victim—confers additional culpability unless this risk is imposed at least negligently. If Mac had no way of knowing that the actual victim (Boris) was present and would be subject to a risk of death from the attempt to kill the intended victim (Abe), then Mac would seem to incur no additional culpability from subjecting the actual victim (Boris) to this risk. Unless Mac at least *should* have known of the risk he imposed on the victim (Boris), (b) would not involve any extra culpability to be added to (a).

[58] I'm inclined to think (a)—the attempt—is already just as culpable as (c) the murder of Abe (provided all else is equal between them and it's a last act attempt). I suggested in Chapter 2 that (a) is just as culpable (c) when they differ only due to luck, as luck likely shouldn't affect culpability. If so, we can already accept that an equal culpability rationale supports the transferred intent doctrine even without aggregating the culpability of (a) and (b). Perhaps this could explain why MPC § 2.03 allows intent to transfer even without negligence in causing the actual death.

Moreover, the insufficient regard manifested in (a) plus that manifested in (b) seems not only as large as that manifested in (c), but both (a) and (b) manifest insufficient regard toward *the very same set of protected interests, rights, and values* as (c) manifests insufficient regard toward. Plausibly, intentional homicide is criminalized in order to protect the value of human life (and I assume this aim actually does provide a sound normative justification for criminalizing intentional homicide). When one intentionally kills a person without any justification or excuse, one reveals that one attached much too little weigh to the value of human life. Moreover, both (a) and (b) manifest insufficient regard for the very same value. Regarding (a), attempting to kill a human being (without justification or excuse) reveals that one did not attach enough weight to the value of human life—that is, to the reasons not to deprive others of the valuable life they would have gone on to lead. For (b), negligently or recklessly exposing someone to an undue risk of death (without justification or excuse) also demonstrates that one did not attach enough weight to the value of human life—that is, the reasons not to impose such risks on others. Thus, (a) and (b) both manifest insufficient regard for the very same protected values as (c) does.

Accordingly, the conditions are met for imputing the missing elements to Mac as needed to convict him of murder. In fact, Mac only did (a) and (b). He didn't literally do (c). Nonetheless, his doing (a) and (b) manifests as much insufficient regard toward the very same protected interests and values as (c) does. Thus, we can impute the missing elements as needed to treat Mac as though he did (c)—namely, the intention to kill Boris. Thus, my theory of equal culpability imputation plausibly supports convicting Mac of murder under the transferred intent doctrine.[59] There may be other justifications for the doctrine, but I think this is one promising strategy.

B. LIMITING SOME IMPUTATION DOCTRINES: FELONY MURDER, VOLUNTARY INTOXICATION, AND PINKERTON

1. Felony Murder

My theory of equal culpability imputation also recommends heavy restriction (if not outright rejection) of some doctrines. Take the felony murder rule. Traditionally, it held that "one whose conduct brought about an unintended death in the commission or attempted commission of a felony was guilty of murder."[60] Modern courts have limited the doctrine

---

[59] Double-counting worries might prevent us from convicting Mac of *both* the attempted murder of Abe and the murder of Boris on the present transferred intent theory. For excellent discussion, *see* Nancy Eherenreich, *Attempt, Merger and Transferred Intent*, 82 Brook. L. Rev. 49, 53 (2016) (arguing that "the merger rule prohibits the practice of allowing conviction of an actor for both murder of an unintended victim and attempted murder as to the original target, whenever the attempt and murder charges flow from the same conduct by the defendant").

[60] LaFave, *supra* note 16. In the United Kingdom this rule (known there as the "constructive malice" rule) was abolished by Section 1 of the Homicide Act of 1957.

in a number of ways—for example, "(1) by permitting its use only as to certain types of felonies [like those that are dangerous to life or at least *malum in se*]; (2) by more strict interpretation of the requirement of proximate or legal cause; (3) by a narrower construction of the time period during which the felony is in the process of commission; (4) by requiring that the underlying felony be independent of the homicide."[61] Thus, suppose Grant is in the midst of a burglary. He is carrying a gun. The homeowner, Hershel, surprises him in the middle of the night, a scuffle ensues, and Grant's gun accidentally goes off, killing Hershel. Under the felony murder rule, Grant is guilty of murder.

How do we explain this result? Equal culpability imputation is one natural strategy (though not the only possibility[62]). As Robinson explains, the "theory of cumulative culpability may also help explain felony-murder cases: The culpability for the underlying felony and for the killing . . . are aggregated to support conviction for a higher degree of homicide than would be justifiable otherwise."[63] Thus, the idea is that when Grant's culpability for the burglary is added to his culpability for recklessly or negligently causing Hershel's death,[64] this sum equals the culpability inherent in murder (i.e., intentional homicide). Although Grant literally lacks the requisite mens rea of intent to kill, this missing mens rea can be imputed because his culpability is as great as it would be if he actually acted with it. In this way, we might try to justify the felony murder rule as an equal culpability imputation principle.

The equal culpability strategy for justifying this rule squares well with many of the limitations courts have subsequently imposed on its use. Some courts only apply the felony murder rule when the underlying felony poses dangers to life and limb, or at least is *malum in se*.[65] We can explain this on an equal culpability theory, since if the underlying felony is not very serious, then it arguably would not confer enough added culpability to get one up to the culpability level of murder. Likewise, if the underlying felony is not independent of the act that causes the killing (e.g., if the underlying felony is manslaughter or aggravated battery),[66] adding the culpability of the killing to that of the underlying

---

[61] LaFave, *supra* note 16.

[62] As Robinson notes, one might try to explain it on evidentiary grounds: "[t]he mental state required for a murder conviction is presumed when the death is caused in the course of certain felonies." Robinson, *supra* note 8, at 654. The idea is that doing the felony is evidence that one intended the killing. Of course, if this theory is adopted, the felony murder should merely create a rebuttable presumption.

[63] *Id.* at 651.

[64] Courts often assume that burglaries generally carry a foreseeable risk of death, which the defendant should know about. The idea is that home invasions foreseeably risk violent confrontations with the owners or occupiers.

[65] LaFave, *supra* note 16 ("In many states, the felony-murder rule has been limited in scope by a requirement that the felony attempted or committed by the defendant must be dangerous to life. Similarly, other courts have required that the felony be one of the few which were felonies at common law (i.e., rape, sodomy, robbery, burglary, arson, mayhem, larceny), or that the felony in question be *malum in se* rather than *malum prohibitum*.").

[66] *Id.* ("Some cases have held that the collateral felony must be a felony which is 'independent' of the conduct which kills; it must involve conduct separate from the acts of personal violence which constitute a necessary

felony would involve illicit double-counting.[67] Thus, the defendant's culpability would not rise to the level inherent in an intentional killing, and there would be no basis for treating him as if he committed such a grave offense.

While equal culpability imputation thus explains many facets of the felony murder rule, my theory raises questions about whether the doctrine really is justifiable on equal culpability grounds. For imputation to be justified on this basis, it's not enough that the defendant's actual conduct manifests *the same amount* of insufficient regard as the crime we're trying to impute liability for, but also that the defendant's conduct manifests this level of insufficient regard *toward the very same set of legally protected interests* as the imputed crime. Above, I called this the Content Restriction on Equal Culpability Imputation. (It will be important in many places in this book.) Thus, it is legitimate to add together the culpability of (a) Grant's burglary and (b) his accidentally killing Hershel only if (a) and (b) both manifest insufficient regard toward the very same set of protected interests as (c) the crime to be imputed—viz., murder.

But it is far from clear that this is so. What (c) manifests insufficient regard for, more or less, is the value of human life: that is, our interest in enjoying a life worth living and our right to not be unjustly killed. While it's plausible that (b)—a negligent or reckless killing—manifests insufficient regard for the same protected values, interests and rights, it's far from clear that (a)—the burglary—does so to a substantial degree. After all, burglary manifests insufficient regard primarily for our property and privacy rights: our right to be secure in our use and enjoyment of our belongings and dwellings. Thus, it's not clear that (a) manifests *as much* insufficient regard for human life as it takes to raise Grant's culpability up from the level of one who does (b) to the level of one who does (c) (i.e., kills intentionally).

To this, one might respond that burglary does manifest insufficient regard for human life. Perhaps illicitly entering the dwelling of another with the intent to commit a felony therein creates a small risk of death as it might lead to a deadly altercation. But this seems to be of only secondary importance. The amount of insufficient regard burglary manifests toward the value of human life pales in comparison to the insufficient regard that it manifests toward property and privacy rights. So it remains unclear whether (a) adds *enough* insufficient regard for the relevant set of interests as it would take to raise Grant's culpability up from the level of (b) to that of (c). Thus, it's at best questionable whether convicting Grant under the felony murder rule is justified on my theory of equal

---

part of the homicide itself. Thus, although rape, arson, robbery and burglary are sufficiently independent of the homicide, manslaughter and aggravated battery toward the deceased will not do for felony murder.").

[67] For example, "[s]uppose *A* recklessly operates his car, unintentionally killing *B*, and thus committing involuntary manslaughter, a felony. Has not *A* committed a foreseeable homicide in the commission of a felony, and therefore is he not guilty of murder rather than of manslaughter? If so, manslaughter has ceased to exist as a separate crime; all manslaughters automatically ride up an escalator to become felony-murders. This is not so, of course; manslaughter will not thus serve as a felony for purposes of the felony-murder doctrine." *Id.*

culpability imputation. (Of course, it might be justified on some other theory besides equal culpability.)

Moreover, similar questions arise for other crimes that can serve as the underlying felony that could bump up one's conviction to murder. Robbery (i.e., violent theft) and rape plausibly manifest insufficient regard toward the same interests concerning the value of life as intentional murder does. As such, they satisfy the Content Restriction on Equal Culpability Imputation. But many other felonies that can trigger the felony murder rule do not (at least not very often)—like larceny, embezzlement, or arson of a building that one believes to be unoccupied.

In this way my theory at least imposes serious scope restrictions on when the felony murder rule can be employed—if it's to be justified on equal culpability grounds. In particular, the underlying felony must be one like rape or robbery that manifests a substantial amount of insufficient regard for the very same legally protected interests and values as murder does: namely, the value of human life and our right not to be unjustly killed.

2. Voluntary Intoxication and the Pinkerton Doctrine

My theory of equal culpability imputation also gives reason to substantially curtail other doctrines—at least insofar as they are justified on culpability aggregation grounds rather than some other rationale. Two are especially important.

My theory supports the voluntary intoxication doctrine only when the defendant's negligent unawareness of the risk she creates, together with her becoming intoxicated in the first place, manifest as much insufficient regard for the very same set of protected interests as acting recklessly as to that same risk does. Very plausibly, this would only be the case when the defendant, when she was getting drunk, was or should have been aware of the underlying risk she later created in her intoxicated state. When you get drunk knowing you'll have to drive home from the bar at closing time, you should know that this will end up creating a risk of death to others. In such a case, recklessness as to the risk you go on to create plausibly can be imputed to you—even though, due to your intoxication, you weren't aware of it at the time you created it.

By contrast, suppose the risk you go on to create while intoxicated is not the sort of risk we'd expect you to realize that you might go on to create. Suppose you get drunk with your friends, and out of the blue, someone asks you to help run an investment scheme. Were you sober, you'd have realized that the prospectus risks misleading investors. But in your intoxicated state, you do not recognize that risk. Should the involuntary intoxication be used to increase your mens rea to recklessness, such that you have the scienter required for some forms of aiding and abetting securities fraud?[68] Probably not, and my

---

[68] Some courts allow a lesser mental state than knowledge to sometimes suffice for liability for aiding and abetting securities fraud. *See* Alan R. Bromberg & Lewis D. Lowenfels, *Aiding and Abetting Securities Fraud: A Critical Examination*, 52 ALB. L. REV. 637, 675–76 (1988).

theory explains why. The act of getting drunk does not seem to manifest any insufficient regard toward the interests that securities fraud is criminalized to protect. Thus, it seems illicit to add together the culpability of your negligent risk creation and the culpability of your getting drunk (if any). They do not manifest insufficient regard toward the same protected interests as the crime to be imputed.

A similar point applies to the Pinkerton doctrine in the law of conspiracy. We can plausibly justify the modest version of the doctrine, on which defendants can be held criminally liable for the foreseeable crimes of co-conspirators within the scope of their criminal agreement. But the same cannot be said for the bolder version of the rule, on which defendants can be held liable for the offenses of co-conspirators even if those offenses are *outside* the scope of their agreement.[69]

Suppose A, B, and C conspire to defraud the IRS—a criminal offense.[70] Suppose one of their employees, D, finds out about the scheme, and so C kills D to prevent her from disclosing the conspiracy. Even if this is foreseeable under the circumstances (perhaps C has a violent past), suppose it's outside the scope of the agreed upon ends. Perhaps A, B, and C even explicitly agree that they will not harm any innocent parties—only the IRS (which they regard as illegitimate).

In such a case, the bold version of the Pinkerton doctrine allows A and B to be held criminally liable for C's actions. But my theory would not sanction this aggressive form of imputation. For one thing, A and B's actions don't seem to manifest the same level of insufficient regard as C's actions—even if C's actions were foreseeable (though not actually foreseen by A and B). Thus, it's questionable whether A and B are as culpable as C in any event. In addition, the bold Pinkerton rule violates the Content Restriction on Equal Culpability Imputation. What A and B actually did—conspire to defraud the IRS—does not manifest insufficient regard toward the same set of protected interests as the crime for which liability would be imputed—namely, murder. The latter manifests tremendous insufficient regard for the value of human life, while A and B's actions in furtherance of the conspiracy manifest insufficient regard toward other protected interests: the interests of taxpayers, and the interest we all have in ensuring a sufficiently well-funded government. This is an additional reason why the bold Pinkerton rule would not be justifiable on my account of equal culpability imputation.

---

69 Jens Ohlin, *Group Think: The Law of Conspiracy and Collective Reason*, 98 J. Crim. L. & Criminology 147, 152 (2007) ("Pinkerton is really two rules rolled into one. The first . . . allows for vicarious liability for the crimes of co-conspirators that fall within the scope of the criminal plan. The second, more extensive . . . rule applies in cases where the actions of a co-conspirator fall outside the scope of the criminal agreement, but are nonetheless attributed to the defendant because they were 'reasonably foreseeable.'").

70 18 USC § 371.

V. In Defense of the Willful Ignorance Doctrine

In closing, return to willful ignorance. Recall that willfully ignorant misconduct decomposes into two parts: (i) deliberately preserving one's ignorance about a suspected risk in breach of the duty to inform oneself (DRI), and then (ii) doing the actus reus while reckless as to whether this risk will materialize. Treating willfully ignorant actors as knowing actors is supposed to be justified on equal culpability grounds: If (i) + (ii) renders one just as culpable as (iii) the analogous knowing conduct, then the missing knowledge may be imputed. For this imputation to be justified on my theory, it must be the case that (i) + (ii) manifests at least as much insufficient regard for *the very same set* of protected interests, values, and rights as (iii) does. That is what it takes for treating willfully ignorant wrongdoers as knowing wrongdoers to be supported by the same underlying rationale as the criminalization of the analogous knowing misconduct.

I argue that willful ignorance *is* similar enough to the mental state of knowledge for punishing them the same to be supported by the same rationale. More specifically, acting in willful ignorance manifests insufficient regard for the same underlying interests, rights, and values as the analogous knowing misconduct does, and willful ignorance can substitute for knowledge when the *amount* of insufficient regard that the former manifests toward these interests is at least as great as the amount the latter manifests.

To see this, first consider knowledge. The reason a criminal act done with knowledge that it will cause a particular harm, H, makes one deserve punishment is this: for a normal person with sufficient regard for others, knowledge that one's conduct will cause H can fairly be expected to give *overriding motivation* not to do that action.[71] When one proceeds to do it anyway, this shows one lacked the motivation against this harmful action one should have had, and thus that one lacks sufficient regard for others.[72] Whatever set of protected interests, rights, or values, P_{IRV}, are threatened or set back by causing H, acting with knowledge that one will cause H manifests insufficient regard for those interests. These are assumed to be the interests, rights, and values that knowingly causing H is legitimately criminalized to protect.

In the same way, acting in willful ignorance of the fact that one's conduct will cause H manifests insufficient regard toward this same set of protected interests, rights or values: $P_{IRV.}$ Willfully ignorant action involves (i) consciously breaching one's duty to

[71] This same reasoning extends to crimes where the inculpatory proposition is not that some harm will occur, but rather that some inculpatory circumstance obtains (e.g., that one possesses drugs, or has a felony conviction while possessing a firearm). It should be obvious how to extend the argument to such cases.

[72] For more on this account of the culpability of knowing misconduct *see* Alex Sarch, *Knowledge, Recklessness and the Connection Requirement Between Mens Rea and Actus Reus*, 120 PENN ST. L. REV. 1 (2015); Kenneth Simons, *Does Punishment for "Culpable Indifference" Simply Punish for "Bad Character"? Examining the Requisite Connection Between Mens Rea and Actus Reus*, 6 BUFF. CRIM. L. REV. 219, 247–57 (2002).

investigate the suspected risk that H will result, and (ii) doing the actus reus with those suspicions intact—that is, recklessly. Let me explain why each manifests insufficient regard the same way knowledge does.

Start with (ii), since it's easier. Being aware that one's contemplated action risks H should produce certain motivations in a normal law-abiding person. It should motivate her to assure herself however she can that she will not bring about H. The obvious way to do this would be to decide not to do the underlying risky action after all. Thus, her awareness that her contemplated action risks bringing about H should provide her with overriding motivation *against* doing that action. If she goes ahead does it anyway, this shows that she lacked the motivations she *should* have had. This is one manifestation of insufficient regard—and it's the same kind of motivational failure manifested in acting with knowledge that H will result. Knowledge and recklessness are closely related mental states, differing only in the degree of confidence the actor has that H will result. Thus, it is unsurprising that recklessly causing H should manifest insufficient regard in just the same way, and toward the same interests, rights, and values, as causing H knowingly does.

When it comes to (i)—the decision not to investigate one's suspicions that H will result—this, too, manifests insufficient regard *toward the same interests, rights, and values*. The reason, as argued in Chapter 4, is that when one suspects one's planned action might cause H and one is in a position to reasonably obtain more information about whether these suspicions are true, the law expects one to do so—assuming one does not abandon the intention to do the underlying act. After all, informing oneself about whether the suspected risk of H really will materialize if one acts as planned is a second way to assure oneself that one will not bring about H. *Either* investigating will reveal that H will not (or is less likely to) materialize, in which case there is no (or a lesser) impediment to acting as planned, *or* investigating will reveal that H will (or is more likely to) materialize, which produces greater normative pressure not to act as planned (and should make one less inclined to do so). Thus, if one deliberately refuses to investigate one's suspicions, one misses yet another opportunity to help assure oneself that one will not bring about H (either by learning that one's planned act is less likely to cause H or by increasing the normative pressure on oneself not to do it).

In this way, willful ignorance involves *two* missed opportunities to help assure oneself that one won't bring about the suspected harm H. Both are failures to be motivated, in the ways one should, by the badness of the suspected risk of H. When one *knows* H will result from one's planned action, the only way to give oneself the required assurance is to not do that action. Similarly, when one acts in willful ignorance, one misses two opportunities to help assure oneself that one won't bring about H. The first is the failure to investigate one's suspicions that H will result, and the second is the failure to pull back from doing the underlying action.

As a result, causing H knowingly and causing H through willful ignorance both manifest insufficient regard *for the very same set of protected interests, rights, and values*. These are the ones that are damaged or set back by harm H, which the knowledge crime in question, it's assumed, was criminalized to protect. Thus, the Content Restriction on Equal Culpability Imputation is satisfied.

It would, of course, not do to add one's culpability for cheating on one's spouse or one's taxes to the culpability of doing the actus reus while reckless as to the risk that it will cause, say, physical harm. The interests and values that the former manifest insufficient regard for are dramatically different from the interests and values implicated by recklessly creating a risk of physical harm. Cheating on spouses or taxes are simply too far afield. Thus, it would be permissible to add together the culpability of a deliberate breach of DRI and the reckless actus reus only if the two are not too far removed in this way.

The analysis I've offered is complex, so let me conclude by summarizing what's been shown. There are two reasons the willful ignorance doctrine does not violate the Content Restriction on Equal Culpability Imputation. *First*, the aggregation involved in the doctrine does not violate this restriction. The restriction prevents adding together the culpability of acts that are too different to manifest insufficient regard for the same set of interests and values. However, as we saw, the two components of willful ignorance—(i) breaching one's duty to learn if H will result, and (ii) doing the actus reus despite suspecting it may cause H—are not too different in this regard. Both manifest insufficient regard for the very same interests and values: namely, those set back by H.

Second, the overall substitution in question—that is, using willful ignorance as the basis for imputing knowledge—does not violate the Content Restriction either.[73] As shown, causing H knowingly and causing H in willful ignorance likewise both manifest insufficient regard for the very same protected interests and values. Had one cared enough about making sure one will not cause H, this would naturally motivate one to investigate whether H will ensue—or at least not do the intended actus reus that may cause H. By consciously declining *both* ways to assure oneself that one will not cause H, one demonstrates *twice over* one's insufficient regard for the interests and values threatened by H—which are, of course, the same ones we're assuming that *knowingly* causing H was criminalized to protect in the first place.

Accordingly, when causing H in willful ignorance is as culpable as causing H knowingly, there is a legitimate basis for imputing to the defendant the knowledge that H would result, such that he may be punished as if he had knowingly caused H. Punishing

[73] Are there really *two* content restrictions here? No, since the content restriction on aggregating different quanta of culpability is just a specific application of the Content Restriction on Equal Culpability Imputation in general. The latter is more fundamental and says we can't impute to someone who does X* the elements missing from crime X unless X* manifests the same amount of insufficient regard *for the same interests ands values* as X does. Applied to aggregation, this idea means we also can't aggregate the culpability of two bits of conduct for imputation purposes unless they both manifest insufficient regard *for the same set of interests and values.*

willfully ignorant misconduct is supported by the same legislative rationale as punishing the analogous knowing misconduct. Therefore, willful ignorance can legitimately satisfy the knowledge element of a crime provided the conditions of equal culpability are met.[74]

[74] Can multiple imputation principles be used in succession to ratchet up the defendant's criminal liability? Suppose Egil deliberately preserves his ignorance of a suspected risk that would occur if he does an actus reus he's contemplating (but doesn't yet intend). He then gets extremely drunk so that when he does the actus reus he's no longer aware of the risks he previously suspected and should have investigated. Can we use the voluntary intoxication rule to substitute in recklessness for his negligence, and then the willful ignorance doctrine to substitute in knowledge for the imputed recklessness? That seems worrisome. (Thanks to Hrafn Asgeirsson for this worry.)

This may not necessarily be *theoretically* problematic if equal culpability really is present. Nonetheless, practical worries remain about misapplication and abuse. Still, we can block the worry as follows. In general, mens rea substitution should be permitted only as between the defendant's *actual* mental state and a nonactual one—not between one nonactual mental state and another. This means that for the imputation of knowledge to succeed in the above hypothetical, we'd have to be able to justify, on equal culpability grounds, substituting out the defendant's actual negligence and imputing knowledge instead. None of the doctrines considered thus far permit such substitution, and because of the risk of misapplication and abuse, I would not advocate negligence-for-knowledge imputation principles. The same reasons suggest that we should not allow imputation doctrines to be stacked on top of one another to achieve this result either. In the above hypothetical, we should not allow the voluntary intoxication doctrine to substitute in recklessness for actual negligence, and then allow the willful ignorance doctrine to use this imputed recklessness plus some willful ignorance to impute knowledge. Such stacking of imputation principles would be a bad policy.

Some cases improperly do just this, however. In *United States v. Fleming*, the defendant got drunk, drove erratically into oncoming traffic, and killed another driver. 739 F.2d 945 (4th Cir. 1984). The Fourth Circuit upheld the murder conviction, relying on the "depraved heart murder" rule, which allows recklessness to satisfy the mens rea for murder (typically at least knowledge). *See id.* at 948. To find the defendant reckless, however, the court appears to have relied on the voluntary intoxication doctrine. *Id.* at 948 (n.3) (observing that even if "subjective awareness of the risk is required to establish murder where the killing resulted from reckless conduct, an exception . . . is made where lack of such awareness is attributable solely to voluntary drunkenness"). Thus, the case is naturally read as invoking voluntary intoxication to justify moving from negligence to recklessness, and the extreme gravity of the risk imposed is then invoked to justify moving from recklessness to knowledge. This would be to apply two imputation principles in succession. Such reasoning is unsound. As the defendant's actual mental state is negligence, the second substitution here—from recklessness to knowledge—involves substituting one nonactual mental state for another. For the previous reasons, such stacking of imputation principles should be disallowed.

III Beyond Willful Ignorance

PART III CONSIDERS a range of ways the law might go beyond the existing willful ignorance doctrine, defending some novel equal culpability imputation principles and rejecting others. Chapter 6 argues that some forms of non-willful ignorance—such as repeatedly and recklessly taking risks of preserving one's ignorance—can also be as culpable as knowing misconduct. Thus, there is reason to permit this form of culpable ignorance to satisfy the knowledge element of the crime as well. However, there are inherent limits on equal culpability imputation. Thus, Chapter 7 argues that no form of culpable ignorance is by itself sufficient for treating the defendant as a purposeful wrongdoer. By contrast, Chapter 8 discusses another form of sub-willful motivated ignorance in which one is not fully aware of the ways one acts to preserve one's ignorance. This, too, can render one culpable, and in limited circumstances may justify treating some negligent actors as if they were reckless. Finally, Chapter 9 shifts to corporate defendants. Starting from the premise that it also can be culpable to preserve the ignorance of others (not just oneself), this chapter argues there is good reason to impute knowledge to some corporations in response to their culpable use of defective information sharing procedures. I extend my theory of criminal culpability to corporate actors and argue that various kinds of culpable ignorance within the corporation can be the basis for imputing knowledge to corporations as well. Thus, Part III demonstrates the wide sweep of equal culpability imputation as a judicial tool, as well as highlighting the inherent limitations on this mode of mental state imputation. As a whole, the book reveals the need for a range of crucial legal reforms, and provides a comprehensive account of when the criminal law may legitimately take equal culpability as the basis for imputing mental states to defendants who lack them.

6 Iterated Reckless Ignorance as a Substitute for Knowledge

THE LAST FEW chapters have been concerned mainly with willful ignorance—which, paradigmatically, is to violate the duty to reasonably inform oneself about a suspected inculpatory proposition with the intention of preserving one's ignorance. But one also might fail to inform oneself about one's suspicions with other mens rea: one might do so while reckless or negligent with respect to the fact that one will remain in ignorance. Such lesser breaches of one's investigatory duties can be culpable too. However, the existing willful ignorance doctrine does not reach these lesser forms of culpable ignorance. That is a problem.

This chapter argues not only that it would be *good* for courts to go beyond the existing willful ignorance doctrine, but that they are *committed* to doing so. The law allows willful ignorance to substitute for knowledge on the theory that acting with the former can be culpable to the same degree and in the same way as acting with the latter. Accordingly, the law is committed also to allowing certain forms of egregious nonwillful ignorance—most importantly, what I call *reckless ignorance*—to substitute for knowledge provided the conditions of equal culpability are met.

However, this chapter doesn't just make a theoretical argument. In addition, I argue that moving beyond the traditional willful ignorance doctrine is especially important to combat the incentives that a range of white-collar professionals—including lawyers, accountants, and corporate managers—have to remain in ignorance of crimes committed by those with whom they work. While the existing willful ignorance doctrine is responsive to *conscious* efforts to remain ignorant of fraudulent practices in one's midst, the criminal law lacks sufficient doctrinal tools to counteract the incentives to *recklessly allow* one's ignorance to be preserved. This is the gap that the rule defended here—the Iterated Reckless Ignorance Principle—is meant to fill.

This chapter proceeds as follows. In Section I, I explain why the existing willful ignorance doctrine does not go far enough. Using the example of criminal liability for lawyers who facilitate client misconduct, I argue that the existing willful ignorance doctrine is too narrow since it incentivizes taking risks of remaining in the dark about client misbehavior. Moving beyond the existing willful ignorance doctrine would be a good way to help combat the troubling incentives created by the existing doctrine.

While Section I thus offers a policy argument, Section II provides the theoretical grounding for moving beyond the existing willful ignorance doctrine. Since courts are doctrinally committed to expanding the doctrine in this way *only if* some forms of nonwillful ignorance are as culpable as the analogous knowing misconduct, to show that my proposed doctrinal expansion is justified, I have to provide reasons to think that acting in nonwillful ignorance *can* actually sometimes be as culpable as knowing wrongs. That is the main task of Section II. Section III bolsters the argument by answering some natural concerns—both practical and theoretical.

I conclude that doctrinal tools are needed to counteract the incentives to structure professional relationships—not only consciously, but *also unconsciously*—in ways that enable parties to pursue lucrative forms of wrongdoing while avoiding liability by claiming ignorance. The willful ignorance doctrine addresses deliberate efforts of this sort, but we lack adequate tools to address reckless or inadvertent versions of the same problem. This is the gap that my proposed doctrinal expansion aims to fill.

I. The Existing Willful Ignorance Doctrine Doesn't Go Far Enough

This section argues that the existing willful ignorance doctrine does not extend far enough. It does not fully address the incentives to remain in ignorance that actors routinely face in corporate contexts where conflicts of interest are a common risk.

To see this, consider how lawyers and accountants, hired to vet a corporation's transactions, can face pressure to remain ignorant of problems within those transactions. If the corporation behaved questionably, it has obvious incentives to keep its lawyers and accountants in the dark. This can lead them to attempt "to use lawyers [or accountants] to paint a gloss of respectability (sprinkle holy water, as it were) on dubious transactions."[1] For their part, the lawyers and accountants are incentivized to please their clients to

[1] Robert W. Gordon, *A New Role for Lawyers?: The Corporate Counselor after Enron*, 35 CONN. L. REV. 1185, 1201 (2003).

retain their business, and thus can end up only too happy to labor away under conditions of imperfect information.[2]

This combination of incentives can be a recipe for disaster. Although many cases prove the point (including, recently, the conduct of ratings agencies hired to evaluate risky securities in the run up to the 2008 financial meltdown[3]), nowhere is the problem more readily apparent than in the infamous Enron scandal. Prior to Enron's collapse, senior executives warned Chairman Kenneth Lay that Enron might be engaged in serious accounting fraud.[4] In particular, Vice President Sherron Watkins informed Lay of her worries that Enron—with the help of accounting firm Arthur Andersen—was executing sham transactions designed to keep debt off Enron's books, thereby inflating company earnings.[5] Watkins recommended having the dubious transactions reviewed by an outside law firm, but Lay retained Enron's traditional law firm, Vinson & Elkins, to review the transactions instead.[6] Moreover, he instructed them not to look too closely at Arthur Andersen's accounting treatment of these transactions.[7] Perhaps unsurprisingly, Vinson & Elkins eventually reported back that the transactions seemed fine, especially since the accountants had signed off on them.[8] Vinson & Elkins proceeded to interview only a handful of senior executives who offered cursory assurances that nothing was amiss, and the law firm declined to interview low-level employees identified as likely sources of information about the problems.[9] Vinson & Elkins cautioned that the transactions might lead to adverse publicity and litigation, but concluded that further investigations were not needed.[10]

---

[2] Max H. Bazerman et al., *Why Good Accountants Do Bad Audits*, 80 HARV. BUS. REV. 97, 99 (2002) ("Auditors have strong business reasons to remain in clients' good graces and are thus highly motivated to approve their clients' accounts. [A]uditors are hired and fired by the companies they audit, and it is well known that client companies fire accounting firms that deliver unfavorable audits. . . . [A]ccounting firms have increasingly treated audits as ways to build relationships that allow them to sell their more lucrative consulting services."). *See also* Donald C. Langevoort, *Reflections on Scienter (and the Securities Fraud Case Against Martha Stewart That Never Happened)*, 10 LEWIS & CLARK L. REV. 1, 15 (2006) (discussing the view "that auditor bias is self-serving, a way of coming to agree with the client in order to maintain and foster the audit relationship").

[3] *See* FIN. CRISIS INQUIRY COMM'N, FINANCIAL CRISIS INQUIRY REPORT 210 (Jan. 2011), http://fcic-static.law.stanford.edu/cdn_media/fcic-reports/fcic_final_report_full.pdf ("If an issuer didn't like a Moody's rating on a particular deal, it might get a better rating from another ratings agency. The agencies were compensated only for rated deals . . . So the pressure came from two directions: in-house insistence on increasing market share and direct demands from the issuers and investment bankers, who pushed for better ratings with fewer conditions.").

[4] Rebecca Roiphe, *The Ethics of Willful Ignorance*, 24 GEO. J. LEGAL ETHICS 187, 189 (2011).

[5] *Id.; see also Text of Letter to Enron's Chairman after Departure of Chief Executive*, N.Y. TIMES, Jan. 16, 2002, at C6.

[6] Roiphe, *supra* note 4, at 189; Gordon, *supra* note 1, at 1187.

[7] Gordon, *supra* note 1, at 1187.

[8] *Id.*; Roiphe, *supra* note 4, at 189.

[9] Roiphe, *supra* note 4, at 189; Gordon *supra* note 1, at 1187.

[10] Gordon, *supra* note 1, at 1187–88 (noting that the lawyers "warned that 'the bad cosmetics' . . . could result in 'a serious risk of adverse publicity and litigation,' but concluded . . . that no further investigation was necessary").

Some form of accountability for actors like the Vinson & Elkins lawyers seems called for,[11] and the criminal law's willful ignorance doctrine is a prime candidate for the job. If it could be shown that lawyers at Vinson & Elkins deliberately preserved their ignorance of the fraudulent nature of the transactions they approved, it would allow courts to treat the lawyers who turned a blind eye to the Enron fraud *as if* they actually knew of it.[12] This, in turn, would allow convictions, say, for fraud,[13] conspiracy to commit fraud,[14] or aiding and abetting fraud.[15]

However, the trouble is that on closer inspection it is not obvious that the lawyers at Vinson & Elkins, while culpable, were genuinely *willfully* ignorant. Willful ignorance requires *deliberately* acting to prevent oneself from learning whether the suspected fraud was occurring.[16] Granted, the lawyers likely suspected fraud—especially given Lay's instructions not to look too carefully into Arthur Andersen's treatment of the transactions. But it is far from clear that the lawyers then proceeded to act with *purpose* to preserve their ignorance. True, they interviewed only a handful of executives, and failed to speak with lower-level employees who might know whether fraud was occurring. But it is not obvious this was a *deliberate scheme* to remain ignorant, as opposed to shoddy investigation manifesting a willingness to tolerate the *risk* of remaining ignorant. Serious professionals generally are averse to conduct that is patently wrong, that can't be rationalized, and that threatens their self-perception as moral.[17] A more charitable reading of the

---

[11] *See id.* at 1189 ("It is likely that some of these lawyers engaged in conduct that may expose them to civil liability. Some may even face criminal liability . . .").

[12] *See* Global-Tech Appliances, Inc. v. SEB S.A., 131 S. Ct. 2060, 2070 n.9 (2011).

[13] United States v. Benjamin, 328 F.2d 854, 862 (2d Cir. 1964) (Friendly, J.) (holding that in securities fraud context, "Government can meet its burden by proving that a defendant deliberately closed his eyes to facts he had a duty to see"); United States v. Epstein, 426 F.3d 431, 441 (1st Cir. 2005) (upholding willful ignorance instructions where defendants were charged with, inter alia, mail fraud). *See also* GEOFFREY C. HAZARD, JR. ET AL., THE LAW AND ETHICS OF LAWYERING 88–91 (5th ed. 2010) (discussing criminal liability for lawyer misconduct).

[14] United States v. Ferrarini, 219 F.3d 145, 155 (2d Cir. 2000) (concluding, where defendants were charged with conspiracy to commit securities and mail fraud, "jury was properly instructed that conscious avoidance could . . . be used to infer knowledge of the conspiracy's unlawful objectives").

[15] United States v. Whitehill, 532 F.3d 746 (8th Cir. 2008) (upholding use of willful ignorance jury instruction, in prosecution for, inter alia, aiding and abetting wire and telemarketing fraud); Bruce Green, *The Criminal Regulation of Lawyers*, 67 FORDHAM L. REV. 327, 355–56 (1998) (discussing aiding and abetting liability for providing legal assistance to ongoing criminal activity).

[16] *See* Chapter 1, Section 3; *Jewell*, 532 F.2d at 700 (requiring "conscious purpose to avoid learning the truth").

[17] *See* Gordon, *supra* note 1, at 1190 ("Like human beings everywhere who want to enjoy self-respect and the esteem of others, [professionals] tell stories about how what they do is all right, even admirable"); Susan P. Koniak, *When the Hurlyburly's Done: The Bar's Struggle with the SEC*, 103 COLUM. L. REV. 1236, 1245 (2003) (explaining that generally "lawyers believe what they are doing is lawful").

facts is that the lawyers did not overtly *aim* to remain in ignorance of the fraud (which is blatant wrongdoing), but merely *risked* it out of a desire to please their clients.[18]

In this more realistic interpretation of events, the willful ignorance doctrine would not permit treating the Vinson & Elkins lawyers as knowing actors. They therefore could not be convicted of crimes like aiding and abetting fraud—despite being significantly culpable.[19] Since the Vinson & Elkins lawyers did not meet the requirements of the existing willful ignorance doctrine, they could not be punished as knowing actors. Thus, they would escape conviction for crimes like aiding and abetting fraud.

Since the willful ignorance doctrine does not cover scenarios of this kind, it falls short of providing an adequate response to the powerful incentives to avoid inculpatory knowledge that exist in white-collar settings. The willful ignorance doctrine is responsive to *deliberate efforts* to prevent oneself from learning inculpatory facts. But in its current form, it is inadequate to counteract the incentives to *nonwillfully allow* the same result to occur.

Accordingly, there is reason to move beyond the existing willful ignorance doctrine to allow some forms of not fully willful ignorance to satisfy the knowledge prong of a crime. Indeed, there is a doctrinal basis for just this. Recall that the "traditional rationale" for the willful ignorance doctrine is that "defendants who behave in [a willfully ignorant] manner are just as culpable as those who have actual knowledge."[20] Courts routinely endorse this *equal culpability thesis* as the substantive justification for the willful ignorance doctrine.[21] If we take this traditional rationale seriously, there is reason to go beyond the existing willful ignorance doctrine. Sometimes defendants act in ignorance, but not because they deliberately preserved their ignorance; rather, they might have only *recklessly* remained ignorant. Such cases fall outside the existing willful ignorance doctrine, but can sometimes intuitively rise to the same level of culpability as the analogous

---

[18] Sung Hui Kim, *The Banality of Fraud: Re-Situating the Inside Counsel as Gatekeeper*, 74 FORDHAM L. REV. 983, 986, 997, 1001–29 (2005) (lawyer acquiescence in corporate fraud often does not result from rational choice, but is produced by cognitive biases that shift the lawyers' perception toward a view that serves client interests).

[19] Generally, aiding and abetting securities fraud requires knowledge of the underlying violation. United States v. Corbin, 729 F. Supp. 2d 607, 620 (S.D.N.Y. 2010). Admittedly, recklessness can sometimes suffice for aiding and abetting fraud. *See* Alan R. Bromberg & Lewis D. Lowenfels, *Aiding and Abetting Securities Fraud: A Critical Examination*, 52 ALB. L. REV. 637, 675–76 (1988). If so, it wouldn't be necessary to rely on the willful ignorance doctrine, as the willfully ignorant are always at least reckless. However, this exception does not apply to Vinson & Elkins. Full knowledge of the underlying violation is required for aiding and abetting in cases like this where the defendant lawyers owe no fiduciary duty to the *victims* of the fraud. Kahn v. Chase Manhattan Bank, 760 F. Supp. 369, 374 (S.D.N.Y. 1991) ("[w]hen the alleged aider and abettor owed no fiduciary duty to the plaintiffs . . . the knowledge requirement is not satisfied by . . . recklessness . . . ; rather . . . the assistance rendered must be knowing and substantial"); SEC v. Collins & Aikman Corp., 524 F. Supp. 2d 477, 491 (S.D.N.Y. 2007); Bromberg & Lowenfels, at 671–77. Since Vinson & Elkins did not owe a fiduciary duty to the victims of Enron's accounting fraud, recklessness doesn't suffice for aiding and abetting; actual knowledge of the underlying violation is required. Thus, the willful ignorance doctrine is the only obvious route to convicting Vinson & Elkins.

[20] *Global-Tech*, 131 S. Ct. at 2069.

[21] *See, e.g., Jewell*, 532 F.2d at 700 ("the substantive justification for the rule is that deliberate ignorance and positive knowledge are equally culpable"). *See* Chapter 1 for many similar cases.

cases of knowing misconduct. Given the traditional rationale, it would be arbitrary not to also allow reckless ignorance to substitute for knowledge—provided the conditions of equal culpability are satisfied. Thus, the traditional rationale gives a doctrinal basis for allowing also some forms of egregious nonwillful ignorance—most importantly, reckless ignorance—to substitute for knowledge in conditions of equal culpability.[22]

Of course, this argument has traction only if some nonwillfully ignorant misconduct *really is* as culpable as the analogous knowing misconduct. Accordingly, the main task of the rest of this chapter is to argue that there actually are such cases.

II. Nonwillful Ignorance Can Be as Culpable as Knowing Misconduct

The claim to be shown is that some nonwillfully ignorant actions can be as culpable as the analogous knowing misconduct. Only then is there a basis, on the traditional rationale, for going beyond the existing willful ignorance doctrine. Toward this end, Section II.A sketches the intuitive case for this claim while Section II.B lays out the theoretical basis for it.

A. THE INTUITIVE CASE

The plausibility of the central claim can be seen most easily by focusing on *recklessly preserved ignorance*. Reckless ignorance (all else equal) is the most serious form of culpable ignorance that is not fully willful, so this is where the argument for going beyond the willful ignorance doctrine is likely to be strongest.

Consider a series of cases based on the allegations against the Vinson & Elkins lawyers: one involving knowledge, the second involving willful ignorance, and the third involving reckless ignorance.[23] All three concern a law firm hired by a corporation to review a series of esoteric transactions whose legality has been questioned. Red flags have come to light, and the attorney heading the investigation is aware of the risk that the transactions might be fraudulent. He visits the client's headquarters to interview employees about the transactions.

First, when Attorney A sits down to interview the employees, they immediately admit they were violating accounting rules. Unfazed, Attorney A writes "true sale" opinions for the transactions despite knowing they are fraudulent.

Second, Attorney B sits down to interview the employees, but before they can say anything, he says, "I don't know what you've been up to with these transactions, but if

---

[22] The argument of this chapter runs in the opposite direction from Chapter 3. There I argued that the traditional rationale requires curtailing the willful ignorance doctrine so it applies only to willfully ignorant defendants who are as culpable as knowing wrongdoers. Now I argue the traditional rationale also supports doctrinal expansions.

[23] I do not claim that any individual at Vinson & Elkins should have been convicted of any offense. I merely use the Vinson & Elkins allegations as the template for a series of hypotheticals that is useful for my argument.

there's been any funny business, I don't want to hear about it." After chatting about the Yankees, he heads back to his office and promptly signs off on the transactions. Attorney B is a classic willfully ignorant actor, who can straightforwardly be convicted of fraud, conspiracy, or aiding and abetting fraud.[24] The traditional rationale supports this, since Attorney B is just as culpable as Attorney A.

Lastly, Attorney C also remains ignorant of fraud—not deliberately, but because he is *recklessly indifferent to the truth*. When Attorney C conducts the interviews, he is blinded by his outsized desire to curry favor with his clients. He is too easily satisfied with the interviewees' flimsy explanations and vague assurances that they did nothing wrong. Suppose Attorney C realizes the employees might be hiding something, since their answers contain many holes. But he is so caught up in a "gold-rush mentality"[25] from the prospect of a lucrative relationship with this client that he concludes it is alarmist and excessive to dig into the weak assurances from the employees.[26] Accordingly, Attorney C conducts only cursory interviews, despite realizing the risk that this might lead him not to uncover any existing fraud.[27] Attorney C thus ends up preserving his ignorance of the fraud due to a reckless disregard for the need to dig deeper into the employees' claims. Instead of cross-examining the employees, he breezes through the interviews and can't be bothered to schedule interviews with others who might have relevant information. None of this is a scheme *aimed* at preserving his ignorance, but is done to avoid irritating his clients. He preserves his ignorance *recklessly*—that is, despite realizing his actions run the risk of preventing him from learning of the fraud.

Is Attorney C as culpable as Attorneys A and B? Were this an isolated incident, probably not. But suppose it's part of a pattern.[28] When the client splinters the legal team vetting the transactions into geographically dispersed offices, Attorney C (as head of the legal team) offers no resistance—*even though* he realizes the risk that this might prevent the lawyers from learning of any fraud.[29] Although he realizes the risk of remaining ignorant, he deems it to be more important to keep the client happy. Although this is not part of a *conscious effort* by Attorney C to remain in ignorance, he recklessly helps create barriers to learning of the fraud. Furthermore, the same thing happens when Attorney C delegates additional interviews about the transactions to a member of his team with a

---

24 *See supra* notes 13–15.

25 *Cf.* Financial Crisis Inquiry Report, *supra* note 3, at 5 (discussing the "gold-rush mentality" at Countrywide).

26 *Cf. Epstein*, 426 F.3d at 440–41 (discussing defendant's claim not to have been willfully ignorant because he asked about the truthfulness of representations to customers, and received flimsy assurances that they were true).

27 *Cf. supra* note 9.

28 Section III.A discusses the importance of requiring a *pattern* of indifference to the truth.

29 Something similar happened to the lawyers doing oversight and compliance work for WorldCom. *Report of the New York Bar Association Task Force on the Lawyer's Role in Corporate Governance* 26 (2006), *available online*: http://www.nycbar.org/pdf/report/CORPORATE_GOVERNANCE06.pdf.

reputation for sloppiness. Again, it's not his aim to remain in ignorance (he just wants to assign an ineffective team member a task where he won't be in the way), but it's another recklessly erected barrier to learning of the fraud in this case. Finally, Attorney C further reduces the chances of learning of the fraud by allowing a culture to take root within his legal team that discourages sharing bad news. He tolerates this culture not because he wants to remain in ignorance, but because he believes shielding the client from bad news keeps them happy.

After all these investigative failures, Attorney C signs off on the transactions. Given all these manifestations of his indifference to the suspected fraud, I submit that Attorney C intuitively is as culpable as Attorney A or B. Attorney C committed a series of acts that recklessly prevented learning of the fraud. It plausibly manifests as little concern for the protected interests of the fraud's victims as Attorney A or B's conduct. (Section II.B further defends this claim.)

Attorney C would escape conviction for the crimes that the willful ignorance doctrine makes Attorney B liable for.[30] However, this result is puzzling if all three attorneys manifested substantially the same degree of indifference to the victims of the fraud. If we take the traditional rationale seriously, Attorney C should be treated the same as Attorneys A and B. Some might be skeptical of convicting Attorney C of knowledge crimes, since he did not actually possess knowledge. But as we've seen, the criminal law adopts other such imputation principles,[31] and Chapter 5 provided an account of why equal culpability imputation of this sort is justified.

Before proceeding, note one limitation of the doctrinal expansion I advocate. Going beyond the willful ignorance doctrine is not the *only* available way to respond to the problems with the attorneys just discussed. One might look to the rules of professional ethics or to civil litigation for a response, or perhaps revisit criminal responsibility for negligent conduct. However, there are concerns about all these responses.[32] Moreover,

---

[30] *See supra* notes 13–15.

[31] The voluntary intoxication and transferred intent doctrines are examples. *See* Chapter 5.

[32] The trouble with relying on professional ethics as a response is that lawyers' ethical obligations are generally even *less* restrictive than the criminal law. The Model Rules of Professional Conduct only prohibit *knowingly* aiding client misconduct, and do not include a willful ignorance doctrine. Roiphe, *supra* note 4, at 190. Moreover, one might doubt that bar associations will substantially expand the scope of these rules, thereby making life more difficult for their members. *Id.* at 199. When it comes to criminal penalties for *negligently* performing one's professional duties, theoretical and practical skepticism threatens. *See, e.g.*, LARRY ALEXANDER & KIMBERLY FERZAN, CRIME AND CULPABILITY 24, 69–71 (2009) (arguing against criminal liability for negligence). I think this skepticism can be answered, but criminal liability for negligence may encounter resistance. Lastly, tort liability could provide a response to the present problem. But tort liability is limited because it requires a plaintiff who not only is willing and able to sue, but also who also can demonstrate that her specific injuries were *proximately caused* by the lawyer or accountant misconduct in question. Private lawsuits for aiding and abetting securities fraud are also heavily restricted. Gordon, *supra* note 1, at 1188 ("the Supreme Court and Congress have eviscerated private actions against lawyers for aiding and abetting under the securities laws"); *Cent. Bank of Denver*, 511 U.S. at 191 ("private plaintiff[s] may not maintain an aiding and abetting suit under § 10(b)").

I do not mean to offer my proposal of moving beyond the willful ignorance doctrine as the *sole* response to these problems. The expansion of the willful ignorance doctrine advocated here is just meant to be one of several responses that would help counteract the incentives to remain in ignorance that actors in white-collar contexts routinely face. Nonetheless, moving beyond the willful ignorance doctrine as advocated here is a particularly promising response because courts are *already committed* to this expansion in virtue of their traditional rationale for the willful ignorance doctrine. Thus, it stands ready to use without legislative action.

B. THE THEORY BEHIND THE SCENES

This section digs deeper to offer a systematic account of how nonwillfully ignorant conduct can be as culpable as analogous knowing misconduct. It builds on my account of the culpability of willful ignorance from Chapter 4, especially the duty to reasonably inform oneself (DRI).

1. The Iterated Reckless Ignorance Principle

There are many ways ignorance might count as nonwillful. If one entirely fails to notice the risks of one's contemplated conduct, one would be ignorant but not willfully so. This would be nonwillful ignorance where DRI is not triggered, since DRI requires awareness of the risks of one's conduct. Here, I focus on cases where DRI *does* apply and was breached. Ignorance may not always be culpable when there is no breach of a particularized duty to learn about recognized risks. But culpability is clearly present when DRI applies and is breached.

Because I aim to identify a form of nonwillful ignorance that is as culpable as knowing wrongdoing, I concentrate on the *most culpable* form of nonwillful ignorance. As shown earlier, willful ignorance requires an intentional or knowing breach of DRI. Since recklessness generally is more culpable than negligence, reckless breaches of DRI will generate the most culpable form of nonwillful ignorance, all else equal. I don't rule out that grossly negligent ignorance could rise to the level of culpability of knowing misconduct, but such cases would be hard to come by. Hence my focus on reckless ignorance.

What, then, *is* reckless ignorance? It occurs when DRI applies, but one takes a substantial and unjustifiable risk of not acquiring information that one should have gotten, and thereby breaches DRI. More specifically, DRI is *triggered* when one recognizes a specific substantial risk, *r*, that one's contemplated act, *a*, would impose and there are reasonable steps one could take to learn whether *r* will materialize if one does *a*. The *breach* of DRI is reckless when one behaves in ways that one is aware impose a substantial risk of preserving one's ignorance about *r*, thereby falling short of what DRI requires. Suppose DRI requires digging up more information about *r*, and being careful not to wall oneself off from information about *r* one normally would receive. If one then only gathers information about *r* in ways one realizes may not be sufficiently effective, thereby running a risk of not learning what one should have, this is a reckless breach of DRI. Likewise, if one creates impediments to obtaining information while realizing that this makes one less likely to learn what one should (i.e., despite realizing it risks preserving one's ignorance), this also constitutes a reckless breach of DRI.[33]

Attorney C illustrates reckless ignorance. He irresponsibly allowed several informational *barriers* to arise that he realized would reduce his chances of learning of the fraud as he should. For a simpler case, consider a doctor who is scheduled to perform complex surgery involving some experimental machinery tomorrow. Crucially, she suspects the machinery might involve new dangers. To stay informed of such dangers, she subscribes to *The Journal of Advanced Surgical Techniques*. Sometimes she reads it; other times her assistant alerts her to relevant articles. The new issue has just arrived. Unbeknownst to the doctor, it contains an article on the dangers of the exact machinery she will use tomorrow. However, she does not read the journal herself because she is late for a tennis match. Given her concerns about the machinery to be used, she hopes instead that her assistant will read the journal (as he sometimes does) and let her know if it contains pertinent articles. Unfortunately, the assistant is away from his desk, so the doctor cannot tell him to do this. Thus, on her way out, she leaves the journal in the common room hoping the assistant will see it. Accordingly, the doctor creates a *substantial risk* that she will remain ignorant of the dangers of the new technology. She does not aim, desire, or decide to remain in ignorance. Nor is she *ensuring* that she will, since her assistant may see the journal and inform her of the article. But suppose he does not. The doctor proceeds with the surgery not having learned of the dangers of the new technology and her patient is harmed as a result.

This is a paradigmatic case of acting with recklessly preserved ignorance. It involves a reckless breach of DRI, which will be culpable if it stems from insufficient regard for the interests of others.[34] Recklessly breaching DRI (e.g., by erecting informational barriers despite recognizing risks that this might prevent one from learning all one should) will

[33] Strictly speaking, recklessly violating DRI requires running the risk that one is investigating in ways that fall short of what DRI requires. For ease of exposition, in what follows I will assume that what DRI generally requires is taking the steps that would *actually lead one to learn conclusively whether the inculpatory proposition, p, is true* provided this is not unduly burdensome. Of course, investigating as reasonably required may not always lead one to learn conclusively whether p is true. But on the assumption that DRI generally requires decisively learning whether p (where one reasonably can), it follows that one breaches DRI *recklessly* when one is aware one is creating a substantial and unjustified *risk* that one will not learn p (where learning p is not unduly burdensome). By contrast, one breaches DRI *knowingly* (the lowest threshold for willful ignorance that has been suggested, see Chapter 1, Section 3) if one is aware one is making it practically certain—that is, *ensuring*—that one will not learn p (where learning whether p is not unduly burdensome). *Purposefully* breaching DRI, then, requires aiming or wanting to remain in ignorance.

[34] The doctor's behavior demonstrates that she places more value on making it to her tennis match on time than on eliminating the risk of remaining ignorant about the dangers of the upcoming surgery. However, the latter is far more important than the former. To risk preserving her ignorance of something she should have learned *only* to get to a tennis match manifests insufficient regard and is culpable.

be *less culpable* than breaching DRI deliberately, as required for willful ignorance. But it still entails *some* additional culpability beyond what one would incur if DRI did not apply. This follows from the Added Culpability Thesis defended in Chapter 4.

Thus, the big challenge is this: How can recklessly breaching DRI *ever* be culpable enough to raise one's culpability level up from (i) the level of purely reckless misconduct when investigation is not reasonably possible (where DRI does not apply) to (ii) the level of knowing misconduct? The clearest answer to this challenge is to employ a particular theoretical device: namely, the idea that one can *repeatedly* recklessly breach DRI and incur more culpability each time.[35] Granted, a single reckless breach of DRI usually will not be sufficient to raise one's culpability for the actus reus up to the level of knowing misconduct (even if this in theory could occur).[36] Still, a *string* of such breaches of one's duty to investigate a given risk *can* together add up to the culpability of the analogous knowing misconduct. Even when one reckless breach is not sufficient, perhaps two such breaches are enough to make one's conduct as culpable as a knowing wrong. Or if two are not sufficient, then perhaps three would do the trick. However culpable the analogous knowing misconduct is, there will be some number of reckless breaches of DRI that, when taken together and added to the culpability of the actus reus, amounts to the culpability of the analogous knowing misconduct.[37]

What is the mechanism at work here? *How*, exactly, is repeatedly breaching DRI supposed to enhance culpability? The thought is that sometimes the *only* plausible explanation for why one repeatedly breaches DRI recklessly is a level of regard for others that is *as low as* the level manifested in knowing misconduct. This idea is related to the view that enhanced punishments can be appropriate for repeat offenders.[38] Sometimes the

---

[35] *Cf.* Paul Robinson, *Imputed Criminal Liability*, 93 Yale L.J. 609, 650 (1984) (suggesting that "imputation of the elements of a serious offense can be justified on a finding of equivalent culpability reached by aggregating the actor's culpability for two or more less serious offenses").

[36] Perhaps one reckless breach of DRI could raise one's culpability up to the level of the analogous knowing wrongdoer if one's credence in the inculpatory proposition is just below the knowledge threshold. In that case, there would only be a small culpability gap to be filled. But it will be difficult to identify such cases in real life. It's hard to pin down actual actors' credences and it's hard to know exactly what credence one must have in the inculpatory proposition to count as being "practically certain" of it and thus knowing it. By contrast, it will be easier to find cases where a string of reckless breaches of DRI raises one's culpability up to the level of a knowing wrongdoer.

[37] Judge Learned Hand expressed a similar idea when, in a mail fraud case, he wrote: "It is true that all these instances, taken singly, do not prove beyond question that White knew that the statements which he prepared were padded with false entries; but logically the sum is often greater that the aggregate of the parts, and the cumulation of instances . . . may have a probative force immensely greater than any one of them alone." United States v. White, 124 F.2d 181, 185 (2d Cir. 1941) (Hand, J.).

[38] Ken Simons discusses the idea of a "recidivist premium," that is, a culpability magnifier to be applied in cases of repeatedly doing the same bad act. Kenneth L. Simons, *Statistical Knowledge Deconstructed*, 92 B.U. L. Rev. 1, 34 (2012). The idea is that "[a]n actor who persists in wrongdoing is legitimately viewed as committing a wrong more serious than the composite wrong that is constituted by the sum of the individual unjustifiable acts." *Id.* at 34. If such a recidivist premium is defensible, it makes my argument even easier. But my argument goes through even without applying a culpability *magnifier* to repeated misconduct. All my argument requires is that the

only way to account for the fact that an offender repeatedly commits a given crime is that he has *even less* regard for his victims than it would take to get him to do the same crime just *once*.[39] Likewise, sometimes defendant D's repeatedly breaching a given investigative duty is *only explainable* by the fact that D has *less* regard for others than would be needed to cause him to breach that duty only once. In this way, D's string of reckless breaches of DRI can manifest more culpability than just one such breach, considered in isolation, would manifest. Thus, repeatedly breaching DRI recklessly can eventually raise one's culpability for doing the underlying actus reus in the resulting state of ignorance up to the level of culpability of doing the actus reus with knowledge.[40]

One caveat is extremely important here. It is key that the reckless breaches of DRI that are added together all pertain to the *same underlying risk*, which the actor suspects his conduct will impose. Otherwise, it would not be legitimate to add together the culpability of each reckless breach of DRI.[41] If one first recklessly breaches the duty to investigate, say, the possibility that one's tax return contains misstatements, and then recklessly breaches the duty to investigate whether one's employees are engaged in insider trading, it would not be appropriate to aggregate the culpability of these two investigative failures. By contrast, if one suspects that one's employees are engaged in insider trading, but recklessly preserves one's ignorance of *this very risk* on a number of separate occasions, then the culpability of these *related* breaches can fairly be added together. They would all be traceable to the same underlying indifference to the risk of insider trading—that is, one's insufficient regard for the same protected interests. Putting all this together, here is the new imputation principle I advocate:

> **Iterated Reckless Ignorance Principle**: If defendant D lacks knowledge of an inculpatory proposition, p, which is required for crime C, D can be treated *as if* D knew that p if:

---

culpability of multiple breaches of one and the same investigative duty can be *added together*, thereby gradually raising one's culpability level over time, even without applying any magnifier.

[39] *See id.* at 34; Youngjae Lee, *Recidivism as Omission: A Relational Account*, 87 TEX. L. REV. 571 (2009).

[40] Is repeatedly recklessly breaching DRI only circumstantial evidence that you *purposefully* preserved your ignorance, thus making you willfully ignorant? (Thanks to Josh Andresen for this worry.) While possible, this will not always be true. My argument focuses on cases where it is clear the defendant did *not* purposefully remain ignorant. Perhaps this is simply conceded by the litigants. Or perhaps the defendant *undermines* his own ignorance by gathering easily avoidable information, thus showing himself not to have the purpose to remain ignorant. Where defendants act *inconsistently* with having purpose to remain ignorant, it would be strained to infer purpose to remain ignorant from merely a string of reckless breaches of DRI. These clear cases of iterated reckless ignorance are what my argument focuses on.

[41] Robinson also recognizes the importance of this relatedness constraint on the aggregation of culpability: "[t]he relation of the two offenses legitimates the aggregation of the two instances of culpability. The requirement of this relationship also avoids an unacceptable precedent: permitting such aggregation in all cases of multiple [unrelated] offenses." Robinson, *supra* note 35, at 650.

(1) D suspected p was true, thus triggering D's duty to inform himself in reasonable ways about whether p is true (i.e., D's duty to gather more information about p as appropriate and not erect barriers to learning whether p);
(2) D performed a series of related, reckless, ignorance-preserving acts or omissions in violation of D's duty to inform himself about p, and these breaches explain why D remained in ignorance of p;
(3) D proceeded to perform the actus reus of C while suspecting (but not knowing) p was true; and
(4) the sum of the culpability incurred from the ignorance-preserving acts or omissions in (2), and the subsequent actus reus in (3), is at least as great as the amount of culpability D would have had if D had performed the actus reus of C under the same circumstances *while knowing p*.

2. An Application of the Iterated Reckless Ignorance Principle

Under this principle, Attorney C can be treated as if he knew of the fraudulent nature of his client's transactions. He repeatedly recklessly breached his duty to investigate his suspicions that the transactions at issue were fraudulent.

The first group of such reckless breaches occurred when he only cursorily interviewed company employees. He was too easily satisfied by their flimsy answers and weak assurances. While recognizing that their answers did not hold water, he displayed reckless indifference to the truth due to his overpowering desire to keep the client content and preserve the profitability of his firm. Cognitively, he remained aware of the problems with the employees' answers, but his desires interfered with his judgment and removed the urgency of his lingering concerns. Thus, he took unjustifiable risks that his ignorance of the fraud would be preserved.

A second reckless breach occurred when he failed to resist the client's decision to split up the legal team into geographically dispersed offices. He recognized this would hamper the legal team's investigations, but his fear of irritating the client again got the better of him. As a result, he aided the creation of further barriers to learning of the fraud. This was not due to a *conscious decision* to remain in ignorance, but demonstrated a willingness to take risks of remaining ignorant of the suspected fraud.

Third, Attorney C recklessly breached DRI when he delegated subsequent interviews to an irresponsible member of his team, despite realizing it risked preventing the team from learning of the suspected fraud. Fourth, the same is true for Attorney C's cultivation of a climate within his team that discouraged sharing bad news that would risk the client's displeasure. This, too, recklessly preserved his ignorance of the fraudulent nature of the transactions.

After all these reckless investigative breaches, when Attorney C signed off on the transactions, he took the final step necessary to warrant treatment as a knowing wrongdoer. This approval of the transactions corresponds to the risky actus reus required under the above-mentioned prong (3).

Since the attorney never *deliberately* preserved his ignorance of the suspected fraud, he does not count as willfully ignorant. Nonetheless, he repeatedly manifested insufficient regard for the protected interests at stake. He did not deliberately blind himself to the truth, but he nonetheless *remained blinded* to it thanks to the distorting influence of his outsized desire to please the client. His conduct amounted to a pattern of recklessly failing to learn the truth about the risks of his chosen conduct, which can only be explained by a significant amount of insufficient regard for the protected interests at stake. Thus, I submit that Attorney C intuitively is no less culpable for his course of conduct than he would have been had he knowingly approved the transactions. As a result, the traditional rationale for the willful ignorance doctrine gives reason to treat Attorney C as if he had known of the fraud. The Iterated Reckless Ignorance Principle entails that Attorney C can be convicted of knowledge crimes like aiding and abetting fraud[42] as well.

III. Objections

A. IS THE REQUIRED ADDITION LEGITIMATE?

One natural objection concerns the legitimacy of adding together the culpability of different reckless breaches of DRI. If these quanta of culpability are not fairly considered together, it would be illegitimate to take a pattern of such breaches to substitute for knowledge.

My response is to emphasize the requirement that the different investigative breaches must all be *related*. They must all breach the duty to investigate *one and the same suspected risk*. It would be illegitimate to add up the culpability of breaching *different* investigative duties concerning unrelated risks. This would violate the Relatedness Constraint on Equal Culpability Imputation from Chapter 5. But repeatedly breaching the *same* investigative duty concerning the *same* suspected risk steadily increases culpability in a way that can be sensibly aggregated.[43]

The reason is that such a pattern of related investigative breaches must be traceable to the same underlying indifference to the truth of a *particular inculpatory proposition*. Breaching one's duty to investigate the same inculpatory proposition again and again

---

[42] *See supra* notes 13–15.

[43] Robinson also recognizes the importance of requiring that the culpability of different breaches cannot be aggregated unless they are sufficiently related. *See* Robinson, *supra* note 35, at 650; *supra* note 41. It is for this reason that courts, when seeking to impute an element of the offense, "often argue that two such related acts are a single course of conduct." *Id.*

manifests even less regard for the same set of interests than just one such breach in isolation. For the reasons given in Chapter 5, a pattern of related breaches of DRI can be aggregated to attribute a greater level of culpability than is manifested by one such breach. Taken together, such a pattern can be the basis for attributing as much culpability as is displayed in doing the actus reus with knowledge.

B. IS THIS MERELY SUBSTITUTING NEGLIGENCE FOR KNOWLEDGE?

One might also worry that the Iterated Reckless Ignorance Principle would allow *mere negligence* to substitute for knowledge. Couldn't enough negligence raise one's culpability up to the level of knowing misconduct? This worry is misplaced. The Iterated Reckless Ignorance Principle only permits a string of *reckless breaches of DRI*, followed by a *reckless* performance of the actus reus, to satisfy the knowledge element of the crime. DRI, moreover, is only triggered when one *suspects* that the relevant inculpatory proposition is true. While one might be ignorant in ways that amount to negligence, DRI does not apply and cannot be breached unless one is aware of a risk of the inculpatory proposition. Thus, the Iterated Reckless Ignorance Principle will never permit a *purely negligent* actor—one who is completely unaware of the unjustified risks of the actus reus—to be treated as a knowing wrongdoer.

What is more, the principle only permits this substitution when the actor displays *more culpability* than a similarly situated purely reckless actor who was not able to reasonably investigate his suspicions. Repeatedly breaching the duty of investigation, I argued, will raise one's culpability level *above* the level of purely reckless misconduct, and sometimes even raise it up to the level of knowing misconduct. Thus, the present worry fails. The Supreme Court, in upholding willful ignorance jury instructions, stressed the importance of willful ignorance having "an appropriately limited scope that *surpasses recklessness and negligence*."[44] The form of iterated reckless ignorance identified in the imputation principle I defend respects this requirement. It, too, demands something that surpasses recklessness and negligence.

C. PRACTICAL CONCERNS

Even those who accept my argument for the Iterated Reckless Ignorance Principle might remain skeptical for practical reasons. Let me consider two such practical worries.

1. Jury Confusion

One concern is that my proposed rule will lead to jury confusion and be unworkable. As we saw in Chapter 4, some argue the willful ignorance doctrine is confusing to

[44] *Global-Tech*, 131 S. Ct. 2060 at 2070 (emphasis added).

juries.[45] This concern might seem at least as forceful for the Iterated Reckless Ignorance Principle.

Several responses are possible,[46] but I remain optimistic about the workability of my proposed rule mainly because it is not hard is to formulate simple jury instructions embodying the Iterated Reckless Ignorance Principle. The idea is to combine traditional willful ignorance jury instructions with a description of the sort of iterated reckless ignorance I've been focusing on. Here is one suggestion for how they might look:[47]

> **Proposed jury instructions:** You may find that the defendant acted knowingly if you find beyond a reasonable doubt that he suspected that [the inculpatory proposition was true], but consciously decided not to learn whether his suspicions were true because he wanted to remain in ignorance and he had no good justification for doing so [i.e., he was willfully ignorant].
>
> Alternatively, even if the defendant did not intend or want to remain in ignorance, you may also find that he acted knowingly if, despite suspecting that [the inculpatory proposition] was true, he *repeatedly* (i.e., on more than one separate occasion) did things he was aware would make it significantly harder to learn the truth and so preserve his ignorance, but he had no good justification for doing so.
>
> However, you may *not* find that he acted knowingly if the defendant was completely unaware of [the inculpatory proposition] due simply to his carelessness or incompetence.

These instructions admittedly involve several simplifications compared to the fully stated, idealized Iterated Reckless Ignorance Principle. Nonetheless, any workable jury instructions in this area will have to involve at least some simplifications, as argued in

---

45 *See, e.g.*, Jessica A. Kozlov-Davis, *A Hybrid Approach to the Use of Deliberate Ignorance in Conspiracy Cases*, 100 MICH. L. REV. 473, 486–87 (2001).

46 My rule makes the jury's job *easier* in some respects than under the willful ignorance doctrine. The existing doctrine requires juries to distinguish between (i) cases where the defendant aimed to, or knew he would, remain ignorant, and (ii) cases where the defendant did not have the purpose or knowledge of remaining ignorant, but was aware he created a *risk* of such ignorance. Knowledge can be imputed based on the former but not the latter. However, empirical work suggests people are not good at distinguishing recklessness from higher mental states. Francis X. Shen et al., *Sorting Guilty Minds*, 86 N.Y.U. L. REV. 1306, 1337–44 (2011) (discussing difficulties test subjects had in separating recklessness from higher mental states); Matthew R. Ginther et al., *The Language of Mens Rea*, 67 VAND. L. REV. 1327, 1337 (2014) (test subjects tended to deem it appropriate to punish the mental states of knowledge and recklessness equivalently). On my proposal, however, juries would not have to distinguish knowingly preserving one's ignorance from merely risking ignorance. Rather, all the jury needs to find is that the defendant repeatedly acted in ways that she was *aware risked preserving her ignorance* (whether ignorance was a practically certain result or not). This seems an easier rule to apply in some ways.

47 This proposal is loosely modeled on the willful ignorance instructions in *Heredia*, 483 F.3d at 917. What's more, I also incorporate several improvements on the traditional willful ignorance instructions that I argued for in Chapter 4.

Chapter 4. Additional refinements may be needed. Still, these instructions at least suggest there is no great difficulty in principle in crafting workable jury instructions reflecting my proposed imputation principle.

One might still worry that juries will misapply the rule to find knowledge even when the evidence does not support such a finding under my proposed rule. Here is one additional suggestion in response. We can increase the workability of my proposed rule by adopting a *burden-shifting framework* similar to an approach some circuits already employ for willful ignorance instructions.[48] The idea is to insist that repeated reckless ignorance can substitute for knowledge only in one narrow litigation scenario: namely, when the defendant has decided to *contest* the prosecution's willful ignorance theory by denying that he, the defendant, *purposefully* remained in ignorance. Suppose in a prosecution for a knowledge crime, the government relies on a willful ignorance theory. Suppose the defendant then counters that his ignorance was not truly *willful*. That is, he contends he did not have the aim or conscious object of remaining ignorant. The proposal is to allow the prosecution under such circumstances—but *only* such circumstances—to use the defendant's repeated reckless ignorance to satisfy the knowledge element of the crime. Thus, it would only be under these limited circumstances (i.e., when defendants contest a willful ignorance theory by denying they *purposefully* remained ignorant) that reckless ignorance jury instructions could be given. This would further reduce the risk of juries misapplying the Iterated Reckless Ignorance Principle.

2. A Reform We Should Bother With?

A final worry is whether it is all that important to expand the equal culpability rationale behind the willful ignorance doctrine as I propose. Should this figure very high on our agenda for reforming the content of the criminal law—especially given the worries about overcriminalization that other legal scholars have forcefully pressed?[49] Do we really need yet another doctrinal tool by which to secure more convictions?

For many offenses involving knowledge, such as drug possession offenses, there is a growing body of literature suggesting that these crimes are prosecuted too aggressively and sentenced too harshly.[50] Accordingly, I doubt there would be grave unfairness in

[48] *See, e.g.*, United States v. Reyes, 302 F.3d 48, 55 (2d Cir. 2002) (noting that willful ignorance jury instructions are given "when a defendant *claims to lack some specific aspect of knowledge* necessary to conviction but where the evidence may be construed as deliberate ignorance" (emphasis added)); United States v. Abbas, 74 F.3d 506, 513 (4th Cir. 1996) ("A willful blindness instruction is appropriate when the defendant *asserts a lack of guilty knowledge* but the evidence supports an inference of deliberate ignorance." (emphasis added)).

[49] Douglas Husak, Overcriminalization: The Limits of the Criminal Law 10–28 (2008) (arguing that there is too much criminal law, inter alia, because the law has grown so complex, with so many surprising crimes, that ordinary citizens lack fair notice of its requirements).

[50] Robert G. Lawson, *Drug Law Reform-Retreating from an Incarceration Addiction*, 98 Ky. L.J. 201 (2010) (arguing the war on drugs "has involved very aggressive law enforcement" and "very harsh punishments"); Shima Baradaran, *Drugs and Violence*, 88 S. Cal. L. Rev. 227, 233 (2015) (contesting the assumed linkage between drugs and violence that underlies harsh sentences in this area); Paul H. Robinson et al., *The Disutility of*

showing leniency and declining, for crimes like these, to extend the equal culpability rationale as far as it can go.

Instead, it might be more prudent to deploy the Iterated Reckless Ignorance Principle not across the board, but rather only as a means to combating problems that independently need solving. Most importantly, the doctrinal expansion I've been arguing for seems especially warranted to combat the incentives to remain in ignorance that actors face in white-collar contexts when potential conflicts of interest loom. The following are characteristic of such cases:

(1) The actor occupies a role that carries with it a duty to detect or prevent fraud or abuse;
(2) The actor knows or ought to know that the party he serves (e.g., his client or employer) has incentives to hamper his efforts to investigate whether fraud or abuse is occurring;
(3) The actor knows or ought to know that he has his *own* incentives to remain in ignorance because this would please his client or employer.

When these three factors are present, heightened accountability is appropriate. The Iterated Reckless Ignorance Principle can be used to provide it.

Why focus on the corporate context in particular? The reason derives form the obvious temptation to structure corporate or professional relationships—whether intentionally or unintentionally—to prevent inculpatory information from being shared, recognized and acted on. As Pettit and List argue, it is

> possible for individuals to incorporate, *consciously or unconsciously*, so as to benefit from this deficit of responsibility [that corporate organization allows]. They might seek to achieve a certain effect, say a certain bad and self-serving effect, while arranging things so that none of them can be held fully responsible for what is done; they are protected by excusing or exonerating considerations [like ignorance].[51]

Similarly, as Khanna argues, because traditional mens rea standards "allow[] corporations to avoid liability by partitioning information, it encourages them to do so, resulting in suboptimal information sharing and a suboptimal level of care."[52]

This danger is equally serious when it comes to the relationship between a corporation and outside professionals like accountants, lawyers, or ratings agencies the corporation

Injustice, 85 N.Y.U. L. Rev. 1940, 1946 & n.12 (2010) (discussing legal scholars who reject desert-based principles because of "what they see as the over-punitiveness of current criminal law"; collecting sources).

[51] C. List & P. Pettit, Group Agency 165–67 (2011) (emphasis added).

[52] Vikram Khanna, *Is the Notion of Corporate Fault a Faulty Notion?: The Case of Corporate Mens Rea*, 79 B.U. L. Rev. 355, 381 (1999).

relies on. Where corporations are engaged in dubious practices, it will be especially tempting "to use lawyers [or accountants] to paint a gloss of respectability . . . on dubious transactions."[53] For their part, lawyers and accountants have incentives to please the parties they serve, and thus may end up being overly tolerant of less than perfect access to the relevant information.[54]

Accordingly, it is especially important to craft judicial tools that counteract the incentives to enter into working relationships with lawyers and accountants that end up perpetuating all the parties' ignorance of wrongdoing that may be occurring. The existing willful ignorance doctrine is one tool that serves this purpose. But it is not a fully adequate solution because it is only responsive to *deliberate* attempts to remain in ignorance. But the problem is not limited to purposeful efforts to avoid inculpatory knowledge. The problem also extends to cases of merely *recklessly allowing* the parties' ignorance to be preserved. To combat this not-fully-deliberate version of the problem, we need tools that go beyond the willful ignorance doctrine. This is the gap that the Iterated Reckless Ignorance Principle is meant to fill.

As a result, it seems especially important to make the Iterated Reckless Ignorance Principle available for criminal prosecutions in settings where the temptation to suppress, avoid, or hinder the acquisition of inculpatory information is known to be acute. Because corporations receive the benefits of using independent firms to vet and approve their activities, it is only fair to subject them, and the outside firms they hire, to heightened forms of accountability. Moving beyond the existing willful ignorance doctrine to adopt the Iterated Reckless Ignorance Principle in the limited circumstances I propose is one way to do this. It is not a silver bullet that will eradicate all harm resulting from the temptation to stay ignorant, but it is an important step toward filling the gap in the criminal law's response to the incentives to remain ignorant of fraud in our midst.

---

53 Gordon, *supra* note 1, at 1201.

54 *See supra* note 2.

7 Substituting Willful Ignorance for Purpose?

THE LAST CHAPTER argued for moving beyond the existing willful ignorance doctrine by allowing some forms of nonwillful ignorance to substitute for knowledge. But where does it end? This chapter considers moving beyond the willful ignorance doctrine in a different direction—by allowing willful ignorance to substitute for purpose—but argues that *this* doctrinal expansion is not justified. Acting with purpose to bring about a bad state of affairs will, all else equal, always be more culpable (or culpable in a different way) than doing so in willful ignorance of whether this state of affairs will result. This precludes the latter from substituting for the former. Thus, this chapter aims to get clearer on the limits of equal culpability imputation.

There are a couple of ways to understand the idea of willful ignorance substituting for purpose. The simplest is illustrated in the conspiracy context, where questions of willful-ignorance-for-purpose substitution have been extensively litigated. Accordingly, I begin by discussing willful ignorance jury instructions in federal conspiracy cases. Courts are generally opposed to allowing willful ignorance of what the goals of the conspiracy are to substitute for purpose to promote the aims of the conspiracy. This rule is sensible, but explaining it reveals a more interesting—and more difficult—question lurking nearby. The real question, therefore, is whether willful ignorance of a particular proposition (e.g., that one's action will cause a certain harm) can legitimately substitute for the purpose to make *that very same proposition* true (i.e., to cause that very harm). I argue that the answer to this question, too, is "no." But this is harder to establish. It requires showing that

Criminally Ignorant. Alexander Sarch.

purposeful misconduct is always more culpable than (or culpable in too different a way from) the analogous willfully ignorant act.

I. Willful Ignorance Instructions in the Conspiracy Context

To sharpen the question we're interested in when asking if willful ignorance can substitute for purpose, I begin by considering conspiracy prosecutions. Related questions have been litigated there, and have been given sensible answers. Explaining these helps home in on the more difficult question we ultimately want to answer.

A. WILLFUL IGNORANCE IN THE CONSPIRACY CONTEXT

Obtaining a conviction under the general federal conspiracy statute[1] requires proving three elements: "(1) an agreement among two or more persons, the object of which is an offense against the United States; (2) the defendant's knowing and willful joinder in that conspiracy; and (3) commission of an overt act in furtherance of the conspiracy by at least one of the alleged co-conspirators."[2] It is "well-settled that the elements of a conspiracy may be proved by circumstantial evidence," since "[c]onspiracies are secretive by their very nature."[3] What matters for us is the second element. This joinder element—also called participation—itself has two components: It requires participating "(1) with some *knowledge* of the conspiracy's unlawful aims and (2) with the *intent* of helping the scheme succeed."[4]

Our question is whether either of these two mens rea elements of participation can be satisfied by willful ignorance. The Second Circuit adopts what I contend is the correct answer: willful ignorance may substitute for knowledge of the unlawful objectives of the conspiracy, but not purpose to further those objectives.[5] Consider *United States*

---

[1] 18 U.S.C. § 371 (it's an offense for "two or more persons conspire . . . to commit any offense against the United States, . . . and one . . . do[es] any act to effect the object of the conspiracy"). Other offense-specific conspiracy statutes have harsher penalties. 21 U.S.C. § 846 (drug trafficking); 18 U.S.C. § 2332b (terrorism).

[2] United States v. Svoboda, 347 F.3d 471, 476 (2d Cir. 2003); *see also* United States v. Ngige, 780 F.3d 497, 503 (1st Cir. 2015) (listing same elements of § 371 conspiracies); United States v. Wright, 215 F.3d 1020, 1028 (9th Cir. 2000) (same). Not all federal conspiracies require an overt act. United States v. Shabani, 513 U.S. 10, 14, (1994) (no overt act required for § 846 drug conspiracies).

[3] *Svoboda*, 347 F.3d at 477.

[4] *Id.* (emphasis added); United States v. Crossley, 224 F.3d 847, 856 (6th Cir. 2000) (requiring proof that defendant "knew the object of the conspiracy and 'voluntarily associated himself with it to further its objectives.' "); Jessica Kozlov-Davis, *A Hybrid Approach to the Use of Deliberate Ignorance in Conspiracy Cases*, 100 MICH. L. REV. 473, 478 (2001).

[5] United States v. Ferrarini, 219 F.3d 145, 155 (2d Cir. 2000) ("conscious avoidance c[an] only be used to infer knowledge of the conspiracy's unlawful objectives, and not of intent to participate"); Kozlov-Davis, *supra* note 4, at 491 ("the Second Circuit forbids . . . deliberate ignorance instruction[s] altogether when intent to further the goals of the conspiracy . . . is at issue").

v. Svoboda, which involved conspiracy to commit insider trading.[6] The defendant's co-conspirator testified that he "had obtained confidential information" and "passed the information to [the defendant], who, in turn, used [it] to make trades."[7] The defendant "denied knowledge of the unlawful source of [the] information."[8] He was convicted, and on appeal challenged the district court's willful ignorance instructions, arguing that "intent to participate may not be proved by . . . conscious avoidance."[9]

The Second Circuit, however, found nothing amiss in the willful ignorance jury instructions at issue. It approved the instructions, holding that "a defendant's conscious avoidance of knowledge of [the conspiracy's] illegal purpose may substitute for knowledge of the illegal purpose."[10] However, "conscious avoidance of such knowledge is [by itself] insufficient" to prove joinder in the conspiracy;[11] in addition, "[t]here must be further proof that the defendant joined in the illegal agreement with the intent of helping it succeed in its criminal purpose."[12] Other circuits endorse the view that willful ignorance of the aims of the conspiracy cannot satisfy the requirement of purpose to help the scheme succeed.[13] Call this the *No-Substitution Rule*.

Some circuits go a bit further. They not only allow willful ignorance to substitute for knowledge of the conspiracy's aims but also allow willful ignorance to constitute *circumstantial evidence* that the defendant acted with purpose to facilitate those aims. Call this the *Evidentiary Rule*.[14] (Other courts may seem to allow willful ignorance to substitute for purpose, but they are more accurately read as just applying the Evidentiary Rule without being very clear about it.[15])

I will have little to say about the Evidentiary Rule in what follows. It is consistent with my view that the No-Substitution Rule is correct. I suspect the Evidentiary Rule risks jury confusion such that willful ignorance may in practice be illicitly standing in

---

6 *Svoboda*, 347 F.3d at 479.

7 *Id.* at 475

8 *Id.*

9 *Id.* at 475–78.

10 *Id.* at 479.

11 *Id.*

12 *Id.*

13 United States v. Fernandez, 553 F. App'x 927, 937 (11th Cir. 2014) (upholding instructions where "district court instructed the jury about deliberate ignorance to help the jury understand the element of *knowledge*, not for the purpose of ascertaining . . . *intent*").

14 United States v. Brodie, 403 F.3d 123, 148, 150 & n.28 (3d Cir. 2005) (allowing evidence of willful ignorance to suffice for inferring defendant knowingly and willfully joined conspiracy to violate Trading With the Enemy Act).

15 *Compare* United States v. Nguyen, 493 F.3d 613, 625 (5th Cir. 2007) ("evidence of [defendants'] continued facilitation of those highly suspicious transactions may constitute 'specific intent' to further an illegal purpose for which they were deliberately ignorant)," *with id.* at 625 ("[t]he evidence for a finding of specific intent can overlap with the evidence establishing the defendant's knowledge that they were acting illegally" and a willful ignorance jury instruction as to knowledge of the conspiracy's aims "is hardly inconsistent with a finding that the defendant intended to further the unlawful purpose'" (internal citations omitted)).

for purpose, but I don't think the rule is *theoretically* unsound. It would be defensible if we could ensure it is applied correctly. (We can help do this by allowing the Evidentiary Rule to be used only where willful ignorance of the conspiracy's objectives is especially probative of purpose to further these objectives.[16]) The aim of this section, however, is to justify the No-Substitution Rule.

B. WHY THE SECOND CIRCUIT'S NO-SUBSTITUTION RULE IS CORRECT

The No-Substitution Rule is correct because the propositional contents of the required knowledge and the required purpose are distinct. To see this, notice how the two elements come apart. The required knowledge is this:

> K: I know that the relevant enterprise aims to accomplish goals G (which actually happen to be criminal, even if I don't know that fact).

I use "enterprise" here instead of "conspiracy" because one needn't conceive of the group in question *as a conspiracy*, which is a negatively loaded concept. Instead, one might just see the group as engaged in a neutral activity. Moreover, to have "knowledge of the enterprise's unlawful aims," one merely has to know what the aims are; one doesn't have to know they would be a crime if accomplished. Next, the requisite purpose can be stated as follows:

> P: I aim for the enterprise to accomplish its goals, whatever they are.

When one possesses both P and K, and puts two and two together, one will also possess the following further purpose:

> P*: I aim for the enterprise to accomplish goals G.

Of course, one cannot possess P* without also possessing K—that is, without knowing what goals the enterprise aims at. To ensure that P and K are separable, the required purpose must be formulated as P was above—as the aim to help the enterprise accomplish whatever goals it has.

How can K and P come apart? First, I might possess P without K if I innocently intend to aid the enterprise (i.e., possess P) without knowing its aims (i.e., lack K). Maybe

---

[16] In particular, the defendant's willful ignorance of the conspiracy's aims should be allowed to serve as evidence of a purpose to facilitate those aims *only if* there is no proof he *lacked* such purpose. What might such proof look like? One example would be if the willfully ignorant defendant actually *hampers* the conspiracy by playing his part in an inefficient way, which seems designed to make the conspiracy less likely to accomplish its aims. To prevent jury confusion and unfair verdicts, the Evidentiary Rule should be applied only when there is no such evidence clearly showing a lack of purpose to promote the aims of the conspiracy.

I think the group just aims to sell flowers, rather than use the flower shop as a front for smuggling drugs. By contrast, I might possess K without P if I know the enterprise aims to accomplish certain (perhaps illicit) goals, but have no intent for the enterprise to succeed. Maybe I know my friends in the flower shop are smuggling stolen goods but do not intend to help them do so (perhaps I even seek to hinder their efforts). In neither case would I be guilty of conspiracy.

Now it should start to become clear why willful ignorance of the proposition in K cannot substitute for P. Of course, such willful ignorance can permit courts to impute K to the defendant. Provided he satisfies all the other elements of the conspiracy including P, it's plausible that his willful ignorance of the proposition in K can make him as culpable as if he joined the conspiracy while actually possessing K.

But what about P? Could willful ignorance of the proposition in K, if culpable enough, be the basis for treating one as if one possessed P as well? It would be odd if it could. Merely knowing what the goals of the conspiracy *are*—or being willfully ignorant thereof—doesn't entail that one also has the purpose that the enterprise should accomplish its goals (or any other pro-attitude toward them). That is a separate matter. One might know—or remain willfully ignorant of—the group's aim of smuggling drugs, but lack any culpability because one has no intent for the scheme to succeed. One might even actively work against it.[17]

Still, doubts might linger. Is it *impossible* for willful ignorance of the proposition in K to confer enough extra culpability in the right way to warrant treating one as if one actually possessed P? There is no predetermined limit on how much culpability deliberately preserving one's ignorance can add. So why not think willful ignorance could confer enough added culpability to make one not just as culpable as a knowing wrongdoer but indeed as culpable as the analogous purposeful wrongdoer?

The main reason willful ignorance of what the aims of the conspiracy are cannot substitute for purpose to promote the conspiracy's aims is that the propositional content of the former (willful ignorance) is not the same as the propositional content of the latter (purpose).[18] The proposition in K is that *the conspiracy aims to accomplish a particular goal, G*. To act with purpose toward *this* proposition would be to aim to make it true that the conspiracy *aims* to accomplish G. But that of course is not the proposition at issue

---

[17] One might object this means there is no *agreement* with the enterprise, which is an independent requirement of conspiracy. *See supra* note 2. Nonetheless, there still could be an agreement with the enterprise that is unrelated to its unlawful goals. Perhaps I know the flower shop boys are smuggling stolen goods, but I agree to have them supply flowers for my wedding. I don't commit conspiracy without intending that their smuggling-related goals succeed.

[18] In addition, one might claim that willful ignorance of the proposition in K cannot be taken to satisfy *two* mens rea requirements: viz., both K and P. Nonetheless, I doubt this is decisive, since in principle willful ignorance—if extensive enough—could make one more culpable than a knowing actor. So one might wonder why it's impossible for willful ignorance of the proposition in K to make one as culpable as if one possessed both these two mental states: K and P. Thus, I think the argument in the main text is better.

in P. To be guilty of conspiracy, the proposition one must aim to make true is not that the conspiracy *aims* to accomplish this or that, but rather that the conspiracy's goals *are accomplished*. For example, suppose the conspiracy aims to make money by smuggling drugs. To be guilty of conspiracy, the proposition one must have the purpose to make true is not:

(1) The conspiracy aims to make money by smuggling drugs,

but rather:

(2) The members of the conspiracy are making money by smuggling drugs.

Willful ignorance of (1) cannot be a basis for imputing purpose to make (2) true because this would violate the *content restriction on equal culpability substitution* defended in Chapter 5. It held that for one mens rea to substitute for another, they both must manifest insufficient regard for the same set of protected interests, rights, and values. But (1) and (2) have different content: (1) is about what the conspiracy *aims* to accomplish, while (2) is about what the conspiracy *accomplishes*. Thus, acting in willful ignorance of (1) does not manifest insufficient regard *toward the same set of protected interests, rights, or values* as acting with the purpose to make (2) true. Simply put, (1) deals with the need to control the aims possessed by groups you belong to, while the interests and values at stake in (2) concern the well-being of those harmed or endangered by drug smuggling. Therefore, it violates the content restriction on equal culpability substitution if willful ignorance of (1) were the basis for imputing the purpose to make (2) true.

Thus, if willful ignorance can plausibly substitute for purpose at all, this could be tolerated *only if* the propositional content of the willful ignorance is the same as that of the purpose to be imputed. Otherwise the two mental states would not be sufficiently closely related for the one to legitimately substitute for the other. This is why the Second Circuit is entirely correct that willful ignorance about what the aims of the conspiracy *are* does not suffice for treating defendants as though they had the purpose that those aims should be accomplished. My theory of equal culpability substitution from Chapter 5 offers a neat explanation of why.

C. THE MORE INTERESTING QUESTION

Nonetheless, there is a more interesting question nearby. There can be scenarios where the proposition the defendant is willfully ignorant of *is* exactly the same as the propositional content of the purpose to be imputed. This naturally occurs when the inculpatory proposition just is the fact that an intended act will have a specific harmful or wrongful consequence. Consider:

(3) My intended act of speeding down the road will cause injury or death to a pedestrian.

One can be willfully ignorant of (3) if one suspects it's true, can investigate, but decides to remain ignorant. One can also act with purpose to make (3) true—as when one acts in order to injure or kill a pedestrian. Thus, we can meaningfully ask whether willful ignorance of (3) can be the basis for imputing not just knowledge of (3) but also purpose to make (3) true.

It is much less clear why speeding down the road in a state of willful ignorance about (3) could not substitute for the purpose to make (3) true provided one's willfully ignorant conduct is as culpable as the analogous purposeful conduct. Since the same proposition is at issue in both the actor's willful ignorance and the purpose to be imputed, substituting the former for the latter would not violate the content restriction on equal culpability substitution. Thus the hurdle to substituting willful ignorance for purpose, seen previously, is no longer present. Since there is no predetermined limit on how much extra culpability is conferred by deliberately preserving one's ignorance, why couldn't willful ignorance of (3) in principle substitute for purpose to make (3) true? For all I've said so far, this has not been ruled out. Thus, the question I address in the rest of this chapter is why willful ignorance of a particular proposition shouldn't be allowed to substitute for purpose *as to the very same proposition*.[19]

In what follows, I offer two arguments that even this form of willful-ignorance-for-purpose substitution is not legitimate. Both rely, in one way or another, on differences between purposeful action and acting with nonpurposeful mental states like knowledge or recklessness.

---

[19] A related question is whether, if knowledge (K) of p is required for guilt, willful ignorance (WI) of some other proposition, q, can satisfy the knowledge element provided q *entails* p (given relevant background beliefs). If a crime requires knowledge that the building you intend to burgle is a dwelling (p), can we impute that knowledge based on the fact that you're willfully ignorant of a different proposition (q)—for example, that personal mail is regularly delivered there? At first blush, it might seem not, since the propositional content of WI and K are different. Nonetheless, as argued in Chapter 1, if p and q are *inferentially linked* in a sufficiently tight way, then WI of q can substitute for K of p. The determinative question for whether WI of q is eligible to substitute for K of p is whether p is something one could reasonably be expected to easily infer (given relevant background beliefs) based on believing q. If so, there is less of a barrier to allowing WI of q to substitute for K of p. On my theory, this is really a question of whether p and q are sufficiently closely related to say that WI of q manifests the same amount of insufficient regard *toward the same set of protected interests, rights, and values* as K of p does. This is a function of what p and q *mean*, so it the matter must be decided on a case-by-case basis. But substituting WI of q for K of p is not categorically ruled out.

II. Willful Ignorance Cannot Substitute for Purpose—First Argument

First, I argue that willful ignorance of p cannot substitute for purpose to make p true because, when all else is equal, willfully ignorant conduct is less culpable than the analogous purposeful conduct. For simplicity, I'll suppose that the inculpatory proposition, p, is the fact that the actus reus one intends will have some harmful consequence—like severe injury or death to a victim. Of course, sometimes it will be only an attendant circumstance (e.g., that a person is in the building one intends to burn down). Nonetheless, the argument carries over. That is, it will also show that acting in willful ignorance that some attendant circumstance obtains cannot be used as a substitute for the purpose to [do the act while that attendant circumstance obtains]. Still, for simplicity, my focus is to argue that willful ignorance of whether one's act will cause a given harm is not a legitimate basis for imputing purpose to bring about that same harm.

A. Why Purposeful Misconduct Is More Culpable Than the Same Willfully Ignorant Misconduct

Under the "traditional rationale," we may substitute willful ignorance of p for knowledge that p only when the equal culpability thesis holds.[20] Similarly, a willful-ignorance-for-purpose substitution principle could be justified only if the equal culpability thesis as between willfully ignorant and purposeful conduct is true. The basic idea behind my first argument, then, is just that this thesis is not true. Acting with purpose to make p true (where p designates the fact that the act will cause a given harm) is *more* culpable than the exactly analogous action done in willful ignorance of p. More specifically, I argue against:

> **Equal Culpability Thesis for Purpose (ECTP)**: Suppose A1 and A2 each do the actus reus of a crime requiring the purpose to make some inculpatory proposition, p, true (e.g., that one's action causes some harmful or prohibited state of affairs). A1 and A2, and their respective actions, are identical in every possible respect except one: while A1's action is done with the purpose to make p true, A2's action is done *in willful ignorance toward p that involves a highly unjustified breach of the duty to reasonably inform oneself.* On these suppositions, A2 is (at least) as culpable for her action as A1 is for his.

The trouble with ECTP is that willfully ignorant actors are not as culpable as their *similarly situated* purposeful counterparts. To show this, I extend an argument I have made

[20] Global-Tech Appliances, Inc. v. SEB S.A., 131 S. Ct. 2060, 2069 (2011).

elsewhere to the effect that there is always one respect in which bringing about a harm purposefully is more culpable than bringing it about only knowingly.[21] What I add here is that the same point also holds between purpose and *willful ignorance*. Purposefully bringing about a bad state of affairs is, all else equal, more culpable than doing so not just knowingly but also in willful ignorance. Assuming all else is equal, the purposeful actor is going to be more culpable.

1. Why Purposeful Harming Is Worse than Knowing Harm

To show this, let me recap the argument I've previously given for the criminal law's adoption of a version of the *doctrine of double effect*—the thesis, roughly, that it's worse to purposefully bring about a harm than to bring about that same harm only knowingly.[22] The idea is that purposeful misconduct involves two strikes against you, while knowing misconduct involves only one. More precisely, an unjustified act of purposefully bringing about a bad state of affairs necessarily involves *two manifestations of insufficient regard*, while the analogous unjustified act of bringing it about knowingly involves just *one* such manifestation.[23] My claim here is only that there is *one respect* in which purposeful misconduct is worse than knowing misconduct. When *all else is equal*—that is, when the harms at issue, the obtainable benefits, the probabilities the actors believe their acts have of bringing about these harms and benefits,[24] etc., are held fixed—then the purposeful act is on balance more culpable than the analogous knowing act.

---

[21] Alex Sarch, *Double Effect and the Criminal Law Culpability Hierarchy*, 11 CRIM. L. & PHIL. 453 (2017).

[22] The criminal law adopts a version of this thesis. Some crimes require full-on purpose to bring about a harm or wrong, and mere knowledge that it will occur does not suffice. Treason is a classic example. Haupt v. United States, 330 U.S. 631, 641 (1947) (requiring purpose to aid the enemy, not mere knowledge an enemy will be aided).

Also note, as Chapter 1 discussed, UK practitioners often insist one cannot have knowledge of future events, only belief. I think we can know some future events, such as that the sun will rise tomorrow, at least sufficiently to satisfy the practical needs of the criminal law. While I thus adopt the US convention here, not much turns on this. My arguments concerning knowledge of future events can be easily translated into talk of belief, if one prefers.

[23] Unlike the traditional doctrine of double effect, my argument does not apply to justified acts, only unjustified ones. *See* Sarch, *supra* note 21, at 460 & n.43. This is similar to Moore's view. MICHAEL S. MOORE, CAUSATION AND RESPONSIBILITY 48 (2009).

[24] Note the perceived likelihood of the possible harms and benefits only needs to be held fixed when comparing purposeful actors to nonpurposeful ones—not when comparing knowing and willfully ignorant actors. The knowing and the willfully ignorant *necessarily* differ as to the perceived likelihood of the harms and benefits. The knowing believe the harm to be practically certain, while the willfully ignorant only believe it to be a substantial risk. But purposeful actors do not necessarily differ from nonpurposeful actors in this way. Thus, for all else to be equal between the purposeful and the nonpurposeful actor, the perceived likelihood of the possible harms and benefits does need to be held fixed.

To see why, note that the main difference between purposefully and knowingly causing harm is that the former involves being *committed* to the harm, while the latter does not.[25] Consider:

> *Arson 1*: Tony offers to pay Alan $5,000 to burn down a building, but it has to be done before midnight or Alan won't get paid. Alan agrees. He arrives at the building at 11:30 p.m., and as he is about to light the fire, he sees that Victor is doing something on the second floor. Victor does not leave, and so Alan proceeds to light the fire knowing (i.e., while practically certain) that this will lead to Victor's death. As expected, Victor dies. Alan regrets it, but he really wanted the money.
>
> *Arson 2*: This case is identical to Arson 1, except that now Tony offers to pay Bobby $5,000 to see to it that Victor dies tonight before midnight. Moreover, Bobby is to kill Victor by making it look like he was killed by a fire in the building. Tony will not give Bobby the money unless Victor *actually* dies. Just before midnight, Bobby lights the building on fire, and Victor dies. Bobby regrets it, but he really wanted the money.

The difference here is that Alan is not committed to causing Victor's death at all, while Bobby is. On the account I've defended,[26] this means Bobby, but not Alan, will feel at least some motivation to take steps that seem to *promote*[27] the occurrence of the death—or at least be on the lookout for such steps. If Bobby knows lighting the fire in the west wing of the building would make Victor's death more likely than lighting it in the east wing, then Bobby would feel some inclination to do the former. But this is not true for Alan. Furthermore, if Victor miraculously does *not* die in the fire, then Bobby but not Alan would be inclined to take further steps to ensure that Victor really dies. After all, Bobby's payment, but not Alan's, depends on Victor's death. Still, note that for both Alan and Bobby, if they could get paid without Victor dying, they would prefer that. Alan has no commitment to the death, and Bobby is only committed to it under the present circumstances (where it's a necessary means to his ends)—not in all possible worlds.

What accounts for Bobby's conduct being more culpable than Alan's? I argue that while Alan's conduct manifests insufficient regard in *one way*, Bobby's commitment to Victor's death means his conduct manifests insufficient regard in this way *as well as in a second way*. Here's why. When you *know* your act will cause a harm, H, you *fail to be sufficiently repelled* by the badness of H. That is, knowing your action A will cause H provides you with a normative reason against A, but you do not have a sufficiently strong

---

[25] *See* Allison Hills, *Defending Double Effect*, 116 PHIL. STUD. 133, 134 (2003) ("an agent intends some state of affairs if she is committed to bringing it about; she merely foresees it if she is aware that she will bring it about, but she is not committed to bringing it about"); MICHAEL BRATMAN, INTENTION, PLANS AND PRACTICAL REASON, at 141–42 (1999) (intending an effect entails being committed to it in three specific ways, while merely foreseeing the effect does not).

[26] *See* Sarch, *supra* note 21, at 464–65 (defending a more precise account of the relevant notion of commitment).

[27] MARK SCHROEDER, SLAVES OF THE PASSIONS 113 (2007) ("X's doing A promotes p just in case it increases the likelihood of p relative to some baseline. And the baseline, I suggest, is fixed by the status quo.").

corresponding motivating reason against A. Thus, your motivating reasons do not coincide with your actual normative reasons: you failed to have a motivating reason that you should have had, or at least not one of the required strength.

By contrast, when you do A with *purpose* to bring about H, and therefore are committed to it in my sense, then you manifest insufficient regard in the same way as doing A knowingly, *as well as* in an additional way. Beyond being insufficiently repelled by H (attaching too little weight to the reasons against it), you also display the further fault of taking it that there are positive reasons in favor of promoting H itself. Your act demonstrates that promoting H is something to which you are *affirmatively attracted* more than you ought to be (assuming H itself is unjustified).[28] Thus, since acting with the commitment to harm involves *two* manifestations of insufficient regard, while merely knowing harm involves only one, this is one respect in which the former is more culpable than the latter. Succinctly stated, the premises supporting this conclusion are:

Premise 1: If you do an unjustified act, A, with a *commitment* to bring about harm H, then you display two distinct faults provided neither your action A nor H itself is justified. Specifically, these are:

(a) you are insufficiently repelled by H (i.e., attach too little weight to the reasons against bringing it about[29]), and
(b) you feel some motivational pressure to affirmatively promote H itself (i.e., adjust your conduct to make H more likely, take further steps to ensuring it, opt for alternatives that make it more likely, etc.), and this is more motivational pressure toward promoting H than you *should* experience.

Premise 2: If in doing the unjustified act, A, you are not at all committed to bringing about H, then your conduct only manifests *one* of the two faults just mentioned: that is, you are only insufficiently repelled by H (and insofar as you do happen to be positively disposed toward H, this will not be *manifested* in your action in a way that impacts your culpability for A[30]).

---

[28] My claim does not hold if the harm in question is justified.

[29] Recall from Chapter 2 this means "too little weight compared to the amount of weight one attaches to the reasons in favor." Suppose I steal to afford a better school for my children, but feel regret about it. I weigh the reasons against the theft at +10, and the reasons in favor at +11. While I attach a lot of weight to the reasons against the theft, I still don't attach *sufficient weight* in the relevant comparative sense. After all, I overvalue my children's interests in attending a good school. (Suppose the correct weighting would be +10 against the theft, and +1 in favor.) Given the large weight I attach to the reasons for the theft, I should attach a correspondingly greater amount of weight to the reasons against. Because I don't, I'm still insufficiently repelled by the theft in the comparative sense.

[30] This parenthetical needs clarification. On my theory of culpability, an action only *manifests* the least bad configuration of mental states we must posit to explain the action under the circumstances (i.e., the least amount of insufficient regard needed to get an otherwise law-abiding citizen to behave that way). Any additional bad mental states you possess, while they bear on your character, do not bear on the insufficient regard *manifested in your action*. This is due to the Principle of Lenity.

Thus, even if Alan greatly dislikes Victor and sees his death as a happy side effect of burning down the building, this additional flaw would not be manifested in Alan's actual conduct. Because Alan by hypothesis *has no commitment* to Victor's death, any attraction Alan might feel to the death would not be manifested. It is

I have defended these claims against numerous objections elsewhere and won't belabor them here.[31] Let me conclude by clarifying that one reason the two faults in purposefully harming are distinct is that they have different objects. The fault that is common to both purposefully and knowingly harming is being insufficiently repelled from the actus reus, A. It amounts to undervaluing the reasons not to do A. In the above scenario, these are that burning down the building will damage property and cause the harm of death. By contrast, the further fault in purposeful harming focuses on *the personal harm itself*. This is the fault of attaching too much weigh to this harm in its own right. That is, one sees greater reason in favor of the harm than one should have, given that the harm itself by hypothesis is unjustified.[32] Since one pursues this harm itself when one shouldn't, we know one sees it as having net positive value when one should not have. Thus, because Bobby acts in pursuit of Victor's death but the death is not justified, we know Bobby sees reasons in favor of Victor's death that he should not have—namely, that it's necessary for his getting paid. In addition, of course, Bobby also fails to see this harm as a sufficiently strong reason against burning down the building, as he should have. So his valuation of burning down the building is messed up too. By contrast, Alan only displays the second fault here. He does not make the further mistake of erroneously seeing positive reasons in favor of the personal harm itself. (As I've argued, if he were to see it as a happy side effect, this would not be manifested in his conduct in a way that affects culpability.[33]) Thus, the two faults in Bobby's conduct are distinct because they have different objects. Alan and Bobby both fail to attach as much weight to the reasons against burning down the building as they should have (and thus have a messed-up valuation of the reasons bearing on or whether to burn down the building), while Bobby makes the further error of seeing greater positive reason in favor of the death itself than he should have (i.e., he also has a messed-up valuation of the reasons bearing on whether the death itself is justified).[34]

---

not needed to explain why he behaved the way he did under the circumstances. If Alan's dislike of Victor really *was* part of what actually motivated him to do what he did—that is, it actually did exert some motivational pull on him that we must appeal to to explain his conduct—then Alan *would count as being somewhat committed to Victor's death*. However, by hypothesis, Alan is *not committed at all* to Victor's death. (An outcome cannot actually exert motivational pull on you without your also being somewhat committed to bringing it about.) Hence, any dislike Alan might feel toward Victor is a free-floating sentiment that does no work in explaining why he did what he did. Thus, this dislike does not affect how much insufficient regard the action manifests.

[31] Sarch, *supra* note 21, at 468–78. *See also supra* notes 29–30.

[32] My account doesn't apply otherwise.

[33] *See supra* note 30.

[34] In Chapter 2, I suggested the basic requirement of the criminal law is not to behave in ways that manifest insufficient repulsion to criminality. Is this consistent with seeing Bobby as displaying the additional fault of overattraction to the harm itself? Yes, because this overattraction can be easily redescribed as a form of insufficient repulsion *in the comparative sense* I'm concerned with. Attaching more weight to the reasons in favor of H itself than one should can be seen as a form of *comparative* underrepulsion. It amounts to attaching too little weight to the reasons against H *compared* to the amount of weight attached to the reasons in favor of H. Thus, if you attach too much weight to the reasons in favor of H and this causes you to act in pursuit of H itself, then that means you failed to attach correspondingly greater weight to the reasons *against* H, as you should have to

2. Extending the Argument to Willful Ignorance

The crucial point for present purposes is that this "two strikes" argument extends beyond knowing misconduct to willfully ignorant misconduct as well. Willfully ignorant conduct is faulty in the same single way as knowing misconduct. So the same argument shows the precisely analogous purposeful misconduct to always be more culpable.

We must tread carefully in extending the "two strikes" argument to willful ignorance, since it is possible for one to be *both* willfully ignorant about whether one's conduct will cause a given harm *and* act with the purpose to cause it. For example, I might suspect that there is a 30 percent risk that a person is inside the building who will be harmed when I burn it down, but then decide not to investigate. But I could simultaneously aim to harm someone through my arson. To avoid this sort of complication, the argument in the last subsection was framed in terms of the distinction between purpose and *mere* knowledge. The same lesson must be applied here too: We must focus on the distinction between purpose and *mere* willful ignorance—that is, someone who is willfully ignorant of p, but who does *not* act with the purpose of bringing about p. In any case, if the actor also had purpose, there would be no need to seek to use willful ignorance as a basis for imputing purpose, as we're now considering.

Thus, the "two strikes" argument carried over to willful ignorance is this. As seen in the previous sub-section, doing an act A with the purpose of causing unjustified harm H involves not only failing to be sufficiently repelled from A to prevent one from doing it but also the further fault of being affirmatively attracted to H itself more than one should. By contrast, suppose one risks H, while being *merely* willfully ignorant of whether one's actions really will cause H—that is, without purpose to cause H, but only having failed to adequately investigate one's suspicions that A might do so. In that case, one would only display the fault of being insufficiently motivated by the prospect of H to ensure that one will not cause it—by either abstaining from A or at least investigating one's suspicions. One would not manifest the further fault of being affirmatively attracted to H itself (i.e., of taking it to have positive net value, when in fact it is unjustified and thus has net negative value). Accordingly, purposefully causing harm will always be more culpable *in at least one respect* than nonpurposeful, merely willfully ignorant misconduct. What follows is that, when all else is equal, purposefully harming will be on balance more culpable than the exactly analogous merely willfully ignorant action.

As a result, ECTP is false. This was the claim that a willfully ignorant actor can be just as culpable as the identically situated purposeful actor. But we have just seen that this is not true. Assuming we are dealing with a pair of cases that differ only in that the one actor is willfully ignorant while the other acts with purpose, and all other relevant factors are held fixed—that is, the harm in question, the obtainable benefits, their

---

prevent yourself from taking H to be of positive value and then acting on that valuation. So the overattraction to H can also be described as a comparative underrepulsion to H. Still, not much of substance turns on which description one prefers.

beliefs about how likely the harm is to ensue, etc.—then the purposeful actor will be on balance more culpable than his merely willfully ignorant counterpart. Accordingly, ECTP does not provide a defensible basis for applying any willful-ignorance-for-purpose substitution.

B. AN OBJECTION

One might object I've misconstrued the equal culpability thesis. ECTP compares purposeful actors and their analogous willfully ignorant counterparts—that is, where all else is equal (harm, benefits, and perceived likelihoods of the outcomes). ECTP says we must compare, for instance:

- D1 does A with purpose to cause +100 units of harm and believes A has a 30 percent chance of doing so;
- D2 lacks this purpose, but believes A has a 30 percent chance of causing +100 units of harm and deliberately, and with sufficient seriousness, breaches his duty to inform himself about whether A really will cause this harm.

ECTP says (albeit falsely) that D2 is as culpable as D1, since D2 is the exactly analogous counterpart of D1.

But one might insist that instead of focusing on the willfully ignorant actor's similarly situated counterpart, the equal culpability thesis should follow the pattern of what Chapter 1 dubbed the indeterminate counterpart version of the thesis. Thus, we'd get this:

> **Indeterminate Counterpart Equal Culpability Thesis for Purpose (IECTP):** Suppose D1 is the *least culpable* purposeful actor who is guilty of crime C, which requires purpose to make inculpatory proposition p true. By contrast, suppose D2 does the actus reus of C, not with purpose, but only with a form of willful ignorance toward p that involves a seriously unjustified breach of the duty to reasonably inform oneself. On these suppositions, D2 is at least as culpable for her action as D1 is for his.

Even I'm right that ECTP is false, IECTP could still be true. Willfully ignorant actors may be as culpable as purposeful actors when all else is *not* equal. Suppose willful-ignorance-for-purpose substitution only requires the willfully ignorant actor charged with purpose crime C to be at least as culpable as *some purposeful actor* who is guilty of C. If so, then even if the willfully ignorant are not as culpable as their identical purposeful counterparts, willful ignorance could still substitute for purpose. That's the idea behind grounding this substitution principle on IECTP.

I won't argue that IECTP is false. I have no idea if it is. Instead, my claim is that even if it's true, it would not be a defensible basis for allowing willful ignorance to substitute for purpose. After all, this logic would suggest that if a crime C requires actus reus A and mens rea M, then anyone who does A can be convicted of C provided only that she is as culpable as the least culpable person who does A with M. Anyone who does A can be convicted of C solely on the ground that she attains the minimum level of culpability required for being guilty of C (whatever that might be). But since many crimes can be committed in ways that do not render one very culpable, this means even *negligent* actors could in principle be convicted of purpose crimes.

Consider treason, which requires purpose to aid the enemy (not mere knowledge).[35] Now compare one actor who *purposefully* aids the enemy in a *tiny* way with another who *negligently* aids the enemy in a *massive* way. Grace gives someone she knows to be a North Korean spy the four-digit passcode to the parking garage at the Sheboygan town hall for the purpose of aiding the enemy. By contrast, Kelly negligently tweets a link to a file containing all the names of every undercover CIA agent and all the tactical data for the movements of the Pacific Fleet. The North Korean government predictably gets a hold of this file and wreaks havoc. Kelly seems *far more* culpable than Grace, even though Kelly negligently aids the enemy, while Grace does so purposefully. All else is not equal as between these two cases.

If IECTP could justify willful-ignorance-for-purpose substitution, then the negligence analog of the same thesis—that is, that negligent actors can sometimes be as culpable as purposeful ones—would justify negligence-for-purpose substitution. But that would be a wholly unacceptable result. The US Supreme Court stressed that willful ignorance, to substitute for knowledge, must have "an appropriately limited scope that surpasses recklessness and negligence."[36] Purpose is of course even more culpable (all else equal) than knowing misconduct. Thus, allowing negligence to substitute for purpose would depart too far from the boundaries of legitimate substitution. But if IECTP could justify allowing willful ignorance to substitute for purpose, the same reasoning would also allow negligence to substitute for purpose. That is an indefensible implication.[37,38]

---

[35] *See supra* note 22.

[36] *Global-Tech*, 131 S. Ct. 2060 at 2070.

[37] Note this problem is not raised by the negligence analog of the *determinate* counterpart ECT. This claim is clearly false. Negligent actors are not as culpable as their exactly analogous purposeful counterparts. Because the negligence analog of determinate counterpart ECT is false, there is no similar worry that it would sanction negligence-for-purpose substitution. This is why determinate counterpart versions of ECT are generally preferable.

[38] What is so bad about this implication? Besides departing from settled criminal law principles, we plausibly have a special right not to be purposefully harmed, which goes beyond our right merely not to be harmed *by accident*, that is, through negligence. Being purposefully harmed—being *targeted*—seems especially disrespectful and provocative. Thus, when I purposefully harm someone, I manifest insufficient regard for an additional right or value, which I do not manifest insufficient regard for when I merely harm negligently. Section III develops this idea further.

III. Willful Ignorance Cannot Substitute for Purpose—Second Argument

Even if my first argument fails to convince you, there is a second way to show that willful ignorance cannot legitimately substitute for purpose. It is based on my theory of equal culpability imputation from Chapter 5. The idea is that purposefully causing a harmful state of affairs, S, manifests insufficient regard toward *different sets of protected interests, rights, and values* than causing S with a nonpurposeful mental state like willful ignorance. This precludes willful ignorance from legitimately substituting for purpose.

On my theory, a defendant who lacks the mens rea, M1, expressly required for a crime, C, may nonetheless be treated *as if* he possessed M1 provided he acted with another mental state, M2, that renders his conduct not only *as culpable*, but also culpable *in the same way*, as acting with M1 and being directly guilty of C. What that means, in turn, is that doing the actus reus of C with M2 must manifest the same amount of insufficient regard *for the same set of interests, rights, and values* as doing the actus reus with M1 would. The interests, rights, and values in this set are, roughly, the ones that C, with its mens rea of M1, was criminalized in order to protect.

I'll argue that acting in willful ignorance of p does not manifest insufficient regard for the same set of protect interests, rights, and values as acting with purpose to make p true. Nonetheless, the argument must remain compatible with Chapter 5's conclusion that willfully ignorant conduct manifests insufficient regard in the same way as knowing misconduct, such that willful ignorance of p can substitute for knowledge of p.

Start by recalling why willful ignorance *can* substitute for knowledge. Knowing p should trigger motivation not to do the actus reus, A, but if it doesn't and one does A, this manifests insufficient regard. The same goes for acting recklessly. What do you manifest insufficient regard *for* when you do A with knowledge or recklessness as to p? The set of interests, rights, and values that the criminal prohibition on [doing A when p is true] aims to protect. This set—call it P_{IRV}—is what gets threatened or damaged by doing [A when p is true]. Now consider willful ignorance. The awareness that p might be true means that P_{IRV} is threatened by your intention to do A, and this *should* (by the law's lights) trigger a motivation to ensure that you don't actualize that threat to P_{IRV}. You could assure yourself of this by dropping the intention to do A. In addition, you can assure yourself that you do not actualize the threat to P_{IRV} by investigating whether p. After all, you might learn that p is false, in which case you would have assured yourself (epistemically) that A won't actually damage P_{IRV}. Thus, you also manifest insufficient regard for P_{IRV} when you decide not to inform yourself whether your suspicions of p are correct. As a result, both the decision not to investigate p, as well as actually doing A despite suspecting that p, manifest insufficient regard for the same set of protected interests: P_{IRV}. Hence these two manifestations of insufficient regard can legitimately be added together.

This explains why willful ignorance can legitimately substitute for knowledge. Knowing and willfully ignorant misconduct both involve failing to do what you can to assure yourself that your conduct won't damage or threaten P_{IRV}. When you know p, there is only one way to ensure that you don't actualize the threat to P_{IRV}: namely, by not doing A. Investigating is not a possible way to assure yourself that your conduct won't actually damage or threaten P_{IRV}. The culpability of doing A in willful ignorance of p is of the very same nature. The only difference is that it involves *two* missed opportunities to assure yourself that your conduct doesn't damage P_{IRV}—not investigating and then doing the actus reus. Hence, under my theory of equal culpability imputation, the culpability of the two parts of willful ignorance can be added together and legitimately substitute for knowledge if the conditions of equal culpability are satisfied. There is no violation of the content restriction here, since both willfully ignorant and knowing misconduct manifest insufficient regard toward P_{IRV}. Both display insufficient regard through rejecting opportunities to ensure that one's conduct does not actually damage P_{IRV}.

The same does not hold for purpose, however. There is at least one interest or right that doing A with *purpose* to bring about p damages that doing A in willful ignorance of p does *not*. Acting with purpose to cause harm H always involves some *commitment* to H (as argued previously in Section II.A). Thus, assuming H is bad and there are no considerations to justify H itself, then when one is committed to causing H, one is going to be more motivationally attracted to H than one should be (since one shouldn't be attracted to it at all). Accordingly, purpose crimes seek to designate conduct involving this special fault, that is, this kind of wrongful attraction to harmful states of affairs. This is a distinct extra wrong, which seems especially disrespectful and provocative. By contrast, misconduct that is merely willfully ignorant (or merely knowing, for that matter) necessarily *does not* display this extra fault.

Thus, purposeful misconduct manifests insufficient regard for an interest, right, or value (however it's best described) that analogous willfully ignorant misconduct does not. There is something especially wrongful or disrespectful about not just being harmed as a side effect of pursuing some other benefit the actor seeks, but rather in the actor aiming to harm us (whether this be as an end in itself or as a means to some further end). When the actor harms us on purpose—that is, when he seeks our detriment and makes this his target (either as an end in itself or as a means to some further end)—this is a distinct kind of injury or disrespect. Moreover, it is one we plausibly have a distinct right or at least interest in not being subject to. Thus, since purposeful harming necessarily manifests insufficient regard for a special interest or right, which mere willfully ignorant misconduct doesn't, my theory of imputation entails that willful ignorance cannot legitimately substitute for purpose. This would violate the content restriction on equal culpability imputation.

This provides a second route to the conclusion that willful ignorance of p should never substitute for purpose to make p true. It would go through even if one thought that in principle willfully ignorant misconduct sometimes could manifest the same *amount* of insufficient regard as the analogous purposeful misconduct. In Section II, I argued against that claim. But even if one doesn't buy my argument there, in Section III I've been arguing that purposeful harming manifests insufficient regard for a different protected interest or right, which merely willfully ignorant harming does not. So this is an independent route to showing that willful ignorance cannot legitimately substitute for purpose. Going into this chapter, this conclusion may have seemed intuitive. Courts are reluctant to sanction this substitution. Now we have a clear understanding of why.

8 Subwillful Motivated Ignorance

THE PREVIOUS CHAPTER dealt with the difficulties for equal culpability substitution at the top end of the mens rea hierarchy. I argued that being willfully ignorant of p cannot legitimately substitute for purpose to make p true. The aim of this chapter is to probe the limits of equal culpability substitution at the low end of the hierarchy. Specifically, I investigate whether some forms of ignorance that fall outside the legal definitions of willful ignorance and recklessness, but fit within negligence, nonetheless might be sufficiently culpable to substitute for higher mental states. I will argue that there is at least one category of such *subwillful motivated ignorance* for which this is true. The same reasoning that underwrites the willful ignorance doctrine suggests that one also should not be able to escape liability by deliberately preventing oneself from forming the *suspicions* one should have had. However, I'll also argue that some forms of subwillful motivated ignorance are too difficult to distinguish from lesser varieties of negligence to substitute for recklessness.

Thus, this chapter aims to demarcate the lower boundary on equal culpability substitution. Section I explains what subwillful motivated ignorance is, while Section II argues that one form of it—*blanket ignorance of a foreseen range of risks*—can legitimately substitute for recklessness as to a specific risk. However, it's doubtful that other kinds of subwillful motivated ignorance—particularly *selective risk recognition*—should substitute for recklessness.

I. Subwillful Motivated Ignorance

A. INTRODUCING THE CONCEPT

By *subwillful motivated ignorance*, I mean self-induced ignorance that may be culpable, but does not fit the criminal law definition of willful ignorance. The legal definition requires (1) serious suspicions of inculpatory proposition p, and (2) deliberately preserving one's ignorance of p.[1] So far in this book, I've been concerned with varieties of self-preserved ignorance that arise from varying prong (2). In Chapter 4, we saw that the duty to reasonably inform oneself (DRI) can be breached with different mental states—"deliberately" (i.e., purposefully or knowingly), as well as recklessly or negligently. Chapter 6 argued that if one breaches DRI while reckless as to the preservation of one's ignorance, this can render one's subsequent conduct as culpable as the analogous knowing wrong—in particular, if one *repeatedly* recklessly breaches DRI. Nonetheless, none of these arguments varied prong (1) of the definition of willful ignorance. DRI itself was formulated to be consistent with prong (1), as seen in the fact that serious suspicions are needed to trigger DRI. However, other species of self-preserved ignorance emerge if we relax prong (1). One can be motivated to remain ignorant of p and be culpable as a result *even without suspecting* p (i.e., being aware of a risk thereof). This chapter focuses on species of culpable ignorance that arise when one lacks suspicions of p.

There are two importantly different cases of this kind. In discussing our moral responsibility for what we believe, Tadros "distinguish[es] two . . . overlapping stages of belief formation": "[t]he first concerns the gathering of evidence," while "[t]he second concerns the evaluation of that evidence: the drawing of inferences."[2] Each stage suggests a different way to prevent oneself from recognizing the risks of one's downstream conduct. First, one might prevent oneself from acquiring evidence one should have received, thus failing to become aware of important risks. Second, one might delude or manipulate oneself into not drawing the right conclusions from information already possessed. Each kind of failure can be self-induced in ways that make one culpable. Let me give examples of each.

The first concerns the information acquisition stage. It involves behavior that functions, consciously or subconsciously, to game the existing willful ignorance rules. Suppose one knows willful ignorance will not get one off the hook for harms one causes. One also realizes one can only be willfully ignorant of specific risks one suspects. This follows from prong (1) of the criminal law definition of willful ignorance. Accordingly, one can circumvent the willful ignorance doctrine by preventing oneself from forming suspicions about *any risks at all*. This prevents one's duty to investigate from being triggered, as DRI

[1] GLANVILLE WILLIAMS, CRIMINAL LAW: THE GENERAL PART 157 (2d ed. 1961) (a willful ignorant actor "has his suspicions aroused but then deliberately omits to make further enquiries"); Global-Tech Appliances, Inc. v. SEB S.A., 131 S. Ct. 2060, 2070 (2011) (giving classic two-pronged definition of willful ignorance).

[2] VICTOR TADROS, CRIMINAL RESPONSIBILITY 245 (2005).

is only activated by awareness of a substantial risk that p. Thus, one might decide to bury one's head in the sand about a *whole swath of possible risks*—not just one specific inculpatory proposition. Here's a hypothetical example:[3]

> ARROGANT CEO: One division of MoveCorp, a logistics company, ships hazardous materials and is subject to strict federal regulations. The *Hazardous Materials Transportation Act of 1975* (HMTA), 49 U.S.C. §§ 5101–5127, requires certification of employee training, plus following specific guidelines for how to package and label the hazardous materials to be shipped. MoveCorp recently appointed a brash new CEO in order to shake things up in the company. Traditionally, the CEO has met with compliance officers from each division in the company twice a week, so the CEO can be informed about urgent legal and safety risks within the company. The new CEO is fully aware of the types of safety and compliance risks these briefings are meant to inform him of. After a few weeks on the job, he says he finds the biweekly briefings repetitive and boring. He'd rather not know about the risks in the company's day-to-day operations so he can focus on his big-picture vision for the company. Thus, he orders these briefings to be held only every six months.
>
> The first meeting he skips includes red flags that MoveCorp's labeling and packaging practices for hazardous materials may not comply with applicable regulations. Their supplier of containment systems and inspection procedures has run into legal trouble, suggesting that its products and services may be dangerous in ways that violate applicable law. The CEO should have recognized these risks immediately, so he could investigate and prevent the problems. However, he fails to take protective actions because he isn't aware of the specific risks. Despite his broad self-induced ignorance, the danger is real: MoveCorp really is imposing safety risks by transporting hazardous material in ways that violate the HMTA. The CEO *should* have been aware of these risks and would have had he attended the briefings.

It is a crime to recklessly violate the HMTA and associated regulations.[4] The CEO isn't knowing, willfully ignorant or even reckless as to the facts constituting the offense. Suppose the inculpatory proposition is that MoveCorp's packaging, labeling, and inspection practices are dangerous to health and safety in ways that violate the HMTA and related regulations.[5] The CEO is not willfully ignorant of this proposition, since he is

---

[3] *Cf.* Louis Nelson, *Trump: I Don't Need Daily Briefings*, POLITICO (Dec. 11, 2016), http://www.politico.com/story/2016/12/trump-briefings-232479 ("Trump said he does not need to receive the presidential intelligence briefing every day, suggesting [they] are repetitive"). If the president skips briefings and fails to learn of specific risks he should have recognized, the argument of this chapter suggests he should be judged as if he were aware of them. Still, presidents are immune from criminal prosecution, so this is not a clean example.

[4] 49 U.S.C. § 5124 (imposing up to five years' imprisonment on "[a] person . . . recklessly violating this chapter or a regulation" issued under it).

[5] *See* 49 C.F.R. 172 (labeling regulations); 49 C.F.R. 173, 178–80 (packaging regulations).

unaware of any chance it is true. How could he suspect that specifically MoveCorp's hazardous material (hazmat) *transportation practices* are dangerous? He prevented himself from becoming aware of *any* specific safety and compliance risks. Thus, he is not reckless as to these specific risks.[6] By skipping the briefings, he avoids virtually all information of the actual risks his company is running.

Although it doesn't amount to willful ignorance or recklessness, this kind of self-induced blindness to a whole category of risks seems culpable. Let *blanket ignorance* refer to blindness to a whole category of risks or suspicions, as the CEO exemplifies here. Although the CEO did not actually suspect the inculpatory proposition, I'll argue that his blanket ignorance makes it appropriate to treat him as if he did. With some important qualifications, blanket ignorance of a broad category of risks makes it apt to treat one as if one were reckless as to specific risks within that category that one blocked oneself from recognizing.

Next, consider an example involving Tadros's second stage: drawing inferences about risks from information already possessed. In this case, one also does not form suspicions of the inculpatory proposition. But this time it is because one engages in motivated reasoning that distorts one's assessment of the applicable risks. Consider:

> Salad Dressing: I'm planning a dinner party, and I was informed by a colleague that one of the guests has a severe seafood allergy. Thus, I should be alert to any risks that my ingredients may contain traces of seafood. Not only should I investigate any such risks I become aware of, but I should be on the lookout for them. However, suppose I strongly dislike this dinner guest. He and I are both competing for the same promotion, and I find him personally abhorrent: he is rude, self-aggrandizing, mean to people behind their backs, and casually racist. Unfortunately, he's a colleague, and I have to include him in the dinner party to make me seem like a team player and help my chances for the promotion. Because I dislike this guest so much (not to mention my subconscious recognition of the benefits of his missing some work due to illness), I end up attending to his preferences and needs as little as possible. Indeed, I try not to think about him at all. I don't want to be reminded of his sure-to-be unpleasant visit, so I push him from my mind and actively focus on other things. I put on some nice music and try to concentrate on the aspects of the evening I'm looking forward to. The unfortunate result is that his seafood allergy loses all salience for me. I try so hard to distract myself from thinking about this person's disagreeable visit that I don't carefully look out for risks of seafood contamination in my cooking. As a result, I don't come to suspect, as I should have, that my Caesar salad dressing might contain traces of seafood. Had I thought about it, I would have noticed this risk and investigated. But because I dislike this guest

[6] *See infra* note 18.

and actively directed my focus elsewhere to avoid upsetting myself, it did not occur to me to check the contents of the Caesar dressing. Unfortunately, it does contain seafood, so when the obnoxious guest eats the salad (thinking I'd been warned of his allergy), he has a bad reaction and suffers permanent kidney damage.

This kind of ignorance I'll call *selective risk recognition*. Unlike blanket ignorance, I don't block myself from having access to information that might generate more concrete suspicions about specific risks. Rather, the ignorance of the relevant risk flows from a failure of attention, one that seems particularly culpable because it stems from animus and a subconscious desire to further my career. Such selective risk recognition also does not satisfy the definition of willful ignorance. Here, I did not actually suspect that the Caesar dressing—or any other ingredient—might contain seafood. I am not willfully ignorant, since the suspicion requirement in prong (1) is not met. (Moreover, DRI is not triggered.) I also do not obviously count as reckless.[7] Nonetheless, there is something very wrong with my assessment of the risks of my conduct. My risk perception in this case was distorted or biased due to motivated reasoning.[8]

Some theorists maintain that one can be willfully ignorant of p even without suspecting that p.[9] On this view, if I merely *should* have been aware of a risk, but then went on—consciously or subconsciously—to block myself from recognizing the risk that p (such that I'd be obliged to inform myself about it), I can still count as willfully ignorant. Nonetheless, because my project starts from the accepted legal definition of willful ignorance (as I've stressed throughout this book), I will continue to take it that both of the previous examples are *not* instances of willful ignorance. Neither actor is willfully

---

[7] Some argue that latent risk awareness also suffices for recklessness. As long as one would have brought the risk to consciousness if one thought about the matter, one is sufficiently aware of it for legal purposes. *See* Kimberly Ferzan, *Opaque Recklessness*, 91 J. CRIM. L. & CRIMINOLOGY 597, 629–30 (2001) (vague awareness can be "preconscious in the sense of easily called to mind if attention is focused on it," which means it "remains part of a person's mental states" (internal quotation marks omitted)); Douglas N. Husak, *Distraction and Negligence, in* PRINCIPLES AND VALUES IN CRIMINAL LAW AND CRIMINAL JUSTICE: ESSAYS IN HONOUR OF ANDREW ASHWORTH 81, 85 (Lucia Zedner & Julian V. Roberts eds., 2d ed. 2012).

To get this example to work for present purposes, we must assume I genuinely am not reckless. Suppose I have so completely pushed the guest from my mind that I would *not* recall his allergy, or form any conscious suspicions about dangers to him, even if I thought about it or were prompted. Thus, I am not aware or suspicious—even latently—of any risk to my guest. There are plausible versions of the case where this is true.

[8] Motivated reasoning is cognition regulated by the desire to arrive at preferred conclusions. It is "the tendency . . . to conform assessments of information to some goal or end extrinsic to accuracy," perhaps paradigmatically the "goal of protecting one's identity or standing in an affinity group that shares fundamental values," which "can generate motivated cognition relating to policy-relevant facts." Dan Kahan, *Ideology, Motivated Reasoning and Cognitive Reflection*, 8 JUDGMENT & DECISION MAKING, 407, 408 (2013).

[9] *See* Jan Willem Wieland, *Willful Ignorance*, 20 ETHICAL THEORY & MORAL PRAC. 105, 115 (2017) ("we need not add a suspicion or awareness requirement on willful ignorance. The latter is compatible with suspicions, but there's also willful ignorance without them").

ignorant in the legal sense because he does not satisfy prong (1) of the legal definition (perhaps also not prong (2)).

Despite not being willfully ignorant in the legal sense, both the above actors are culpable. Their self-caused ignorance is *motivated* in that it's traceable to their desires and interests. In ARROGANT CEO, by avoiding forming suspicions of specific risks, the CEO effectively circumvents the willful ignorance doctrine. Just as deliberately refusing to investigate suspected risks can make one culpable, so too can it be culpable to avoid information one intuits might generate actionable suspicions. This can manifest insufficient regard for affected others. SALAD DRESSING, by contrast, involves an insidious form of motivated reasoning. Wishful thinking is one familiar example, but the concept generally covers cognitive bias or information processing that is guided by the desire to further one's own goals rather than epistemic aims like accuracy or truth. If such motivated reasoning prevents one from forming suspicions about risks one should have appreciated, it can make one culpable. In particular, it can be culpable when such blind spots in one's awareness are self-caused in ways that stem from one's insufficient regard for others.

One might object that all subwillful motivated ignorance—including blanket ignorance and selective risk recognition—just is garden-variety negligence. Subwillful motivated ignorance of p consists in causing oneself to fail to suspect p although one should have (a) possessed such a suspicion, and then (b) gone on to reasonably inform oneself about p. Isn't this just failing to notice risks one should have been aware of—that is, paradigmatic negligence? Under the Model Penal Code (MPC), a "person acts negligently with respect to a material element of an offense when he should be aware of a substantial and unjustifiable risk that the material element exists or will result from his conduct."[10] Further, not perceiving this risk must involve "a gross deviation from the standard of care that a reasonable person would observe in the actor's situation."[11] Doesn't this perfectly describe subwillful motivated ignorance?

Subwillful motivated ignorance is indeed a type of negligence, but one worth paying special attention to. It is an especially culpable form of negligence that sometimes can legitimately substitute for recklessness—as I'll argue in Section II. Regular negligence simply involves failing to become aware of risks one should have noticed. This could be due to regular cognitive failures like laziness, sleep deprivation, or lack of intelligence. But the special kind of negligence I'm concerned with involves taking steps, consciously or subconsciously, to prevent one from becoming aware of such risks. This could stem from a conscious effort not to see *any* red flags, as in ARROGANT CEO, or it could be a subconscious version of the same. Likewise, in SALAD DRESSING my ignorance was induced by the subliminal effects of my attitudes on my regular cognitive processes.[12]

[10] Model Penal Code § 2.02(2)(d).

[11] *Id.*

[12] *See, e.g.*, NOMY ARPALY & TIM SCHROEDER, IN PRAISE OF DESIRE 226–31 (2014) (showing how desires can influence attention and cognition even if it is not through a conscious choice); Stephen P. Garvey, *What's Wrong with Involuntary Manslaughter?*, 85 TEX. L. REV. 333, 337–38 (2006) (arguing it can be culpable to fail "to exercise . . . control over desires that influence the formation and awareness of one's beliefs").

Although both are forms of negligence, they are especially pernicious because they involve *causing oneself*—either strategically or though the distorting influence of desires one should have controlled—to remain unaware of important red flags one ought to have seen. This special source of culpability, I'll argue, can make it appropriate for some subwillful motivated ignorance to substitute for recklessness.

B. AN ACCOUNT OF SUBWILLFUL MOTIVATED IGNORANCE

I'll only argue that some, not all, subwillful motivated ignorance should substitute for recklessness. To home in on the kind I have in mind, I need to analyze the phenomenon more precisely. I offer a general account of the culpability of subwillful motivated ignorance, and then distinguish several varieties of blanket ignorance and selective risk recognition.

My account is structurally similar to the account of willful ignorance defended in Chapter 4. I argued that willful ignorance involves breaching DRI, where DRI was triggered by suspicions that one's conduct would be risky. By contrast, the defining feature of subwillful motivated ignorance is that it involves interference with one's own ability to recognize relevant risks. Rather than a pro tanto duty to inform oneself about *suspected* risks, the present account posits a pro tanto duty to *recognize* salient risks of one's conduct.[13] More precisely:

> **Duty to Recognize Risks (DRR)**: If one is intending or planning to perform action A and given the evidence one possesses or has straightforward access to, a reasonable person would realize that A would impose certain legally cognizable risks, then one has a *pro tanto* obligation (conditional on continuing to intend or plan to do A) to *actually become sufficiently aware* of the relevant risks to be able to respond to them appropriately (assuming unawareness of them is not justified). This not only means one must draw relevant inferences, reason, and pay attention as needed to actually become aware of the risks of A but also that one must refrain from actively creating barriers to becoming aware of such risks.

The subwillful motivated ignorance I'm concerned with involves violating this pro tanto duty to become aware of the risks of one's planned conduct as needed to respond appropriately. Such breaches can involve not paying attention or reasoning sufficiently, or walling oneself off from relevant information sources.

---

[13] Tadros likewise thinks a duty to investigate applies not just to those who suspect the inculpatory proposition, but even to actors who were completely unaware of the relevant risks and merely objectively should have investigated (or become aware of the relevant risks). *See supra* note 2, at 246–47. Thus, my view is in good company. Nonetheless, Tadros's aims are differ from mine. He aims to determine whether the failure to be aware of certain risks one should notice can fairly make one subject to criminal liability at all. My question is more doctrinal: Can the unjustified failure to be aware of certain risks legitimately substitute for a reckless awareness of such risks? I am concerned with the defensibility of an imputation principle, while Tadros seeks to delineate the outer limits of criminal liability.

As with DRI, several factors impact the culpability of breaching DRR. These more or less track those that affect the breach of DRI, so I merely summarize them:

Factors enhancing the gravity of breaching DRR:

(a) *The harm or wrong at stake*: The breach of DRR is more serious, all else equal, the more harmful or wrongful the risks of one's planned action, A, are that one failed to recognize.

(b) *The costs of complying*: The legally cognizable costs (to oneself or others) involved in coming to recognize the relevant risks of A can provide full or partial justification for remaining unaware of these risks, thus reducing culpability of breaching DRR. Thus, the breach of DRR is more serious, all else equal, the easier or less costly it would be for a person under the circumstances to actually become aware of the risks of A.

(c) *One's mens rea*: The breach of DRR is more serious, all else equal, (i) the higher one's mens rea (if any) with respect to the fact that one is not recognizing relevant risks as one should, and (ii) the more clearly one attends to or is aware of *what type and how serious* the risks are that one is keeping oneself ignorant of.

The last two factors are particularly important here. Focusing on DRR shows that for both self-induced blanket ignorance as well as selective risk recognition, two sub-categories of each must be distinguished.

1. Two Kinds of Blanket Ignorance

The self-induced blanket ignorance in ARROGANT CEO involves a serious breach of DRR. The CEO deliberately blocks himself from recognizing any safety risks posed by the company's operations. But there are two varieties of blanket ignorance: one where the actor is aware of the general type and gravity of the risks he keeps himself in the dark about and one where he is not.

In ARROGANT CEO as presented in sub-section A, it was stipulated that the CEO knows what sort of risks he is blocking himself from learning about and generally how serious such risks tend to be. He knows the biweekly briefings typically deal with red flags of ongoing threats posed by the company's operations, and he is aware that such risks—if they exist and materialize—can be quite harmful. Call this version of the case ARROGANT CEO—FORESEEN RISKS. The relevant inculpatory proposition, p, is that MoveCorp's packaging, labeling, and inspection practices are dangerous to health and safety in ways that violate the HMTA's substantive provisions and regulations. The key feature of this case thus is that p falls within a broad class of risks that the CEO is aware he is walling himself off from.[14]

---

[14] By refusing the briefing, he shows himself willing to *take the risk* that risks of this type exist (i.e., that propositions like p might be true). This starts to show why it is culpable.

The other type of blanket ignorance is where the actor doesn't foresee the category of risks he could learn about from the information source he rejected. Thus, we get:

> Arrogant CEO—Unforeseen Risks: The CEO refuses to receive the biweekly safety briefings as before, but now is a complete novice. He spent his career in another field and knows nothing about how complex transportation operations work. (He was promoted in a wave of anti-elite sentiment because of his "fresh perspective" and perceived ability to "shake things up.") He has no idea what kind of information is presented in such briefings—and his staff (who don't trust compliance officers) do not tell him. The case is otherwise exactly like the first version. The briefing would have revealed risks that MoveCorp's hazmat operation might involve faulty packaging, labeling, and inspection procedures. Thus, the CEO fails to learn what he should have, and doesn't take necessary precautions.

Such cases may be rare, since few CEOs this uninformed will keep their jobs for long. The point, however, is that it seems less culpable than the first version. The difference is that in Arrogant CEO—Foreseen Risks, the CEO knows the general type of risk he prevents himself from learning of, while in Arrogant CEO—Unforeseen Risks, he doesn't. In the latter case, this may be the CEO's fault or it may not. If he's not at fault for it, he may not be culpable at all for his ignorance-preserving conduct. However, even if he is a bit at fault for failing to know what kind of risks he would learn of in the briefings, this version still plausibly is less culpable than the first version, when the CEO foresees the type of risks he avoids learning of. This difference in culpability between the two versions is captured in culpability-enhancing factor (c).

2. Two Kinds of Selective Risk Recognition

There are also two types of selective risk recognition. For simplicity, they can also be illustrated using Arrogant CEO. I'll circle back to Salad Dressing in a moment. Selective risk recognition occurs when the actor receives information about the red flags in question, but fails to recognize them *as red flags* (i.e., as salient or actionable risks). This might be due to wishful thinking, cognitive bias, or other kinds of motivated reasoning—or it might not be. It's important to distinguish these two groups of cases.

In cases of the first kind, one receives information containing red flags about p, but due to motivated reasoning, one doesn't recognize this information *as a substantial risk requiring action*. Perhaps one rationalizes away the information. Or perhaps one just doesn't notice it due to selectively focusing one's attention elsewhere. Thus, consider:

> Arrogant CEO—Selective Risk Recognition: The CEO receives the biweekly safety and compliance briefings. In today's briefing, he receives information suggesting that MoveCorp's hazmat packaging, labeling, and inspection procedures are faulty. (As before, he is told the company supplying these systems to MoveCorp

> is facing serious legal trouble.) Nonetheless, the CEO does not want to believe this bad news, as it would hurt his fortunes in the company. Accordingly, in processing this information, he focuses on his intense distrust of accountants, lawyers, and compliance officers, whom he regards as timid bean counters. He feels they have been disloyal to him personally by standing in the way of his grand vision for MoveCorp. However, his distrust is based not on evidence of their unreliability, but rather on his feeling hurt by what he regards as disloyalty. Thus, the CEO concludes the compliance officers are lying to undermine him. So he dismisses what they tell him as untrustworthy. This lets him reach his desired conclusion: that the bad news is not true. Instead, he concludes there is no serious chance that MoveCorp's hazmat transportation procedures impose unlawful risks. However, he is wrong. The company is creating many such risks.

The CEO does not suspect p although he was presented with information from which a reasonable person in the circumstances would have inferred that there is a significant risk that p. He failed to see the information for what it is because of his motivated reasoning. He desires to believe a particular result and relies on the weak story of the compliance officers' disloyalty to rationalize away recalcitrant evidence. Thus, the CEO in this case did not see the red flags *as red flags* due to motivated reasoning.

Still, the CEO plausibly is culpable here because he *could* and *should* have controlled these cognitive biases. He could have done better, epistemically, and the reason he didn't is because he cared more about not having to confront his fears of bad professional consequences if the news is true than he did for the interests of potential victims who would be exposed to risk. This form of ignorance is culpable because it is caused by a failure to control or correct for one's own cognitive biases. Adults in general have a fairly good (if imperfect) ability to control such cognitive biases and mistakes, and they plausibly are culpable when they fail to do so due to insufficient regard.[15] What's more, the responsibility to guard against the distorting effects of motivated reasoning is even more stringent when one occupies high positions of authority. Hence, it is more culpable for the CEO to fail to control or correct for his cognitive biases than the average person.

Not all selective risk recognition is this culpable. Sometimes the failure to recognize relevant risks has nothing to do with motivated reasoning. Consider:

> Arrogant CEO—Regular Inattention: The CEO attends the biweekly briefings. However, he was up all night negotiating a lucrative contract for the company, and so doesn't process the information from today's briefing as he should. He misunderstands crucial evidence indicating flaws in MoveCorp's hazmat packaging, labeling, and inspection procedures (i.e., reports of the supplier's legal troubles).

---

[15] *See* Garvey, *supra* note at 12, at 337–38.

Had he been in better shape, he would have recognized the risk that the hazmat operations may be dangerous, unlawful, and in need of reform. However, he doesn't because of sleep deprivation.

This is also a case of not coming to suspect p as one should have, despite being presented with evidence from which a reasonable person would have inferred a risk that p. However, now the explanation is not motivated reasoning or biases we can be expected to control. Even if DRR applies here (since a reasonable person would have become aware of the relevant risks), this breach of DRR is still on the less culpable end of the scale. It is not done with any mens rea as to the fact that the CEO is failing to learn what he should. It is perhaps not even a negligent breach of DRR if it's not a *gross* departure from the conduct of a reasonable person to make mistakes due to sleep deprivation incurred from important company work. In any case, this breach of DRR is less culpable than if it were driven by motivated reasoning. ARROGANT CEO—SELECTIVE RISK RECOGNITION is more culpable than ARROGANT CEO—REGULAR INATTENTION.

Now what about SALAD DRESSING? I contend this case is closer to ARROGANT CEO—SELECTIVE RISK RECOGNITION. In SALAD DRESSING, I failed to correctly process available information due to motivated reasoning—specifically, my dislike of the obnoxious guest and my subconscious desire to improve my chances of promotion. Admittedly, I didn't rationalize away conflicting evidence as blatantly as the CEO in ARROGANT CEO—SELECTIVE RISK RECOGNITION. The CEO there showed himself willing to invent outlandish conspiracy theories to preserve his desired conclusion. In SALAD DRESSING, I merely was distracted due to my wish not to think about the obnoxious guest at all. Rather than actively blinding myself to easily discernable risks in the face of people telling me otherwise, in SALAD DRESSING I am just inattentive to the risks due to motivated reasoning. The self-induced failure to notice risks in SALAD DRESSING seems less culpable than the sort of active blindness in ARROGANT CEO—SELECTIVE RISK RECOGNITION.[16] Nonetheless, the selective risk recognition in SALAD DRESSING is still culpable. It lies between the two versions of the CEO case sketched in this subsection.

II. Substituting Subwillful Ignorance for Recklessness

The actors in the previous examples are negligent: they are either fully unaware of substantial and unjustified risks that they should have recognized, or they are aware of them,

[16] One might object that the amount of harm risked is not the same in the two cases. But suppose we equalize the magnitude and likelihood of harm in both. Even so, the motivated ignorance in SALAD DRESSING seems less culpable than the kind of *actively cultivated* blindness in ARROGANT CEO—SELECTIVE RISK RECOGNITION.

but do not regard them as substantial (as required for recklessness).[17] My aim in this section is to argue that blanket ignorance of a foreseen range of risks can legitimately substitute for recklessness. The actor in ARROGANT CEO—FORESEEN RISKS can be legitimately treated *as if* he were aware of the risks of MoveCorp's hazmat operation. I mount this argument in subsection A, but in subsection B I express doubts about the analogous argument for selective risk recognition. Even if the actors in ARROGANT CEO—SELECTIVE RISK RECOGNITION and SALAD DRESSING could in theory be treated as reckless actors, I have doubts that this rule is workable in practice. Thus, I only advocate taking blanket ignorance of a foreseen range of risks—not selective risk recognition—to be grounds for treating one as a reckless wrongdoer.

A. BLANKET IGNORANCE OF A FORESEEN RANGE OF RISKS CAN SUBSTITUTE FOR RECKLESSNESS

In this subsection, I argue that self-induced blanket ignorance of a foreseen range of risks can legitimately substitute for recklessness. But no analogous argument can plausibly be made for cases like ARROGANT CEO—UNFORESEEN RISKS, where the actor has no idea of the general type and gravity of the risks he blocks himself from learning of.

Return to ARROGANT CEO—FORESEEN RISKS. There is a particularly pressing need to treat such actors as reckless, even though they are not actually aware of the particular risks in question. This imputation rule is needed because the definition of recklessness can be gamed through blanket ignorance—just as the definition of knowledge can be gamed in ways that the willful ignorance doctrine is designed to block. One core benefit of the willful ignorance doctrine is that it prevents people from escaping knowledge-crime punishments by deliberately avoiding knowledge of an inculpatory proposition they only suspected. The same reasoning suggests that we should not allow people to escape recklessness-crime punishments by deliberately preventing themselves from becoming aware of particular risks, which would have rendered them reckless. Currently, if one blocks oneself from recognizing the specific risk, one can avoid punishment as a reckless wrongdoer, instead dropping oneself into the lesser category of negligence.[18] By

[17] David M. Treiman, *Recklessness and the Model Penal Code*, 9 AM. J. CRIM. L. 281, 362 (1981) (arguing that the drafters of the Model Penal Code intended its definition of recklessness to require that "a person must be aware of the risk *and its substantiality*, but awareness of the unjustifiability of the risk is partially objective"—that is, one need not believe the risk is unjustified) (emphasis added).

[18] Recklessness requires awareness of the particular risk at issue (described with some specificity), not just vague uncertainty or generally wondering about possible dangers. *See* MODEL PENAL CODE, § 2.02 (One "acts recklessly with respect to a material element . . . when he consciously disregards a substantial and unjustifiable risk that *the material element exists or will result* from his conduct" (emphasis added)); People v. Hall, 999 P.2d 207, 220 (Colo. 2000) ("recklessness requires that [one] consciously disregard a substantial and unjustifiable risk *of*

treating blanket ignorance as a substitute for recklessness, we return such defendants, who are effectively gaming the law, to the higher category of recklessness.

Of course, this is legitimate on my theory of mens rea imputation only when blanket ignorance actually renders the negligent actor as culpable as the analogous reckless wrongdoer. For this imputation rule to be justified, we must be confident that negligent actors who preserve their ignorance of a range of risks in blanket fashion really manifest the same amount of insufficient regard toward the same set of protected interests and values as the analogous reckless actors do.

This is plausible for blanket ignorance of a foreseen range of risks. In ARROGANT CEO—FORESEEN RISKS, the CEO knows the general type and gravity of the specific risks he prevents himself from becoming aware of. The CEO blinds himself to a broad category of risks while having a general sense of the typical nature and seriousness of what is within this category. Accordingly, we can treat him as being aware that *some* particular risk of this general type and gravity exists (which is not to say he knows that harm will ensue, just that there is a risk thereof).

Let's be more precise. Suppose if the CEO had attended today's compliance briefing, he would have received information that would make him aware of a 20–30 percent chance of p—that MoveCorp's hazmat operation is dangerous in ways that violate the law. However, he does not actually become aware of this risk since he skipped the briefing. Thus, he continues to have credence 0 in p. Suppose further that the disvalue if p were true would be around 500–1,000 units. (This is a measure of the gravity of the harm or wrong in p.)

Nonetheless, when deciding not to attend the briefing, the CEO is aware of the general *type* and *gravity* of risk that these briefings provide information about. That is, he is aware that there is a range of *possible* risks, {R1 . . . Rn}, any of which may or may not exist, and the risk of the dangerous hazmat operation he'd have learned about is of this same general type and gravity. The CEO is aware that {R1 . . . Rn} are *substantial*—in terms of likelihood and gravity—since they otherwise wouldn't make it into the briefing. So suppose the CEO expects the briefing would make him aware of risks involving at most a roughly 20–30 percent likelihood of harms with about 500–1,000 units of disvalue. The CEO doesn't specifically contemplate dangers or legal problems with the hazmat operation—this possibility doesn't occur to him. But the problems with the hazmat operation are of a type and gravity that make this risk fall squarely within the broad category of risks he does foresee: {R1 . . . Rn}.

Although the CEO doesn't know what specific risks the briefing would make him aware of, he expects it to reveal *some particular risk or other* that is of the same type and

a particular result," which for manslaughter is "death to another person" (emphasis added)); Commonwealth v. Coggeshall, 46 N.E.3d 19, 24 (Mass. 2016) (recklessness "requires . . . defendant's subjective state of mind with respect to the risk involved").

seriousness as the problems with the hazmat operation. At the risk of oversimplifying, I'll model the situation by saying he (at least vaguely or loosely) believes there is a substantial (i.e., 20–30 percent) chance that a harm of this general type and gravity (i.e., one with about 500–1,000 units of disvalue) will occur. While he doesn't know the specific nature of the risk, his expectation that the briefing would alert him to some risk of this type and seriousness means he is aware, at least in the abstract, that the same degree of harm has roughly the same chance of occurring.

This, I contend, can be sufficient to substitute for recklessness as to the company's problems with the hazmat operation. His self-induced blanket ignorance of the foreseen range of risks, which *encompasses* the risk of problems with the hazmat operation, can serve as the basis for treating the CEO as if he *were* actually aware of this specific risk. This, in turn, is because he is as culpable as if he actually were aware of this risk. The CEO decides not to attend the briefing despite being aware of a comparable chance of a comparable harm. He is aware that *some similar* harm of this same magnitude (i.e., 500–1,000 units of disvalue) has a similar chance of materializing (i.e., 20–30 percent). There are many ways this could be true, and had he attended the briefing, he would have learned which was correct. Still, attending the briefing would not have significantly changed his overall estimate of the amount or likelihood of the harm risked. He just blocked himself from learning precisely how and why it is true that this foreseen type and gravity of risk is present.

Accordingly, he is just as culpable as if he were aware of the particular risk of problems with the hazmat operation. He manifests just as much insufficient regard toward the same broad set of interests as if he actually had recognized these problems. True, he doesn't know precisely *whose* interests or *which* values he is manifesting insufficient regard for. But in general, one needn't know precisely what interests one is threatening, or whose interests they are, in order for one to genuinely threaten them—or manifest insufficient regard for them. While it's possible that not being aware of the nature of the *particular* risk one runs might make one's conduct manifest slightly less insufficient regard for the interests at stake than if one had vividly recognized it, the shortfall of culpability can be made up for by the added culpability involved in one's self-induced blanket ignorance in violation of DRR (i.e., walling oneself off from information about the particular risks in the broad category at issue). Thus, we can be confident that the CEO manifests the same degree of indifference toward the same amount and likelihood of harm as if he'd actually been aware of the red flags about the hazmat operation. Moreover, because he foresees the same general *type* of risk as the one that really exists, there also is no violation of the content restriction on equal culpability substitution (defended in Chapter 5). He manifests insufficient regard for the same set of interests, rights, and values as he would have done were he aware of the specific risk posed by the hazmat operation.

Because the CEO is as culpable as the analogous reckless actor, I contend, he may legitimately be treated as if he were reckless with respect to the problems with MoveCorp's hazmat operation—even though in fact he was unaware of the specific risks it posed. Accordingly, it would be appropriate to convict the CEO of recklessly violating the HMTA[19] even though he strictly speaking is only negligent as to the particular risk of problems with the hazmat operation's licensing, labeling, and inspection procedures. The especially culpable form of negligence the CEO displays here—that is, self-induced blanket ignorance of a foreseen range of risks—can legitimately be the basis for imputing recklessness to him.[20]

By contrast, blanket ignorance of an *unforeseen* range of risks should not substitute for recklessness. In Arrogant CEO—Unforeseen Risks, the CEO does not know even the general type and gravity of the risks typically discussed in compliance briefings. Therefore, no comparable argument is available here. When the CEO has a sense of the general category of problems and dangers he prevents himself from coming to suspect, he displays insufficient regard for the same broad set of interests and values as he would were he aware of a particular risk within that category. However, this is not so when the CEO is unaware of the kind of issues he is walling himself off from. Granted, he *should* recognize additional risks by going to the briefings. But if he lacks even a general sense of the type and gravity of risk he is preventing himself from learning about, then we can't be sure his estimate of the harmfulness of his conduct (its likelihood and amount) would be roughly the same as it would were he reckless (i.e., actually aware of the risk of problems with the hazmat operation). Nor can we be sure he is manifesting insufficient regard for the same interests, rights, and values as he would if he'd recognized the particular risk at issue—which would generate a violation of the content restriction on mental state imputation from Chapter 5. Thus, there is no guarantee that preserving his ignorance by not going to the briefing will manifest the same degree of insufficient regard toward the same set of interests, rights, and values as his conduct would have manifested were he aware of the particular risk in question. Thus, in Arrogant CEO—Unforeseen Risks we cannot use a similar line of reasoning for imputing recklessness as we could in Arrogant CEO—Foreseen Risks.

---

[19] *See supra* notes 4–5 and accompanying text.

[20] Does my argument only show that generalized suspicions of a category of possible risks are *evidence* of awareness of a particularized risk within that category? (Thanks to Josh Andresen for this worry.) I think not. Recklessness normally requires awareness of the *particular* risk one creates (its nature described with at least some specificity). *See supra* note 18. But we cannot *infer* awareness of a particular risk from vague, general suspicions that one may be running *some risks or other*. The former does not follow from the latter. Awareness of a particular risk cannot reliably be proved by showing generalized suspicions that something may be amiss. Instead, I argue the latter can sometimes make one as culpable as the former, such that particularized risk-awareness can be *imputed* based on self-induced ignorance of a general category of possible risks of a comparable magnitude. Thus, I am defending an imputation principle, not an inference rule.

B. SELECTIVE RISK RECOGNITION COULD BUT PROBABLY SHOULDN'T SUBSTITUTE FOR RECKLESSNESS

I do not advocate treating the actors in ARROGANT CEO—SELECTIVE RISK RECOGNITION and SALAD DRESSING as if they were reckless. Still, this is for practical not theoretical reasons.

I see nothing *in principle* that would prevent these actors' motivated reasoning from sometimes rendering them as culpable as analogous reckless wrongdoers. This plausibly can happen where the motivated reasoning that keeps one from recognizing the relevant risks (or from seeing them as substantial) stems from insufficient regard—that is, the distorting influence of one's bad attitudes, which one could and should have controlled. In ARROGANT CEO—SELECTIVE RISK RECOGNITION, the CEO attends the compliance briefings, but rationalizes away the red flags discussed as an attempt by the compliance officers to mislead him. This was motivated reasoning. He did not want to believe there was a risk that the company might be acting dangerously, since, if true, this would hurt his career. The conspiracy theory about the compliance officers being out to get him is the mechanism he invents to allow himself to reach his desired conclusion. This is why he ends up believing there is no substantial risk that MoveCorp's hazmat operations are dangerous and unlawful.

This kind of motivated reasoning can be culpable to the extent that it is due to insufficient regard for the interests of others or other protected values. If the CEO in this case had cared sufficiently about protecting people from the dangers of the company's hazmat operation, he would have controlled the distorting influence of his career aspirations, as well as his doubts about his colleagues' loyalty. As normal well-adjusted adults, I suggest, we can and should be able to guard against this kind of motivated reasoning—particularly where harm to others or violations of law are concerned. That is, we generally should be able to resist the temptation to rationalize away bad news or invent stories to preserve our desired conclusions—especially where learning the truth is crucial to avoid harming others. Likewise, when seeking the truth is essential to avoid causing harm, we also typically can and should prevent our assessment of the evidence from being influenced by our negative feelings about the people who gave us that evidence. Normal adults can be expected to largely block the effects of such non-truth-oriented factors on their reasoning. The CEO, however, failed to control these factors, which he would have done if he'd had enough regard for the interests of others. Thus, the best explanation for why he did not recognize the risk here (or recognize it as substantial) is insufficient regard.

Accordingly, the CEO's failure to recognize a substantial risk that MoveCorp's hazmat operation might be dangerous is culpable. It makes him more culpable than if he had just failed to notice this risk due to regular inattention (e.g., tiredness or distraction), which is not traceable to insufficient regard. Thus, the CEO's culpability plausibly can rise to the same level as if he'd been a reckless actor.

A similar story explains why, in Salad Dressing, I incur extra culpability from my inattention to the risk that my salad might be harmful to the guest I dislike. Here, too, the failure to recognize a substantial risk of harm to the obnoxious guest must be chalked up to heightened insufficient regard. It should be fairly clear how this story goes.

While there thus can be *theoretical* grounds for treating actors who engage in selective risk recognition as reckless actors, I do not advocate this substitution rule. This is because of the obvious difficulty courts will face in distinguishing selective risk recognition due to culpable motivated reasoning from cases where the actor's failure to recognize relevant risks stems from more benign causes like laziness, forgetfulness, distraction, or other thoughtlessness not due to disregard for protected interests and values. In short, I suspect it will be too difficult for courts to distinguish cases like Arrogant CEO—Selective Risk Recognition from Arrogant CEO—Regular Inattention.

This is not just a worry about putting conceptually hard questions before judges or juries. They confront complex questions all the time. Rather, my concern is more structural. In any case of insufficient-regard-driven motivated reasoning, what is to stop the defendant from simply *asserting* that he really just was being dumb, or distracted, or lazy? I suspect it would often prove exceedingly difficult for prosecutors to contest such assertions. Were the CEO in Arrogant CEO—Selective Risk Recognition charged with recklessness crimes under the proposed imputation rule, he would simply claim that it wasn't a concern for his career or animosity toward compliance officers that prevented him from recognizing a substantial risk of danger in MoveCorp's hazmat operations; rather, he would insist it was due to something more benign like tiredness, distraction, or laziness as in Arrogant CEO—Regular Inattention. Defendants would routinely try such strategies to avoid being treated as reckless actors, and prosecutors would have to work exceedingly hard to rebut their claims.

Thus, the worry is that judges and juries with normal human epistemic limitations will not *reliably* be able to tell the difference between these two types of cases. Perhaps psychologists with the benefit of repeated therapy sessions could distinguish pernicious motivated reasoning issuing in selective risk recognition from more benign inattention. But particularly given the risk of deceit by defendants regarding the details of their own mental states, I suspect this is more than we can safely ask of judges and juries in the normal run of things.

Accordingly, I do not advocate allowing selective risk recognition to substitute for recklessness—even if in principle it could. Instead, all I advocate is allowing blanket ignorance of a foreseen range of risks to substitute for recklessness. It is much easier to discern when the defendant has blocked himself from learning about a whole category of risks whose general nature and gravity he antecedently recognized. As the willful ignorance doctrine demonstrates, courts are already called on to determine when defendants prevent themselves from obtaining knowledge of suspected facts. It does not seem much more difficult to tell when they are preventing themselves from developing suspicions about a contemplated category of risks in the first place. Accordingly, I see no reason it would be unworkable to allow blanket ignorance of a foreseen range of risks to substitute for actual awareness of a particular risk within that range.[21]

[21] As with many of the doctrinal revisions recommended in this book, I am happy to make this conclusion conditional on its not being rebutted by empirical findings. If empirical work reveals that courts cannot reliably apply such a rule, then I would retract my endorsement of it.

9 Corporations Keeping Themselves in the Dark

SOMETIMES CORPORATIONS KEEP themselves in the dark. This chapter argues that a corporation can incur culpability when its employees block themselves or others within the corporation from obtaining knowledge they should have had. This, I argue, can provide an equal culpability rationale for imputing the missing knowledge to the corporation itself.

One obvious way this could happen is through willful ignorance. If a company employee deliberately keeps herself in the dark about suspected inculpatory facts, the corporation—through familiar respondeat superior principles—can be convicted of crimes requiring knowledge thereof. Beyond this, I argue, knowledge can be imputed to the corporation when employees keep *others* within the company from obtaining information they should have had. Perhaps an employee decides to withhold crucial information he had a responsibility to share. Perhaps management interferes with the natural flow of information within the company, thus blocking other employees from learning of risks they should have uncovered and prevented. This, I argue, can also be the basis for treating the corporation as though it possessed the knowledge it would have had but for the culpable interference of its employees.

Determining when corporations can be deemed to know what their employees kept themselves or others from learning is the task of this chapter. I argue that both the above kinds of interference with the information flow within the corporation can, in extreme cases, ground the imputation of knowledge to the corporation. Perhaps controversially,

I argue this can sometimes be done even for knowledge that *no individual within the company actually possessed.*

This may be controversial because traditional respondeat superior principles assume a mental state can be attributed to a corporation only if an employee possessed that mental state.[1] As one court put it, "a corporation acts with a given mental state in a criminal context only if at least one employee who acts (or fails to act) possesses the requisite mental state at the time of the act (or failure to act)."[2] Call this the *Individualist Constraint* on corporate mental state attribution.

As should be clear by this point in the book, this claim cannot be quite right as stated. Given the willful ignorance doctrine, if an employee deliberately blocks himself from acquiring salient knowledge during his employment with a corporation, the missing knowledge can be imputed to him, and from there, to the corporation. Thus, some mental states that no single employee possesses can be imputed to the corporation. Consider:

> CarCo v.1: Manny, a manager at CarCo, suspects his employees are improperly applying emissions testing equipment, such that the cars the company produces may be violating applicable regulations. But he decides to wall himself off from information that could confirm whether his suspicions are correct. In fact, they are. The cars violate applicable emissions standards, though he deliberately prevented himself from learning this fact.

The willful ignorance doctrine permits imputing knowledge to Manny that CarCo cars violate applicable emissions standards. As detailed in Section III.A, this knowledge may then be imputed on to the corporation under standard agency principles. No surprises here.

Nonetheless, I argue the same reasoning that supports this result in willful ignorance cases also supports imputing mental states to a corporation *beyond* classic willful ignorance. This can be done, I contend, when employees act not to keep themselves in ignorance, but rather to keep *others* in the corporation in the dark of crucial information they should have had. Consider:

> CarCo v.2: Mindy is a CarCo manager. She's aware of a body of data that she suspects might reveal to scientists in another division that CarCo cars are violating applicable emissions standards. She knows the scientists would learn of the existence of the data set from the data security report she is supposed to write. If they find out about the data set and investigate, Mindy thinks there is a substantial risk it would reveal emissions violations. She isn't certain it would, since she can't analyze the information herself. But it might.

---

[1] *See infra* notes 34–35, 41–43.

[2] Com. v. Life Care Centers of America, Inc., 926 N.E.2d 206, 212 (Mass. 2010).

> If it does and the scientists realize it, she thinks it could hurt the finances of the company so badly that her $20,000 bonus would be jeopardized. She would not learn the results of the data analysis, or of any possible emissions violations, in the regular course of her work, since such information is not shared with people in her role. She would only find out about it on the news like anyone else. But she thinks that because a scandal would seriously harm the company's finances, her bonus—like that of other employees—could be imperiled.
>
> Thus, to reduce the chance of this happening, she writes her report with obscure language and downplays the importance of the data in question. She references it only in an appendix, and includes other irrelevancies that could distract even careful readers. Moreover, she buries the data itself on a third-party server that is harder for the scientists to access. Thanks to Mindy's efforts, they don't learn about the data or uncover its significance. However, Mindy's suspicions are correct: The data does contain obvious evidence that CarCo's cars violate emissions standards. But for Mindy's interference with the regular information flow in the company, the scientists would have easily discovered the emissions problems.[3]

Mindy is not willfully ignorant. She does not aim to preserve *her own* ignorance. Nonetheless, she culpably preserved the ignorance of others within the company. She had a duty to share important information that could reveal legal problems for the company, but she deliberately prevented it from reaching company experts who should have had access to it. She deliberately keeps them in the dark. I don't argue that this supports imputing *to Mindy* the knowledge she blocks others from acquiring.[4] After all, Mindy would never be expected to know of the emissions violations and her job description confers no responsibility for such issues. Nor should the scientists, who in principle should have learned of the emissions violations, be treated as if they knew. Instead, I argue *the corporation* should be treated as if one of its employees knew of the emissions violations, meaning this knowledge can be imputed to the corporation itself.

Making this argument stick is the task of this chapter. In doing so, I consider how the willful ignorance doctrine overlaps with another infamous principle used to construct corporate mental states: the *collective knowledge doctrine*. Roughly, this rule permits different pieces of information known separately by various employees in the corporation to be stitched together to impute the aggregate of this knowledge to the corporation, thus satisfying the mens rea of a particular knowledge crime.[5]

---

[3] The case might be varied. Perhaps Mindy doesn't prevent others from learning about existing data, but rather prevents others from initially *collecting* it.

[4] Mindy would not be properly convicted of crimes requiring knowledge of the emissions violations, but she might have committed recklessness or negligence offenses.

[5] *See infra* notes 38–39.

The collective knowledge doctrine, I argue, is best seen as an equal culpability imputation principle. Thus, it can justifiably be used to impute knowledge required for a crime to the corporation *only if* the corporation, through its employees, acts in ways that together are as culpable as if an individual employee had possessed the requisite knowledge. If equal culpability is lacking, however, the collective knowledge doctrine cannot justifiably be employed.

Accordingly, I argue that the same rationale that underlies the willful ignorance doctrine also supports applying the collective knowledge doctrine at least sometimes. The two doctrines rest on similar normative principles. This may be why some see the collective knowledge doctrine as just the willful ignorance doctrine by another name.[6] Nonetheless, this overstates the reality. The two doctrines come apart: In some cases, the willful ignorance doctrine would not support imputing knowledge to the corporation, while the properly constrained collective knowledge doctrine *would*. Thus, the two doctrines are best seen as different applications of the same normative principle: equal culpability imputation.

Section I formulates a duty to inform others that grounds my analysis of the cases discussed later. While Chapter 4 defended a duty to reasonably inform *oneself* (DRI), now I contend that breaching the duty to inform *others* can also be culpable. There are few (if any) cases where it makes sense to treat my failure to inform others as grounds for imputing missing mental states to *me*, so I don't posit an analog of the willful ignorance doctrine for individuals who culpably fail to inform others. But matters are different for corporations. The rest of the chapter argues that one employee's failure to inform another can be the basis for imputing mental states to the corporation employing them.

Section II unpacks corporate criminal culpability. I set aside some skeptical objections to corporate culpability before showing how my theory of culpability applies to corporations. Section III then explains how the analysis of corporate culpability is to be carried out against the background of existing criminal law doctrine. Courts generally use the respondeat superior model, with its Individualist Constraint, to construct corporate mental states. But this simple model is called into question by the collective knowledge doctrine.

While most courts are wary of the collective knowledge doctrine, Section IV argues they shouldn't always be. The collective knowledge doctrine rests on the same normative foundation as the willful ignorance doctrine. Both are equal culpability imputation principles, and can be legitimately employed when, but only when, the conditions of equal culpability are met.

---

6 Thomas A. Hagemann & Joseph Grinstein, *The Mythology of Aggregate Corporate Knowledge: A Deconstruction*, 65 Geo. Wash. L. Rev. 210 (1997) ("the collective knowledge rule has simply acted as a corollary to . . . the doctrine of willful blindness").

This might suggest that the collective knowledge doctrine just is the willful ignorance doctrine by another name, but I show that the two doctrines come apart. Specifically, they diverge when corporate employees act to keep others (as opposed to themselves) in the dark. Thus, the willful ignorance and collective knowledge doctrines are distinct applications of the same underlying idea: Interfering with proper information flow can be culpable in ways that justify the imputation of knowledge.

I. The Duty to Inform Others

This book so far has focused mostly on the duty to inform *oneself* about risks posed by one's conduct. This chapter unpacks the mirror image duty. One also plausibly has obligations to inform *others* when important interests or values are at stake, and one can be culpable (at least *pro tanto*) in failing to do so.

Granted, one might have strictly moral obligations to inform others—perhaps a moral duty to whistle-blow about serious wrongdoing. But morality is not my concern here. Rather, my focus (as in most of this book) is the sort of obligations that are properly encoded in criminal law.

Existing law contains many examples of liability for breaching information-sharing obligations. Some jurisdictions criminalize the failure to report known felonies to the proper authorities—so-called *misprision of felony*. The offense exists in US federal law,[7] where it requires active concealment, not merely the failure to report.[8] This restriction to cases where active steps were taken to conceal the felony makes sense on my view of culpability from above. It is sensible because it will typically be more difficult and costly—and pro tanto more culpable on my account—to take affirmative steps to cover up a crime than to merely sit by and omit to report it.[9] In the United Kingdom, misprision of felony remains only in a restricted form that requires having been compensated for one's silence.[10] The demand to spread important information to those who should have it is discernable in other crimes too. Withholding information can be criminal fraud, particularly where the defendant owes fiduciary duties to disclose.[11]

Outside criminal law, duties to inform others abound. For example, US Securities and Exchange Commission rules, issued under the Sarbanes-Oxley Act, require attorneys

[7] 18 U.S.C. § 4.

[8] *See* Lancey v. United States, 356 F.2d 407, 410 (9th Cir. 1966) ("[m]ere silence, without some affirmative act, is insufficient evidence" of a § 4 violation); United States v. Cefalu, 85 F.3d 964, 969 (2d Cir. 1996) (defendant must "t[ake] steps to conceal the crime").

[9] We saw a similar idea in Chapter 4. Costly affirmative efforts to block otherwise freely available information make one's willful ignorance more culpable, all else equal, than not spending effort or money to investigate.

[10] Criminal Law Act of 1967 ch. 58, § 5.

[11] United States v. Brown, 459 F.3d 509, 532 (5th Cir. 2006) ("a breach of fiduciary duty . . . involving a violation of the duty to disclose could only result in criminal mail fraud where the information withheld from the employer was material") (internal citations omitted).

representing issuers of stock to report known evidence of material violations—first up the chain of command within the corporation, and if that fails, then to regulators outside the corporation.[12] Likewise, a lawyer can breach her ethical duties to the court if she learns that perjury has been committed but doesn't disclose it.[13]

The duty to inform others does not always require actively sharing information. It can also require not *preventing* others from obtaining information they otherwise could or should have received. That is, one might be required not to block others from becoming appropriately informed. It can be criminal to impede or obstruct law enforcement investigations or court proceedings.[14] The Sarbanes-Oxley Act likewise criminalizes destroying or falsifying records with "intent to impede, obstruct, or influence the investigation . . . of any matter within the jurisdiction of any . . . agency of the United States."[15]

From such examples, we can extrapolate a general principle that captures their spirit and motivation. We can see in the penumbra of laws of this sort a general duty (that is, a legally cognizable reason) to inform appropriate others when one knows or has suspicions of inculpatory facts—at least if they are well placed to respond to the harms or wrongs involved in this inculpatory information. This idea complements the *duty to inform oneself*, which figured into earlier chapters. Just as breaching one's duty to inform *oneself* can be a source of culpability (sometimes enough to ground equal culpability imputation), the same can hold for breaching one's duty to inform *others*. Here is an explicit statement of the duty with several details and caveats included to make it as normatively plausible as possible:

Duty to Reasonably Inform Others (DRIO): If an actor, A,

(i) at least suspects some inculpatory proposition, p, is true and p falls within A's domain of reasonable responsibilities (and A lacks reason to think the risk of p's truth is somehow justified), and

(ii) A should believe (based on her evidence) that she reasonably can see to it that relevant information about p (that she possesses, has access to, or controls) is shared with appropriate others who should act to address p or lessen the harm of p (and A's doing this is not so burdensome as to not be a reasonably available course of action),

---

[12] 17 CFR § 205.3 (specifying attorneys' "reporting up" obligations and authorizing "reporting out" as a last resort).

[13] Model Rule of Professional Responsibility 3.3(a)(3) (requiring lawyers to take remedial measures if they know their clients or witnesses gave material false evidence "including, if necessary, disclosure to the tribunal").

[14] 18 U.S.C. § 1503(a) (making it criminal to "corruptly or by threats or force . . . influences, obstructs, or impedes, or endeavors to influence, obstruct, or impede, the due administration of justice"); Denis v. Attorney General of U.S., 633 F.3d 201, 212 (3d Cir. 2011) (§ 1503(a) also covers evidence tampering); 18 U.S.C. § 1512(c) (imposing up to twenty years' imprisonment for related forms of tampering with documentary evidence).

[15] 18 U.S.C. § 1519.

then A has a *pro tanto* obligation to (at least try to) take the reasonably available steps (if any) needed to see to it that this information about p is shared with the appropriate others.[16]

Breaching DRIO is culpable for the same reasons as DRI: It manifests insufficient regard for interests, rights, or values that are properly protected by law. If I fail to share inculpatory information as appropriate when this can help mitigate the harms in question, then this shows me to not be sufficiently concerned with the threatened interests and rights of others (assuming I have no justification or excuse). Thus, I am more culpable if I breach DRIO, all else equal, than if I don't (either because I comply or because it doesn't apply).

As with DRI, several factors impact the culpability of breaching DRIO:

Factors enhancing the gravity of breaching DRIO:

(a) *The harm in p*: Breaching DRIO is more serious, all else equal, the more serious harms or wrongs the truth of p would involve (given the anticipated conduct of others and other background conditions over which one has no control).

(b) *The costs of sharing information*: The legally cognizable costs, for oneself or others, of sharing information about p one possesses or has access to can provide a full or partial justification for not sharing it, thus reducing culpability of breaching DRIO. This means the breach of DRIO is more culpable, all else equal, the easier or less costly it would be under the circumstances to share one's information about p with appropriately situated others.

(c) *One's mens rea*: The breach of DRIO is more serious, all else equal, (i) the higher one's mens rea is as to the fact that one is preventing appropriately situated others from acquiring relevant information about p that they should receive, and (ii) the more clearly one is aware of what type and how serious the risks are that one is keeping appropriately situated others in the dark about.

Factors (a) and (c) play out the same way as the analogous factors in previous chapters. Factor (b) deserves more discussion in this context. Suppose I know my friend has committed a serious crime, but threatens harm to more people. He has software that allows him to hack into people's bank accounts and withdraw funds in difficult to detect ways. He's already done this for twenty victims, but intends to do it for hundreds more. Should I alert the authorities?

---

[16] Just as DRI requires both investigating and not blocking information from reaching oneself, it follows from DRIO that one must both share the relevant information and not block it from reaching appropriate others.

Under DRIO, if I have no reasonably available way to share my inculpatory information with the authorities, then I wouldn't have any obligation to do so. Nor would I incur extra culpability for failing to. If my friend is notoriously violent and alerting the authorities would likely get me killed, then DRIO as formulated would not be triggered.

However, if the costs of informing are not so high that it's unreasonable to expect me to do so, then DRIO applies. Even if I'm reasonably able to inform, however, there can still be substantial costs to doing so, and, as factor (b) notes, these can help reduce my culpability for breaching DRIO. Suppose my alerting the authorities only risks causing my friend (or his friends) to retaliate by slashing my car tires—or depleting my bank account. In that case, I might still be a bit culpable for breaching DRIO (given the massive harm to others I could prevent by informing), but not as culpable as if sharing my information were costless.

If I'm right that breaching DRIO makes one more culpable, this can support equal culpability imputation. That is what I'll argue in the rest of this chapter. However, I'll contend, it most naturally grounds imputing mental states to corporate defendants, not individuals.[17]

[17] One might object that the law does not endorse DRIO as formulated. DRIO requires both actively sharing information and not blocking people from receiving information they should have. The law might demand the latter, but would shy away from the former. (Thanks to Will Thomas for this objection.)

Nonetheless, I remain committed to DRIO at least where normative culpability is concerned. The notion of culpability I'm working with is a *normatively cleaned-up version* of the legal concept employed in jurisdictions like ours. Thus, while I hew to the broad contours of existing law, I also deploy normative considerations to evaluate and criticize the law. There can be daylight between normative culpability and the culpability attributions of this or that jurisdiction (or "posited culpability"). Thus, it's within bounds for me to recommend principles that go somewhat beyond existing law—provided they have solid normative support. This is so for DRIO—for two reasons.

First, it's hard to distinguish between failing to actively share information and blocking others from receiving it. Suppose I have information I think the scientists in my company may need to analyze, but I email them without bothering to rewrite the message to urge them to look at this data. Am I blocking them from obtaining information they should have? Or merely failing to actively inform them? It's unclear. Perhaps both. My inability to draw this distinction is one reason I formulate DRIO to demand *both* actively sharing information (where appropriate) and not blocking others from obtaining it. Second, under natural assumptions, the same fairness or procedural considerations support both a pro tanto obligation (a) to avoid blocking others from obtaining information, and (b) to share that information (to the extent these are separable). In other words, the two components of DRIO—the obligation to share information and the obligation not to obstruct others from receiving it—often are grounded in similar, mutually reinforcing considerations.

Thus, there is support for DRIO as formulated. However, even if this diverges somewhat from actual legal practice, that is fine for me. I am concerned with normative culpability for use in critiquing and improving the law. Even if existing law doesn't often demand sharing information, there is reason to think it culpable to fail to do so when required by DRIO. The law should adopt this position, or at least go further in this direction.

II. What Is Corporate Criminal Culpability?

To argue that breaching DRIO can support equal culpability imputation of mental states to corporations, I must clarify the notion of corporate criminal culpability.

A. SIDESTEPPING SOME THEORETICAL CHALLENGES

My argument rests on a crucial presupposition about corporate culpability: It exists. It's beyond the scope of this project to defend the view that corporations are appropriate objects of criminal liability. Instead, I simply assume that a plausible case can be made for this view. The ship has largely sailed on this debate within our own criminal justice system. At least since the early twentieth century, we have routinely convicted corporations of crimes.[18] I mean to remain consistent with the basic contours of criminal law practice in jurisdictions like ours, so I will not reopen this debate about the theoretical soundness of holding corporations criminally liable. (As explained in Chapters 2–5, I seek to map out the contours of a notion of culpability that is a normatively cleaned-up version of the concept at work in our legal practices.[19])

In presupposing the defensibility of corporate culpability, I skate over difficult theoretical worries. Two are worth mentioning. First, I assume corporations can have the kind of capacities for practical reasoning and decision-making required to be apt targets of criminally responsibility. Many theorists suggest that corporations (despite being artificial entities) can possess the requisite deliberative capacities for it to be sensible to hold them liable—both civilly and criminally.[20] Corporations often have complex deliberative structures permitting them to consider different plans, weigh reasons for and against each, settle on an intended plan of action, and then execute it.[21] It is hard to see what more could be needed for criminal culpability.[22]

---

[18] N.Y. Cent. & Hudson River Ry. v. United States, 212 U.S. 481 (1909) (recognizing the aptness of imposing criminal responsibility on corporations). *See also U.S. Sentencing Guidelines Manual*, Ch. 8, Sentencing of Organizations (2016), http://www.ussc.gov/guidelines/2016-guidelines-manual/2016-chapter-8.

[19] More precisely, I aim to hew to the general understanding of culpability used in systems like ours, and then illuminate the normatively best version of that concept. This normatively cleaned-up concept of culpability can then be used to critique, evaluate, and reform existing law.

[20] C. List & P. Pettit, Group Agency 153–63 (2011); Will Thomas, *The Ability and Responsibility of Corporate Law to Improve Criminal Punishment*, 78 Ohio St. L. Rev 601 (2017).

[21] List and Pettit argue corporations satisfy the main requirements for responsibility: (1) "fac[ing] a normatively significant choice," (2) "ha[ving] the *understanding* and *access* to evidence required for making normative judgments about the options" and (3) "ha[ving] the *control* required for choosing between the options." List & Pettit, *supra* note 20, at 158. *See also id.* at 158–63 (explaining how groups with formalized decision-making procedures satisfy these conditions).

[22] Will Thomas puts it nicely: "If all . . . critics have in mind is that corporations must be responsive to the sorts of normative considerations that arise in the criminal law, then I see no basis for their complaints. (. . .) Corporations . . . can deliberate and act consistent with their self-identified interests and . . . are willing

A second worry I set aside concerns whether corporate criminal liability is really needed, given that we already punish individuals. A skeptic about corporate criminal liability might argue that any time it seems apt to blame a corporation for some misconduct, this can be fully reduced to blame that properly belongs to individual actors for their separate actions. While this is a fair worry particularly as regards moral blame,[23] it does not carry over to the notion of culpability that operates in law. Existing law would not allow us to secure *criminal convictions* for all the minute bits of individual action that go together to constitute a wrongful act by a corporation. Where legal liability is concerned, it's less plausible that whenever it seems apt to hold a corporation liable, this legal liability can always be reduced to separate bits of individual liability that fully account for the total responsibility to be doled out for the wrong in question. Individual liability plausibly does not go far enough to guarantee that there will be no such "responsibility deficit"—to borrow List and Pettit's term—that remains to be apportioned because of the wrongs done to victims.[24]

To this, the skeptic might reply that this is merely a problem with our law. If individual legal liability doesn't suffice to capture all the blame to be allocated for some wrongful conduct by the corporation, then the law should be *amended* so there always are enough crimes for individuals on the books to ensure that all the blame that is merited can be attributed to individual actors.

While I can't fully answer this worry here, here is the sort of reply I think is needed. Amending the law to expand individual liability so it always accounts for all the blame that seems warranted, thus guaranteeing that there is never a "responsibility deficit" that makes corporate liability needed, *would be a very bad policy*. Doing so would likely require criminalizing minute conduct—like momentary lapses of attention, failing to notice emerging structural problems that are difficult for any one person to notice alone, a bit of carelessness here or there, natural mistakes in prioritizing one's time, getting too invested

participants in broad swaths of our normative practices, even if they may not be objects of moral consideration in . . . themselves. For example, through contract law, corporations routinely participate in a normatively laden practice akin to promising." Thomas, *supra* note 20, at 612–13.

[23] *See, e.g.*, Andras Szigeti, *Are Individualist Accounts of Collective Responsibility Morally Deficient?*, INSTITUTIONS, EMOTIONS, AND GROUP AGENTS: CONTRIBUTIONS TO GROUP ONTOLOGY (A. Konzelmann Ziv & H.B. Schmid eds., 2014).

[24] On List and Pettit's view, group responsibility is needed because of "responsibility deficits"—cases where adding up the culpability of all individuals in the group doesn't fully account for the total blame that seems apt in response to the relevant group-caused harm. LIST & PETTIT, *supra* note 20, at 165–67. Suppose a group harms many victims, which warrants an amount of blame, X. However, most of the individuals in the group have excuses (like duress or ignorance) given how the group's activities were structured. Thus, if we add up the blame attributable to all the individuals, we might get a total that is less than X. Where is this missing blame—the responsibility deficit—to be directed? List and Pettit think it goes *to the group itself* (provided it meets the minimum requirements for agency). Responsibility deficits are especially likely, they think, when the individuals have justifications or excuses (like ignorance, lack of legal causation, or duress) that mitigate individual culpability. *Id.* at 165.

in projects, or not being sufficiently skeptical of the group's agenda. Criminalizing such minute failures—bringing them into the public sphere and deploying the heavy sanctions of the criminal law in response—would be highly invasive and threaten other values we hold dear, such as autonomy, or freedom of expression and association. Moreover, this expansion of individual liability would provide further avenues for overprosecution and other abuses of the criminal law. For these reasons, I suspect it would be a dangerous policy to expand individual criminal liability as far as necessary to ensure responsibility deficits never arise that corporate criminal liability is needed to fill.

What I've said here admittedly will not settle the matter, but space does not allow me to give a complete defense of corporate culpability. Instead, I press on under the assumption that answers to the corporate culpability skeptic can be given.

B. SKETCHING AN ACCOUNT OF CORPORATE CRIMINAL CULPABILITY

Next we need to understand how the idea of criminal culpability applies to corporations. This subsection explains in broad outline how my theory from Chapter 2 carries over to corporations, thus sketching how to determine the level of culpability for a bit of corporate misconduct.

On my account, some piece of misconduct is culpable to the extent it manifests insufficient regard for relevant interests, rights, and values. If we want a descriptive account capturing the culpability attributions in a given jurisdiction, we'd focus on the interests rights and values actually protected by the law in this jurisdiction. If we want a normative account for use in critiquing the law, we'd focus on the interests, rights, and values that properly should be protected. Like most of this book, this chapter employs the latter notion.

My account applied to corporate conduct involves two stages. To figure out how culpable a corporation is for an action, *step one* is to determine just what the corporation did. Since corporations necessarily act through agents—like their officers, managers, and employees—we need to determine which acts of its employees can be included in a proper description of what the corporation did. To answer this question, I take an inclusive approach, which is also is the simplest. Specifically, I propose to rely on familiar agency principles, so I take it that any conduct carried out by an agent of the corporation within the scope of his or her employment can be imputed to the corporation.[25] This goes both for actions done and mental states possessed (like knowledge) within the scope of one's employment.[26] The sum total of what the corporation did just is the aggregate of

---

[25] RESTATEMENT (THIRD) OF AGENCY § 1.01 ("[a]gency is the fiduciary relationship that arises when one person (a 'principal') manifests assent to another person (an 'agent') that the agent shall act on the principal's behalf and subject to the principal's control, and the agent manifests assent or otherwise consents so to act").

[26] Deborah DeMott, *When Is a Principal Charged with an Agent's Knowledge*, 13 DUKE J. COMP. & INT'L L. 291, 293 (2003) (principal charged with "legal consequences of knowledge of a fact known by an agent when knowledge of the fact is material to the agent's duties to the principal and to the principal's legal relations with third parties"); RESTATEMENT (THIRD) OF AGENCY § 5.03, cmt. b (Principals "charged with the legal

acts performed and mental states possessed by agents of the corporation within the scope of their employment (i.e., those which are imputable to the corporation under the most defensible agency principles, whatever they are). Thus, what the corporation *did*, on the occasion in question, just is the relevant subset of these actions and mental states. To proceed with determining criminal culpability, we must select the relevant unit (e.g., a time slice or subset) of the sum total of what the corporation did. It is that unit whose culpability then is assessed in the second step of the procedure.

Accordingly, *step two* is to determine how much insufficient regard is manifested by the relevant unit of conduct by the corporation. This is to be assessed, on my theory, by asking what the least amount of insufficient regard is that it would take to get an otherwise law-abiding corporation to perform that conduct under the circumstances. In other words, the insufficient regard this conduct, C, manifests equals the smallest possible departure from the way a similarly situated perfectly law-abiding corporation, comprising perfectly law-abiding employees, would weigh the applicable reasons that would be needed to get a corporation to do C under the circumstances. This level of departure from the correct weighing of reasons is what the culpability of the corporation's actual conduct, C, equals.

If something like this two-step, manifestation-based account is the right approach to determining the culpability of a corporation for what it did, it follows that assessing corporate criminal culpability is a process of *charitable reconstruction*. Determining what a corporation counts as having done, and how culpable it is therefor, will necessarily involve some degree of choice by the theorist or adjudicator when selecting what should count and what shouldn't. In this regard, my theory is no different when applied to natural persons. On my account of individual culpability from Chapter 2, we peg a person's culpability for an action to the amount of insufficient regard that action manifests. The amount manifested, in turn, is partly a function of normative assumptions—like the principle of lenity, which says the amount manifested equals the least degree of insufficient regard needed to get an otherwise law-abiding person to behave similarly. Thus, I think ascribing criminal culpability to individuals is already a normatively laden process, involving assumptions about fair attribution. Corporate culpability is no different in this respect. Although corporations are artificial, such that their culpability must be legally constructed through normatively infused processes, this is not different in kind from assessing the culpability of natural persons. My view thus preserves continuity between the ascription of culpability to individuals and corporations.

---

consequences of having actual knowledge of" facts their agents know. "Imputation . . . reduces the risk that a principal may deploy agents as a shield against the legal consequences of facts the principal would prefer not to know."). In re Hellenic Inc., 252 F.3d 391, 395 (5th Cir. 2001) ("An agent's knowledge is imputed to the corporation where the agent is acting within the scope of his authority and where the knowledge relates to matters within the scope of that authority.").

III. Constructing Corporate Culpability

What I've said about corporate culpability thus far is very general. To appreciate how this works in practice, we must consider how corporate culpability tends to be constructed under existing law. As this section explains, the respondeat superior model is the law's starting point for attributing culpability to corporations. This model contains an Individualist Constraint on mental state attribution. However, this constraint is called into question by the (in)famous collective knowledge doctrine. While many courts are skeptical of the collective knowledge doctrine, Section IV argues this is a mistake. In fact, the collective knowledge doctrine is sometimes legitimately employed on equal culpability grounds. Thus, courts have good reason to rethink their strict adherence to respondeat superior.

A. THE STARTING POINT: RESPONDEAT SUPERIOR

The standard approach to determining corporate criminal liability is the respondeat superior model.[27] It is a vicarious liability theory. Under the simplest version, all and only the crimes that individual employees of the corporation directly commit, while acting in the course of their employment and for the corporation's benefit, will be imputed to the corporation.[28] Additional restrictions are sometimes added,[29] but the basic principle is this:

> **Strict Respondeat Superior Model**: A corporation may be convicted of a crime, C, if and only if there is some individual employed by the corporation who commits

[27] Ashley Kircher, *Corporate Criminal Liability versus Corporate Securities Fraud Liability: Analyzing the Divergence in Standards of Culpability*, 46 Am. Crim. L. Rev. 157, 157 (2009) ("In the United States, the doctrine of respondeat superior has been the most traditionally accepted method of imputing criminal liability to a corporation.").

[28] Eli Lederman, *Models for Imposing Corporate Criminal Liability: From Adaptation and Imitation Toward Aggregation and the Search for Self-Identity*, 4 Buff. Crim. L. Rev. 641, 654–55 (2000) (under respondeat superior "a corporation is liable for the deeds of any of its agents or employees . . . as long as two cumulative conditions are fulfilled: [1] '[T]he agent was acting within the course and scope of his or her employment, having the authority to act for the corporation with respect to the particular corporate business which was conducted criminally; (2) the agent acting, at least in part in furtherance of the corporation's business interests'").

[29] The Model Penal Code restricts its respondeat superior model to acts of high corporate officials. Model Penal Code § 2.07(1)(c) (requiring that "the commission of the offense was authorized, requested, commanded, performed or recklessly tolerated by the board of directors or by a high managerial agent . . ."); Pamela H. Bucy, *Trends in Corporate Criminal Prosecutions*, 44 Am. Crim. L. Rev. 1287, 1290 (2007) (noting the MPC uses respondeat superior in "limited fashion: a corporation is liable for the conduct of only some agents (its directors, officers, or other higher echelon employees)"); Lederman, *supra* note 28, at 655 (discussing the same limitation).

> C—that is, satisfies all the actus reus and mens rea requirements herself—within the scope of her employment while acting at least in part for the corporation's benefit.

Consider the federal crime of knowingly making false statements to the US government.[30] Suppose I work for Big Oil Corp., and as part of my work, I submit a report to the Environmental Protection Agency stating that the company's Texas plant releases no more of the carcinogen benzene than 1 milligram per cubic meter, although I know this is false. In fact, I know the amount released into the air is twice this.[31] Thus, I have committed a crime in my own right—that is, I satisfy the mens rea and actus reus elements. Under the Strict Respondeat Superior Model, my crime can be imputed to Big Oil Corp. (Likewise, if several employees conspire to submit the report containing this false statement, the conspiracy could be imputed to the corporation.)

The Strict Respondeat Superior Model clearly is too narrow to capture existing practice. Crimes can be imputed to the corporation even if the mens rea was possessed by a different person than the one who physically performed the actus reus—at least provided the mens rea and actus reus are sufficiently closely connected to satisfy the concurrence[32] requirement.[33] Consider the crime of hauling nuclear waste without a permit.

---

[30] 18 U.S.C. § 1001.

[31] As with all my examples herein, assume there are no problems of proof.

[32] Wayne LaFave, 1 Subst. Crim. L. § 6.3 (2d ed.) (guilt requires that the "defendant's mental state actuate[] the physical conduct"); Joshua Dressler, Understanding Criminal Law (6th ed.) 199 ("[t]he defendant's conduct that caused the social harm must have been *set into motion or impelled by* the thought process that constituted the *mens rea* of the offense").

[33] Several commentators note that the concurrence requirement is a challenge for any theory of corporate mens rea beyond the Strict Respondeat Superior Model. *See, e.g.*, Patricia Abril & Ann Morales Olazába, *The Locus of Corporate Scienter*, Colum. Bus. L. Rev. 81, 85–86 (2006) ("respondeat superior do[es] not apply neatly to corporations" when "the act and the intent do not coincide in a single corporate actor"); Lederman, *supra* note 28, at 674 (suggesting "that aggregating elements of one offense from the thinking of various corporate agents . . . is detrimental to the principle of simultaneity required between actus reus and mens rea").

Here, I will always assume the concurrence requirement is satisfied in my examples. Moreover, it is an implicit requirement of the imputation principles I have defend throughout this book that criminal liability cannot be imposed unless the concurrence requirement between actus reus and mens rea is also satisfied.

I cannot offer a full theory of the concurrence requirement for corporate action, but the basic idea is that the mens rea of the crime must be causally active in producing the actus reus. As I've argued elsewhere, this means that for crimes requiring knowledge, the actus reus must be done "in light of" this knowledge—that is, the knowledge must reasonably be expected to trigger the motivation not to do the actus reus, but doesn't. Alex Sarch, *Knowledge, Recklessness and the Connection Requirement Between Actus Reus and Mens Rea*, 120 Penn. State L. Rev. 1 (2015). For example, knowing a report contains a falsehood should provide sufficient motivation not to submit it to the government, and if I do so despite possessing this knowledge, I've acted in light of the knowledge. The knowledge was part of the causal story producing my action, and the concurrence requirement is satisfied. The same holds when the CEO has the requisite knowledge for the crime and orders an employee to physically do the actus reus. The action is causally traceable to the knowledge, and the concurrence requirement is satisfied.

How does the concurrence requirement apply for willful ignorance? In the same way as for knowledge. Suspecting the inculpatory proposition p should provide sufficient motivation to investigate and then, upon learning that p is true, refrain from doing the actus reus. If one neither investigates, nor refrains from the

I'm the boss, and I know our company doesn't have the right permit. Nonetheless, I instruct an employee to drive a truck filled with nuclear waste to a disposal plant four hundred miles away. I have the mens rea for the crime, but don't physically do the actus reus. The driver—a company employee under my authority—does the actus reus on my instructions. He does it *for me*. Regular agency principles allow his action to be imputed to me. Thus, the crime of knowingly hauling hazardous waste without a permit can also be imputed to the corporation—although the actus reus was done by someone else than the person with mens rea. To capture this wrinkle, the respondeat superior model must be refined:

> **Refined Respondeat Superior Model**: A corporation may be convicted of a crime, C, if and only if
> (1) there is some individual employed by the corporation (acting within the scope of her employment and for the corporation's benefit) who possesses the whole mens rea required for C, and
> (2) there is some person employed by the corporation (acting within the scope of her employment and for the corporation's benefit)—perhaps the same person as in (1), or perhaps not—who does the actus reus of C in a way that is sufficiently causally connected to the mens rea of C for the concurrence requirement to be satisfied. (If the person in (1) is not the person in (2), then (2) will be satisfied, for example, if the actus reus is done on the instructions of the person who possessed the requisite mens rea in (1).)

This is a more precise and plausible statement of the respondeat superior principle, and it is what I employ in what follows. Still, prong (1) will be most important for present purposes. What's key is that under any plausible respondeat superior model, corporate criminal liability requires one and the same person to possess the *full mens rea of C* (before either doing the actus reus himself, or ordering or requesting someone else to do it).

For ease of reference, call this last assumption the *Individualist Constraint* on corporate mens rea attribution. Case law is rife with such statements.[34] One New York court captured it especially well when holding that a "corporation can be held to have a particular

---

actus reus, then part of the causal explanation of one's conduct is the absence of motivation to the contrary (a repulsion failure). This is what it means for the actus reus to be caused by (or done in light of) one's willful ignorance. So that's what it takes for the concurrence requirement to be satisfied.

The same applies where one acts to preserve the ignorance of others, as discussed in this chapter. Concurrence is satisfied when your suspicions of p should motivate you to share information with others in the corporation, but you don't and these others go on to do the actus reus in a benighted state that you caused. Provided your suspicions are sufficiently related to the actus reus done by others, the concurrence requirement is satisfied.

[34] Com. v. Life Care Centers of America, Inc., 926 N.E.2d 206, 212, (Mass. 2010) ("a corporation acts with a given mental state in a criminal context only if at least one employee who acts (or fails to act) possesses the requisite mental state at the time of the act (or failure to act)").

state of mind only when that state of mind is possessed by a single individual" within the corporation.[35] While the Individualist Constraint is a good default rule, I will argue it should not apply in all cases.

In what follows, I focus on knowledge crimes. To formulate the Individualist Constraint for these crimes, we must not forget individual imputation doctrines like the willful ignorance doctrine. An employee's willful ignorance of p can also be the basis for imputing knowledge that p to the corporation employing her.[36] Thus, the Individualist Constraint that matters to us will be:

> **Individualist Constraint on Knowledge Attribution to Corporations:** A corporation possesses the knowledge that p as required for being guilty of a crime, C, *only if* there is at least one individual employee of the corporation who, acting within the scope of her employment and for the corporation's benefit, either (i) actually knows that p, or else (ii) can have the knowledge that p imputed to her (e.g., because she was willfully ignorant).

B. CALLING RESPONDEAT SUPERIOR INTO QUESTION: THE COLLECTIVE KNOWLEDGE DOCTRINE

Serious questions have been raised about even the refined versions of the Individualist Constraint and the respondeat superior model on which it rests. Specifically, the *collective knowledge doctrine*, which numerous courts and theorists have at least flirted with accepting, casts doubt on the Individualist Constraint.

The collective knowledge doctrine rejects the Individualist Constraint built into respondeat superior, and instead would allow courts to aggregate the different pieces of information possessed separately by different employees in order to *impute to the corporation* the full knowledge required for conviction.[37] That is, it permits stitching together

---

[35] First Equity Corp. of Florida v. Standard & Poor's Corp., 690 F. Supp. 256, 259–60 (S.D.N.Y. 1988) (denying that "the corporation may be deemed to have a culpable state of mind when that state of mind is possessed by no single employee").

[36] United States v. St. Michael's Credit Union, 880 F.2d 579, 583–86 (1st Cir. 1989) (finding sufficient evidence for convicting individual under willful ignorance jury instructions for violating IRS filing requirements, and imputing this knowledge to the corporation that employed her, which was convicted of the same offenses—although the convictions were vacated on other grounds). *See id.* at 583 (finding "[t]he liability of the [corporation] is . . . measured by the liability of [the individual employee]"); *id.* at 586 (holding the "evidence and inferences permissibly drawn therefrom were sufficient to support . . . willful blindness instruction" for said individual employee).

[37] *See* Abril & Olazába, *supra* note 33, at 115–16 (collective knowledge theory permits corporate criminal liability "when several actors, none of whom could be found guilty individually, each have committed one or more requisite elements of a crime such that their actions, when taken as a whole, constitute criminal conduct. This represents a significant departure from the respondeat superior doctrine. . . . The doctrine also may apply . . . where no single agent knows all of the facts, but multiple agents hold pieces of information that together would amount to the corporation's guilty knowledge.").

different pieces of knowledge possessed by different individuals in the corporation, who could not themselves be individually convicted, in order to construct the requisite knowledge and impute it to the corporation. To see how this works, consider:

> SEPARATE KNOWLEDGE: Big Oil Corp. is charged with knowingly making false statements to the US government in violation of 18 U.S.C. § 1001. Alice, an employee of Big Oil Corp., writes and submits a report to a government agency, which asserts that p, where "p" denotes the fact that the company's benzene emissions level is below one milligram per cubic meter. Unbeknownst to Alice, it turns out that Betty, another employee of the company, knows that not-p. Alice and Betty do not talk or share information. Alice never learns that not-p, and Betty never learns of the report's statement that p. So neither actually knows that which is required for conviction, namely, the fact that the report contains a statement that is false.

Under the collective knowledge doctrine, Big Oil Corp. could be convicted of violating the statute. It would allow Alice's knowledge that the report states that p to be combined with Betty's knowledge that not-p in order to impute the mens rea of the crime to Big Oil Corp. Accordingly, Big Oil Corp. could be deemed to *know* that the report contained a certain statement and that it is false, as required to be guilty.

Some criminal cases appear to adopt this doctrine—most notoriously, *United States v. Bank of New England*,[38] where the court stated:

> A corporation cannot plead innocence by asserting that the information obtained by several employees was not acquired by any one individual who then would have comprehended its full import. Rather the corporation is considered to have acquired the collective knowledge of its employees and is held responsible for their failure to act accordingly. Since the Bank had the compartmentalized structure common to all large corporations, the court's collective knowledge instruction was not only proper but necessary.[39]

This conflicts with the Individualist Constraint, under which a corporation can be convicted of a crime only if there is at least one individual within the company who actually possesses the whole mens rea for the crime or could have it imputed to her personally.

Although much discussed by theorists and clearly favored by prosecutors (and plaintiffs in civil contexts[40]), the collective knowledge doctrine has been mostly rejected

---

[38] 821 F.2d 844, 856 (1st Cir. 1987). However, it's doubtful this case really adopted the collective knowledge doctrine. *See infra* note 44.

[39] *Id.* (quotation marks, amendments, and citations omitted).

[40] Civil and criminal corporate mens rea function similarly, as Judge Learned Hand observed a century ago. United States v. Nearing, 252 F. 223, 231 (S.D.N.Y. 1918) (Hand, J.) ("[T]here is no distinction in essence between the civil and the criminal liability of corporations, based upon the element of intent or wrongful purpose. Each is merely an imputation to the corporation of the mental condition of its agents.").

by American courts. This seems especially apt where there is no foul play that prevented employees from pooling their knowledge and drawing obvious inferences. If Betty and Alice never talk because it's not reasonably expected that they would communicate as part of their jobs, and no one prevented them from talking, then it would seem perverse for a court to intercede and pretend as if they had shared their knowledge, and from there impute this combined knowledge to their employer.

I suspect it is mostly due to this worry that so many courts reject the collective knowledge doctrine. Moreover, they have done so even in civil contexts, which one would expect to be less exacting than the standards for criminal guilt. The Eleventh Circuit rejected the collective knowledge doctrine in 2013.[41] Similarly, the D.C. Circuit in 2010 expressed doubts about "the legal soundness of the 'collective intent' theory, under which . . . a corporation's specific intent to defraud can be inferred if the company's public statements contradict the accumulated 'collective knowledge' of the corporation's employees."[42] The court held the collective knowledge doctrine was inconsistent with the language and purpose of the False Claims Act.[43] Accordingly, the Individualist Constraint built into the respondeat superior model is fairly regarded as the default position taken by courts.

There are some cases that *seem* to adopt something like the collective knowledge doctrine. Nonetheless, these can be explained in ways that are consistent with the Individualist Constraint. First, some courts merely adopt the evidential rule that the collective knowledge of multiple employees can be *circumstantial evidence* of actual knowledge held by an individual within the corporation. This seems true of the leading collective knowledge doctrine case: *Bank of New England*.[44] Second, other cases adopt the collective knowledge doctrine only as a pleading rule—that is, a simplifying assumption used at early stages of civil litigation in connection with a Motion to Dismiss—not a rule that governs whether liability is ultimately to be imposed.[45] Both these ways of coming close

[41] McGee v. Sentinel Offender Servs., LLC, 719 F.3d 1236 (11th Cir. 2013) (noting that other circuits had encountered "attempt[s] to weave the fragmented actions of various agents into corporate *mens rea*," but "[w]hatever the theory's status in other jurisdictions, . . . we decline to recognize it here").

[42] United States v. Sci. Applications Int'l Corp., 626 F.3d 1257, 1274 (D.C. Cir. 2010) (quotation marks omitted).

[43] *Id.* (expressing "skepticism about corporate intent theories that rely on aggregating the states of mind of multiple individuals").

[44] 821 F.2d at 856. The D.C. Circuit claims *Bank of New England* only endorsed an evidential version of the collective knowledge rule. *Science Applications*, 626 F.3d at 1274. The court suggested *Bank of New England* only used collective knowledge as an evidentiary shortcut that allowed juries to *infer* that one individual possessed the full mens rea *if* other employees possessed different pieces of knowledge that, when combined, amounted to knowledge of the fraud. *Id.* If this reading of *Bank of New England* is right, it would not license true knowledge aggregation. Rather, it would just allow the inference that some employee believes q from the fact that two other employees believed p and p entails q, respectively. This still respects the Individualist Constraint as a liability rule.

[45] Teamsters Local 445 Freight Div. Pension Fund v. Dynex Capital Inc., 531 F.3d 190 (2d Cir. 2008). The court held that to survive a corporate defendant's motion to dismiss under the PSLRA, a plaintiff must plead facts that "create a strong inference that someone whose intent could be imputed to the corporation acted with the requisite scienter," although "it is possible to raise the required inference with regard to a corporate defendant

to the collective knowledge doctrine are still consistent with *rejecting* this doctrine as a substantive liability rule, thus preserving the Individualist Constraint. Accordingly, the Individualist Constraint currently is the majority view among courts as to the proper standard for liability.

Why am I going on about the collective knowledge doctrine when it has met with such resistance from courts? Because this resistance is often mistaken. There is a deep insight behind the collective knowledge doctrine, which is akin to the normative basis for the willful ignorance doctrine. In what follows, I'll argue that there is a strong normative foundation for the collective knowledge doctrine at least when the corporation is seriously culpable.

IV. The Equal Culpability Basis for the Collective Knowledge Doctrine

A. THE INSIGHT BEHIND THE COLLECTIVE KNOWLEDGE DOCTRINE

Despite courts' antipathy toward it, the collective knowledge doctrine embodies an insight worth defending—if only it can be formulated to apply within reasonable limits. Thomas Hagemann and Joseph Grinstein suggest something similar. While arguing that the collective knowledge doctrine can be carried to excess, they point out an important connection between this doctrine and willful ignorance.[46] They think the collective knowledge doctrine, with the knowledge aggregation it permits, *is justified as a judicial response to willful ignorance*. They contend "the collective knowledge rule has simply acted as a corollary to . . . the doctrine of willful blindness. Before courts will collectivize knowledge, they will first demand a showing that corporations deliberately attempted . . . to compartmentalize or avoid inculpatory information."[47]

There is something importantly right about this. Although Hagemann and Grinstein don't explicitly spell out *why* aggregating knowledge possessed separately by different employees is justified in response to willful ignorance, this late in the present book the answer should be clear. Willful ignorance by employees can be culpable, so there is an equal culpability rationale in the offing for aggregating bits of information these employees deliberately prevented themselves from obtaining. Thus, in conditions of equal culpability, the corporation employing these individuals can be treated as if they knew what they prevented themselves from learning.

without doing so with regard to a specific individual defendant." *Id.* at 195. Thus, *Dynex* recognizes that a version of the collective knowledge doctrine can apply at the pleading stage. (A similar rule was adopted by the Seventh Circuit in Makor Issues & Rights, Ltd. v. Tellabs Inc., 513 F.3d 702, 710 (7th Cir. 2008) (Posner, J.).) However, this is still consistent with the Individualist Constraint construed as a liability rule.

[46] Hagemann & Grinstein, *supra* note 6.

[47] *Id.* at 237–38.

Thus, one of my aims is to explain the theoretical basis for Hagemann and Grinstein's claim. I argue that knowledge aggregation is justified because—but only to the extent that—it is justified on equal culpability grounds. Compartmentalizing information within the company so employees remain in the dark can make the corporation as culpable as if it had acted, though its agents, with full knowledge.

In addition to elucidating the normative basis for the collective knowledge doctrine, properly constrained, I also want to avoid the weaknesses of Hagemann and Grinstein's view. Their claim that the "collective knowledge rule has simply acted as a corollary to . . . the doctrine of willful blindness"[48] suggests that the collective knowledge doctrine is *unnecessary* since we already have the willful ignorance doctrine.[49] However, this is a mistake. I argue that the collective knowledge doctrine, if justified on equal culpability grounds, properly applies *beyond* the scope of the existing willful ignorance doctrine.

B. THE PROPER SCOPE OF THE COLLECTIVE KNOWLEDGE DOCTRINE

The collective knowledge doctrine is best seen as an equal culpability imputation principle that may be used only when the corporation is as culpable as if it had the relevant knowledge. Accordingly, the first thing to note is that there are cases where aggregating knowledge is clearly inappropriate. Consider this version of SEPARATE KNOWLEDGE:

> INNOCENT SEPARATE KNOWLEDGE: Alice, an employee of Big Oil Corp., writes and submits a report to a government agency, which asserts that p. Unbeknownst to Alice, Betty, another employee of Big Oil Corp., knows that not-p. Alice and Betty do not talk or share information. Alice never learns that not-p, and Betty never learns of the report's statement that p. But this is due to no fault of theirs or anyone else within the company. Alice and Betty don't work together, have no routine interactions, and therefore would not reasonably be expected to share information.

Because neither Alice nor Betty (nor anyone else) is culpable for failing to communicate and discover the falsehood in the report, it would be extremely harsh to convict the corporation of the offense of knowingly making a false statement to the government.[50] This is the sort of excess that make Hagemann and Grinstein legitimately worried about the collective knowledge doctrine.[51] Punishing innocent actors, or the corporation employing them, as knowing wrongdoers clearly goes too far.

---

[48] *Id.*

[49] In fairness, they don't explicitly state that the collective knowledge doctrine is unnecessary. This is at most strongly implied by their discussion. *See also infra* notes 54–55.

[50] Assume Alice was not negligent in preparing the report. But even if she were, that would of course not be enough to justify convicting her or the corporation of a knowledge crime.

[51] Hagemann & Grinstein, *supra* note 6, at 237 (suggesting with only some hyperbole that corporate executives are fairly "terrified that the collective knowledge bogeyman will creep up on them and convict their companies

But matters are different where willful ignorance is involved. Consider:

> SEPARATE KNOWLEDGE—WILLFUL IGNORANCE: This case is the same as before except that Alice is willfully ignorant. As before, Alice writes and submits the report to a government agency asserting that p, while Betty knows that not-p. But now Alice suspects some of the statements in the report are false, but doesn't want to jeopardize the company. So she tells the other employees, including Betty, that she doesn't want them to tell her about their work—particularly if they encounter possible bad news for the company. Thus, Alice intends to keep herself ignorant about the truth of the statements in the report. She is willfully blind of the fact that not-p.

Here, there is no unfairness in aggregating Alice's knowledge that the report asserts p with Betty's knowledge that not-p—that is, that the company's benzene emissions are above what the report asserts. As a willfully ignorant actor lacking any justification, Alice seems just as culpable as if she had known not-p. Thus, knowledge that not-p can be imputed to her on equal culpability grounds, and from there, to the corporation by respondeat superior.

However, notice that in this case, there actually is no need to appeal to the collective knowledge doctrine. The same result—imputing knowledge that not-p to the corporation, together with knowledge that the report asserts p—can be accomplished through the traditional willful ignorance doctrine together with regular respondeat superior principles. The result is the same if we use the collective knowledge doctrine to combine Alice's knowledge of the contents of the report with Betty's knowledge that not-p *or* if we impute knowledge that not-p to Alice directly thanks to her willful ignorance, and then impute this (together with her knowledge that report says p) to the corporation via the refined respondeat superior model. Either way, the corporation can be treated as if it knowingly submitted a false statement to the government.

If this were the only type of case we encountered, there wouldn't be much need for the collective knowledge doctrine. Instead, we could simply rely on the willful ignorance doctrine and convict the corporation on a willful ignorance theory under respondeat superior principles. Thus, there would be no call to abandon the Individualist Constraint. Nonetheless, this is not the only case we encounter. In other cases, the willful ignorance doctrine does not apply, and there *is* a genuine need for the collective knowledge doctrine. It is to such cases I now turn.

---

of criminal acts that neither they nor any employee had any intention of committing: innocent individual behavior wholly transmogrified into corporate guilt").

C. Knowledge Aggregation beyond Willful Ignorance

I offer two kinds of case where the collective knowledge doctrine is justified on equal culpability grounds, but the willful ignorance doctrine doesn't generate the same results. Here the collective knowledge doctrine is genuinely needed. One such case involves the aggregation of existing knowledge, the other the construction of new knowledge—that is, imputing mental states that no individual within the corporation possesses. Neither case involves willful ignorance, which requires breaching the duty to inform *oneself*. Rather, they involve breaching the duty, sketched earlier, to reasonably inform *others* (DRIO). Both undercut the Individualist Constraint.

To see the first of these cases, consider the following variation of our working example:

> Separate Knowledge—Keeping Others in the Dark: As before, Alice writes and submits the report knowing that it asserts p, while Betty separately has knowledge that not-p. But now they *do* routinely collaborate on projects like this and can be expected to share their knowledge in the normal course of their work. But management interferes with the normal flow of information. Management knows Alice and Betty sometimes poke around looking for legal problems, and this has cost the corporation significant amounts of money in the past. So management—while they generally have nothing to do with submitting such reports and have no specific suspicions about this one—try to split up Alice and Betty by assigning them offices in different buildings and giving Betty another major assignment so she won't get curious about Alice's work. Management hopes this will prevent them from talking and discovering problems that might delay or undermine Alice's projects. Thus, Alice and Betty never talk about the report, and it never comes to light that not-p actually is the case. They are both innocent victims of management's scheme to compartmentalize potentially damaging information. Management creates a structure designed to prevent people like Alice and Betty from talking and sharing information on their projects, in the hopes of preventing knowledge of legal violations from rising to the surface, so the company can have plausible deniability.

In this case, Alice and Betty do not seem culpable. Neither was willfully ignorant. Instead, management put informational barriers in place to prevent Alice and Betty from talking and getting curious about possible problems in the company. Acting this way, I submit, is culpable. In particular, they breached their duty of reasonable information toward others, DRIO. Management did not fail to disclose information, but they created obstacles that they knew would prevent others—Alice and Betty—from receiving the information that they should have gotten. I argued earlier that erecting such informational roadblocks without any justification (e.g., solely to create plausible deniability) can be culpable. Accordingly, because of this culpable interference by management, the company plausibly is as culpable as it would have been had Alice actually found out that the report contained a falsehood and submitted it anyway. There are plausible equal culpability grounds for aggregating the *existing* knowledge of Alice and Betty—viz., (a) Alice's knowledge that the report asserts p, and (b) Betty's knowledge that not-p—in order to impute the conjunction thereof to the corporation. Thus, using the collective knowledge doctrine is justified, and the corporation can be convicted of knowingly submitting a false report.

However, the willful ignorance doctrine does not support the same result. Management was not itself willfully ignorant. This is for two reasons. First, they did not act with the intention of preserving *their own* ignorance about possible falsehoods in the report. Management, it was stipulated, would not be involved with writing such reports and would not be expected to learn of their contents. So rather than acting to preserve its own ignorance, it sought to preserve the ignorance *of others* in the corporation. Thus, there is no breach of the duty to inform oneself (DRI), but a derogation of the duty to see to it that others are informed (DRIO).

The second reason management is not willfully ignorant of the falsehoods in the report is that they had no specific suspicions about problems in the report. Management merely acted to prevent Alice and Betty from getting curious and potentially finding a range of possible legal problems—as they had done in the past to the annoyance of management and expense of the corporation. Since management itself lacked suspicions about the inculpatory proposition (or anything relevantly similar), management would not itself qualify as willfully ignorant.[52]

Thus, this is one case where the collective knowledge doctrine is justifiably applied to impute knowledge to the corporation, although the willful ignorance doctrine does not yield the same result. Accordingly, Hagemann and Grinstein are mistaken that the collective knowledge doctrine is merely "a logical corollary to the doctrine of willful blindness."[53] As seen, there is a normative basis for applying the doctrine even where the willful ignorance doctrine doesn't support the same result.[54] Hagemann and Grinstein exaggerate the extent to which the collective knowledge doctrine is duplicative of the willful ignorance doctrine.[55]

---

[52] See the "basic" legal definition of willful ignorance from Chapter 1. Global-Tech Appliances, Inc. v. SEB S.A., 131 S. Ct. 2060, 2070 (2011) (willful ignorance has "two basic requirements: (1) the defendant *must subjectively believe that there is a high probability that a fact exists* and (2) the defendant must take deliberate actions to avoid learning of that fact") (emphasis added).

[53] Hagemann & Grinstein, *supra* note 6, at 256

[54] Indeed, some scholars have criticized Hagemann and Grinstein for "applying the concept of willful blindness inaccurately." Lederman, *supra* note 28, at 670 (2000). They apply the notion of willful ignorance too broadly. They use it to cover not just cases where employees "wanted or intended not to know" but also (and incorrectly) cases where employees were merely negligent in "fail[ing] to examine or match information." *Id.* at 670–71.

[55] Confusingly, Hagemann and Grinstein may actually be open in practice to aggregating existing knowledge here to impute knowledge of the falsehoods in the report to the corporation. They claim "[w]hen a corporation deliberately structures itself to avoid the accumulation within one individual of all the pieces of inculpatory information necessary to commit a crime knowingly, courts may defeat such machinations by aggregating information possessed by persons within the corporation." Hagemann & Grinstein, *supra* note 6, at 245. Moreover, as an illustration of how this might happen, they mention a "policy or procedure to avoid the corporation's collection of knowledge." *Id.*

Although the willful ignorance and the collective knowledge doctrines are not coextensive, it's important to bear in mind that they flow from the same animating principles. Both are equal culpability imputation principles, and are motivated by similar policy concerns. Both are ways of responding to actors—whether individuals or corporations—who preserve ignorance and keep people (whether themselves or others) in the dark of important information they should have had.

D. KNOWLEDGE GENERATION BEYOND WILLFUL IGNORANCE

1. The Basic Picture

The case just discussed involved aggregation of *existing knowledge* for imputation to the corporation. However, there are structurally similar cases where the same results are appropriate, but where there is no *existing knowledge* to aggregate and we instead have to construct *new knowledge* to be imputed to the corporation. This goes a step further than the previous case.

Hagemann and Grinstein think this marks a difference between the willful ignorance and collective knowledge doctrines. While they claim these doctrines largely do "the same work," "[t]he only difference between the two is that in noncorporate contexts, the willful blindness doctrine imputes to defendants knowledge that they never actually acquired," while this is not so for the collective knowledge rule, which only aggregates "knowledge that does exist, albeit in separate locations."[56] However, in this, too, Hagemann and Grinstein are wrong. The same reasoning that supported the collective knowledge doctrine in the previous example sometimes also supports the generation of *new knowledge* to be imputed to the corporation. Sticking with our same working example, consider:

> Missing Inference: This case is the same as the previous one except for the pieces of knowledge Alice and Betty possess. Alice again submits a report that she knows asserts p. She also knows p entails q. Betty, by contrast, knows that not-q, but doesn't know p entails q. Alice and Betty do routinely collaborate on projects like this and can be expected to share their knowledge in the normal course of their work. But, again, management interferes with the normal flow of information. To prevent the team working on the report from discovering problems with the corporation's business practices, management (again while having no specific suspicions about this report or similar ones) assigns Alice and Betty offices in different buildings and gives Betty a big assignment so she won't get too involved in Alice's work (just as before). Thus, Alice and Betty never talk about the report. They never combine their knowledge, and neither one draws the inference that not-p. Again, Alice and Betty are innocent victims of management's scheme to compartmentalize sensitive information.[57]

---

[56] *Id.* at 246.

[57] The example clearly could proceed in terms of modus ponens, or any other sufficiently simple inference rule, instead of modus tollens. Perhaps I know p, and you know p entails q. If you knew q, you would have to take

This case is identical to the last one except for the inferential structure of the information at issue. If one agrees it would be justified on equal culpability grounds in SEPARATE KNOWLEDGE—KEEPING OTHERS IN THE DARK to impute knowledge to the corporation that although the report says p, actually not-p is the case (i.e., the benzene emissions actually are over the limit), then one should have no trouble accepting that the same knowledge should be imputed to the corporation in MISSING INFERENCE too. If one thinks the collective knowledge doctrine applies in the former case, there should be no basis for denying that it also applies in the latter.

The only difference between them is that SEPARATE KNOWLEDGE—KEEPING OTHERS IN THE DARK involved aggregating existing knowledge while MISSING INFERENCE involves generating *new knowledge*—that is, a mental state no individual actually possesses. To see why, recall the proposition one must know to be guilty of knowingly making a false statement to the government. It has two parts: one must know both that (a) there is a statement made to the government, and (b) this statement is false. In SEPARATE KNOWLEDGE—KEEPING OTHERS IN THE DARK, for each component, there was at least one person who knew it. Alice knew (a), and Betty knew (b). Thus, imputing knowledge to the corporation of (a) + (b) only required aggregating Alice's and Betty's different bits of knowledge, which management had culpably kept separate.

By contrast, in MISSING INFERENCE, no individual actually knows (b). Thus, applying the collective knowledge doctrine in this case requires constructing *new knowledge* to be imputed to the corporation. To impute the requisite knowledge for the crime to the corporation, we must pretend as if Alice, besides knowing the report asserts p and that p entails q, also was informed that not-q, so she could infer that not-p. We can suppose she reasonably would have done so but for the culpable interference of management with the natural flow of information in the corporation. Thus, there is a plausible equal culpability rationale for imputing to the corporation not only Alice's actual knowledge that the report asserted p but also knowledge of the second half of the inculpatory proposition—namely, not-p.

Notice that the extra culpability needed to support this imputation does not come from Alice. Alice did not keep herself ignorant. Rather, management acted in ways that prevented Alice from coming to know not-p. In this, management breached DRIO—its duty to see to it that others receive the information they should have. Management's breach of DRIO is plausibly attributed to the corporation. After all, management's interference with the natural flow of information was within the scope of their employment, and so the corporation can be charged with it under respondeat superior. Thus, the extra culpability from management's breaching DRIO is attributable to the corporation. Because of this extra culpability, it is a plausible that *the corporation* is as culpable

---

protective actions. I should share my knowledge that p with you, but culpably decide not to. Thus, the corporation can be treated as if you knew q. Thus, it can be held responsible for failing to take the associated protective actions.

for what it did—that is, interfering with the information flow and then submitting the report in ignorance of its falsehoods—as the corporation would have been had one of its employees submitted the report while actually knowing of these falsehoods. Thus, we have another case where the collective knowledge doctrine is justified on equal culpability grounds, despite involving not the aggregation of existing knowledge but the construction of *new knowledge*, which no individual possessed or could have imputed to her.

Again, the willful ignorance doctrine does not generate the same result here. Neither Alice nor Betty was willfully ignorant. They did not block themselves from obtaining knowledge that not-p, and in fact were victims themselves. Moreover, management was not willfully ignorant—again for two reasons. First, they did not suspect the report might contain any false statements. Perhaps they were not even aware of this specific report, since it was assumed their jobs generally do not pertain to such reports or the details of compliance issues. Thus, there is nothing that would trigger their own duty to inform themselves about whether p was true. Second, the managers did not act to preserve their *own* ignorance. They did not breach DRI, since, as just seen, this duty wasn't triggered, as they lacked the requisite specific suspicions. Rather, their culpability comes from their acting to keep others in the dark—specifically, Alice and Betty. The managers breached their duty to see to it that others are reasonably informed—that is, DRIO. Thus, there is no basis for imputing knowledge to the managers under the willful ignorance rule either.

One can imagine courts, faced with such a case, twisting the willful ignorance doctrine to *claim* that management was willfully ignorant. A court might stretch the willful ignorance doctrine to suggest the managers really were trying to remain ignorant about what was in the reports. But as the facts of *this* case were stated, this would do violence to the willful ignorance doctrine. It was stipulated that the managers would never know ex ante about problems with specific statements in such reports. It was assumed they never concern themselves with the content of these reports (which is why others are hired to write and submit them). The managers were stipulated to have no suspicions about any misstatements in this or similar reports that trigger a duty to investigate. So they are not willfully ignorant on the legal definition.

Thus, instead of twisting the willful ignorance doctrine to find a hook for treating the managers as knowing actors, the better strategy is to recognize that this is a case calling for the direct application of the distinct collective knowledge doctrine. Like the willful ignorance doctrine, it is justified on equal culpability grounds. But unlike the willful ignorance doctrine, knowledge in MISSING INFERENCE should be imputed to the corporation in response to the managers keeping *others* in the dark—not themselves—of facts the managers did not even suspect.

Accordingly, I contend that the proper predicate for applying the collective knowledge doctrine, and thus imputing knowledge to the corporation, is the culpable interference with the proper flow of information within the corporation. Sometimes this will overlap with the willful ignorance doctrine—as when this informational interference involves preventing *oneself* from receiving information one should have obtained (thus violating DRI). But, as shown, this is not the only way it can happen. One also can culpably interfere with the proper information flow in the corporation by preventing *others* from receiving information *they* should have had (thus violating DRIO). This, too, can make the corporation as culpable as if its employees had done the actus reus with actual knowledge of the requisite inculpatory facts. Accordingly, this knowledge can be fairly imputed to the corporation itself—even if not to any of the individuals within the corporation under existing law, like to Alice, Betty, or the managers.

2. Fleshing Out the Model

The previous picture derives support from the theories of corporate culpability and equal culpability imputation defended earlier. Thus, I conclude by connecting the account to these theories. To do so, return to CarCo v.2 from the start of the chapter, as Missing Inference is not an isolated example. Some actual court cases are plausibly analyzed this way too (though they involve factual ambiguity, so I relegate them to a footnote).[58]

---

[58] Consider a classic collective knowledge case: United States v. TIME-DC, Inc., 381 F. Supp. 730 (W.D. Va. 1974). I also discussed it in Alex Sarch, *Beyond Willful Ignorance*, 88 U. Colo. L. Rev. 97 (2016), suggesting it exemplified the Iterated Reckless Ignorance Principle from Chapter 6. That was a mistake. It is better read as an instance of management culpably preventing others from being properly informed.

TIME-DC was charged with knowingly letting employees drive on the highway while dangerously ill, thus violating federal regulations. Under TIME-DC's new attendance policy, driver absences would be unexcused without a doctor's note. The government claimed TIME-DC didn't properly explain that unexcused absences could be expunged from the driver's record with a doctor's note. This allegedly created an "aura of confusion," which induced employees to drive even when overly ill. *TIME-DC, Inc.*, 381 F. Supp. at 736.

One evening, the wife of one driver Brown called to report her husband was too sick to work. The dispatcher, Giles, told her the absence would be unexcused under the new policy. It was disputed whether he mentioned that a doctor's note could later expunge the absence. Several hours later, driver Brown asked to work after all. After driving 110 miles, he became too sick to proceed and went to the emergency room.

The issue was whether the government had proved "the Company acted knowingly" as to Brown's violation of the highway regulations. *Id.* at 738. The company accepted it knew of the regulations, so the question was only whether it knew its employees were driving while impaired. Reasoning that a "corporation is considered to have acquired the *collective knowledge* of its employees," *id.*, the court concluded that "the Company had sufficient information . . . , through its various employees, to know that driver Brown's ability to drive was impaired . . . [so] as to make it unsafe for him to begin his trip." *Id.* at 739. The company's rollout of the new policy was confusing, and "[c]ognizant of this situation . . . the Company could not simply rely on driver Brown's subsequent request to be placed back on duty as absolving it from its responsibility to ensure that the [highway laws] were not ignored." *Id.* at 740. TIME-DC was convicted.

Here, management breached DRIO. It culpably interfered with employees properly sharing information. Management created an informational barrier to dispatchers becoming fully informed of relevant dangers. Still, none of the parties were willfully ignorant. Giles might have suspected Brown was sick, but Brown's assurances that he could drive were enough to extinguish any duty to investigate further. Management also was not willfully ignorant. They did not keep *themselves* in the dark about instances of driving while impaired due to sickness. They would not have found out about such instances in the normal course of their work—and certainly not at a time when they could do anything about it. Instead, this was the dispatchers' job. Their task is to assign routes safely. Thus, the managers were not keeping *themselves* ignorant of violations of the highway regulations; they were keeping *dispatchers* ignorant thereof. Management created a situation—perhaps to create plausible deniability—where dispatchers might be misled by drivers wanting to work despite being too ill to do so safely.

Instead, return to CarCo v.2, a cleaner case. There, Mindy had suspicions about a data set and worried that subjecting it to proper analysis might lead CarCo into financial trouble, thus jeopardizing her bonus. So she prevented company scientists from finding and analyzing it—including by burying the data in her report and storing it off-site. Had the scientists dealt with it in the normal way, they would have realized the cars CarCo manufactured violate applicable emissions standards. Mindy did not preserve her *own* ignorance of the violations. She is a mid-level employee who would never be informed of such facts in her normal work. She only preserved the ignorance of others.

Mindy is in a similar position to the managers in Missing Inference. As before, it is appropriate to impute knowledge *to the corporation* of the inculpatory facts—although no one within the corporation actually knows it or could have such knowledge imputed to them. For clarity, here is a schematic formulation of the equal culpability rationale for imputing knowledge to CarCo. It applies the theory of corporate culpability sketched in Section II.B.

Equal Culpability Rationale for Imputing Knowledge to CarCo:

(1) *Mindy breached DRIO.* Mindy culpably interfered with the natural information flow within the corporation. She breached DRIO with high mens rea. (Note that she was not willfully ignorant because did not act to preserve her own ignorance. She merely kept others in the dark. Thus, Mindy should not herself be treated as if she knew of the violations. She would not have learned of them in the course of her work. It would be perverse to hold her personally responsible for knowingly allowing the emissions standards to be violated—even if she should lose her job.)

(2) *Mindy's breach of DRIO can be imputed to the corporation under respondeat superior.* Under step one of my theory of corporate culpability (i.e., determining what the corporation did), Mindy's act of preserving the ignorance of others is attributable to the corporation. The act was done within the scope of Mindy's employment for the benefit of the company.

Thus, management did not violate DRI, but DRIO—the duty to ensure that others are reasonably informed of relevant risks. Accordingly, although management was not willfully ignorant, there is an equal culpability basis for treating *the corporation* as though it knew of Brown's offense of driving while impaired. Applying the collective knowledge doctrine in this way is to combine (a) management's knowledge of the highway regulations with (b) the knowledge dispatcher Giles should have had that Brown was too sick to drive, but which he was blocked from obtaining by management's culpable informational interference. This is the best explanation of why the court is justified in imputing knowledge of Brown's violation to TIME-DC.

Nonetheless, one might push back and insist the managers really did design the absentee policy with the intent to keep *themselves* ignorant of instances of driving while impaired. This was the government's assertion, but it was contested by the defense. Accordingly, the case involves some factual ambiguity and may not be a clean case.

Thus, the relevant unit of corporate conduct to be assessed—that is, the relevant part of *what the corporation did*—includes Mindy's breach of DRIO.

(3) *This adds culpability*. Given (2), the corporation's conduct with Mindy's breach of DRIO included is more culpable than it would be had she not breached DRIO within her employment. A greater degree of insufficient regard is needed to get an otherwise law-abiding corporation to behave the same way. That is, Mindy's breach of DRIO makes the corporation's conduct a greater departure from the standard of a similarly situated perfectly law-abiding corporation, comprising perfectly well-motivated employees, than if Mindy hadn't breached DRIO.

(4) *Equal culpability claim*. The extra culpability the corporation incurs from Mindy's breach of DRIO renders the corporation as culpable as it would have been had the scientists actually analyzed the data and come to know of the emissions violations, but the company continued manufacturing them nonetheless. I cannot *prove* this equal culpability claim here. But given that Mindy knew what was at stake—she had suspicions about what the data she hid from the scientists might reveal—and had no legally cognizable justification for keeping the scientists in the dark, her conduct was highly culpable, and this extra culpability is fairly attributed to the corporation. Thus, I submit it is intuitively plausible that what the corporation did, with Mindy's breach included, is roughly as culpable as the corporation would have been had it manufactured the vehicles while individual employees actually knew the cars violated the emissions standards.

(5) *Relatedness claim*. There is no violation of the relatedness constraint on equal culpability imputation, as presented in Chapter 5. Deliberately keeping appropriate others in the dark, despite recognizing a risk of the inculpatory information involved, shows insufficient regard for *the very same protected interests, rights, and values* that knowingly violating the emissions standards would manifest insufficient regard for. Here, these are the interests and values the relevant criminal statute seeks to protect, which are associated with environmental protection and honest dealing with the government.

(6) *Conclusion*. Therefore, knowledge of the emissions violations can be fairly imputed to the corporation itself (although not to Mindy personally).

If I'm right, it's justified to depart from the Individualist Constraint in such cases. Through equal culpability imputation, CarCo can be treated *as if* it possessed all the knowledge required for the crime—although no individual employees possess it at the time or could have it imputed to them. This shows why courts are sometimes justified in departing from the Individualist Constraint. While generally plausible, this constraint should be rejected for cases of this sort. The following exception should be carved out from the Individualist Constraint:

> **Nonindividualist Knowledge Imputation**: Imputing a piece of knowledge, K, to the corporation—even though K was not possessed by and could not be imputed to any individual within the corporation—is justified if its employees interfere with the proper flow of information (which otherwise could have led other appropriate employees to acquire K) *provided*
> (a) this interference is within the scope of the actor's employment and done for the benefit of the corporation, and thus can be attributed to the corporation (i.e., is part of *what the corporation did*), and
> (b) this interference was sufficiently culpable to render the corporation as culpable as it would have been had an individual possessed K and the company acted analogously (and the relatedness constraint is not violated).

This covers both knowledge aggregation as in SEPARATE KNOWLEDGE—KEEPING OTHERS IN THE DARK, and constructing new knowledge as in MISSING INFERENCE and CARCO V.2.

E. AN OBJECTION

Some might doubt my conclusion that the willful ignorance and collective knowledge doctrines diverge. Recall SEPARATE KNOWLEDGE—KEEPING OTHERS IN THE DARK. Although the managers may not have been willfully ignorant, since they didn't preserve their own ignorance, couldn't we say the corporation preserved *its* ignorance? Couldn't one insist that knowledge aggregation requires at least willful ignorance *by the corporation*—if not individual members? Perhaps this lets us insist the collective knowledge doctrine just is the willful ignorance doctrine by another name.

I actually have nothing against this way of talking, provided it doesn't lead to sacrificed clarity or a misunderstanding of the willful ignorance doctrine for individuals. Indeed, it might be quite catchy to say that willful ignorance *by the corporation* grounds treating the corporation as though it had knowledge. The trouble is that this obscures the applicable conceptual structure, which is better left explicit. Specifically, it must be clear what "willful ignorance by the corporation" means. We need some process for constructing the *conduct of the corporation* ("what it did") out of the individual actions of its agents, and determining when this counts as "willful ignorance by the corporation." We need a theory to fill this gap. The present way of talking obscures this key question.

By contrast, my account leaves no explanatory gap.[59] Willful ignorance involves breaching the duty to inform oneself, DRI, which can be culpable. If one's breach of

[59] Alternatively, my account can be said to fill this gap and explain what "willful ignorance by the corporation" means.

DRI is within the scope of one's employment, it can be imputed to the corporation via respondeat superior. Call this *Method 1* for imputing missing knowledge to the corporation. But sometimes people in the corporation culpably interfere with the information flow without breaching DRI, but by preventing *others* from properly obtaining information, thus breaching DRIO. This is not true willful ignorance by the individual. Still, it can be culpable—particularly when it's a deliberate attempt to seek unfair benefits for oneself or the corporation. If such interference with others' ability to inform themselves falls within the scope of one's employment, this act—and its culpability—can also be attributed to the corporation. This is *another* basis for imputing missing knowledge to the corporation. Call it *Method 2*.

For both methods, the individual conduct triggering knowledge imputation—either breaching DRI or DRIO—might loosely be described as "willful ignorance by the corporation." But this way of talking threatens to erase the analytical distinction between Method 1 and Method 2. We retain greater analytical clarity if we talk in terms of Method 1 and Method 2 directly, rather than making the less precise claim that knowledge is to be imputed to the corporation based on "willful ignorance by the corporation."

At bottom, not much besides terminology hangs in the balance. If it turns out that using the catchy phrase "willful ignorance by the corporation" more clearly conveys the relevant idea, then go for it. Either way, the important point is that a corporation can *itself* be willfully ignorant even if there is no individual within it who is willfully ignorant. That's what we saw in SEPARATE KNOWLEDGE—KEEPING OTHERS IN THE DARK, MISSING INFERENCE, and CARCO V.2.

In the end, we should not let terminological questions overshadow the central conclusions of this chapter. The take-home message is that the collective knowledge doctrine for corporations and the willful ignorance doctrine for individuals are two emanations of the same underlying normative idea: *Equal culpability grounds the imputation of missing mental states*. It has been the aim of this book to show why this is true and where the proper limits of this powerful idea belong.

Conclusion

LET'S BE HONEST: YOU'LL probably sneak a peak at this conclusion without having read most of the book because you want to know what the takeaways are. Why is this relevant to me? Is there anything here I can use? Assuming that's right, here's what I've been up to in this book.

Most simply, this is a book about a common legal fiction: the criminal law's practice of pretending we know what we don't. Maybe you instinctively feel scandalized by legal fictions. It's natural to want the law to be honest and accurate. Nonetheless, in this book I've tried to give reasons not to be so worried and actually get on board with the kind of legal fiction at issue here. It's a *justified* fiction, I've argued, that promotes valuable aims. At least when properly constrained, it is justified for the law to treat you as if you had certain culpability-relevant mental states (like knowledge of inculpatory facts or awareness of risks) that you didn't literally possess. What justifies it? The same purposes the criminal law generally serves: protecting our core interests, rights, and values.

Thus, my primary aim has been to defend a *theory of equal culpability mental state imputation*. The point of the theory (presented in Chapter 5) is to say when imputing missing mental states to defendants is justified on the basis of their being as culpable as if they had possessed those mental states—and when it's not justified on that basis. My claim was roughly this: when you lack a mental state required for a crime, but you acted in ways that made you just as culpable, and culpable in the same way, as if you had possessed it, then imputing this mental state to you, and punishing you accordingly, is supported by the same rationale as the criminalization of the underlying crime. This rationale, in turn, is the protection of the very same interests, rights, and values that the underlying criminal prohibition serves to safeguard.

This theory shows why what at first might seem like a brazen legal lie—imputing mental states we actually lack—in fact makes good normative sense. I extracted my theory from the equal culpability rationale courts offer in support of the existing willful ignorance doctrine. I explicated the normative foundations of this rationale, articulated its limitations, and generalized it into a theory of mental state imputation. In so doing, I hope to have shown why equal culpability mental state imputation, when used properly, is a legitimate way to further the aims of the criminal law.

My theory of equal culpability imputation is not just meant to explain the weird workings of the law—it also has normative bite. It tells us how to *evaluate* particular imputation doctrines that are already in use—or could be. As we've seen, the theory yields recommendations about particular doctrines and tells us whether they should be retained, rejected, or reformed—at least insofar as they are to be construed as equal culpability imputation rules. Granted, some rules my theory recommends rejecting might still be defended on, say, consequentialist grounds. However, consequentialism as a justificatory strategy in the criminal law has familiar drawbacks, which make it better seen as a strategy of last resort. Better to see how far we can get in justifying specific imputation rules through the equal culpability route, which sits more easily with the culpability-focused internal perspective of criminal law doctrine. This is the task my theory aims to help accomplish.

Come on, I thought we were going to get some takeaways! What are they already? OK, OK, here are the main substantive upshots from the book. My theory simultaneously recommends doctrinal contraction in some places and expansion in others. Some existing imputation doctrines should be restricted, while new imputation rules should be recognized. Here's what we should do, more specifically:

- **Restrict the existing willful ignorance doctrine**: Chapters 3–4 argued that since not all willfully ignorant misconduct is as culpable as the analogous knowing misconduct, willful ignorance should satisfy the knowledge element of crimes *only* when the conditions of equal culpability are met. To prevent punishing in excess of culpability while maintaining workability, juries should be told (roughly) that willful ignorance may substitute for knowledge only when the defendant (1) had serious suspicions that the inculpatory proposition was true, (2) reasonably could have learned the truth but deliberately didn't, and (3) was not aware of anything that helped justify the decision not to learn more. (Other conditions could be added for greater protection of defendants, though this could also become excessive.)
- **Allow repeated reckless ignorance to substitute for knowledge**: As Chapter 6 argued, repeatedly taking unjustified risks that you'll preserve your ignorance of

the inculpatory proposition can make you as culpable as a knowing wrongdoer, which would justify treating you as though you had knowledge. I argued there is a particular need to adopt this rule to avoid attempts by sophisticated actors to game the existing willful ignorance doctrine and escape liability for knowledge crimes.

- **Allow "blanket ignorance" of a known range of risks to substitute for recklessness:** Chapter 8 recommended another new form of equal culpability imputation: one kind of subwillful motivated ignorance—blanket ignorance—should substitute for recklessness, despite being only an egregious form of negligence. This is needed to prevent the definition of recklessness from being gamed by blocking oneself from recognizing a broad category of particular risks one should have appreciated. Recklessness should be imputed to such actors in conditions of equal culpability to prevent them from escaping liability for recklessness crimes.
- **Don't allow willful ignorance to substitute for purpose:** Chapter 7 argued we mustn't get carried away with equal culpability imputation. There are clear bounds on when equal culpability imputation is permitted on my theory. These limits are transgressed if willful ignorance of p is allowed to substitute for purpose to make p true.
- **Recognize a restricted collective knowledge doctrine for corporations:** Equal culpability imputation is a doctrinal tool that legitimately applies not just to individuals but also to corporations. As Chapter 9 argued, courts should be less worried about the collective knowledge doctrine, which allows stitching together the mental states of individual employees to impute the aggregate thereof to the corporation. There is a sound equal culpability rationale in the offing for doing just this in response to seriously culpable interference with the normal flow of information within the corporation. Such interference by employees can make the corporation as culpable as it would have been had it possessed the knowledge that it was prevented from acquiring. Nonetheless, this is not just an application of the willful ignorance doctrine for individuals. It is a distinct imputation rule for corporations even where no individual was willfully ignorant.

My theory of equal culpability imputation thus recommends a range of reforms. Criminal law doctrine should be updated to reflect the normative landscape I've been mapping out (subject to reasonable practical constraints, of course). I've sought to provide a more solid normative foundation for the criminal law's practice of imputing mental states on equal culpability grounds. This project required giving a detailed account of the notion of criminal culpability underlying this imputation. This was the business of Chapter 2. There I articulated a refined version of the familiar insufficient regard theory of culpability, and showed that, when supplemented with a proper account of manifesting insufficient regard, it is an attractive framework with significant explanatory power and normative plausibility. The account makes room for both (a) the descriptive notion of culpability that tracks specific jurisdictions' actual culpability attributions, and (b) the more important notion of *normative culpability*, which theorists deploy when evaluating and proposing reforms to existing law. Moreover, despite distinguishing normative culpability (a legal notion) from moral blameworthiness, the insufficient regard theory reveals deep continuities between these two notions. Thus, my inquiry into the normative foundations of equal culpability imputation not only has practical payoffs but also reaps deeper theoretical rewards.

I initially got pulled into these questions by investigating the willful ignorance doctrine and the equal culpability rationale behind it. The general theory of equal culpability imputation this inquiry generated, however, has upshots well beyond the willful ignorance doctrine. If you come away remembering one conclusion from this book, let it be this: equal culpability imputation is a valuable and defensible judicial tool, but it is an especially powerful tool that must be used with great care within strict limits to avoid unjustly punishing people in excess of what they deserve.

Index of Cases and Legal Authorities

CASES

LEGAL AUTHORITIES

Index